Divine Scapegoats

Divine Scapegoats

Demonic Mimesis in Early Jewish Mysticism

ANDREI A. ORLOV

SUNY PRESS

Cover painting entitled “The Great Red Dragon and the Woman Clothed with the Sun” by William Blake; courtesy of the National Gallery of Art.

Published by State University of New York Press, Albany

Printed in the United States of America

For information, contact State University of New York Press, Albany, NY
www.sunypress.edu

Production, Diane Ganeles
Marketing, Michael Campochiaro

Library of Congress Cataloging-in-Publication Data

Orlov, Andrei A., author.
Divine scapegoats : demonic mimesis in early Jewish mysticism / Andrei A. Orlov.
pages cm
Includes bibliographic references and index.
ISBN 978-1-4384-5583-9 (hc : alk. paper)—978-1-4384-5582-2 (pb : alk. paper)
E-ISBN 978-1-4384-5584-6 (ebook)
1. Jewish demonology. 2. Azazel (Jewish mythology). 3. Scapegoat. 4. Mysticism—Judaism. 5. Apocalypse of Abraham—Criticism, interpretation, etc. 6. Slavonic book of Enoch—Criticism, interpretation, etc. I. Title.

BM645.D45O755 2015
296.3'16—dc23 2014020288

10 9 8 7 6 5 4 3 2 1

"And Abram went down to Egypt" . . . This verse hints at wisdom and the levels down below, to the depths of which Abraham descended. He knew them but did not become attached.

—*Zohar* I.83a

Contents

Preface

Along with seven unpublished studies, this book contains one essay previously published in a collection inaccessible to many interested readers. A shorter version of the essay "Adoil Outside the Cosmos: God Before and After Creation in the Enochic Tradition" appeared in *Histories of the Hidden God: Concealment and Revelation in Western Gnostic, Esoteric and Mystical Traditions* (eds. A. DeConick and G. Adamson; Durham, NC: Acumen, 2013) 30–57. I am thankful to Acumen Publishing for permission to reuse the material. The format and style of the essay have been changed to comply with the standards of this collection.

I would like to express my appreciation to Rick Barry, Moshe Idel, Oleg Makariev, Ivan Miroshnikov, Fr. Joseph Mueller, S.J., Paul Pasquesi, Nikolai Seleznyov, and Brian Sigmon, who read various parts of the manuscript and offered numerous helpful suggestions. I am especially grateful to my research assistants Jeff Walkey and Jim Wykes, who worked very hard through different versions of the manuscript to help improve the text in both style and substance.

I am grateful to the National Gallery of Art, Washington for permission to use a digital reproduction of William Blake's painting "The Great Red Dragon and the Woman Clothed with the Sun" as the cover image.

Sincere thanks are also due to Nancy Ellegate, Diane Ganeles, and the editorial team of the SUNY Press for their help, patience, and professionalism during preparation of this book for publication.

Andrei Orlov
Milwaukee
The Great Feast of Theophany, 2014

Abbreviations

ÄAT	Ägypten und Altes Testament
AAWG	Abhandlungen der Akademie der Wissenschaften in Göttingen
AB	Anchor Bible
ABRL	Anchor Bible Reference Library
AGAJU	Arbeiten zur Geschichte des antiken Judentums und des Urchristentums
AJSR	*American Jewish Studies Review*
ANRW	*Aufstieg und Niedergang der römischen Welt*
AOAT	Alter Orient und Altes Testament: Veröffentlichungen zur Kultur und Geschichte des Alten Orients und des Alten Testaments
ArBib	Aramaic Bible
ASOR	American Schools of Oriental Research Series
AUSS	*Andrews University Seminary Studies*
BAR	*Biblical Archaeology Review*
BBB	Bonner Biblische Beiträge
BETL	Bibliotheca Ephemeridum Theologicarum Lovaniensium
Bib	*Biblica*
BIS	Biblical Interpretation Series

BJS	Brown Judaic Studies
BKAT	Biblischer Kommentar Altes Testament
BN	*Biblische Notizen*
BR	*Bible Review*
BSac	*Bibliotheca sacra*
CBQ	*Catholic Biblical Quarterly*
CBQMS	Catholic Biblical Quarterly Monograph Series
ConBOT	Coniectanea biblica: Old Testament Series
ConBNT	Coniectanea biblica: New Testament Series
CRINT	Compendia rerum iudaicarum ad Novum Testamentum
CSCO	Corpus scriptorum christianorum orientalium
EA	*Etudes Asiatiques*
EB	*Estudios Bíblicos*
EE	*Estudios eclesiásticos*
EJL	Early Judaism and Its Literature
EKKNT	Evangelisch-Katholischer Kommentar zum Neuen Testament
Ekstasis	Ekstasis: Religious Experience from Antiquity to the Middle Ages
ErJb	*Eranos Jahrbuch*
ET	*Expository Times*
ETR	*Études Théologiques et Religieuses*
FAT	Forschungen zum Alten Testament
FRLANT	Forschungen zur Religion und Literatur des Alten und Neuen Testaments
GAP	Guides to Apocrypha and Pseudepigrapha
HBM	Hebrew Bible Monographs
HBT	*Horizons in Biblical Theology*

HSM	Harvard Semitic Monographs
HTR	*Harvard Theological Review*
HUCA	*Hebrew Union College Annual*
Imm	*Immanuel*
JAAR	*Journal of the American Academy of Religion*
JAOS	*Journal of the American Oriental Society*
JATS	*Journal of the Adventist Theological Society*
JBL	*Journal of Biblical Literature*
JCPS	Jewish and Christian Perspectives Series
JCS	*Journal of Cuneiform Studies*
JHI	*Journal of the History of Ideas*
JJS	*Journal of Jewish Studies*
JR	*Journal of Religion*
JRS	*Journal of Roman Studies*
JSHRZ	Jüdische Schriften aus hellenistisch-römischer Zeit
JSJ	*Journal for the Study of Judaism in the Persian, Hellenistic and Roman Period*
JSJSS	Journal for the Study of Judaism in the Persian, Hellenistic and Roman Period: Supplement Series
JSNT	*Journal for the Study of the New Testament*
JSNTSS	Journal for the Study of the New Testament. Supplement Series
JSOTSS	Journal for the Study of the Old Testament. Supplement Series
JSOR	*Journal of the Society of Oriental Research*
JSQ	*Jewish Studies Quarterly*
JSP	*Journal for the Study of the Pseudepigrapha*
JSPSS	Journal for the Study of the Pseudepigrapha: Supplement Series

JSSSS	Journal of Semitic Studies Supplement Series
JTS	*Journal of Theological Studies*
JU	Judentum und Umwelt
JZWL	*Jüdische Zeitschrift für Wissenschaft und Leben*
KAW	Kulturgeschichte der antiken Welt
LCL	Loeb Classical Library
LSTS	Library of Second Temple Studies
NHMS	Nag Hammadi and Manichaean Studies
NHS	Nag Hammadi Studies
NICOT	New International Commentary on the Old Testament.
NIVAC	NIV Application Commentary
NovT	*Novum Testamentum*
NovTSup	Supplements to Novum Testamentum
NTTS	New Testament Tools and Studies
NSBT	New Studies in Biblical Theology
NTOA	Novum Testamentum et Orbis Antiquus
NTS	*New Testament Studies*
OBO	Orbis biblicus et orientalis
OS	Oudtestamentische Studiën
PEQ	*Palestine Exploration Quarterly*
PTS	Patristische Texte und Studien
QD	Quaestiones disputatae
RB	*Revue biblique*
RBS	Resources for Biblical Study
REJ	*Revue des études juives*
RevExp	*Review and Expositor*

RevQ	*Revue de Qumrân*
RSR	*Recherches de Science Religieuse*
SAALT	State Archives of Assyria Literary Texts
SBLDS	Society of Biblical Literature Dissertation Series
SBLMS	Society of Biblical Literature Monograph Series
SBLSP	Society of Biblical Literature Seminar Papers
SHR	Studies in the History of Religions
SJ	Studia Judaica
SJJTP	Supplements to the Journal of Jewish Thought and Philosophy
SJLA	Studies in Judaism in Late Antiquity
SJS	Studia Judaeoslavica
SJT	Studies in Jungian Thought
SO	Sources Orientales
SOR	Studies in Oriental Religions
SP	*Studia patristica*
SPHS	Scholars Press Homage Series
SSLJM	Sources and Studies in the Literature of Jewish Mysticism
STDJ	Studies on the Texts of the Desert of Judah
StudNeot	Studia Neotestamentica
SVC	Supplements to Vigiliae Christianae
SVTP	Studia in Veteris Testamenti Pseudepigrapha
TB	*Tyndale Bulletin*
TBN	Themes in Biblical Narrative
TCS	Text-Critical Studies
TED	Translations of Early Documents

TSAJ	Texte und Studien zum antiken Judentum
UBL	Ugaritisch-Biblische Literatur
VC	*Vigiliae christianae*
VT	*Vetus Testamentum*
WBC	Word Biblical Commentary
WMANT	Wissenschaftliche Monographien zum Alten und Neuen Testament
WUNT	Wissenschaftliche Untersuchungen zum Neuen Testament
YJS	Yale Judaica Series
ZAW	*Zeitschrift für die alttestamentliche Wissenschaft*
ZCP	*Zeitschrift für celtische Philologie*
ZDPV	*Zeitschrift des deutschen Palästina-Vereins*
ŹM	Źródła i monografie
ZNW	Zeitschrift für die Neutestamentliche Wissenschaft und die Kunde der älteren Kirche

INTRODUCTION

The Right in the Left

The Divine and the Demonic in the *Apocalypse of Abraham* and *2 Enoch*

> . . . there is a right above and there is a right below; there is a left above and there is a left below. There is a right above in the realm of supernal holiness, and there is a right below in the realm of the Other Side. . . .
>
> —*Zohar* I.53a

This collection of studies continues the inquiry initiated several years ago in *Dark Mirrors: Azazel and Satanael in Early Jewish Demonology*, published by SUNY Press in 2011. The essays in that volume explored the parallels in early Jewish apocalyptic literature between heavenly and demonic realities in which antagonists reflect and mirror not only the features of angelic characters but even the attributes of the Deity himself. I argued that this paradoxical symmetry between the divine and the demonic often encompassed a distinctive sacerdotal dimension in the antagonists' cultic roles, which stemmed from the traditional liturgical and priestly settings of Jewish Temple services, including the Yom Kippur ritual. This mirroring is not entirely novel or surprising, as it echoes the fundamental principle of Jewish religious tradition in which the earthly cultic realities are seen as the reflection of the heavenly ones. The main thrust of this cultic symmetry has often been expressed by the phrase "on earth as in heaven," a concept that envisions the earthly sanctuary as a structure created in accordance with the heavenly pattern and sustained by divine reality.

Like the earthly abode, the demonic realm sustains its existence by imitating the heavenly sacerdotal settings and its cultic retinue. Cultic mirroring affects both negative and positive characters of the apocalyptic stories. In this inverse correspondence, a character literally takes the place of his opponent by acquiring the peculiar attributes and conditions of his counterpart. Some of these correlations stem from early biblical priestly patterns in which positive and negative actors of the cultic drama were portrayed symmetrically. One such early biblical priestly *topos* was the Yom Kippur ceremony. In *Dark Mirrors* I explored the inverse symmetry in the apocalyptic Yom Kippur rite found in the *Apocalypse of Abraham* between the angelic high priest Yahoel and the demonic scapegoat Azazel.

The mirroring of the divine and the demonic in the Slavonic apocalypse has another significant motif, also prominent in the Yom Kippur rituals, namely, the dichotomy of left and right, where the divine side is associated with the right and the demonic side with the left. In the *Apocalypse of Abraham*, the eschatological opposition between the divine "right" and the demonic "left" unfolds in the antagonism between the two "lots" or "portions" of humanity. Such imagery is strikingly reminiscent of that found in the ceremony of the goats' selection on Yom Kippur. This sacerdotal symbolism receives an eschatological reinterpretation in the Slavonic apocalypse where the left lot has become associated with the demonic scapegoat, the fallen angel Azazel, while its right counterpart is associated with the eschatological "goat for YHWH," the patriarch Abraham.

As in the earthly version of the Yom Kippur rite, in which the goats for YHWH and Azazel were similar to each other, in the apocalyptic version of the ritual, the divine "right" becomes imitated by the demonic "left," and vice versa. The presence of the "right" in the "left" and the "left" in the "right" eventually becomes a prominent topic in later Jewish mysticism, especially in the Castilian Kabbalah and the Zoharic tradition.[1] It appears that the early roots of this conceptual development had already been manifested in early Jewish pseudepigrapha, including the *Apocalypse of Abraham* and *2 Enoch*. In such works, the divine blueprints were mysteriously imitated by sacerdotal, messianic, and creational dimensions of the demonic realm.

The *Apocalypse of Abraham* and *2 Enoch* belong to a very special cluster of Jewish apocalyptic texts that exhibit features not only of the apocalyptic worldview but also of the symbolic universe of early

Jewish mysticism. Both of them were preserved completely only in the Slavonic language and belonged to the group of early Jewish writings often labeled as the Slavonic pseudepigrapha. With an enigmatic history of transmission, this group of texts has a highly developed mystical imagery that makes them stand out in the corpus of early pseudepigrapha. *Apocalypse of Abraham* and *2 Enoch* share unique theophanic and mediatorial language, which is very different from the mainstream of early apocalyptic and pseudepigraphic writings. These Slavonic sources bear witness to the lost conceptual development that bridges the matrix of early Jewish apocalypticism as it was manifested in the early Enochic circle with the matrix of early Jewish mysticism as it became manifest in rabbinic Merkabah and Hekhalot materials. Thus, for example, the portrayal of Enoch in various sections of *2 Enoch* appears to be more elaborate than in the early Second Temple Enochic tractates of *1 Enoch*. For the first time, the Enochic tradition seeks to depict Enoch not simply as a human taken to heaven and transformed into an angel but as a celestial being exalted above the angelic world. In this attempt, one may find the origins of another image of Enoch (very different from the early Enochic literature) developed much later in rabbinic Merkabah and Hekhalot mysticism—namely, the image of the supreme angel Metatron, "the Prince of the Presence." The transformations, reminiscent of later Jewish mystical developments, encompass not only positive characters of the Slavonic pseudepigraphical texts but also their infamous antagonists, including the fallen angel Azazel. As noted, these antagonistic figures often attempt to imitate the attributes of heavenly beings. This nefarious mimesis exhibits striking similarities to later Jewish mystical developments in Hekhalot and Zoharic literature in which the Other Side attempts to imitate the messianic and cultic attributes of heavenly figures.

The current collection of studies continues exploration of the symmetry between the demonic and the divine found in the *Apocalypse of Abraham* and *2 Enoch* by concentrating on sacerdotal, messianic, and creational aspects of this imagery.

The first part of the collection deals with the demonological developments in the *Apocalypse of Abraham*. This section, continuing from *Dark Mirrors*, focuses on the attributes and features of the demonic scapegoat Azazel and his conceptual counterparts, namely, the eschatological high priestly and messianic figures.

"The Curses of Azazel" continues the examination of the inverse symmetrical correspondence between the sacerdotal attires of the protagonist and the antagonist of the *Apocalypse of Abraham*. It explores the conceptual connections between the high priest's endowment with the divine Name and the scapegoat's endowment with the aural counterpart of the Name, the cultic curses bestowed on the animal during the atoning rite. The study also explores one of the central clothing symbols of the Yom Kippur ceremony—a crimson band tied around the head of the scapegoat, a puzzling piece of clothing that, like the garment of the high priest, is transformed during the atoning rite.

"The Cosmological Temple in the *Apocalypse of Abraham*" explores the cosmological account in chapter 21 of the *Apocalypse of Abraham*. The essay discusses how the text portrays the whole creation as a macrocosmic temple with its sacred chambers represented by heaven, earth, and the underworld. One of the paradoxical features of this account is the portrayal of the demonic sea as the courtyard of the macrocosmic temple and of its chief inhabitant, Leviathan, as the sacred foundation of the sanctuary, comparable to the Foundation Stone.

"The Demise of the Antagonist in the Apocalyptic Scapegoat Tradition" explores rabbinic and early Christian portrayals of the final moments of the Yom Kippur ritual, in which, after the removal of the crimson band, the scapegoat was pushed from a rugged cliff. The essay argues that these rabbinic and early Christian descriptions appear reminiscent of the motifs in the eschatological reinterpretations of the scapegoat rite in the *Book of the Watchers*, the *Apocalypse of Abraham*, and other early Jewish apocalyptic accounts.

"The Nourishment of Azazel" explores the motifs of angelic and demonic sustenance found in the *Apocalypse of Abraham*, in which Abraham is fed on the presence of Yahoel, while Adam and Eve receive ominous nourishment from the hands of Azazel. Such eating habits on the part of the protoplasts inversely mirror the nourishing mode of the patriarch. While Abraham transitions to the celestial prelapsarian condition of humanity, renouncing the associated conventional nourishment, Adam and Eve head in the opposite direction through consumption of earthly food. The study demonstrates that the symbolism of nourishment found in the *Apocalypse of Abraham* plays an important conceptual role in the dualistic framework of the entire text.

"The Messianic Scapegoat in the *Apocalypse of Abraham*" continues to examine the parallels between the divine and the demonic by concentrating on the tradition of the two messiahs found in chapter 29 of the *Apocalypse of Abraham*, one of which is envisioned as a messianic scapegoat. The study argues that the symbolism of the messianic scapegoat attempts to unify both messianic and cultic dimensions. An analysis of the two messiahs affirms an important feature of the symmetrical correspondences between the divine and the demonic, namely, the existence of peculiar dyads in which one character acts as the representative of the divine portion, and the other as an agent of the demonic side. In *Dark Mirrors*, I explored in detail one example of such a dyad: the two eschatological portions or lots represented by Abraham and Azazel in the *Apocalypse of Abraham*. The current collection continues the exploration of the dyad imagery, not only in the *Apocalypse of Abraham* but also in another apocalyptic work, *2 (Slavonic) Enoch*. The second part of the book includes three essays dealing with this early Jewish pseudepigraphon.

"Adoil Outside the Cosmos: God Before and After Creation in the Enochic Tradition" explores an extensive creational account situated in the central portion of *2 Enoch*. The narrative exhibits dualistic features by unveiling the dyad of primordial aeons, one of which is associated with divine light, and the other with divine darkness. Just as the divine light is personalized in the Slavonic apocalypse through the imagery of the primordial aeon Adoil, similarly, *2 Enoch* depicts darkness as a preexistent and divine entity with its own personified agent, namely, Arukhas, who is the foundation of the "lowest things." The creational dualism of *2 Enoch* is quite different from the dyadic material found in the *Apocalypse of Abraham*. In contrast to the *Apocalypse of Abraham*, in which the right is paradoxically present in the left through the demonic imitation of the divine, in *2 Enoch*, the left is present in the right. Later Jewish mysticism would eventually call this the "left side" of the divine—a domain not properly demonic but rather a realm of divine darkness from which the demonic takes its power. The darkness in *2 Enoch*, however, stems from the Godhead and remains fashioned according to the Deity's command. Further, besides exploring the symmetry of divine darkness and divine light, this essay also explores another symmetrical correspondence: the relation between *Endzeit* and *Urzeit*, when the disintegration of the primordial aeon of light in the beginning of creation is juxtaposed with the aeon's symmetrical eschatological restoration at the end of time.

"The Veneration Motif in the Temptation Narrative of the Gospel of Matthew: Lessons from the Enochic Tradition" examines the veneration motif in the third temptation of the Gospel of Matthew and its connection with the extra-biblical apocalyptic traditions in Adamic and Enochic lore. Satan's request for veneration, I argue, is patterned according to the theophanic accounts found in *2 Enoch* and the *Primary Adam Books* in which Enoch and Adam are first ordered to venerate the Deity and then, in turn, to be venerated by angelic hosts. In Matthew's gospel, however, this motif of angelic veneration becomes deconstructed. The deconstruction affects Satan's unusual roles and actions during his temptation of Jesus in the wilderness, including his roles as a transporting and interpreting angel (a *psychopomp* and an *angelus interpres*), offices well known from Jewish apocalyptic stories.

Finally, "Primordial Lights: The Logos and Adoil in the Johannine Prologue and *2 Enoch*" returns to the tradition of the primordial aeon Adoil, depicted in *2 Enoch* as demiugic light and a helper at God's creation. The essay argues that Adoil's attributes and functions are reminiscent of certain functions of the *Logos* in the Johannine Prologue. Further, the study also continues the exploration of the motif of divine darkness in *2 Enoch* and its role in the dualistic framework of the Slavonic apocalypse.

PART I

Studies in the *Apocalypse of Abraham*

The Curses of Azazel

> . . . Aaron shall lay both his hands on the head of the live goat, in this fashion: his right hand upon his left. He shall confess over it all the iniquities of the children of Israel and all their rebellions, whatever their sins; he shall put them on the head of the goat with a declared and explicit oath by the great and glorious Name.
>
> —*Targum Pseudo-Jonathan* to Leviticus 16:21

Introduction

The second part of the *Apocalypse of Abraham*, a Jewish pseudepigraphon written in early centuries of the Common Era,[1] deals with the ascent of the eponymous hero to the heavenly Holy of Holies. On this celestial journey, Abraham and his angelic companion Yahoel encounter a strange demonic creature, namely, the fallen angel Azazel, who attempts to interfere, warning the patriarch about the grave dangers that a mortal might encounter upon ascending to the abode of the Deity. In response to Azazel's challenge, Yahoel rebukes and curses the fallen angel. The curses imposed on the fallen angel are often seen as having cultic significance.[2] In the sacerdotal framework of the Slavonic apocalypse, which is permeated with the dynamics of the Yom Kippur ritual,[3] the cursing formulae delivered by the angel Yahoel, whom the text depicts as the celestial cultic servant,[4] appear reminiscent of those curses bestowed on the scapegoat by the high priest on the Day of Atonement.[5] Thus some have argued that the fallen angel bearing the conspicuous name Azazel[6] is depicted here as the celestial scapegoat predestined to take upon itself the sins and transgressions of Abraham in order to carry them into the realm of his exile. This chapter will explore Azazel's curses and their role in the sacerdotal framework of the Slavonic apocalypse.

The Cursing of Azazel in the Apocalypse of Abraham 13 and 14

Preliminary analysis of the relevant passages in the *Apocalypse of Abraham* reveals that the curses on the celestial scapegoat in the text can be divided in two major groups: (1) curses bestowed on Azazel directly by Yahoel in chapter 13 and (2) the reaffirmation of these sacerdotal actions taking place when the angel instructs Abraham in chapter 14.

Chapter 13: Curses bestowed by Yahoel

In *Apocalypse of Abraham* 13:7–14, the following mysterious encounter between the heavenly high priest Yahoel and the celestial scapegoat Azazel takes place:

> . . . Reproach is on you, Azazel! Since Abraham's portion is in heaven, and yours is on earth, since you have chosen it and desired it to be the dwelling place of your impurity.[7] Therefore the Eternal Lord, the Mighty One, has made you a dweller on earth. And because of you [there is] the wholly-evil spirit of the lie, and because of you [there are] wrath and trials on the generations of impious men.
>
> Since the Eternal Mighty God did not send the righteous, in their bodies, to be in your hand, in order to affirm through them the righteous life and the destruction of impiety. . . . Hear, adviser! Be shamed by me, since you have been appointed to tempt not all the righteous!
>
> Depart from this man! You cannot deceive him, because he is the enemy of you and of those who follow you and who love what you desire. For behold, the garment which in heaven was formerly yours has been set aside for him, and the corruption which was on him has gone over to you.[8]

In view of the aforementioned sacerdotal affiliations of Yahoel, it is possible that his address to the fallen angel bearing the name of the scapegoat has cultic significance, since it appears reminiscent of some of the actions performed by the high priest on the Day of Atonement. Similarly, some of the technical terminology found in this passage may be related to terminology associated with Yom Kippur.[9] The most crucial aspect of the text is that Yahoel's address contains utterances that are reminiscent of curses bestowed on the scapegoat during the great atoning rite. One of these pronouncements is found in *Apocalypse of Abraham* 13:12–14 (quoted above), where the transference of the patriarch's sin onto the celestial scapegoat coincides with the command to depart. Scholars note that this address is reminiscent of the earlier form of the scapegoat's curse imposed on the animal by his handlers during the Yom Kippur celebration.[10] *M. Yoma* 6:4 reads:

> . . . And they made a causeway for it because of the Babylonians who used to pull its hair, crying to it, "Bear [our sins] and be gone! Bear [our sins] and be gone!"[11]

This mishnaic passage includes two cultic elements: (1) a bestowal of sins ("bear [our sins]") and (2) a command of departure ("be gone").[12] The Apocalypse of Abraham exhibits a very similar constellation of motifs, as the transference of the sins on Azazel[13] ("the corruption which was on him has gone over to you") appears simultaneously with the command to depart ("depart from this man"). It is noteworthy, however, that, in contrast to the mishnaic tradition, the Slavonic apocalypse situates the departing formula not after the action of the sins' transference but before.

Further details related to the bestowal of curses onto the scapegoat are found in *Apocalypse of Abraham* 13:7–14 and 13:11, 15 which describe Yahoel's reproach and shaming of Azazel. Moreover, his utterances may be related to the ritual curses bestowed upon the scapegoat. The language of cursing or "shame" found in verse 11 is especially significant because it precedes the similar formulations within mishnaic traditions.

Chapter 14: Curses in Yahoel's Instruction to Abraham

After Yahoel bestows the curses in Chapter 13, the great angel explains both the handling of the scapegoat to Abraham and the ritual curses. Several details must be considered with respect to the peculiar sacerdotal settings of this portion of the text. Scholars have proposed that in the *Apocalypse of Abraham* Yahoel appears to function as a senior cultic celebrant explaining and demonstrating rituals to a junior sacerdotal servant, namely, Abraham.[16] This parallelism between the instructions of the teacher and the actions of the apprentice is already clear in the beginning of the apocalyptic section of the text, where the patriarch faithfully follows the orders of his angelic guide to prepare the sacrifices.[17] The same pattern of sacerdotal instruction, in which the orders of the master are followed by the disciple's performance, is also discernible in the depiction of the ritual of dispatching the scapegoat. *Apocalypse of Abraham* 14:1–8 describes how, after Yahoel's own "handling" of Azazel, the angel verbally instructs Abraham about dealing with the scapegoat:

> And the angel said to me, "Abraham!" And I said, "Here am I, your servant." And he said, "Know by this that the Eternal One whom you have loved has chosen you. Be bold and have power, as I order you, over him who reviles justice, or else I shall not be able to revile him who scattered about the earth the secrets of heaven and who conspired against the Mighty One.
>
> Say to him, "May you be the fire brand of the furnace of the earth! Go, Azazel, into the untrodden parts of the earth. Since your inheritance are those who are with you, with men born with the stars and clouds. And their portion is you, and they come into being through your being. And justice is your enmity. Therefore, through your own destruction vanish from before me!" And I said the words as the angel had taught me.[18]

This address again contains elements intended to further denigrate and humiliate the fallen angel bearing the name of the scapegoat, depicting him as an enemy of justice and a damned celestial creature predestined for destruction in the lower abode.

It is also important that in this narrative we again encounter the formulas of departure that constitute the crucial element in the previously mentioned mishnaic curse. Moreover, these commands of departure appear to be even more decisive and forceful than in the passage from chapter 13, as it now includes such commands as "Go" (Slav. иди)[19] and "Vanish from before me" (Slav. буди от мене исчезлъ).[20]

The description of the handling of the scapegoat recorded in *m. Yoma* 4:2 reveals that the high priest was to place the scapegoat in the direction of his future exile, likely to indicate its destination. Thus, *m. Yoma* 4:2 reads: "He bound a thread of crimson wool on the head of the scapegoat and he turned it towards the way by which it was to be sent out. . . ."[21] This tradition of showing the scapegoat the place of his banishment appears to be reflected in the Slavonic apocalypse when the celestial high priest Yahoel informs Azazel about his future destination: "Go, Azazel, into the untrodden parts of the earth." The word "untrodden" (Slav. *беспроходна*, lit. "impassable")[22] is significant because it designates a place uninhabitable to human beings, reminiscent of the language of Leviticus 16, where the scapegoat is dispatched "to the solitary place" (אל ארץ גזרה) "in the wilderness" (במדבר).[23] Commenting on this terminology, Jacob Milgrom observes that "the purpose of dispatching the goat to the wilderness is to remove it from human habitation."[24] Later exegetical traditions, too, often emphasize this "removing" aspect of the scapegoat rite.[25] For example, in his *De Spec. Leg.* I.188, Philo explains that the goat was sent ". . . into a trackless and desolate wilderness bearing on its back the curses which had lain upon the transgressors who have now been purified by conversion to the better life and through their new obedience have washed away their old disobedience to the law."[26]

Abraham's repetition of the words he received from Yahoel in the concluding phrase of the passage from chapter 14 seems to align with our earlier suggestion that Abraham is depicted in this text as a type of priestly apprentice receiving instructions from his great master, and then applying this knowledge in dispatching the scapegoat.[27]

The Scarlet Band of the Scapegoat and Azazel's Garment

As mentioned above, the *Apocalypse of Abraham* reinterprets many features of the scapegoat rite with complicated eschatological imagery, translating earthly attributes of the cultic animal into a new apocalyptic dimension.[28] This profound paradigm shift affects several distinctive features of the scapegoat ritual, including the crimson band that, according to some traditions, was placed on the head of the cultic animal during the Yom Kippur celebration. In the intricate web of apocalyptic reformulations which took place in the Slavonic pseudepigraphon, this animal's emblematic headgear becomes his garment of sins.[29]

Early Jewish and Christian Traditions about the Crimson Thread

The origin of the scarlet band imagery is shrouded in mystery.[30] Rabbinic passages often connect the symbolism of the band with Isa 1:18: "[T]hough your sins are like scarlet, they shall be like snow; though they are red like crimson, they shall become like wool."[31] Their use of the Isaiah passage indicates that the band was intended to manifest the forgiveness of Israel's transgressions by changing it from red to white, an important cultic motif. Several mishnaic passages relate that during the Yom Kippur ceremony, the crimson band—tied either to the rock or to the door of the sanctuary—would turn white as soon as the goat reached the wilderness,[32] fulfilling Isaiah's prophecy.[33]

Although the description of the scapegoat ritual found in the Book of Leviticus does not mention the band of the cultic animal, later Jewish and Christian sources provide a plethora of references to this mysterious item. A number of mishnaic passages, including *m. Yoma* 4:2, 6:6, and 6:8, mention the scarlet ribbon.[34] For instance, *m. Yoma* 4:2 contains the following tradition:

> He bound a thread of crimson wool on the head of the scapegoat and he turned it towards the way by which it was to be sent out; and on the he-goat that was to be slaughtered [he bound a thread] about its throat.[35]

This passage portrays the high priest marking two chief cultic animals for the Yom Kippur ordinance by designating one as the goat for YHWH and another as the goat for Azazel, then placing the scapegoat in the direction of his exile, as mentioned previously.

The tradition of the crimson wool is further expanded in *m. Yoma* 6:6, which reads:

> What did he do? He divided the thread of crimson wool and tied one half to the rock and the other half between its horns, and he pushed it from behind; and it went rolling down, and before it had reached half the way down the hill

> it was broken in pieces. He returned and sat down beneath the last booth until nightfall. And from what time does it render his garments unclean? After he has gone outside the wall of Jerusalem. R. Simeon says: From the moment that he pushes it into the ravine.[36]

While *m. Yoma* 4:2 describes the beginning of the scapegoat ritual where an animal was chosen and then marked with the crimson thread, *m. Yoma* 6:6 deals with the conclusion of this rite, a climactic moment when the scapegoat is pushed down the hill by his handlers. Most notably, before the end of the ritual the scapegoat's band was temporarily removed by his handlers. After the animal's cultic headgear was removed, one half of the band was tied to the rock and the remaining half was returned to the scapegoat's head before his final plunge into the abyss. Some new features of this tradition appear in *m. Yoma* 6:8, which reads:

> R. Ishmael says: Had they not another sign also?—a thread of crimson wool was tied to the door of the Sanctuary and when the he-goat reached the wilderness the thread turned white; for it is written, Though your sins be as scarlet they shall be as white as snow.[37]

In contrast to *m. Yoma* 6:6, this passage insists that the crimson thread was to be tied not to the rock but instead to the door of the sanctuary. Furthermore, in this passage, the crimson wool of the scapegoat seems to be understood as the deposit of the human sins carried by the scapegoat into the wilderness. When this burden is safely removed from the human *oikoumene*, the thread changes its color from red to white.

Early Christian exegetes also display their familiarity with this tradition of the cultic band. For instance, the *Epistle of Barnabas* speaks about the crimson thread using very similar terminology to the mishnaic testimonies.[38] *Barnabas* 7:6–11 reads:

> Pay attention to what he commands: "Take two fine goats who alike and offer them as a sacrifice; and let the priest take one of them as a whole burnt offering for sins." But what will they do with the other? "The other," he says, "is cursed." Pay attention to how the type of Jesus is revealed.

> "And all of you shall spit on it and pierce it and wrap a piece of scarlet wool around its head, and so let it be cast into the wilderness." When this happens, the one who takes the goat leads it into the wilderness and removes the wool, and places it on a blackberry bush, whose buds we are accustomed to eat when we find it in the countryside. (Thus the fruit of the blackberry bush alone is sweet.) And so, what does this mean? Pay attention: "The one they take to the altar, but the other is cursed," and the one that is cursed is crowned. For then they will see him in that day wearing a long scarlet robe around his flesh, and they will say, "Is this not the one we once crucified, despising, piercing, and spitting on him? Truly this is the one who was saying at the time that he was himself the Son of God." For how is he like that one? This is why "the goats are alike, fine, and equal," that when they see him coming at that time, they may be amazed at how much he is like the goat. See then the type of Jesus who was about to suffer. But why do they place the wool in the midst of the thorns? This is a type of Jesus established for the church, because whoever wishes to remove the scarlet wool must suffer greatly, since the thorn is a fearful thing, and a person can retrieve the wool only by experiencing pain. And so he says: those who wish to see me and touch my kingdom must take hold of me through pain and suffering.[39]

This passage describes a ritual in which the priest wraps a piece of scarlet wool around the scapegoat's head, followed by the handler of the scapegoat removing the wool and placing it on a blackberry bush.[40] It parallels both *m. Yoma* 4:2, where the celebrant binds a thread of crimson wool on the head of the scapegoat, and *m. Yoma* 6:6, where the handler of the scapegoat divides the thread of crimson wool and ties one half of the cultic band to the rock.

Another early Christian author, Tertullian, is also familiar with the tradition that the scapegoat was bound with scarlet thread.[41] In *Against Marcion* 3:7, he writes:

> If also I am to submit an interpretation of the two goats which were offered at the Fast, are not these also figures of

> Christ's two activities? They are indeed of the same age and appearance because the Lord's is one and the same aspect: because he will return in no other form, seeing he has to be recognized by those of whom he has suffered injury. One of them however, surrounded with scarlet, cursed and spit upon and pulled about and pierced, was by the people driven out of the city into perdition, marked with manifest tokens of our Lord's passion: while the other, made an offering for sins, and given as food to the priests of the temple, marked the tokens of his second manifestation, at which, when all sins have been done away, the priests of the spiritual temple, which is the Church, were to enjoy, as it were, a feast of our Lord's grace, while the rest remain without a taste of salvation.[42]

Both *Epistle of Barnabas* and Tertullian use the symbolism of the crimson band, the same imagery that receives new meaning in the *Apocalypse of Abraham*'s reinterpretation of the atoning rite.

Hippolytus of Rome is also cognizant of the traditions of the scarlet wool of the scapegoat. A fragment of his *Catenae on Proverbs* reads:

> And a goat as leader of the flock
> Since, it says, this is
> Who was slaughtered for the sins of the world
> And offered as a sacrifice
> And send away to the Gentiles as in the desert
> And crowned with scarlet wool (κόκκινον ἔριον) on the
> head by the unbelievers
> And made to be ransom for the humans
> And manifested as life for all.[43]

The scarlet band is, thus, for the early Christians, envisioned as the crown of Christ, receiving novel messianic and liturgical significance.

The Crimson Thread and Human Sins

As one can see, early Christian authors sometimes attempted to link the symbolism of the crimson thread with the cultic or messianic accouterment of Christ by describing it as either his robe or his crown.

This Christian understanding of the thread as a part of the cultic vestment or even as the vestment itself is remarkably similar to the Slavonic apocalypse, where the crimson band appears to be understood as a garment. More precisely, in the *Apocalypse of Abraham* (see chapter 12), it is the garment of the patriarch's transgressions, the deposit of human sins, placed upon Azazel by Yahoel.[44] The arrangement and details of this narrative are evocative of the scapegoat ritual, as all actors of the eschatological drama appear to be endowed with the peculiar cultic roles of the atoning rite.

Earlier it was noted that the text from *Apocalypse of Abraham* seems to portray Yahoel as the heavenly high priest handling the angelic scapegoat. Scholars have also suggested that the second apocalyptic portion of the text envisions Abraham as the second cultic animal of the Yom Kippur ordinance, namely, the goat for YHWH.[45] Moreover, the Slavonic apocalypse might envision the ascent of Abraham with his angelic companion into heaven as the entrance of the celestial high priest into the upper Holy of Holies, with the soul of the immolated goat, represented by his blood.[46] If such an understanding of these cultic actions is present in the Slavonic apocalypse, and Abraham is indeed imagined in *Apocalypse of Abraham* 12 as the goat for YHWH, then the setting of the whole scene is reminiscent of the depiction found in the aforementioned passage from *m. Yoma* 4:2, where the high priest, standing between two cultic animals, places the deposit of the sins, symbolized by the crimson thread, on the head of the scapegoat.

The tradition of Azazel's garment found in the *Apocalypse of Abraham* may provide additional insights into the "clothing nature" of the cultic band, which is the only known material that the scapegoat wore during the atoning rite. Moreover, if it is assumed that the crimson-dyed wool on the horns of the scapegoat represents a "garment," the mishnaic passage, then, seems to indicate that the immolated goat receives its own "garment," namely, a piece of wool tied around its neck.[47] Consequently, in the reinterpretation of the Yom Kippur ritual found in *Apocalypse of Abraham* 12, both "goats" receive "garments" when Azazel is endowed with the garment of sins and Abraham receives the garment stripped from the former celestial citizen.

The aforementioned analysis hints at a potential connection between the tradition of the scarlet band as the deposit of the human iniquities and the garment of sins given to the fallen angel Azazel in the Slavonic apocalypse. It is possible that the mishnaic accounts understand the scarlet band as a sort of a garment of sins carried by the scapegoat into the uninhabited realm where, according to some mishnaic testimonies, he was then "disrobed" by his handlers and his ominous headgear was either fully or partially removed.[48]

An important connection to the *Apocalypse of Abraham* here is that both the garment of Azazel in the Slavonic pseudepigraphon and the crimson band of the mishnaic testimonies are understood as a fabric that symbolizes the deposit of human sins. For instance, *m. Yoma* 6:8[49] and *m. Shabbat* 9:3[50] connect the tradition of the crimson band to a passage from Isaiah that speaks about the forgiveness of the sins. Elsewhere, a connection was made between the scarlet thread and human sins, as Jewish lore often associated the color red with sin and white with forgiveness. The *Book of Zohar* II.20a-b neatly summarizes this understanding of the color symbolism:

> Sin is red, as it says, "Though your sins be as scarlet"; man puts the sacrificial animal on fire, which is also red; the priest sprinkles the red blood round the altar, but the smoke ascending to heaven is white. Thus the red is turned to white: the attribute of Justice is turned into the attribute of Mercy.

A very similar appropriation of the color imagery also appears to be reflected in the scapegoat ritual. The band's transformation from red to white,[51] signaling the forgiveness of Israel's sins, strengthens the association of the red coloration with sin.[52] Numerous mishnaic and talmudic passages attest to the whitening of the band[53] during the scapegoat ritual in which it signifies the removal of sins.[54]

Loosing the crimson band at the end of the scapegoat rite might also signify the forgiveness of sins. Indeed, some scholars point out the semantic overlap between formulae of loosing and forgiving in Semitic languages, stressing the fact that "there is a semi-technical use of language of loosing (שרי) in the Palestinian Aramaic of the Targums to mean forgiving."[55]

Moreover, the close ties between the scarlet band and human sins can be further illuminated by referring to another significant procedure during the Yom Kippur celebration, the ritual during which the high priest transferred Israel's iniquities by placing his hands on the head of the scapegoat. For instance, Leviticus 16:21 describes the chief cultic celebrant placing his hands upon the head of the scapegoat and confessing over him all the sins of the people of Israel.[56]

The connection between the placement of the scarlet band on the head of the scapegoat and the placement of sins on the head as well by hand-leaning should be explored further. Jacob Milgrom suggests that the hand-leaning rite acts as the ritual of the transference of human sins. He notes:

> [T]he fact that the text stresses that the hand-leaning rite is executed with both hands is the key to understanding the function of Azazel's goat. It is not a sacrifice, else the hand-leaning would have been performed with one hand. The two-handed ceremonial instead serves a transference function: to convey, by confession, the sins of Israel onto the head of the goat.[57]

David Wright, likewise, argues that the two-handed rite identifies the scapegoat as the recipient of the sins. He notes:

> [T]wo-handed handlaying is distinct in form and meaning from the one-handed handlying found in sacrifice (cf. Lev 1:4; 3:2, 8, 13: 4:4, 24, 29, 33). The two-handed rite identifies the scapegoat as the recipient of the ritual action (in this case, as the recipient of the sins, cf. Lev 24:14; Num 27:18, 23) while the one-handed rite in sacrifice identifies the animal as belonging to the offerer. . . .[58]

It is of great importance that both the sins and the crimson band are placed *on the head* of the animal, once again strengthening the connection between the band of the cultic animal and the transgressions it is intended to bear.

Crimson Band and Clothing Metaphors

Distinguished students of Jewish ritual have pointed out that the imagery of sacred vestments plays a pivotal role in the Yom Kippur ordinance. They underline the transformational thrust of the atoning rite in which all celebrants were predestined to undergo the dramatic breach of their former limits, shepherding them into novel ontological conditions. The anthropological significance of such transformations is especially noticeable in the chief sacerdotal celebrant of the Yom Kippur rite, the high priest, whose reclothing during the ritual proleptically anticipates the transition from the garments of skin to the garments of light, signifying the return of humanity to its original state—that is to say, the prelapsarian condition of the protoplast.

Later apocalyptic reinterpretations of the atoning rite, like the *Apocalypse of Abraham* and other Jewish visionary accounts, make the transformation signaled by the change of garments a privilege not only for the high priestly figure but also his ominous cultic counterpart. In the *Apocalypse of Abraham*, for example, the celestial scapegoat Azazel receives an unclean garment of sins from Yahoel.[59]

In attempting to reconstruct the possible roots of this clothing metaphor, it should be noted that the earliest nonbiblical accounts of the scapegoat ritual juxtapose the imagery of the crimson wool with the symbolism of the unclean garments. Thus, *m. Yoma* 6:6 reveals that handling the scapegoat and its crimson band renders the garments of the handler unclean; again, it reads:

> . . . He divided the thread of crimson wool and tied one half to the rock and the other half between its horns, and he pushed it from behind; and it went rolling down, and before it had reached half the way down the hill it was broken in pieces. He returned and sat down beneath the last booth until nightfall. And from what time does it render his garments unclean?[60]

There is thus a peculiar mirroring when the scapegoat's "attire" appears to be paralleled by the garments of his handlers. Moreover, in these accounts another feature can be found, namely, the correspondence between the removal of the scapegoat's crimson band and the subsequent stripping of the unclean garment of the handler.[61] Leviticus 16:26 appears aware of this procedure, as it commands that the animal's handlers must wash their clothes.[62]

Early reinterpretations of the Yom Kippur imagery found in some prophetic accounts also seem to underline the importance of clothing in the scapegoat ritual. One such account is found at Zechariah 3:1–5:

> Then he showed me the high priest Joshua standing before the angel of the Lord, and Satan standing at his right hand to accuse him. And the Lord said to Satan, "The Lord rebuke

> you, O Satan! The Lord who has chosen Jerusalem rebuke you! Is not this man a brand plucked from the fire?" Now Joshua was dressed with filthy clothes as he stood before the angel. The angel said to those who were standing before him, "Take off his filthy clothes." And to him he said, "See, I have taken your guilt away from you, and I will clothe you with festal apparel." And I said, "Let them put a clean turban on his head." So they put a clean turban on his head and clothed him with the apparel; and the angel of the Lord was standing by. (NRSV)

Strikingly, this account depicts the high priest as situated between two creatures, one of whom bears the name of YHWH and the other, the one who is cursed.[63] The whole scene appears to draw on a set of Yom Kippur motifs.[64] Indeed, the account is reminiscent of some depictions of the high priest's actions during the atoning rite dealing with two goats, one of whom was the goat for YHWH, and the other the cursed scapegoat. Similar to the traditions found in the *Apocalypse of Abraham*, both cultic animals are now depicted as spiritual agents, one angelic and the other demonic. This depiction is remarkably similar to the roles of Yahoel and Azazel in the Slavonic apocalypse. In the prophetic account, as in the *Apocalypse of Abraham*, the attire of the human sacerdotal subject is changed from the defiled garments of sin to festal apparel. Although in Zechariah's account, unlike in the Slavonic apocalypse, the human's filthy clothes are not transferred to the demonic creature, the ritual of Satan's cursing might suggest that the antagonist becomes the recipient of the Joshua's vestments of impurity.

These early references to the changing of cultic attire in connection with the scapegoat ritual are important for our study. It is also significant that such parallelism in the removal of garments of the sacerdotal characters affects the high priest, who is the most important celebrant of the rite and is required to be purified and vested into the new, now golden garments after sending the scapegoat away.[65]

The Garment of Darkness

Our previous analysis demonstrated that early biblical and extra-biblical accounts of the scapegoat ritual were filled with a panoply of clothing metaphors. Some mishnaic passages even develop the peculiar parallelism between the crimson band of the scapegoat and the garments of its handlers. Such developments provide an important interpretive framework for understanding the tradition of the garment of Azazel in the *Apocalypse of Abraham*. Yet the fallen angel's attire of sins attested in the Slavonic apocalypse appears to stem not only from biblical and mishnaic testimonies but also from some apocalyptic accounts that reinterpreted the scapegoat rite eschatologically. One of these formative accounts is found in one of the earliest Enochic books, the *Book of the Watchers*, where the fallen angel Asael, as the celestial scapegoat, is depicted as being "clothed" with a dark garment. Thus, in *1 Enoch* 10 the Deity orders one of his angelic executors to throw Asael into the abyss and to cover him with darkness.[66]

Although scholars have previously reflected on features of Asael's punishment in *1 Enoch* 10 that are similar to the scapegoat ritual, they often fail to notice the Yom Kippur motif in the fallen angel's covering with darkness.[67] As in the Jewish atoning rite, this may be correlated to both the placement of the scarlet band on the scapegoat and the transference to it of the sins of the Israelites by the laying of hands, the sacerdotal action that symbolizes the endowment of the cultic animal with the deposit of the human transgressions.[68]

It is also important that in Enochic lore, as in the later *Apocalypse of Abraham*, the antagonist's clothing in darkness inversely correlates with the protagonist's clothing in light. We find one such correlation in *1 Enoch* 10, with a peculiar mention of the fallen angel's face clothed in darkness, which may recall a series of transformational motifs involving God's luminous *Panim* and the shining *panim* of the visionary. This terminology is quite well known in the Jewish apocalyptic literature. Rather than symbolizing the luminous visage or face of the figure, such terminology symbolizes the complete covering of the protagonist or Deity in luminous attire. Reception of the heavenly garment by the human protagonist recalls also the realities of the Yom Kippur rite in which the high priestly celebrant receives white clothes during the atoning ceremony.

The parallelism between the demonic garment of darkness and high priestly garment of light returns us again to the Christian testimonies cited earlier, in which the imagery of the crimson band often signifies both the garment of sins that Christ wore on behalf of humankind and his sacerdotal clothes.[69] Thus, Daniel Stökl Ben Ezra notes[70] that in *Barnabas* 9 the scarlet band appears to be the high priestly robe of Jesus during his second coming.[71] As demonstrated by this tradition of the priestly robe of Christ and its association with the crimson band, the band and the priestly accoutrement were often paired together, a pairing which now must be explored further in our study.[72]

The Scarlet Band of the Scapegoat and the Front-Plate of the High Priest

One of the characteristics of the Yom Kippur ordinance previously noted by scholars is the mirroring that takes place between the two main characters in the atoning rite, in which case the actions and attributes of one celebrant are mocked and deconstructed by the actions and attributes of the other. It has been suggested that the Yom Kippur ritual reflects the dynamics of two inversely symmetrical movements, one represented by the progression of the high priestly figure into the Holy of Holies, and the other embodied by the banishment of the scapegoat into the wilderness. Regarding this spatial arrangement, Daniel Stökl Ben Ezra notes that the Yom Kippur ritual

> . . . consisted of two antagonistic movements . . . centripetal and centrifugal: the entrance of the High Priest into the Holy of Holies and the expulsion of the scapegoat. As the first movement, the holiest person, the High Priest, entered the most sacred place, the Holy of Holies of the Jerusalem Temple, burned incense, sprinkled blood and prayed in order to achieve atonement and purification for his people and the sacred institutions of the Jewish cult. As a second movement, the scapegoat burdened with the sins of the people was sent with an escort to the desert.[73]

In view of this inverse sacerdotal symmetry of the chief celebrants of the atoning rite, it is possible that the scarlet band of the scapegoat is intended to "mock" and deconstruct some of the attributes of the high priest. Since the clothing metaphors affect both celebrants of the rite—one of which receives the garment of light, and the other the garment of darkness—the scapegoat's scarlet band was intended possibly to mirror the garment of the high priest.

Later rabbinic accounts of the Yom Kippur ritual often speak about the garments of the high priest, who, for instance, was girded with a sash of fine linen and wore a turban of fine linen on his head.[74] One particular piece of the high priestly accouterment—which, like the ominous scarlet band of the scapegoat, was put on the head of the cultic servant—deserves special attention.

Both biblical and extrabiblical materials often make reference to the high priest's front-plate (ציץ) worn on the forehead.[75] Made of gold and inscribed with the divine Name, the plate is said to have shone like a rainbow. As a result, Jewish accounts often describe heavenly and earthly priestly figures with the imagery of a rainbow in a cloud. This tradition of "the rainbow in the cloud" is known from several texts, including the description of the high priest Simeon in the *Wisdom of Jesus ben Sira* 50:7:

> Greatest of his brothers and the beauty of his people was Simeon the son of Johanan the priest . . . how honorable was he as he gazed forth from the tent, and when he went forth from the house of the curtain; like a star of light from among clouds, and like the full moon in the days of festival; and like the sun shining resplendently on the king's Temple, and like the rainbow which appears in the cloud. . . .[76]

It is important to emphasize that the high priestly front-plate was decorated with the divine Name, that is to say, the Name by which the Deity once created heaven and earth. The portrayal of the ציץ given in one of the later Jewish mystical compendiums, known today as *Sefer Hekhalot*, underlines the demiurgic functions of the divine Name. Chapter 14 of *Sefer Hekhalot* describes the forehead of the heavenly priest Metatron as decorated with the letters by which heaven and earth were created. *3 Enoch* 12:1–2 reads:

> R. Ishmael said: The angel Metatron, Prince of the Divine Presence, the glory of highest heaven, said to me: Out of the abundant love and great compassion wherewith the Holy One, blessed be he, loved and cherished me more than all the denizens of the heights, he wrote with his finger, as with a pen of flame, upon the crown which was on my head, the letters by which heaven and earth were created; the letters by which seas and rivers were created; the letters by which mountains and hills were created; the letters by which stars

> and constellations, lightning and wind, thunder and thunderclaps, snow and hail, hurricane and tempest were created; the letters by which all the necessities of the world and all the orders of creation were created. Each letter flashed time after time like lightnings, time after time like torches, time after time like flames, time after time like the rising of the sun, moon, and stars.[77]

The imagery of the ציץ also appears in the *Apocalypse of Abraham*, when the angelic high priest Yahoel wears headgear reminiscent of a rainbow in the clouds, recalling similar descriptions given in the *Wisdom of Jesus ben Sira* 50:7 and rabbinic literature. It is also significant that in Jewish accounts, the imagery of the front-plate of the high priest often appears in the context of the Yom Kippur rituals in which the scarlet headgear of the scapegoat is also mentioned. It is thus possible that the scarlet band of the scapegoat is envisioned in the inverse symmetrical patterns of the atoning rite as an ominous counterpart to the front-plate of the high priest.[78]

The first important connection here is that both cultic items are situated on the heads of the sacerdotal agents. Exodus 39:30–31 states that the plate was fastened to the turban of the high priest, a tradition that is reflected in the *Apocalypse of Abraham*, as it also appears on the turban of the great angel. The crimson band is also placed on the head of the scapegoat, as both Jewish and Christian sources suggest: namely, two passages found in *m. Yoma*[79] and the *Epistle of Barnabas*.[80] Moreover, Hippolytus of Rome, likewise, speaks of crowning the scapegoat with scarlet wool.

It is also noteworthy that both the scarlet thread bound around the head of the scapegoat and the ציץ of the high priest become peculiar markers of the sin and righteousness of the Israelites. As mentioned earlier, the scarlet band is said to change its color during the atoning ritual in order to signal the forgiveness of the sins of the Israelites and the restoration of righteousness. This metamorphosis acts as a litmus test to indicate the change in moral status of the Israelites. It appears that the front-plate of the high priest served a very similar function. Some Jewish descriptions of the ציץ indicate that the front-plate, like the scarlet band, would change its appearance depending on the sinfulness or righteousness of the Israelites who came into contact with the plate.

One of the most extensive descriptions of the unusual qualities of the ציץ is found in the *Book of Zohar* II.217b; it reads:

> He opened saying, *They made* ציץ *(tsits), the medallion of, the holy diadem of pure gold . . .* (Exodus 39:30). Come and see: Why is it called *tsits*? Well, looking to see. Since it was intended for human observation, it is called *tsits*. Whoever looked at that *tsits* was thereby recognized. In the *tsits* were letters of the Holy Name, inscribed and engraved. If the one standing before it was virtuous, then those letters engraved in the gold protruded from below upward, rising from that engraving radiantly, and they illumined that person's face—a scintillation sparkled in him and did not sparkle. The first moment that the priest looked at him, he would see the radiance of all the letters in his face; but when he gazed intently he saw nothing but the radiance of his face shining, as if a sparkle of gold were scintillating. However, the priest knew from his first momentary glimpse that the blessed Holy One delighted in that person, and that he was destined for the world that is coming, because this vision issued from above and the blessed Holy One delighted in him. Then when they gazed upon him, they saw nothing, for a vision from above is revealed only for a moment. If a person stood before the *tsits* and his face did not display momentarily a holy vision, the priest would know that he was brazen-faced, and he would have to plead for mercy on his behalf and seek atonement for him.[81]

We see, then, according to this text, the front-plate of the high priest served to indicate the righteousness or sinfulness of the person standing before the cultic servant; that is to say, the reflection of the letters of the plate, on the face of the individual, differed according to the moral condition of the person.

Finally, another important parallelism between the front-plate of the high priest and the crimson band of the scapegoat is the connection of each to the divine Name. As suggested earlier, the crimson thread, representing the transgression of Israel, appears to be closely connected to the ritual of laying hands, during which the priest performs the transference rite by laying the sins of the people on the head of the cultic animal. If both the ritual of hand-laying and the crimson band are indeed interconnected, a tradition found in *Targum Pseudo-Jonathan* is helpful for understanding the important conceptual link between the crimson band and the divine Name. *Targum Pseudo-Jonathan* to Leviticus 16:21 reads:

> Aaron shall lay both his hands on the head of the live goat, in this fashion: his right hand upon his left. He shall confess over it all the iniquities of the children of Israel and all their rebellions, whatever their sins; he shall put them on the head of the goat with a declared and explicit oath by the great and glorious Name. . . .[82]

Here, during the rite of the hand-laying, the high priest was not only obliged to transfer to the scapegoat the iniquities of the children of Israel, but also to seal the head of the cultic animal with a great oath containing the divine Name.

The Divine Name and the Curse

Although mishnaic and early Christian testimonies do not directly associate the imposition of the curses with the figure of the high priest, the Slavonic apocalypse insists on such a function, depicting Yahoel as the one who places curses on Azazel during the transference rite.

It is important for our study that the curses come, not coincidentally, from the angelic cultic servant associated with the divine Name. This motif evokes the association of the high priest with the divine Name, which was worn on the forehead of the sacerdotal agent.

It is possible that the divine Name's inverse counterpart is the crimson band of the scapegoat, depicted by *Targum Pseudo-Jonathan* as being sealed with the Name. Furthermore, this connection between the divine Name and the curse might already be present in Zechariah 3's parallelism between the angelic being bearing the divine Name and the antagonistic creature who is rebuked. The tradition of the divine Name found in the *Apocalypse of Abraham* appears to be able to explain further the symmetry of the atoning rite, revealing another link between the divine Name of the high priest and the curse of the scapegoat, described in *Targum Pseudo-Jonathan* 16:21 as an "oath"—that is to say, an ominous cultic utterance possibly representing an aural antipode to the divine Name.[83]

The *Apocalypse of Abraham* appears to strengthen this link between the divine Name and the curse when it depicts its chief cultic servant not as one who simply wears the turban decorated with the divine Name but rather as the embodiment of the divine Name, defining the great angel as the mediator of "my [God's] ineffable name."[84] Even apart from this explanation of the angel's spectacular office, the peculiar designation Yahoel (Slav. *Иаоилъ*) in itself identifies the angelic creature as the representation of the divine Name. The curse for the scapegoat comes literally from the very depth of the hypostatic aural expression of the Deity. Thus the curse might be envisioned as the inverse aural counterpart of the divine Name, an important conceptual marker of the aural ideology that permeates the Slavonic apocalypse. This conspicuous opposition between two aural expressions might also paradoxically reflect the initial aural cultic symmetry of the two goats of the Yom Kippur rite in which one animal is accursed but the other manifests the divine Name in being designated as the goat for YHWH.[85]

Although the Slavonic apocalypse only hints at the profound connection between these two aural expressions, early Enochic lore, a development crucial for the theological universe of the *Apocalypse of Abraham*, provides further insights into the conceptual link between the divine Name and the curse of the fallen angel.

The Curse of the Fallen Angels

As demonstrated in our study, the scapegoat imagery receives an angelological refashioning in the Slavonic apocalypse. This modification, however, is not a novelty of this text. Rather, as suggested, it is deeply rooted in the apocalyptic hermeneutics of the scapegoat imagery found in early Enochic lore. One of the earliest Enochic booklets, the *Book of the Watchers*, reinterprets the scapegoat rite by incorporating certain details of the sacrificial ritual into the story of its main antagonist, namely, the fallen angel Asael. *1 Enoch* 10:4–7 constitutes an important nexus of this conceptual development:

> And further the Lord said to Raphael: "Bind Azazel by his hands and his feet, and throw him into the darkness. And split open the desert which is in Dudael, and throw him

> there. And throw on him jagged and sharp stones, and cover him with darkness; and let him stay there forever, and cover his face, that he may not see light, and that on the great day of judgment he may be hurled into the fire. And restore the earth which the angels have ruined, and announce the restoration of the earth, for I shall restore the earth. . . .[86]

Several distinguished scholars of these apocalyptic traditions have convincingly argued that some details of Asael's punishment are reminiscent of the scapegoat ritual. They point to a number of parallels between the Asael narrative in *1 Enoch* and the wording of Leviticus 16, including "the similarity of the names Asael and Azazel; the punishment in the desert; the placing of sin on Asael/Azazel; the resultant healing of the land."[87]

Although scholars have often been eager to reflect on the aforementioned parallels between the atoning rite and the apocalyptic account, they have neglected an important aspect of the scapegoat imagery found in the Enochic narrative, namely, the curse associated with the fallen angels and their leaders. Already in the *Book of the Watchers*, Asael and his rebellious companions are closely tied to the imagery of the curse, which is an important link, given the role that curses play in the scapegoat tradition.

The curse's symbolism looms large already in the beginning of the Watchers' story, during their preparation for entrance into the earthly realm and their descent on Mount Hermon. *1 Enoch* 6:1–7 reads:

> And it came to pass, when the sons of men had increased, that in those days there were born to them fair and beautiful daughters. And the angels, the sons of heaven, saw them and desired them. And they said to one another: "Come, let us choose for ourselves wives from the children of men, and let us beget for ourselves children." And Semyaza, who was their leader, said to them: "I fear that you may not wish this deed to be done, and (that) I alone will pay for this great sin." And they all answered him and said: "Let us all swear an oath, and bind one another with curses not to alter this plan, but carry out this plan effectively. Then they all swore together and all bound one another with curses to it. And they were in all two hundred, and they came down on

> Ardis which is the summit of Mount Hermon.[88] And they called the mountain Hermon, because on it they swore and bound one another with curses.[89]

Poised at the threshold of their realm, the angelic band makes a momentous decision: to ensure mutual responsibility for their risky action, their angelic leaders demand that they bind each other with curses. This fascinating act of "binding" with curses before the entrance into the lower earthly realm appears to have a cultic significance.[90] It is reminiscent of certain elements of the scapegoat ritual in which the animal was "bound" with the crimson band, representing the "curse" of Israel's sin, in preparation for its departure to the lower realm, symbolized by wilderness and the mountainous cliff. It recalls also the Azazel tradition found in the *Apocalypse of Abraham* in which the fallen angel, just prior to his banishment into the earthly realm, is cursed by Yahoel and Abraham.

The binding of the Watchers with a curse before their descent in *1 Enoch* 6 also represents a curious parallel to the binding of Asael a few chapters later, in *1 Enoch* 10, when the rebel is bound by the angelic priest before his banishment into the subterranean realm.

The Demiurgic Curse and the Divine Name

An interesting aspect of *1 Enoch* 6 is that it mentions not only curses but also an oath. It depicts the fallen angels as "swearing the oath" while "binding themselves with curses"; such phrases occur repeatedly, in tandem[91] throughout the text.[92] In view of these connections, scholars often see the symbolism of curse and oath in *1 Enoch* 6 as interchangeable.[93] If it can be assumed that these concepts are indeed connected, and indeed interchangeable, a significant link between the symbolism of curse and the concept of the divine Name might be revealed.

Interestingly, the same connection might also be present in the *Apocalypse of Abraham* in which the curses for Azazel come from the mouth of Yahoel, an angelic creature who is also the representation of the divine Name.

This link between the divine Name and the curse of the fallen angel(s) may already underlie *1 Enoch*'s narratives, in which the curse/oath of the Watchers appears to possess the same demiurgic powers as the divine Name. Here, as in the case of the crimson band of the scapegoat and the front-plate of the high priest, two opposite spiritual realities, one divine and another demonic, are closely interconnected.

In order to grasp the conceptual link between the powers of the demonic oath and the divine Name we must again return to *1 Enoch* 6, in which the fallen angels are depicted as binding each other with a mysterious oath. Although it does not provide any direct connection between the oath/curse and the divine Name, the retelling of the Watchers' story in the *Book of the Similitudes* hints at this possibility. *1 Enoch* 69:2–20 further expands the tradition about the great oath of the Watchers:

> And behold the names of those angels. And these are their names: the first of them (is) Semyaza. . . . And this is the task of Kesbeel, the chief of the oath, who showed (the oath) to the holy ones[94] when he dwelt on high in glory, and its name. . . . And this one told the holy Michael that he should show him the secret name, that they might mention it in the oath, so that those who showed the sons of men everything which is secret trembled before that name and oath. And this (is) the power of this oath, for it is powerful and strong; and he placed this oath Akae in the charge of the holy Michael.[95] And these are the secrets of this oath . . . and they are strong through his oath, and heaven was suspended before the world was created and for ever. And through it the earth was founded upon the water, and from the hidden (recesses) of the mountains come beautiful waters from the creation of the world and for ever. And through that oath the sea was created, and as its foundation, for the time of anger, he placed for it the sand, and it does not go beyond (it) from the creation of the world and for ever. And through that oath the deeps were made firm, and they stand and do not move from their place from (the creation of) the world and for ever. And through that oath the sun and the moon complete their course and do not transgress their command from (the creation of) the world and for ever.[96]

In this passage, as in *1 Enoch* 6, we find references to the familiar names of the fallen angels responsible for the antediluvian corruption of humanity[97] as well as to the imagery of the oath. Yet, unlike in the earlier narrative, here the oath is now not simply a sign of commitment[98] but an instrument of creation with which God once fashioned the heaven and earth.[99] *1 Enoch* 41:5 reaffirms the significance of the oath for the destiny of all creation, suggesting that various elements of creation are made to exist and be bound by this demiurgic oath. It depicts the heavenly luminaries (the sun and moon) keeping their proper course according to the oath that they have sworn.[100] The *Book of Jubilees*[101] also reflect the idea that the demiurgic oath was once used by the Deity in his creative work and since then is predestined to hold creation together. It is noteworthy that in some passages, such as *1 Enoch* 41, the demiurgic oath[102] is used interchangeably with the divine Name.[103] Later rabbinic accounts reflect extensively on the demiurgic functions of the Tetragrammaton[104] and its letters,[105] often interpreting them as the instruments through which the world came into being.[106] These traditions often construe God's command יהי at the creation of the world as an abbreviation of the divine Name.[107]

It is striking that the fallen angels traditions found in *1 Enoch* 69 also try to negatively reinterpret this demiurgic understanding of the divine Name/Oath by putting it in the hands of the celestial rebels.[108] In this respect *1 Enoch* 69 further illuminates initial obscure allusions to the demiurgic powers of the great oath/curse. Moreover, such cryptic allusions might already be present in *1 Enoch* 6,[109] hinted at in the name of one of the Watchers' leaders, Shemihazah (שמיחזה), an angelic rebel who is often interpreted by scholars as a possessor or a seer of the divine Name.[110] The demiurgic connotations in the name of the chief leader of the angelic group do not appear to be coincidental, considering the irreparable havoc that the group is able to cause in God's creation, necessitating new creative activity by the Deity.

Another name—that of Asael (עשאל), the second leader of the fallen Watchers—possesses possible demiurgic connotations of the same sort. In fact, his very name is often translated by scholars as "God has made,"[111] providing further links to the "creational" task of the fallen angels who decided to "refashion" the earthly realm through the revelations of mysteries and the conjugal unions of the celestial and earthy creatures.

In this context, the oath uttered by the fallen angels bearing peculiar demiurgic names acts as a curious parallel to the oath of the Creator. While the demiurgic powers of the divine Name bring the world into existence, and sustain its harmony, the Watchers' oath creates chaos and allows them to unlock the boundaries of the created order in order to refashion it. It also demonstrates their extraordinary access to the deepest mysteries of the universe, the faculties that enable them to replicate and mimic the creative faculties of the Deity. As later rabbinic testimonies often suggest, they literally "fall down with open eyes."[112]

While the possibility of the fallen angels possessing the demiurgic oath remains only in the background of early Enochic texts, it comes to the forefront in some other materials; for instance, later Jewish and Islamic traditions often directly connected the "mighty" deeds of Shemihazah and Azael with their possession of the divine Name. Some passages even depict them as the one who unlawfully revealed the divine Name to humans.[113]

It has been noticed by scholars that in *1 Enoch* 8:3 the names of the fallen angels indicate their illicit revelatory functions,[114] including the type of instruction they offered.[115] In light of this, it seems no accident that in later Watchers traditions Shemihazah is often posited as the one who is responsible for passing on illicit knowledge of the divine Name.[116] *The Midrash of Shemhazai and Azael* 3–5, for instance, depicts the fallen angel teaching a girl named Esterah the Ineffable Name; it reads:

> They said before Him: "Give us Thy sanction and let us descend (and dwell) among the creatures and then Thou shalt see how we shall sanctify Thy name." He said to them: "Descend and dwell ye among them." . . . Forthwith Shemhazai beheld a girl whose name was Esterah; fixing his eyes at her he said: "Listen to my (request)." But she said to him: "I will not listen to thee until thou teachest me the Name by which thou art enabled to ascend to the firmament, as soon as thou dost mention it." He taught her the Ineffable Name. . . ."[117]

Later Muslim accounts of the fallen angels found in the *Tafsirs* attest to a similar cluster of traditions portraying Shemihazah (*'Aza*) and Asael (*Azazil*) as the culprits responsible for the illicit revelation of the divine Name to a woman named Zuhra.[118]

Conclusion

Chapters 12 and 13 of the *Apocalypse of Abraham*, where the celestial creature bearing the divine Name teaches the young hero of faith how to impose ritual curses on the celestial scapegoat, constitute one of the important conceptual nexuses of the Slavonic pseudepigraphon, a work permeated with the aural ideology. This distinctive ideological stand attempts to fight the anthropomorphic understanding of God by putting emphasis on the audial expression of the Deity, who manifests Himself through His Voice and Name. For this reason, Yahoel, the personified manifestation of the divine Name, plays a paramount role[119] and highlights some new aural potentials of the Yom Kippur rite. The chief celebrant of the atoning rite here is not simply a bearer of the front-plate with the divine Name; rather, he himself becomes the embodiment of the Name. Likewise, other aural realities of the atoning rite, such as those in the early Enochic reinterpretations of the Yom Kippur ritual, are solidified here around the figure of this pivotal sacerdotal servant.

In this respect it is significant that, although the biblical and mishnaic accounts are silent about the duties of the high priest in imposition of the curses on the scapegoat, the *Apocalypse of Abraham* openly assigns the execution of these duties to the heavenly priest Yahoel.

Another significant aspect is the inverse aural settings found in the text. The previously discussed connection between the divine Name and curse appears to be already manifested in the initial aural cultic symmetry of two goats of the Yom Kippur rite in which one animal was accursed but the other was predestined to manifest the divine Name as the goat for YHWH. The *Apocalypse of Abraham*, which closely follows the Enochic demonological patterns, even further identifies the curse as the inverse counterpart of the divine Name, connecting the angelic bearer of the divine Name with the curses of the scapegoat. Here there is not merely a goat bearing the divine Name that serves as the counterpart of the accursed animal, but rather it is the hypostatic divine Name itself that now presents a foil for the infamous scapegoat standing in opposition to his angelic representation.

Does this paradoxical positioning of the celestial scapegoat vis-à-vis the embodied manifestation of the divine Name found in the

Slavonic apocalypse envision Azazel as an inverse counterpart of the divine Name, similar to Shemihazah's position in early Enochic accounts? The *Apocalypse of Abraham* is unwilling to provide a clear answer to this question.

The Cosmological Temple in the *Apocalypse of Abraham*

> A monster below, on the left side, swims in all those rivers. He comes with his mighty scales, each one as strong as iron, and he arrives there in order to draw water and defile the place. All the lights are darkened before him; his mouth and his tongue flame with fire; his tongue is as sharp as a mighty sword until he gets as far as entering the sanctuary within the sea, and then he defiles the sanctuary, and the lights are darkened, and the supernal lights disappear from the sea.
>
> —*Zohar* I.52a

> For, as the nut has a shell surrounding and protecting the kernel inside, so it is with everything sacred: the sacred principle occupies the interior, whilst the Other Side encircles it on the exterior.
>
> —*Zohar* II.233b

Introduction

In chapter 18 of the *Apocalypse of Abraham*, Abraham, having entered into the celestial throne room, receives a vision of all creation and the entire human history from the beginning to the end. This disclosure accounts for much of the apocalypse, stretching from chapter 19 to chapter 31. Although the main portion of the vision is devoted to describing the history of humankind, from the fall of Adam and Eve until the appearance of its eschatological messianic figures, the beginning of this vision is concerned with cosmological matters. In the cosmological revelations situated in chapters 19 and 21, the seer contemplates the complex architecture of the heavenly realm and learns about the structure and features of the lower realms, which include earth and the underworld. In the lowest region, Abraham sees Leviathan, who is depicted as the foundation of the world.

Although certain details of this cosmological portrayal have been explored in previous studies, one important question that has not been addressed is how this vision fits into the overall sacerdotal framework of the Slavonic apocalypse. It appears that certain details of the disclosure account, including peculiar references to the imagery of the Garden of Eden and others, are distinctive sacerdotal motifs. Indeed, the Slavonic apocalypse may intend to apply its sacerdotal vision to the entire created order. From this perspective, the whole universe is envisioned as one macrocosmic temple, with heaven, earth, and underworld as its sacred chambers. The aim of this chapter is to explore in depth the cosmological revelation found in *Apocalypse of Abraham* 19–21 and its possible connections to the sacerdotal traditions.

Waters of the Sacred Courtyard[1]

Abraham's vision begins in the initial verses of chapter19 when the patriarch receives the divine command from the theophanic furnace to look beneath his feet and explore the lower levels of heaven. As the divine voice speaks, the "levels" under his feet open up to reveal the lower heavens.[2] Multitudes of angelic beings are situated on some of the lower heavens. On the lowest heavenly level, he sees stars and "the elements of earth obeying them."

The revelation, however, is not limited to heavenly realities. After contemplating the various levels of heaven and their inhabitants, Abraham receives another command from the Deity, this time the command to "contemplate creation." Following God's order, he again looks beneath his feet at the expanse and sees what the text calls the "likeness of heaven,"[3] the lower realms including the earth and the underworld:

> And he said to me, "Look now beneath your feet at the expanse and contemplate the creation which was previously covered over. On this level there is the creation and those who inhabit it and the age that has been prepared to follow it." And I looked beneath the expanse at my feet and I saw the likeness of heaven and what was therein. And I

> saw there the earth and its fruits, and its moving ones, and its spiritual ones, and its host of men and their spiritual impieties, and their justifications, and the pursuits of their works, and the abyss and its torment, and its lower depths, and the perdition which is in it. And I saw there the sea and its islands, and its animals and its fishes, and Leviathan and his domain, and his lair, and his dens, and the world which lies upon him, and his motions and the destruction of the world because of him. I saw there the rivers and their overflows, and their circles. And I saw there the tree of Eden and its fruits, and the spring, the river flowing from it, and its trees and their flowering, and I saw those who act righteously. And I saw in it their food and rest.[4]

Some features of this depiction, including the portrayal of Leviathan as the foundation of the world, indicate that the vision is not merely a "historical" disclosure like those that are revealed to the seer in the later chapters of the apocalypse, but rather a distinctive cosmological revelation of a different nature intending to communicate to the patriarch the structure of the entire world. Several details of this depiction are subtly connected to cultic traditions and indicate that here one might have a sacerdotal vision of the entire creation understood as the cosmological temple rather than simply a depiction of the universe. This macrocosmic sacred structure reflects the tripartite division of the earthly temple wherein heaven is conceived as the macrocosmic Holy of Holies; earth, the holy place; and the underworld—represented by the sea—the courtyard. This concept of the cosmological temple, attempting to connect creation and cult, is quite ancient, stemming from early Mesopotamian[5] and Egyptian[6] traditions. In Jewish materials, this conceptual trend is often associated with the cluster of protological motifs in which the Garden of Eden is understood as the celestial Holy of Holies[7] where the first human was ministering as the high priest.[8]

Scholars have noted that a conception of the cosmological temple is already implicit in some biblical materials, including Ezekiel's formative depiction of the eschatological sanctuary, which paradoxically juxtaposes cosmological and paradisal imagery.[9] Ezekiel's portrayal of the eschatological temple provides a crucial aid to discerning the possible sacerdotal dimensions of the cosmological narrative found in the

Slavonic apocalypse. For instance, one important cultic motif that is equally important in both Ezekiel and the *Apocalypse of Abraham* is the imagery of the primordial waters.

Abraham reports that he sees under his feet "the sea and its islands, and its animals and its fishes, and Leviathan and his domain, and his lair, and his dens, and the world which lies upon him, and his motions and the destruction of the world because of him . . . the rivers and their overflows, and their circles."[10] In addition to the text's use of the sea to represent the underworld, this watery imagery appears to betray several cultic connections as well.

In Jewish sacerdotal reinterpretations of creational imagery, the sea often symbolizes the courtyard of the sanctuary of the world. *Numbers Rabbah* 13.19 states that the court encompasses the sanctuary just as the sea surrounds the world.[11] *B. Sukkah* 51b likewise tells how the white and blue marble of the temple walls were reminiscent of the waves of the sea.[12] The association between the sacred chamber and the sea may also be suggested by the symbolism of the bronze tank in the courtyard of Israel's temple, designated in some texts as the "molten sea."[13] It has been suggested that "the great size of the tank . . . in conjunction with the fact that no practical application is offered for the 'sea' during the time of Solomon, supports the supposition that the tank served symbolic purpose.[14] Either the 'cosmic waters' or the 'waters of life,' which emanated from below the garden of Eden, or the 'great deep' of chaos is most often cited as the underlying symbolism of the molten sea."[15]

It appears that depictions of the eschatological temple in the Book of Ezekiel reflect the cosmological meaning of the sacred courtyard, connecting it to the imagery of living water. Victor Hurowitz notes that "Ezekiel's temple of the future has a river flowing from under the threshold (Ezekiel 47:1). . . . The river envisioned by Ezekiel seems to replace the basins in Solomon's temple—basins that may have symbolized the rivers of a divine garden."[16] Ezekiel 47:1–8 offers the following description of the sacred waters:

> Then he brought me back to the entrance of the temple; there, water was flowing from below the threshold of the temple toward the east (for the temple faced east); and the water was flowing down from below the south end of the threshold of the temple, south of the altar. Then he brought me out by

> way of the north gate, and led me around on the outside to the outer gate that faces toward the east; and the water was coming out on the south side. Going on eastward with a cord in his hand, the man measured one thousand cubits, and then led me through the water; and it was ankle-deep. Again he measured one thousand, and led me through the water; and it was knee-deep. Again he measured one thousand, and led me through the water; and it was up to the waist. Again he measured one thousand, and it was a river that I could not cross, for the water had risen; it was deep enough to swim in, a river that could not be crossed. He said to me, "Mortal, have you seen this?" Then he led me back along the bank of the river. As I came back, I saw on the bank of the river a great many trees on the one side and on the other. He said to me, "This water flows toward the eastern region and goes down into the Arabah; and when it enters the sea, the sea of stagnant waters, the water will become fresh." (NRSV)

The flowing rivers of this passage evoke the cosmological account found in the Slavonic apocalypse where the sea is depicted alongside rivers and their circles. Like the great prophetic account, the *Apocalypse of Abraham* is familiar with the paradisal provenance of the sacred waters since it connects the Edenic tree with "the spring, the river flowing from it." In both passages, the waters of the Paradise are portrayed as "flowing."[17] The origin of the paradisal imagery of the circulating waters can be traced to Genesis 2:10,[18] in which a river flows from Eden to water the garden.[19] In Ezekiel, however, the image of flowing Edenic waters receives further cultic meaning. Yet such an emphasis is not unique to Ezekiel. Gregory Beale notes[20] that the similar sacerdotal imagery of "rivers" can also be found in the description of Israel's Temple in Psalm 36:8–9.[21] Scholars have additionally discerned[22] a similar sacerdotal motif of sacred waters in various Jewish extrabiblical accounts, including the *Letter of Aristeas* 89–91[23] and *Joseph and Aseneth* 2.[24] Christian materials also display acquaintance with the sacerdotal tradition of flowing waters. Revelation 22:1–2, for example, portrays a river of the water of life flowing from the throne of God.[25]

If we again turn our attention to the foundational Ezekiel account, it is notable that in Ezekiel 47:12, the imagery of the water is conflated with other distinctive symbols, including arboreal imagery:

> And on the banks, on both sides of the river, there will grow all kinds of trees for food. Their leaves will not wither nor their fruit fail, but they will bear fresh fruit every month, because the water for them flows from the sanctuary. Their fruit will be for food, and their leaves for healing.

This portrayal is evocative of the constellation of motifs found in the Slavonic apocalypse, particularly where the tree of Eden is mentioned in conjunction with other trees:

And I saw there the tree of Eden and its fruits, and the spring, the river flowing from it, and its trees and their flowering, and I saw those who act righteously. And I saw in it their food and rest.[26]

One cannot ignore the panoply of striking similarities between Ezekiel and the *Apocalypse of Abraham*, both of which combine the imagery of flowing rivers, Edenic trees, and the fruits of these trees that will serve as nourishment for the elect.[27] In both accounts, the Edenic imagery appears to hint at the motif of eschatological restoration of the harmony of creation, known in various traditions as the paradise of the righteous. Paradisal imagery, as mentioned, permeates the Ezekelian account. In the Slavonic account, too, the patriarch sees "those who act righteously" near the tree of Eden. Some early Jewish texts often interpret this restored, uncorrupted, paradisal state of creation in cultic terms, envisioning it as the eschatological temple.[28]

The host of similarities between Ezekiel and the *Apocalypse of Abraham* suggests that the portrayal of the eschatological temple found in the great prophetic book appears to exercise some influence on the cosmological narrative of the apocalyptic work. Moreover, Ezekiel's cultic concerns may also underlie the Slavonic apocalypse's account, especially considering its own priestly concerns.[29]

Chambers of the Macrocosmic Temple

Let us now return to the motif of the sacred courtyard symbolically representing the primordial sea. In Jewish lore, the courtyard of the macrocosmic temple was identified with the sea, whereas the other chambers of the sanctuary of creation were associated with heaven and earth, respectively. A late rabbinic tradition that circulated in the name of Rabbi Pinhas ben Ya'ir states that "the Tabernacle was made to correspond to the creation of the world. . . . The house of the Holy of Holies was made to correspond to the highest heaven. The outer

Holy House was made to correspond to the earth. And the courtyard was made to correspond to the sea."[30] This arcane cosmological speculation is not a late rabbinic invention but a tradition with ancient roots. Josephus, in his *Jewish Antiquities* 3.121–123, suggests that the tripartite division of the earthly sanctuary was a reflection of the tripartite structure of the entire creation,[31] with its sacred chambers that corresponded to heaven, earth, and sea:

> Internally, dividing its length into three portions, at a measured distance of ten cubits from the farther end he set up four pillars, constructed like the rest and resting upon similar sockets, but placed slightly apart. The area within these pillars was the sanctuary; the rest of the tabernacle was open to the priests. Now this partitionment of the tabernacle was withal an imitation of universal nature; for the third part of it, that within the four pillars, which was inaccessible to the priests, was *like heaven* devoted to God, while the twenty cubits' space, even *as earth and sea* are accessible to men, was in like manner assigned to the priests alone.[32]

Likewise, *Jewish Antiquities* 3.180–181 affirms a similar tradition:

> For if one reflects on the construction of the tabernacle and looks at the vestments of the priest and the vessels which we use for the sacred ministry, he will discover that our lawgiver was a man of God and that these blasphemous charges brought against us by the rest of men are idle. In fact, every one of these objects is intended to recall and represent the universe, as he will find if he will but consent to examine them without prejudice and with understanding. Thus, to take the tabernacle, thirty cubits long, by dividing this into three parts and giving up two of them to the priests, as a place approachable and open to all, Moses signifies *the earth and the sea*, since these too are accessible to all; but the third portion he reserved for God alone, because *heaven* also is inaccessible to men.[33]

The idea that cult and creation corresponded was also known to another prominent Jewish interpreter, Philo, who suggests that the holy temple of God represents the whole universe in his *De Specialibus*

Legibus 1.66.[34] This belief that the earthly temple is a replica of the entire creation is rooted in biblical materials; the creation of the world in Genesis 1–2 is set in conspicuous parallel with the building of the tabernacle in Ex 39–40. Moshe Weinfeld notes that "Gen 1:1–2:3 and Ex 39:1–40:33 are typologically identical. Both describe the satisfactory completion of the enterprise commanded by God, its inspection and approval, the blessing and the sanctification which are connected with it. Most importantly, the expression of these ideas in both accounts overlaps."[35] Scholars often suggest that, in view of these parallels, the earthly sanctuary is envisioned as a microcosm of the world, imitating the sacerdotal structure of the entire creation.

Keeping in mind these intriguing connections, let us return to the *Apocalypse of Abraham*. If a cultic dimension is indeed present in its cosmological depiction, then the Slavonic apocalypse might also be aware of the threefold sacerdotal structure of the universe—heaven, earth, and watery underworld—as the visionary account found in chapters 19–21 mentions all three realms. In these chapters, the seer first sees the heavenly levels, and then the earth and the sea. Moreover, Abraham's position in the upper heaven, which represents the macrocosmic Holy of Holies, provides an elevated vantage point from which he is able to glimpse into the other chambers of the cosmological temple. This spatial arrangement provides additional insights about the structure of the macrocosmic sanctuary, which exhibits some similarity to the earthly temple.

Much like the earthly shrine, whose inner sanctum was shielded from the less holy parts of the sanctuary, the macrocosmic temple seems also to possess a sacred border between its Holy of Holies, identified with the heavenly realm, and its less sacred chambers, with the earth and the sea. Such a boundary, represented in the Slavonic apocalypse by the firmament, appears to be understood as equivalent to the *Pargod*, the mysterious curtain of the celestial Holy of Holies, an entity which, according to some traditions, reflects all human history from the beginning to the eschatological end. We should now explore more closely this imagery of the cosmic fabric.

The Veil of the Cosmological Sanctuary

Assuming that the idea of the macrocosmic temple is indeed present in the cosmological depiction found in the Slavonic apocalypse, it is possible that this macrocosmic structure, similar to the earthly shrine, has its own sacred veil that separates the adytum of the sanctuary from other less sacred enclosures.

It has been noted that the patriarch's revelations in the heavenly throne room are reminiscent of the vision of the *Pargod*, the heavenly counterpart of the veil of the terrestrial sanctuary.[36] Later Jewish mystical accounts often depict the *Pargod* as the mystical textile that miraculously reflects the history of creation. The patriarch's placement in the celestial Holy of Holies, gazing on the firmament under his feet, situates him behind the curtain that separates the heavenly adytum from the rest of the macrocosmic sanctuary.

Further, some researchers have commented that the unique way in which Abraham receives the vision of the ages is reminiscent of the disclosures to the Hekhalot mystics on the celestial curtain and the apocalyptic seers on the heavenly tablets.[37] Specifically, it recalls the revelation of the *Pargod* to R. Ishmael[38] in *Sefer Hekhalot*,[39] where the rabbinic seer beholds the whole span of human history on a cosmic curtain.[40]

The mystical screen of *3 Enoch*, like the medium of revelation in the *Apocalypse of Abraham*, reveals the order of events from the generation of the protological couple until the generation of the Messiah. However, as noted previously, in the *Apocalypse of Abraham* the vision of the *Pargod* encompasses not only historical but also cosmological subjects, attempting to reveal the structure of the entire universe.

In this respect, it is curious that some early Jewish texts state that even the veil guarding the terrestrial Holy of Holies was to be understood as the fabric that somehow mirrors the entire universe. Josephus's *Jewish War*, for example, explains that the veil of the Jerusalem temple was an image of the entire universe; it reads:

> Before these hung a veil of equal length, of Babylonian tapestry, with embroidery of blue and fine linen, of scarlet also and purple, wrought with marvelous skill. Nor was this mixture of materials without its mystic meaning: it typified the universe. For the scarlet seemed emblematic of fire, the fine linen of the earth, the blue of the air, and the purple of the sea; the comparison in two cases being suggested by their colour, and in that of the fine linen and purple by their origin, as the one is produced by the earth and the other by the sea. On this tapestry was portrayed a panorama of

> the heavens, the signs of the Zodiac excepted. (*Jewish War* V. 212–214)[41]

The account noticeably emphasizes the combination of the colors of the veil, which the author asserts symbolize the four elements of the universe: fire, earth, air, and water. He also underlines the familiar tripartite structure of the universe, in other words, the heavenly realm, the earth, and the sea. Josephus's reflection on the curtain of the tabernacle in his *Jewish Antiquities* contains a similar portrayal, again alluding to the cardinal elements and their corresponding colors:

> The tapestries woven of four materials denote the natural elements: thus the fine linen appears to typify the earth, because from it springs up the flax, and the purple the sea, since it is incarnadined with the blood of fish; the air must be indicated by the blue, and the crimson will be the symbol of fire. (*Jewish Antiquities* III. 183)[42]

Creation's projection onto the sacerdotal fabric, the veil of earthly sanctuary, may represent an important contribution to the concept of the heavenly curtain, *Pargod*, which shows the entire universe to apocalyptic or Hekhalot seers.

After this short excursus into early *Pargod* traditions, let us return to the developments found in the Slavonic apocalypse. Before proceeding to a close analysis of the revelation given to the patriarch, it will be important to discuss certain spatial aspects of this disclosure. Consider, for instance, *Apocalypse of Abraham* 21:1–2, which reports the Deity's command received by the visionary immediately before the disclosure is given to him; we read:

> And he said to me, "Look now beneath your feet at the expanse and contemplate the creation which was previously covered over. On this level there is the creation and those who inhabit it and the age that has been prepared to follow it." And I looked beneath the expanse at my feet and I saw the likeness of heaven and what was therein.[43]

Here the Deity orders the seer look beneath his feet. At first, the vision's arrangement appears to be strange and quite different from the customary appearance of the *Pargod*, which in rabbinic accounts is usually depicted as a vertical barrier. In the Slavonic apocalypse, however, the curtain of the celestial Holy of Holies, unlike the *paroket* of the earthly adytum, is not a vertical entity but a horizontal one. The arrangement of the vision stresses the fact that Abraham looks down from the heavenly Holy of Holies onto the medium of the divine revelation, which is situated under his feet. It affirms a paradoxical spatial structure of the macrocosmic sanctuary in which the upper Holy of Holies is separated from the lower realms by a horizontal boundary called "a spreading under one's feet"—in Slavonic, простертие ножное.[44] This horizontal orientation of the heavenly veil is not unique to the Slavonic apocalypse and is found in other Jewish documents. Some rabbinic traditions understand one of the heavens as a veil that separates the celestial Holy of Holies from the lower realms/heavens, often envisioned as the less sacred chambers of the heavenly Temple. George MacRae, in his in-depth investigation of the imagery of the heavenly veil,[45] draws attention to a passage from the Babylonian Talmud in which the lowest heaven, Wilon (וילון),[46] is understood as the cosmic veil.[47] The relevant passage from *b. Hag.* 12b reads:

> R. Judah said: There are two firmaments, for it is said: Behold, unto the Lord thy God belongeth heaven, and the heaven of heavens. Resh Lakish said: [There are] seven, namely, Wilon, Rakia', Shehakim, Zebul, Ma'on, Makon, 'Araboth. Wilon serves no purpose except that it enters in the morning and goes forth in the evening and renews every day the work of creation, for it is said: That stretcheth out the heavens as a curtain, and spreadeth them out as a tent to dwell in. Rakia' is that in which sun and moon, stars and constellations are set, for it is said: And God set them in the firmament [Rakia'] of the heaven.[48]

According to the rabbinic tradition, then, the cosmic curtain represented by Wilon, the lowest of the seven firmaments,[49] draws back every morning, revealing the light of day to the world, and in the evening, the same cosmic veil closes and hides the daylight.[50]

The biblical roots of Wilon's imagery are usually traced to Isaiah 40:22, in which the Deity is depicted as stretching heavens like a curtain: "It is he who sits above the circle of the earth, and its inhabitants are like grasshoppers; who stretches out the heavens like a curtain, and spreads them like a tent to live in. . . ."[51]

B. Ber. 58b also connects the imagery of the celestial veil with Wilon: "R. Huna the son of R. Joshua said: Wilon was torn asunder and rolled up, showing the brightness of Rakia."[52] It is significant that both talmudic passages connect the symbolism of Wilon to the imagery of firmament (רקיע). This connection is important in light of the tradition found in the *Apocalypse of Abraham*, in which the seer beholds the mysteries of creation and human history by gazing on the firmament at his feet:

> And he said to me, "Look now beneath your feet at the *expanse* (простертие) and contemplate the creation which was previously covered over. On this level there is the creation and those who inhabit it and the age that has been prepared to follow it." And I looked beneath the *expanse* (простертие) at my feet and I saw the likeness of heaven and what was therein. (*Apoc. Ab.* 21:1–2)[53]

In the biblical materials, the firmament or expanse (רקיע) is often understood as the diaphragm that separates upper waters from lower waters. Genesis 1:6 records that the Deity created a firmament (רקיע) in the midst of the waters in order to separate "the waters from the waters." In a fashion similar to the *Apocalypse of Abraham*, some midrashic materials appear to envision the firmament's separating function as the cosmic curtain by tracing the etiology of the sacerdotal veil to the division of upper and lower waters at that crucial point of creation. Thus, in *Midrash Bereshit Rabbati* on Exodus 26:33, the veil of the terrestrial sanctuary is put in parallel with the firmament as the dividing line between upper and lower waters:

> In the Tabernacle the veil divided between the Holy Place and the Holy of Holies, and in body the diaphragm divides the heart from the stomach, and in the world it is the firmament which divides between the upper waters from lower waters. . . .[54]

Numbers Rabbah 12:13 preserves a similar conceptual development:

> . . . It is written, In the beginning God created the heaven, etc. (Gen. I, 1), and it is written, Who stretchest out the

> heaven like a curtain (Ps. CIV, 2), while of the Tabernacle it is written, And thou shalt make curtains of goat's hair for a tent over the Tabernacle, etc. (Ex. XXVI, 7). It is written in connection with the second day, Let there be a firmament . . . and let it divide, etc. (Gen. I, 6), and of the Tabernacle it is written. The veil shall divide unto you (Ex. XXVI, 33). Of the third day we read, Let the waters under the heaven be gathered together (Gen. I, 9). . . .[55]

A passage from the *Book of Zohar* underlines the sacerdotal significance of the firmament as the curtain by stating that it separates the more sacred realm from the less sacred:

> Rabbi Yehudah said, "From here we learn that every division of opinion for the sake of heaven is destined to endure, for here is a division for the sake of heaven, and through it heaven endured, as it is written: *God called the expanse Heaven* (Genesis 1:8). In a waterskin of lofts they appear by the pint and endure. For we have learned that it is written: *The curtain shall serve you as a partition between the Holy and the Holy of Holies* (Exodus 26:33), precisely, for this is an *expanse* dividing in the middle. (*Zohar* I.33a)[56]

It appears that in the aforementioned passages from *Midrash Rabbah* and the *Zohar* there is found a peculiar parallelism in which the dividing line between upper and lower waters is understood as the cosmic veil. This rabbinic understanding of the curtain as the cosmic diaphragm between the more sacred upper regions and the less sacred lower realms, a boundary represented either by the lowest heaven or the firmament, appears to have early conceptual roots. MacRae draws attention to some Nag Hammadi materials in which the cosmic veil is understood as the threshold that separates the divine Pleroma from the world of matter. One text, the *Hypostasis of Archons* (NHC, II, 94, 9–14) states that "a veil exists between the world above and the realms that are below; and shadow came into being beneath the veil; and that shadow became matter; and that shadow was projected apart."[57] Here, as in the Jewish texts attesting to the Wilon imagery, the veil is understood as the horizontal entity dividing the divine realm from its material "shadow." Another passage, *Hypostasis of Archons* (NHC, II, 95, 19–22), again envisions the cosmic veil as the dividing border between upper and lower abodes: "And Sophia and Zoe caught him up and gave him charge of the seventh heaven, below the veil between above and below."[58] In these heterodox Christian traditions, similar to the aforementioned rabbinic developments in which the lowest firmament Wilon serves as the macrocosmic veil, the lowest region/aeon of the divine Fullness, Sophia, is often understood as the curtain separating the realm of the Pleroma from the realm of humans. *On the Origin of the World* (NHC, II, 98, 21–23) another Nag Hammadi text, informs its readers that "she (Sophia) functioned as a veil dividing mankind from the things above. . . ."[59]

As we see, these texts often endow their cosmic veils with a cultic function, serving as a boundary between the more sacred and the less sacred realms. The horizontal spatial arrangement of the macrocosmic "veil" in the *Apocalypse of Abraham* possesses both cosmological and cultic significance. It might suggest that the lower realms portrayed in the patriarch's vision can be understood as exterior chambers of the temple of the universe, which correspond to the less sacred chambers of the terrestrial sanctuary known as the holy place (*hekhal*) and the vestibule (*olam*).[60]

The Leviathan as the Foundation Stone

Returning to the motif of the sacred courtyard, which the Slavonic apocalypse associates with the sea, another feature demands some attention, namely, the mysterious oceanic inhabitant, Leviathan, whom the text portrays as the foundation of the world. Exploring this motif of the primordial monster sustaining the earth leads to a cluster of Jewish traditions in which the world's protological foundation often has cultic connotations, being closely associated with the sacred base of the Temple. The idea of the sacerdotal and cosmological groundwork received its crystallization in the notion of the Foundation Stone (the *Eben Shetiyah*),[61] the primordial entity with which, according to some Mesopotamian[62] and Jewish texts, creation began and which became the cornerstone not only of the entire world[63] but also of the temple.[64] This idea of the primordial foundation of the sanctuary is reflected in *2 Enoch,* in which the primordial aeon Adoil becomes the foundation of the upper temple, represented by the divine throne.[65]

In rabbinic lore, the Foundation Stone was often identified both with the foundation of the upper sanctuary[66] and with the rock in the earthly Holy of Holies of the Jerusalem Temple. *Mishnah Yoma* 5:2 tells us that "after the Ark was taken away a stone remained there from the time of the early Prophets, and it was called '*Shetiyah*.' It was higher than the ground by three fingerbreadths."[67]

Moreover, in Jewish lore, the primordial stone additionally becomes the cosmic plug, intended to subdue and seal the waters of chaos. One can find such idea of the primeval waters' sealing in the *Prayer of Manasseh* 1–3, in which the Deity seals the abyss with his glorious Name:

> O Lord, God of our fathers, God of Abraham, Isaac, Jacob, and their righteous offspring; He who made the heaven and the earth with all their beauty; He who bound the sea and established it by the command of his word, He who closed the bottomless pit and sealed it by his powerful and glorious name. . . .[68]

Although the Foundation Stone is not mentioned in this early passage, the reference to the divine Name parallels this entity insofar as the *Eben Shetiyah* was often associated with the Name. *Targum Pseudo-Jonathan* on Exodus 28:30 states that, in the beginning, God sealed up the mouth of the Tehom with the Foundation Stone, on which the divine Name was engraved.[69] In the Babylonian Talmud,[70] this protological act of the Deity was later replicated by King David, who similarly seals the waters of chaos with the stone inscribed with the Tetragrammaton.[71] Here the primordial act of subduing of the chaotic waters is linked to the Temple's foundation.[72] Michael Fishbane notes that

> . . . the waters of Tehom are held in check by a stone . . . and this is the foundation stone upon which the Temple itself was established. . . . Thus . . . the Temple serves as an *axis mundi*, or point of connection and intermediation between the divine realms above and the chaotic waters below. There is also a palpable trace in these accounts of the ancient mythic theme of the establishment of the world and the heavenly shrine upon the defeated waters of chaos. This topic is most famously known from the great battle and building scenes found in *Enuma elish* iv-v; but one will also recall

> the striking link between the divine combat against the sea and the references to the building of a temple recorded in Exod. 15:6–8, 17.[73]

The imagery of the Foundation Stone, envisioned as the primordial solid point, brings us back to the cosmological account of the Slavonic apocalypse, in which Leviathan is depicted as the foundation of the world.[74] Like the *Eben Shetiyah,* Leviathan too serves as the cosmic dam against the turbulent waters. Rabbinic lore also often describes Leviathan not only as the cornerstone of the world[75] but also, similar to the Foundation Stone, as the barrier against the waters of chaos.[76] *Pesikta Rabbati* 48:3 claims that if Leviathan did not lie over the abyss and press down upon it, the abyss would eventually destroy the world and flood it.[77] In view of these traditions, scholars suggest that the Jewish materials appear to describe Leviathan as "a plug over the primordial waters, preventing a world-threatening flood from arising from the netherworld."[78] Similar imagery is used with respect to the Foundation Stone.[79] Thus both Leviathan and the Foundation Stone are envisioned as the cosmic boundaries predestined to "block the primordial waters."[80] William Whitney notes that rabbinic tradition about Leviathan "places him at a focal point in the cosmic order. He is the one solid point on which the cosmos might be founded in the midst of the watery depths."[81] This, again, evokes the rabbinic understanding the Foundation Stone as an initial solid point of cosmos, thrown by the Deity into the primordial abyss.[82] In this respect, it is intriguing that the Leviathan tradition preserved in *1 Enoch* 60:9 depicts God throwing the monster into the depths of the sea during the process of creation, an act strikingly reminiscent of the protological casting of the Foundation Stone into the abyss.[83]

The position of Leviathan as the sacred foundation of the cosmological temple might also be hinted at in *Apocalypse of Abraham* 10:9–10 in which the Leviathans are paired with the Cherubim/*Hayyot.*[84] Ezekiel's vision depicts the *Hayyot* as the holders or foundation of the celestial sanctuary represented by the divine Chariot. Their counterparts are the Cherubim of the Holy of Holies, who hold the divine Presence in the earthly adytum. Pairing the Leviathans with these sacerdotal "holders" provides additional insight into the cultic functions of the monsters of the sea.[85]

Appointing Yahoel, the angelic embodiment of the divine Name, as the stabilizing force over the Leviathans is also instructive. Whitney notes that *Apocalypse of Abraham* 10:9–10 is concerned with the stability of the *Axis Mundi*, since Yahoel—the angelic representation of the Name—rules over the Leviathans and is portrayed as "the one who guarantees the stability of the cosmic axis."[86] Juxtaposing the themes of divine Name and the *Axis Mundi*, represented by Leviathan(s), again calls to mind the tradition of the Foundation Stone in which this primordial entity is sealed with the divine Name to suppress the watery chaos under the sanctuary. Whitney notes the same stabilizing function of Yahoel in relation to the *Hayyot*; besides taming the Leviathans, he also reconciles the rivalries of the Living Creatures of the Cherubim against one another. Whitney suggests that "here the power of the name of God serves to suppress dark and threatening forces beneath the throne of God."[87] The hypostasized divine Name thus tames chaotic forces both in the foundation of the upper sanctuary as well as the sanctuary of the world.

It is also possible that, in some traditions, Leviathan is envisioned not only as the Foundation Stone that provides the cultic base and seals the primordial waters but also as the cosmological courtyard of the macrocosmic temple that, like the outer sacerdotal chamber, circumscribes the sacred realm. In some traditions, Leviathan encompasses the entire world, acting as "*Circuitus Mundi.*"[88]

Leviathan "embodying" the sacred structure also seems to be found in the Babylonian Talmud, which tells that Leviathan will represent the building material for the eschatological Tabernacle. *B. Baba Bathra* 75a speaks of the following tradition: "Rabbah in the name of R. Johanan further stated: The Holy One, blessed be He, will in time to come make a tabernacle for the righteous from the skin of Leviathan; for it is said: Canst thou fill tabernacles with his skin."[89] Here the eschatological tabernacle of the righteous will be constructed from the skin of Leviathan.

Conclusion

Examining the cultic dimensions of the cosmological account found in chapter 21 of the *Apocalypse of Abraham*, we have suggested that this chapter portrays the macrocosmic temple, with the sacred chambers corresponding to heaven, earth, and the underworld. The presence of such sacerdotal imagery reflects the cultic concerns that permeate the Slavonic apocalypse. Written shortly after the destruction of the Jerusalem Temple, the text offers an alternative, idealized vision of the sanctuary in order to mitigate the catastrophic loss of the earthly shrine. It portrays the young hero of the faith as an adept of otherworldly priestly praxis, receiving revelation about the true upper prototype of the earthly temple. In this respect, the portentous cultic disclosure of the macrocosmic temple in the very beginning of Abraham's vision in the celestial Holy of Holies appears to envision him as an archetypal sacerdotalist to whom God reveals the "idea of priesthood." The sacerdotal developments taking place in the *Apocalypse of Abraham* and other Jewish apocalyptic writings will influence later Jewish mystical developments, as rabbinic seers will also receive visions of the idealized sanctuaries.[90]

Another distinctive feature of the sacerdotal universe of the *Apocalypse of Abraham* that will play a similarly prominent role in later Jewish mysticism is the cultic dimension of the demonic side that attempts to mirror the sacerdotal realities of the divine realm. It has been previously noted that the chief antagonist of the Slavonic apocalypse, the fallen angel Azazel, appears to possess his own "glory," or *kavod*, an attribute that is reserved almost exclusively for the depiction of the Deity in apocalyptic accounts.[91] The transference of divine theophanic attributes to the story's antagonist seems part of the broader ideological tendency of the Slavonic apocalypse, which builds paradoxical symmetry between the good and evil realms. Leviathan's role as the foundation stone of the macrocosmic sanctuary appears also to belong to the similar cluster of ideas that attempt to envision the prominent agents of the Other Side as counterparts to the divine realities.

The Demise of the Antagonist in the Apocalyptic Scapegoat Tradition

> What was that vision? Uzza and Azael, who were "falling down and having eyes open."
>
> —*Zohar* III.194a

Introduction

As has been already noted in our study in the *Apocalypse of Abraham*, the reader encounters an eschatological reinterpretation of the chief sacerdotal event of the Jewish tradition, namely, the Yom Kippur ceremony. In particular, chapter 13 utilizes this enigmatic rite, in which the angel Yahoel, depicted as the celestial high priest, bestows the garment of sins upon the main antagonist of the story, the fallen angel Azazel, who is then sent into the lower realm.

Previous studies note that the peculiar details of this account evoke the scapegoat ritual, the annual atoning ordinance of the Jewish tradition outlined in the Book of Leviticus, during which the transgressions of the Israelites were heaped upon a goat who was then banished into the wilderness.[1] According to Leviticus, in the Yom Kippur ordinance, the exile of the cultic animal into an uninhabitable realm coincided with another significant progression, namely, the entrance of the high priestly celebrant into the divine presence—that is to say, into the Holy of Holies.

By adding several nuances, the Slavonic apocalypse offers a unique apocalyptic understanding of the purifying ordinance. In this eschatological reinterpretation of Yom Kippur, the main hero of the story does not simply enter the sacred chamber of the earthly Temple made by human hands, but rather the celestial throne room, represented by the highest heaven. His ominous counterpart, on the other hand, namely, the fallen angel bearing the name of the scapegoat, is exiled to the subterranean sphere. Such refashioning ushers the enigmatic rite into an entirely new conceptual dimension. Some traces of this novel apocalyptic framework also appear in rabbinic and early Christian accounts, suggesting that later interpretations of the Yom Kippur imagery may have been shaped by not only biblical patterns but also early apocalyptic developments. Indeed, later rabbinic and Christian testimonies betray obvious similarities with the apocalyptic currents.

It is even possible that the determinative biblical version of the ritual may not have completely escaped the influence of the apocalyptic worldview. After all, even the early version found in Leviticus appears to deal with certain themes also found in apocalyptic literature, such as the transformation and the breaching of the boundaries of sacred realms, as well as alongside purification and atonement.

The conceptual roots of the Yom Kippur ritual are shrouded in mystery. In their attempts to clarify the origin of this enigmatic rite, scholars have often focused on Mesopotamian traditions, which are permeated by a complex apocalyptic worldview, including visions, initiations, and heavenly journeys. Although the Mesopotamian materials yield some useful information, a great deal of uncertainty remains. This uncertainty is reflected in the proposed rationale behind the ritual described in Leviticus. On one hand, it has been proposed that the ritual was developed as a dialogical reaffirmation of the practice of heavenly ascent, as the earthly complement to the visionary's eschatological entrance into the celestial Holy of Holies. On the other hand, the opposite approach has been articulated as well—it has been suggested that the Levitical ritual may have arisen as a polemic against such practices, in order to discourage the praxis of the heavenly priesthood by establishing an alternative cultic framework that limits the access to the divine presence on earth to the members of certain priestly clans.[2]

While there are no clear answers to the questions about the account found in the Book of Leviticus, it is possible that later accounts of the atoning rite, those in the Mishnah and early Christian authors, were influenced by the apocalyptic reinterpretations of Yom Kippur found in early apocalyptic texts such as the *Book of the Watchers*, the *Animal Apocalypse*, and the *Apocalypse of Abraham*.

In this respect, it is important to note several possible "apocalyptic" features of the atoning ritual that seem present in the later descriptions of the scapegoat ordinance. For instance, several enigmatic additions to the Levitical blueprint of the scapegoat ritual appear in later interpretations of the atoning rite found in mishnaic, targumic, and talmudic accounts, especially in the description of the conclusion of the scapegoat ceremony. Some of these accounts insist that in the final moments of the ritual in the wilderness the crimson band of the scapegoat was removed and then placed back onto the animal. The scapegoat was then pushed off the cliff by its handlers. These traditions are not attested to in the biblical description from Leviticus, yet they figure into many rabbinic and early Christian interpretations. *M. Yoma* 6:6, for example, contains this tradition:

> What did he do? He divided the thread of crimson wool and tied one half to the rock and the other half between its horns, and he pushed it from behind; and it went rolling down, and before it had reached half the way down the hill it was broken in pieces. He returned and sat down beneath the last booth until nightfall. And from what time does it render his garments unclean? After he has gone outside the wall of Jerusalem. R. Simeon says: From the moment that he pushes it into the ravine.[3]

This account depicts the climax of the scapegoat ceremony in which the handlers of the scapegoat stripped away the infamous crimson band from the cultic animal, and then, according to the Mishnah, the band was divided into two pieces, one of which was tied to a rock and the other to the animal's horns. The scapegoat was finally pushed off the cliff by its handlers. Scholars have suggested that the scarlet band was envisioned as an impure garment or, more specifically, as the attire of sins[4] that the cultic animal was predestined to carry in an uninhabitable realm, in this case, the wilderness.[5] Loosing the cultic band possibly signifies the forgiveness of the sins of the Israelites,[6] since, in some Jewish accounts, the imagery of loosing is closely connected to the forgiveness of transgressions.[7]

The aforementioned mishnaic passage also hints to the fact that the final destination of the scapegoat's exile was not merely the desert but rather the underworld or abyss, a descent symbolically expressed by the pushing of the animal off the cliff.

Other Jewish and Christian sources, both preceding and contemporaneous with the aforementioned mishnaic testimony, attest to the scapegoat's dramatic descent and the ritual function of the crimson band. For instance, in *De plantatione* 61, Philo speaks about the fall of the scapegoat.[8] Similarly, although Justin Martyr does not directly mention the act of pushing the cultic animal off the cliff, his statements regarding the scapegoat's death in *Dialogue with Trypho* hint at his knowledge of the ritual:

> Likewise, the two identical goats which had to be offered during the fast (one of which was to be the scapegoat, and the other the sacrificial goat) were an announcement of the two comings of Christ: Of the first coming, in which your priests and elders send him away as a scapegoat, seizing him and putting him to death. . . . (40:4)[9]

Further, *The Epistle of Barnabas* 7:6–11 repeats the tradition of disrobing the scapegoat by removing the cultic band, connecting the crimson thread to the messianic or sacerdotal garment of Christ.[10] It relates a version of the ritual in which the priest wraps a piece of scarlet wool around the scapegoat's head; its handler subsequently takes the goat into the wilderness and removes the wool, placing it on a blackberry bush. This depiction parallels both *m. Yoma* 4:2, in which the celebrant places a thread of crimson wool onto the head of the scapegoat, and *m. Yoma* 6:6, in which the handler of the scapegoat divides the thread of crimson wool and ties one half of it to the rock.[11]

Later rabbinic testimonies found in the targumic and talmudic literature are also cognizant of the disrobing and rerobing of the cultic animal, as well as its forced descent from the cliff into the abyss. In these rabbinic accounts, this cliff is often called the Zok (Heb. צוק).[12] One such example is found at *b. Yoma* 67a:

> What did he do? He divided the thread of crimson wool, and tied one half to the rock, the other half between its horns, and pushed it from behind. And it went rolling down and before it had reached half its way down hill it was dashed to pieces. He came back and sat down under the last booth

> until it grew dark. And from when on does it render his garments unclean? From the moment he has gone outside the wall of Jerusalem. R. Simeon says: from the moment he pushes it into the Zok.[13]

Y. Yoma 6:3 also contains such a motif:

> . . . All during Simeon the Just's lifetime he [the scapegoat] did not fall down half the mountain before he dissolved into limbs; after Simeon the Just's death he fled to the desert and was eaten by the Saracens.[14]

As shown above, both the Babylonian and Jerusalem Talmuds make reference to the high places as the animal's final destination. Both accounts also portray its violent descent, culminating in the dramatic disintegration of the scapegoat's body.

Targum Pseudo-Jonathan on Leviticus 16:21–22 provides a specific location from which the scapegoat was to be pushed—the mountains of Beth Haduri:

> Aaron shall lay both his hands on the head of the live goat, in this fashion: his right hand upon his left. He shall confess over it all the iniquities of the children of Israel and all their rebellions, whatever their sins; he shall put them on the head of the goat with a declared and explicit oath by the great and glorious Name. And he shall let (it) go, in charge of a man who has been designated previously, to go to the desert of Soq, that is, Beth Haduri. The goat shall carry on himself all their sins to a desolate place; and the man shall let the goat go into the desert of Soq, and the goat shall go up on the mountains of Beth Haduri, and the blast of wind from before the Lord will thrust him down and he will die.[15]

The intriguing reference to "the blast of wind from before the Lord" causing the scapegoat's demise may represent a spiritual or angelic agent pushing the goat into the abyss, which is reminiscent of the story found in the *Book of the Watchers* in which the archangel Raphael executes Asael's punishment. Indeed, as Lester Grabbe notes, although in this passage "the goat dies, as in the Mishnah," his final demise "is ascribed to a supernatural force rather than to the human agent."[16]

These traditions—hurling the scapegoat off the cliff and the alteration of his "attire," the crimson band, immediately before his death—are strikingly reminiscent of the eschatological reinterpretations of the scapegoat rite in the *Book of the Watchers*, the *Apocalypse of Abraham*, as well as other Jewish apocalyptic material. As mentioned, the *Apocalypse of Abraham* reflects the tradition of sending the scapegoat into the lower realm when Yahoel banishes Azazel first to the earthly realm and eventually into the fiery abyss of the subterranean sphere.[17] It is noteworthy that, much like the scapegoat in mishnaic testimonies, the antagonist's exile in the Slavonic apocalypse coincides with his disrobing and rerobing. The text tells us that the fallen angel was first disrobed of his celestial garment and then reclothed in the ominous attire of human sins; it reads: "For behold, the garment which in heaven was formerly yours has been set aside for him, and the corruption which was on him has gone over to you."[18]

Azazel's ontological garments are likely altered from angelic to demonic in order to prepare for the new conditions of his exile, indicated by the connection between his transition to the lower realm and his disrobing and rerobing. As we see, then, such clothing metaphors in this text serve as important markers for the characters' transitions to different habitats or realms.

The traditions of the scapegoat's garments and his descent into the lower realm must now be explored in detail in the search of their possible apocalyptic roots.

The Reinterpretation of the Yom Kippur Ritual in the Jewish Apocalypticism

As noted, one of the earliest apocalyptic reinterpretations of the scapegoat ritual in Jewish tradition can be found in the *Book of the Watchers*, in which the story of the cultic gatherer of impurity receives a novel conceptual makeup. This early Enochic booklet refashions the scapegoat rite in a paradoxical angelological way, incorporating details from the sacrificial ritual into the story of its main antagonist, the fallen angel Asael.

1 Enoch 10:4–7 presents a striking depiction laden with the familiar sacerdotal details; it reads:

> And further the Lord said to Raphael: "Bind Azazel by his hands and his feet, and throw him into the darkness. And split open the desert which is in Dudael, and throw him there. And throw on him jagged and sharp stones, and cover him with darkness; and let him stay there forever, and cover his face, that he may not see light, and that on the great day of judgment he may be hurled into the fire. And restore the earth which the angels have ruined, and announce the restoration of the earth, for I shall restore the earth. . . .[19]

Several scholars have noticed numerous details of Asael's punishment that are reminiscent of the scapegoat ritual. Daniel Olson, for instance, argues that "a comparison of 1 Enoch 10:4–8 with the Day of Atonement ritual (cf. Lev 16:8–26), where we find a goat sent off 'to Azazel,' leaves little doubt that Asael is indeed Azazel."[20] Additionally, Daniel Stökl Ben Ezra observes that "the punishment of the demon resembles the treatment of the goat in aspects of geography, action, time and purpose."[21] Furthermore, the place of Asael's punishment designated in *1 Enoch* as *Dudael* is reminiscent of the terminology used for the designation of the ravine of the scapegoat (בית הדורו/הדודו) in later rabbinic interpretations of the Yom Kippur ritual.[22] This is reflected in, for example, *m. Yoma* and *Targum Pseudo-Jonathan*.[23]

Asael's special execution in *1 Enoch* 10, especially in comparison with the undifferentiated punishment of the other leader of the fallen angels, Shemihazah, which takes place with the rest of the celestial rebels,[24] strengthens the cultic interpretation of his punishment, perhaps envisioning him as a sort of expiatory offering for the sins of fallen angels and the giants,[25] or as a sacrifice to remove the impurity and defilement caused by the celestial rebels and their offspring.[26] Józef Tadeusz Milik draws attention to one such motif found in fragments from the *Book of Giants* (*4Q203*), in which Asael/Azazel seems to be an expiatory agent; it reads:[27]

> . . . and [yo]ur power . . . Blank Th[en] 'Ohyah [said] to Hahy[ah, his brother . . .] Then he punished, and not us, [bu]t Aza[ze]l and made [him . . . the sons of] Watchers, the Giants; and n[o]ne of [their] be[loved] will be forgiven . . . he has imprisoned us and has captured yo[u]. (*4Q203*, frag. 7, col. I)[28]

Moreover, some Qumran materials appear aware of the angelological interpretation of the scapegoat figure. In particular, they depict Azazel as the eschatological leader of the fallen angels,[29] incorporating him into the story of the Watchers' rebellion.[30] All these strands of evidence demonstrate that the conceptual link between the scapegoat and the fallen angel is documented in a number of important materials across a substantial span of history.

Placing the Scapegoat into the Abyss

Although biblical materials are silent about the demise of the scapegoat, later rabbinic testimonies often insist on the fact that the cultic animal was pushed by his handlers off the cliff, hurtling into the abyss. The apocalyptic versions of the Yom Kippur ritual in the *Book of the Watchers*, the *Animal Apocalypse*, and some other Enochic materials often contain some features of the scapegoat ritual that are absent from the Levitical description but which are present in the mishnaic testimonies. One of the important details here is the placement of the antagonist into a pit situated in the wilderness. As mentioned, in *1 Enoch* 10, the Deity orders Raphael to open the pit in the desert and throw Asael into the darkness. The text further describes the celestial scapegoat's fall into the depths of the abyss.[31] It should be noted that, although *m. Yoma* 6:6 also informs its readers about the descent of the animal from the desert cliff, this account is much later than the tradition found in the *Book of the Watchers*, the *Animal Apocalypse*, and other Jewish apocalyptic works. The latter were written several centuries before the composition of the Mishnah.

The roots of the Enochic tradition of the angelic scapegoat's punishment in the abyss are shrouded in mystery. Some scholars believe that this motif may have its origin in a set of earlier developments connected with another infamous Enochic rebel, namely, Shemihazah. *1 Enoch* 10:11–15[32] tells how the other rebellious angels, including their leader Shemihazah, will eventually be shepherded into the abyss:

> "Go, inform Semyaza and the others with him who have associated with the women to corrupt themselves with them in all their uncleanness. When all their sons kill each other, and when they see the destruction of their beloved ones, bind them for seventy generations under the hills of

> the earth until the day of their judgment and of their consummation, until the judgment which is for all eternity is accomplished. And in those days they will lead them to the abyss of fire;[33] in torment and in prison they will be shut up for all eternity. And then he (Semyaza) will be burnt and from then on destroyed with them; together they will be bound until the end of all generations."[34]

Scholars suggest that *1 Enoch* 6–11 represents a fusion[35] of two[36] originally distinct traditions, one of which was associated with Shemihazah and the other with Asael.[37] Some studies argue that the Shemihazah material may have had priority over the Asael material,[38] suggesting that the Shemihazah narrative did not originally include the Azazel episode in 10:4–8.[39] George Nickelsburg, for instance, proposes that the interpolation of material about Asael was drawn "largely from an independent myth about the rebellion of a single angelic figure."[40] Some researchers attempt to explain the cultic overtones of *1 Enoch* 10 by suggesting that the tradition of Asael's punishment arose as a conflation of Leviticus 16 and the Shemihazah narrative.[41] An in-depth discussion of the editorial history of *1 Enoch* 10 transcends the boundaries of the current investigation, but it is important to emphasize that the final constellation of the sacerdotal traditions reflected in chapter 10 most certainly took place before the composition of *m. Yoma*, with its peculiar understanding of the scapegoat ritual.

The incarceration of the fallen angels in the abyss is also reflected in other booklets of *1 Enoch*, which largely draw on the formative accounts found in the *Book of the Watchers*.[42] For instance, the tradition of confining the celestial rebels to the depth of the abyss looms large in the *Animal Apocalypse* in which the story of the fallen angels is clothed in obscure cosmological and zoomorphic imagery.[43] Thus, *1 Enoch* 90:24 designates the abyss as the place of the punishment of the fallen "stars":

> And the judgment was held first on the stars, and they were judged and found guilty; and they went to the place of damnation, and were thrown into a deep (place), full of fire, burning and full of pillars of fire.[44]

As in the *Book of the Watchers*, this Enochic booklet seems to pay special attention to the penalization of the leaders of the fallen angels. *1 Enoch* 88:1 further refashions the story of Asael's punishment, shrouding it in even more esoteric imagery.[45] Despite the cryptic embellishments, however, the place of the demonic scapegoat's punishment is described as a narrow, deep, dark, and desolate abyss, just as in the *Book of the Watchers*.[46]

The *Book of Jubilees*, another Second Temple Jewish text that tries to reconcile the Mosaic revelation with the Enochic tradition, contains the same motif.[47] *Jubilees* 5:6, for instance, reads:

> Against his angels whom he had sent to the earth he was angry enough to uproot them from all their (positions of) authority. He told us to tie them up in the depths of the earth; now they are tied within them and are alone.[48]

Similarly, *Jubilees* 5:10 reads:

> Now their fathers were watching, but afterwards they were tied up in the depths of the earth until the great day of judgment when there will be condemnation on all who have corrupted their ways and their actions before the Lord.[49]

In both passages, the condemned angels are restrained in the place of their punishment, a *topos* designated in *Jubilees* as the depth of the earth. Moreover, *Jubilees* provides another striking reinterpretation of the scapegoat symbolism relevant to our study. *Jubilees* 34:18–19, as others have noted, connects the story of Joseph and his brothers to the scapegoat ritual:

> For this reason, it has been ordained regarding the Israelites that they should be distressed on the tenth of the seventh month—on the day when (the news) which made (him) lament Joseph reached his father Jacob—in order to make atonement for themselves on it with a kid—on the tenth of the seventh month, once a year—for their sins. For they had saddened their father's (feelings of) affection for his son Joseph. This day has been ordained so that they may be saddened on it for their sins, all their transgressions, and all their errors; so that they may purify themselves on this day once a year.[50]

Some studies even argue for the formative value of the biblical Joseph story in the development of the original account of the atoning rite.[51] It is additionally important that the biblical account of Joseph's ordeal includes the motifs of binding the "human scapegoat" and placing him in the pit.[52]

Scholars note that besides the early Jewish pseudepigraphical works, the tradition of pushing the scapegoat off the cliff may also appear in Philo's *De Plantatione*, 6.[53] While speaking about the scapegoat ritual, Philo mentions "rocky chasms" in the wilderness. Some have suggested that such an interpretation may reflect an early Midrash on the meaning גזר (cut, split up) in ארץ גזרה (Lev. 16:22) and/or the historical memory of the actual cliffs in the mountains of Jerusalem.[54] However, although Philo's early testimony is significant, it is not entirely novel, since the early Enochic booklets, written several centuries before the great Alexandrian author, already attempt to connect the figure of the celestial scapegoat to the motifs of ruggedness and the abyss.

It should be noted that the motif of the angelic antagonists' exile into the subterranean pits is not confined to the Enochic currents but can also be found in Adamic lore. In these Adamic accounts we can see the formative influence of the Enochic aetiology of evil. Thus, Revelation 20:1–3,[55] an account that some scholars believe to be patterned after the Enochic scapegoat tradition,[56] sentences its chief antagonist, Satan, to the bottomless pit.[57] The later Satan traditions, reflected in the *Primary Adam Books*, perpetuate the narrative of the antagonist's expulsion.[58] It is also intriguing that, in the *Primary Adam Books*, the antagonist's demotion coincides with the use of distinctive clothing metaphors, such as the removal of the opponent's angelic garment[59] and his rerobing into the animal skins of the Serpent and the Beast.[60]

2 (Slavonic) Enoch also elaborates on this tradition of Satan's exile into the abyss with a complex mix of Adamic and Enochic trends. *2 Enoch* 24:4–5 reads:

> But one from the order of the archangels deviated, together with the division that was under his authority. He thought up the impossible idea, that he might place his throne higher than the clouds which are above the earth, and that he might become equal to my power. And I hurled him out from the height, together with his angels. And he was flying around in the air, ceaselessly, above the Bottomless.[61]

This account represents a curious intersection of the Enochic and Adamic aetiologies of evil, since the features of the chief character of one mythology of corruption are transferred to the antagonist of the other. Both conceptual developments, however, exhibit their independent, ancient roots. Besides its reliance on the familiar Enochic motifs, the tradition of Satan's fall into the pit in *2 Enoch* 24 also seems to draw upon some early biblical themes found in Isaiah[62] and Ezekiel.[63]

The aforementioned conceptual developments demonstrate that the early tradition of the scapegoat's exile into the wilderness found in Leviticus was enhanced by other prophetic and apocalyptic reinterpretations, which eventually led to a more complex understanding of the scapegoat's removal. This understanding grew to encompass two stages: (1) its exile into the wilderness and (2) its fall into the subterranean realm, represented by the abyss. It is this novel and more complex understanding of the cultic animal's removal that plays a prominent role in later mishnaic and early Christian understandings of the scapegoat ritual.

Clothing the Scapegoat with the Dark Garment

As we saw in previous chapters, another important feature absent in Leviticus but quite prominent in the rabbinic and early Christian depictions of the scapegoat ritual is the symbolism of the crimson band. Tied around the cultic animal's head, the ribbon was said to miraculously change color at the climax of the atoning ceremony in order to signify the forgiveness of Israel's sins. Early interpretations suggest that the scarlet band decorating the scapegoat's head was often intended to be a garment, the attire of human sins, carried by the animal into the uninhabitable desert. There, according to Christian and mishnaic testimonies, the cultic animal was "disrobed" by its handlers when its ribbon was either fully or partially removed.[64]

In the search for the possible roots of this complex and ambiguous tradition, some prophetic and apocalyptic accounts that deal with the motif of the spiritual scapegoats' attire are very useful. A peculiar reinterpretation of the Yom Kippur ritual found in the Book of Zechariah provides an important conceptual development that will be often used by later interpreters in their speculation about the garment of the scapegoat. Zechariah 3:1–5 gives the following description:

> Then he showed me the high priest Joshua standing before the angel of the Lord, and Satan standing at his right hand to accuse him. And the Lord said to Satan, "The Lord rebuke you, O Satan! The Lord who has chosen Jerusalem rebuke you! Is not this man a brand plucked from the fire?" Now Joshua was dressed with filthy clothes as he stood before the angel. The angel said to those who were standing before him, "Take off his filthy clothes." And to him he said, "See, I have taken your guilt away from you, and I will clothe you with festal apparel." And I said, "Let them put a clean turban on his head." So they put a clean turban on his head and clothed him with the apparel; and the angel of the Lord was standing by.

As I argued in the first chapter, this prophetic passage is permeated with Yom Kippur symbolism. It contains several characters that hold familiar cultic roles and attributes evocative of the atoning rite, namely, a human high priest who is reclothed during the ceremony, a character bearing the divine Name, and an accursed antagonist.

Already, the familiar constellation of cultic motifs can be discerned here, motifs that later play a prominent role in *Apocalypse of Abraham* 13. In particular, the spiritual creatures of Zechariah, like the *Apocalypse of Abraham*, are reminiscent of the two emblematic animals of the atoning rite, one of whom was endowed with the divine Name and another who was cursed. Similar too are the functions and actions of the actors of the prophetic account when compared to those of the Slavonic apocalypse. In Zechariah 3, as in the *Apocalypse of Abraham*, the attire of the human sacerdotal celebrant is changed from the defiled garments of sin to pure vestments. Conducting this transferal is the Angel of the Divine Name. Unlike the Slavonic apocalypse, the filthy human clothes are not directly transferred to Satan in Zechariah; nonetheless, his presence during the ceremony and his cursing represent important conceptual steps toward associating the demonic scapegoat with the attire of human sins.

The antagonist in Zechariah is not clothed with the dark vestment of human sins, but it is possible that this does take place in the *Book of the Watchers*. Asael, the celestial scapegoat, appears to receive a garment of darkness in *1 Enoch* 10:

> . . . And throw on him jagged and sharp stones, and cover him with darkness; and let him stay there forever, and cover his face, that he may not see light. . . .[65]

The symbolism of the scapegoat's covering, enhanced by the dichotomy of light and darkness, parallels another cluster of clothing metaphors often found in Jewish apocalyptic accounts, namely, the imagery of the seer's endowment with garment of light, received upon his entrance into upper realm. Asael seems to undergo a similar, albeit reverse, transformation when he is covered with darkness to prepare for his forced exile into the subterranean realm.

In view of these transformational correspondences, it is especially significant that Asael's *face* is covered. It appears that, here, like in the metamorphoses of Jewish patriarchs and prophets, the term "face" serves as a *terminus technicus* for designating the character's entire "extent." Moreover, the ontological refashioning of the visionary's "face" leads to his new status vis-à-vis the Deity when his face literally becomes the reflection of the glorious Face of God. Covering the antagonist's "face" leads to the opposite metamorphosis. In this context, therefore, the covering of Asael's "face" may suggest that he receives a new ontological garment that deprives him from access to or vision of the Deity.[66]

Elsewhere in the early Enochic booklets, too, these clothing metaphors are equally important. Asael and other fallen angels are often depicted as changing their angelic celestial vestments, even before their punishment in the abyss. This theme receives special attention in the *Animal Apocalypse*, a work permeated with intense transformational patterns. The distinct zoomorphic codes found in this enigmatic apocalypse allow its readers to easily discern the change of the ontological "costumes" of the main characters. Thus, in contrast to the *Book of the Watchers*, the *Animal Apocalypse* begins Asael's story with an account of his transformation and ontological "reclothing." *1 Enoch* 86:1 portrays a fallen star's celestial form changed into earthly "animal garments" upon his entrance in the lower realm:

> And again I looked with my eyes as I was sleeping, and I saw heaven above, and behold, a star fell from heaven, and it arose and ate and pastured amongst those bulls.[67]

The same cluster of clothing metaphors permeates the portrayal of the descent of other Watchers:

> And again I saw in the vision and looked at heaven, and behold, I saw many stars, how they came down and were thrown down from heaven to that first star, and amongst those heifers and bulls; they were with them, pasturing amongst them. And I looked at them and saw, and behold, all of them let out their private parts like horses and began to mount the cows of the bulls, and they all became pregnant and bore elephants and camels and asses.[68] (*1 Enoch* 86:3–4)

As in the *Book of the Watchers*, the *Animal Apocalypse* contains the familiar transformational pattern in which a change in the fallen angels' clothes coincides with the metamorphosis of the hero's ontological garments. The animal garments of skin into which the fallen angels are forced to change constitutes a striking contrast to the metamorphosis of Moses and Noah, who undergo the reverse process, changing their animal dress to angelic clothes.

This Enochic tradition appears to have played a formative role in later Adamic currents, in which its antagonist also receives the animal attires. Satan traditions, reflected in the *Primary Adam Books*, speak of his expulsion, which, as above, coincides with the removal of his angelic garment and his rerobing into the animal skins of the Serpent and the Beast.

The Binding of the Scapegoat

Along with his garment of darkness and exile to the abyss, *1 Enoch* 10 also speaks about the binding of Asael. Although the biblical account of the scapegoat ritual found in Leviticus does not mention any bindings for the scapegoat, it is very prominent in the mishnaic accounts, such as *m. Yoma* 4:2, in which the scapegoat is bound with the scarlet thread upon his selection by the high priest. Another tradition, found in *m. Yoma* 6:6, tells us that, in the final moments of the ceremony, the scapegoat was unbound and then retied with the crimson band.[69]

The features that mishnaic authors weave into the fabric of the ancient rite are intriguing, and seemingly novel. Yet it should not be forgotten that, several centuries before the composition of the Mishnah, some apocalyptic accounts already link the scapegoat ritual with the symbolism of binding, including *1 Enoch* 10.[70] In *1 Enoch 10*, the handler of the celestial scapegoat, the archangel Rafael, is instructed to bind the demon by his hands and feet immediately before throwing him into the subterranean pit. This is similar to *m. Yoma* 6:6 in which the cultic animal is bound with a crimson band *immediately* before his demise.

One interesting detail in Asael's binding is that he is bound by his hands and his feet, a peculiar sacerdotal custom that hints at the fallen angel's role as a cultic animal predestined for sacrifice. Likewise, Jewish tradition attests to rituals in which animals were bound before being offered as sacrifices. Moreover, some halakhic regulations even forbid the sacrifice of animals without binding. *2 Enoch*, for example, heavily emphasizes the binding of the sacrificial animal before its offering. In that text, the seventh antediluvian hero warns his children not to forget to bind their sacrifices.[71]

Besides the obvious cultic connotations, the theme of binding also seems to be connected with the exorcistic practice of "binding" the unclean spirits.[72] This practice is widely attested to in early Jewish literature, including, for instance, Tobit 8:3, in which the archangel Raphael binds a demon bearing the name Asmodeus.[73] An intriguing detail, here, is that, as in the *Book of the Watchers*, it is the archangel Raphael who binds the demon. The method of the antagonist's binding is also similar in both accounts—that is, like Asael, Asmodeus is bound by hand and foot.

It thus appears that it is no coincidence that the practice of binding demons come to the fore in the *Book of the Watchers*, a text focused primarily on the fallen angels. Moreover, in this work, the theme of binding is not confined solely to Asael's punishment but includes Shemihazah and other fallen angels as well. There the familiar constellation of peculiar details can be found in conjunction with the motif of banishment into the subterranean pit:[74]

> Go, inform Semyaza and the others with him who have associated with the women to corrupt themselves with them in all their uncleanness. When all their sons kill each other, and when they see the destruction of their beloved ones, bind

> them for seventy generations under the hills of the earth until the day of their judgment and of their consummation, until the judgment which is for all eternity is accomplished. And in those days they will lead them to the abyss of fire; in torment and in prison they will be shut up for all eternity. And then he (Semyaza) will be burnt and from then on destroyed with them; *together they will be bound* until the end of all generations. *(1 Enoch* 10:11–15; my italics)[75]

Paul Hanson has argued that "the details unique to the Azazel episode can be recognized as stemming from the expository techniques of interpreters writing from the perspective of apocalyptic eschatology as they now relate their narrative to yet another biblical text, Lev 16."[76] Hanson traces the roots of the motif of Asael's binding to Mesopotamian apocalyptic traditions.[77] He suggests that prophetic authors attempted to shepherd these traditions into a Jewish context by adopting the motif of binding to portray the capture of the rebel. Hanson argues that "Ezek 32, by combining the motifs of binding, casting into the pit, blotting out light, covering with darkness, and final healing of the earth, illustrates the important position assumed by late prophecy in mediating these archaic motifs from the ancient myths of rebellion in heaven to the writers of the Shemihazah story and the Azazel elaboration."[78]

Further, the motif of Asael's binding appears again in the *Animal Apocalypse* (*1 Enoch* 88:1–3), in which it is mentioned that the fallen star's hands and feet are tied. In fact, the *Animal Apocalypse* extends this tradition of sacrificial binding of the hands and the feet to all the "stars" who are similar to Asael:

> And I saw one of those four who had come out first, how he took hold of that first star which had fallen from heaven, and *bound it by its hands and its feet, and threw it into an abyss*; and that abyss was narrow, and deep, and horrible, and dark. And one of them drew his sword and gave (it) to those elephants and camels and asses, and they began to strike one another, and the whole earth shook because of them. And as I looked in the vision, behold, one of those four who had come out cast from heaven and gathered and

> took all the large stars whose private parts (were) like the private parts of horses, and *bound them all by their hands and their feet, and threw them into a chasm of the earth.*[79] (my italics)

Another Enochic booklet included in *1 Enoch*, the *Book of the Similitudes*, is also cognizant of the tradition of the Watchers' binding. In particular, in *Similitudes* 54:4–6, the *angelus interpres* discloses to the seer the purpose of the chain-instruments prepared for the fallen angels:

> And I asked the angel of peace who went with me, saying: "These chain-instruments—for whom are they being prepared? And he said to me: "These are being prepared for the hosts of Azazel, that they may take them and throw them into the lowest part of Hell; and they will cover their jaws with rough stones, as the Lord of Spirits commanded. And Michael and Gabriel, Raphael and Phanuel—these will take hold of them on that great day, and throw them on that day into the furnace of burning fire, that the Lord of Spirits may take vengeance on them for their iniquity, in that they became servants of Satan and led astray those who dwell upon the dry ground.[80]

Other pseudepigraphical texts reflect the same motif. For instance, *Jubilees*, at 5:6 and 5:10, depicts the binding of the fallen angels in the abyss:

> Against his angels whom he had sent to the earth he was angry enough to uproot them from all their (positions of) authority. He told us to tie them up in the depths of the earth; now they are tied within them and are alone. (*Jub.* 5:6)[81]

> Now their fathers were watching, but afterwards *they were tied up in the depths of the earth* until the great day of judgment when there will be condemnation on all who have corrupted their ways and their actions before the Lord. (*Jub.* 5:10)

Similarly, *Testament of Levi* 18:12 places the motif of binding in a cultic context when it portrays its antagonist bound by a high priestly figure.[82]

The theme of the antagonist's binding also appears in some New Testament materials, subtly revealing its formative Enochic roots. This is most obvious in the telling of the execution of angelic servants, the darkness to which they have been exiled, and their subsequent placement into the abyss. Thus, in Revelation 20:1–3, the antagonist's enchaining coincides with the now familiar motif of his banishment to the subterranean pit by an angelic executor.[83] Jude 6 also reveals a tradition of binding of the fallen angels; it reads:

> And the angels who did not keep their own position, but left their proper dwelling, he has kept in eternal chains[84] in deepest darkness for the judgment of the great Day. (NRSV)[85]

Here, too, the same elements can be found: the celestial rebels are bound and situated in the depths of darkness.[86] 2 Peter 2:4, which draws on Jude 6,[87] repeats this tradition of binding the fallen angels, carefully preserving motifs of darkness and abyss.[88]

Conclusion

Having explored the apocalyptic refashioning of the final moments of the scapegoat ritual, we return to the account of the antagonist's demotion found in the *Apocalypse of Abraham.* This Jewish pseudepigraphon, which was most likely written during the period in which the mishnaic descriptions of the atoning rite received their conclusive textual codification, provides us with a unique glimpse into the final stages of the ever-changing scapegoat imagery that began many centuries earlier in the Enochic booklets. Although the early traits of the Enochic apocalyptic blueprint still play a formative role in the Slavonic account,[89] this conceptual core is now greatly enhanced by some novel developments that are essential in mishnaic and early Christian versions of the atoning ritual. Thus the imagery of the celestial scapegoat's clothing, only vaguely alluded to in the early Enochic booklets, in the symbolism of covering the antagonist with darkness, now receives its distinctive conceptual expression as the impure vestment of human sins.

The details of the demonic scapegoat's exile into lower realms found in the Slavonic apocalypse are similarly indebted to the early Enochic blueprint. As with Asael in the Enochic tradition, the antagonist's exile in the *Apocalypse of Abraham* encompasses two movements:

first, to the earth, and second to the fiery abyss of the subterranean sphere. Although early versions of the scapegoat ritual found in the Book of Leviticus attest to only a one-step removal of the goat to the wilderness, the tradition of the two-step removal plays a prominent role in later mishnaic versions of the rite in which the cultic animal will be first taken to the wilderness and then further pushed into the abyss from the cliff.

All these developments point to the paramount importance of apocalyptic patterns for the later rabbinic and early Christian understandings of the scapegoat ritual. Such influence of Second Temple apocalypticism upon the development of the scapegoat imagery is not universally recognized; scholars have more often understood the presentations of the Yom Kippur ritual found in the Mishnah as an ideal form of the cult, based solely on biblical texts.[90] In contrast to these studies, our investigation suggests that these mishnaic accounts were profoundly influenced by the apocalyptic reinterpretations of the atoning rite found in such early Enochic writings as the *Book of the Watchers* and the *Animal Apocalypse*, the works that led the traditional biblical imagery into a new eschatological dimension.

The Nourishment of Azazel

> . . . after God cast Uzza and Azael down from their holy place, they went astray after the womenfolk and seduced the world also. It may seem strange that being angels they were able to abide upon the earth. The truth is, however, that when they were cast down the celestial light which used to sustain them left them and they were changed to another grade through the influence of the air of this world. Similarly the manna which came down for the Israelites in the wilderness originated in the celestial dew from the most recondite spot, and at first its light would radiate to all worlds and the "field of apples," and the heavenly angels drew sustenance from it, but when it approached the earth it became materialized through the influence of the air of this world and lost its brightness, becoming only like "coriander seed."
>
> —*Zohar* III.208a

Introduction

A large portion of the *Apocalypse of Abraham* is devoted to Abraham's celestial journey to the divine throne room. During this ascent, God assists the seer, appointing the great angel Yahoel to be the patriarch's companion on this dangerous trip into the upper realm. Yahoel's tasks include not simply guiding the patriarch to the divine abode but also preparing the visionary for his entrance into his new heavenly habitat. Consequently, en route to the divine presence, Abraham undergoes a series of initiations and transformations that reshape his ontology into an eschatological state suitable for the upper realm. One of the most striking stages in his metamorphosis comes from *Apocalypse of Abraham* 13:4 in which Yahoel tells Abraham about his future endowment with the angelic garment stripped from the former heavenly dweller, namely, the fallen angel Azazel.[1] This promise of the new celestial attire anticipates Abraham's transition to the state of a newly born heavenly citizen. Further, along the way, the seer learns how to abstain from earthly provisions and become nourished in a new, celestial way. *Apocalypse of Abraham* 11:1–2 relates the following tradition:

> And we went, the two of us alone together, forty days and nights. And I ate no bread and drank no water, because [my] food was to see the angel who was with me, and his speech with me was my drink.[2]

This passage, which recounts the patriarch's initiatory fast, is preceded by *Apocalypse of Abraham* 9:7 in which the Deity himself orders the seer to abstain from food and drink for forty days and nights.[3] During this exercise in self-denial, the hero of the faith learns how to be sustained in a new celestial way, not through food and drink but through his visual and audial contemplation of the great angel and his words. Scholars have noted the uniqueness of this imagery of nourishment on the angelic being, arguing, for instance, that "this description of an angel providing the kind of nourishment otherwise attributed to the *Shechinah* is quite unique and without parallel."[4]

The motif of celestial provisions appears, again, later in chapter 13, when Abraham prepares his animal sacrifices according to the instructions of the Deity and Yahoel. While the patriarch waits for the evening offering, the "impure bird"—that is to say, the fallen angel Azazel—descends upon the seer's sacrifices. In the antagonist's speech, delivered at this point and only once, the subject of human sustenance in heaven is again mentioned. This time, however, the theme of heavenly provisions is overshadowed by ominous overtones. The demoted celestial creature specifically warns the visionary about the perils of his upcoming heavenly journey, specifically, the lack of human food "on the holy heights." Here again the theme of nourishment appears in the midst of an encounter with a celestial being—this time, however, an encounter with the antagonistic one. *Apocalypse of Abraham* 13:36 reads:

> And an impure bird flew down on the carcasses, and I drove it away. And the impure bird spoke to me and said, "What are you doing, Abraham, on the holy heights, where no one eats or drinks, nor is there upon them food of men. But these will all be consumed by fire and they will burn you up. Leave the man who is with you and flee! Since if you ascend to the height, they will destroy you." And it came to pass when I saw the bird speaking I said to the angel, "What is this, my lord?" And he said, "This is iniquity, this is Azazel!"[5]

While this passage, as one found in chapter 11, deals with the subject of celestial provisions, one can easily detect an inversion. Here, a human person, rather than being nourished by the sight and speech of the celestial creature, can become, according to Azazel, "food" for heavenly creatures, doomed to be "consumed," like the animal sacrifices, through fiery annihilation.[6] The fallen angel, therefore, clearly disbelieving the possibility that a human being could survive in the upper regions, warns the seer of his catastrophic demise if he were to dare to cross into the heavenly realm.

It is clear that the passages about celestial nourishment, found in chapters 11 and 13, stand in a striking conceptual opposition. Such opposition, specifically between Yahoel and Azazel, depicted in the midst of traditions of human sustenance, is not limited to the passages found in these chapters. For example, later in the text, the Deity relates to Abraham the puzzling account in which the fallen angel nourishes Adam and Eve with grapes taken from the Tree of the Knowledge of Good and Evil.[7] Here, like the angelic protagonist of the story, the antagonist too is portrayed as a spiritual being who nourishes human beings. Yet while Yahoel's sustenance of Abraham, by means of sight and hearing, leads the patriarch into a celestial state, reminiscent of the prelapsarian condition, Azazel's feeding causes the corruption of the protoplasts, dooming them to exile from their elevated domicile in the Garden of Eden.

Such inverse patterns play a prominent role in the conceptual universe of the Slavonic apocalypse. This chapter will explore motifs of angelic and demonic nourishments found in the *Apocalypse of Abraham*, as well as their connections with the main theological currents of the text as a whole.

Roots of the Angelic Nourishment Motif

As previously mentioned, the theme of the seer's heavenly sustenance occurs in the context of Abraham's preparation for his visitation to the upper realm. It is important that the celestial nourishment through visual and audial contemplation coincides, in the text, with abstinence from normal human food. Such cessation appears to signal the seer's transition to a new ontological state as an angelic being.

Scholars have recognized the established Jewish tradition according to which the angels are not able to consume earthly food.[8] One early testimony to this tradition is found in the *Book of Judges*. Judges 13:15–16, in particular, depicts the Angel of the Lord openly rejecting human food, asking, instead, for a burnt offering.[9] In Judges 6:19–21 one finds a similar development when the angel first asks Gideon to prepare a meal but then, instead of eating it, annihilates the food with fire:

> So Gideon went into his house and prepared a kid, and unleavened cakes from an ephah of flour; the meat he put in a basket, and the broth he put in a pot, and brought them to him under the oak and presented them. The angel of God said to him, "Take the meat and the unleavened cakes, and put them on this rock, and pour out the broth." And he did so. Then the angel of the Lord reached out the tip of the staff that was in his hand, and touched the meat and the unleavened cakes; and fire sprang up from the rock and consumed the meat and the unleavened cakes; and the angel of the Lord vanished from his sight. (NRSV)

Such biblical witnesses bring to mind the interaction between Azazel and Abraham found in chapter 13 in which the fallen angel tells the patriarch about the absence of human food on the holy heights, and at the same time warns the patriarch that he himself can become the angelic food, burned together with his animal sacrifices.

Nonbiblical Jewish texts also contain the motif of the angels' abstinence from human food. A reference is found, for example, in the *Testament of Abraham* 4:9, in which the archangel Michael cannot be nourished by human food.[10]

Some Jewish texts, furthermore, argue that although the angels sometimes give the impression that they consume human food, in reality they do not. One early testimony to this belief is found in the *Book of Tobit*, in which the angel Raphael first partakes in a human meal but later tells the protagonist that his consumption of earthly food was just an illusion.[11] Similarly, Philo[12] and Josephus[13] argue that the angelic beings only create an appearance of eating human food.[14] Similar testimonies are found in pseudepigraphical[15] and targumic sources.[16]

Elsewhere, in the Jewish pseudepigrapha, one finds the belief that humans who achieved a celestial state, akin to the angelic beings, are not able to consume human food. For instance, in *2 Enoch*, a Jewish apocalypse written in the first century CE, a gesture toward the angelic status of its hero is indicated by his refusal to participate in a human meal.[17] Chapter 56 of this work depicts the return of the seventh antediluvian hero from his celestial trip. Upon his arrival, Enoch is asked by his son Methuselah to share food with close relatives. In response to this offer, the patriarch politely declines the invitation of his son, offering him the following reasons:

> Listen, child! Since the time when the Lord anointed me with the ointment of his glory, food has not come into me, and earthly pleasure my soul does not remember, nor do I desire anything earthly.[18]

Here, Enoch does not reject just any kind of food but rather rejects specifically *earthly* food, hinting to his son that he has already been transformed into a celestial creature who is satiated in a different way. It is also noteworthy that, in *2 Enoch* 56, the theme of rejecting earthly food is set in parallel with the motif of Enoch's anointment with ointment of God's Glory. This striking parallelism between an inability to partake in a human meal and angelic anointing might provide a portentous clue indicating the ways in which angels are nourished in the heavenly realm. We should therefore take a closer look at the scene of Enoch's anointing in *2 Enoch* 22.

2 Enoch 22:9 portrays the archangel Michael disrobing Enoch and anointing him with delightful oil. The text says that the oil's appearance is "greater than the greatest light and its ointment is like sweet dew, and the fragrance like myrrh; and it is like rays of the glittering sun."[19] The anointing with the oil effects the patriarch's transformation from his garments of skin to the luminous garment of an immortal angelic being. It is noteworthy that here the ointment of glory, also identified in the text as the paradisal dew, transforms the earthly being into a celestial creature who no longer enjoys earthly food.[20]

Moreover, the paradisal dew motif is noteworthy since it is present in another pseudepigraphical account of celestial nourishment attested in *Joseph and Aseneth* 16:14, in which the angels' food is said to be made from the dew from the paradise of God:

> . . . For this comb is (full of the) spirit of life. And the bees of the paradise of delight have made this from the dew of the roses of life that are in the paradise of God. And all the angels of God eat of it and all the chosen of God and all the sons of the Most High, because this is a comb of life, and everyone who eats of it will not die for ever (and) ever.[21]

Scholars have noted that the honeycomb that Pentephres's daughter consumes from the angel's hand is reminiscent of manna, the celestial provision once sent from heaven[22] to the Israelites in the wilderness.[23] It is also noteworthy that in *Joseph and Aseneth* 15, as in *2 Enoch* 56, the motif of nourishment of the seer coincides with her anointing when the honeycomb is identified as "ointment of incorruptibility."[24] Like Enoch's, Aseneth's anointing also grants immortality to the recipient.[25]

The constellation of motifs found in *2 Enoch* and *Joseph and Aseneth* might provide an important insight into how the angels are actually "fed" in heaven. It is often assumed that they are nourished through the vision of the divine light. Yet it cannot be excluded that other traditions are also at play in various Jewish materials. It is possible, then, that the celestial creatures are, during their anointment with divine light, fed not only through their eyes but through the whole of their angelic bodies. *2 Enoch*'s account of the patriarch's anointing gestures toward such a possibility. *2 Enoch* 22 clearly depicts the source of the patriarch's metamorphosis as the light coming from the luminous divine form, designated in the text as the divine Face. From *2 Enoch*, one learns that the light proceeding from the divine Face causes dramatic changes in Enoch's appearance. His body endures irreversible transformations as it becomes covered with the divine light. In this account, the luminous body of a newly born celestial citizen is literally "nourished" by the luminosity of the divine form.[26] This anointing of angelic bodies from the splendor of the divine Presence, His *Shechinah,* can be viewed as an example of angelic sustenance. A later rabbinic tradition appears to affirm just such a nourishing function. Thus, from *Numbers Rabbah* 21:16, one learns the following:

> . . . You can learn the answer by analogy with the ministering angels, of whom it says, His ministers are a flaming fire (Ps. CIV, 4). Whence do they derive their sustenance? R. Judan, citing R. Isaac, said: From the lustre of the *Shechinah* they derive their sustenance; as it says, In the light of the king's countenance is life (Prov. 16:15).[27]

Here, the fiery nature of the angels' bodies is put in parallel with the splendor of the divine form. Similarly, *Pesikta of Rav Kahana* reads:

> His ministers are a flaming fire. And how is their fire nourished? By the flame-like splendor of God's presence, for it is written "In the light of the King's countenance is life" (Prov. 16:15).[28]

Here again the angels are satiated by the splendor of the Deity's form which, as in *2 Enoch*, is depicted as the divine presence—that is to say, as the Face of God.

While the humans transported to the upper realm are taught how to be nourished in a new celestial way, the once-celestial creatures of heaven, exiled to the lower realm, are forced to survive on a different provision, namely, earthly food.[29] In this respect it is important that the formative biblical narrative of the Fall, found in Genesis 3, indicates a change in the mode of nourishment for both human beings and the serpent. For instance, in Genesis 3:17–18, the Deity tells Adam the following: "[I]n toil you shall eat of it all the days of your life; thorns and thistles it shall bring forth for you; and you shall eat the plants of the field."[30]

The theme of Adam and Eve's new means of sustenance, after the Fall, is also reflected in the *Primary Adam Books*, which depict a change in the mode of sustenance of the protoplasts, after their eviction from the Garden of Eden.[31] The *Primary Adam Books* mention the hunger experienced by Adam and Eve as they found themselves on earth. The cause of their hunger does not appear to be the absence of food on earth but, rather, the dining habits of the first humans, who were accustomed to different, celestial sustenance during their stay in Paradise. It is thus significant that the Armenian, Georgian, and Latin versions of the *Primary Adam Books* emphasize the difference between the two foods: the angelic food,[32] which Adam and Eve ate in paradise, and the food that lies before them on the earth.[33] The key aspect of these versions of the *Primary Adam Books* is their common emphasis that *earthly* food is unsuitable for those who just came from the celestial realm. As the *Primary Adam Books* states, "[Adam and Eve] did not find food like the food by which they had been nourished in the Garden." In particular, Eve's discourse in the *Primary Adam Books* 4:2 emphasizes this difference between earthly and celestial food, referring to earthly food as nourishment for the beasts.[34]

It is also noteworthy that, in the *Primary Adam Books*, one can find the motif of anointing with the oil of the Tree of Life—the arboreal symbol that stands in striking opposition to the infamous Tree of Corruption from which the protoplasts once tasted the forbidden fruit. Thus, the *Primary Adam Books* portray Eve and Seth traveling to paradise in order to bring the oil to the dying Adam. Here, as in *2 Enoch* and *Joseph and Aseneth*, the anointing which comes from the Tree of Life might be understood as an eschatological sustenance of the restored humanity. Yet, this provision is denied to Adam; the archangel Michael tells Eve and Seth that the oil will be used for the restoration of the original condition of humankind in eschatological time.

The Mosaic Background of Abraham's Angelic Sustenance

Having provided a brief excursus on the early traditions of celestial nourishment, it will be fruitful now to return to the *Apocalypse of Abraham*. More specifically, in this regard, a question remains: from which cluster of early Jewish traditions about heavenly food have our authors drawn their inspiration? For instance, recall that some of these traditions, especially those found in the *Testament of Abraham*, are directly associated with the patriarch and his close family by its emphasis on the biblical tale of Abraham's table fellowship with the angels. Yet, although some aforementioned pseudepigraphical interpretations of angelic nourishment are connected with Abraham's story, especially as reflected in Genesis 18:8, the tradition that lay behind the *Apocalypse of Abraham* appears to be drawing on a different set of conceptual currents, namely, the lore associated with the son of Amram, another prominent visionary of the Jewish tradition, who, like Abraham, had an encounter with the Deity on Mount Sinai.

The sustenance of Moses on Mount Sinai, as a theme, received unprecedented attention from later Jewish interpreters. One encounters a panoply of rabbinic witnesses that links the theme of heavenly nourishment to the figure of the great Israelite prophet. For example, *Exodus Rabbah* 47:7 communicates that, during his reception of the Torah from the Deity on Mount Sinai, Moses was satiated by a vision of the luminous divine form:

> It was for the benefit of Moses that he fasted a hundred and twenty days, so that he might receive the Torah; and from whence did Moses receive nourishment? From the splendor of the *Shechinah*, for it says, Thou preservest them all (Neh. 9, 6).[35]

Here, as in the *Apocalypse of Abraham*, the seer's feeding on the celestial form coincides with the abstinence from human food.[36] *Exodus Rabbah* 47:5 even compares Moses' celestial nourishment to the sustenance of the living creatures of the divine Throne, namely, the *Hayyot*:

> . . . He did neither eat bread, nor drink water, that is, in this world; but in the World to Come he will eat of the bread of the Torah and drink of its waters. For this reason he did neither eat bread, etc. Whence did he derive his nourishment? From the lustre of God's presence. Lest this seem surprising, then remember that the *Hayyot* who bear the Divine Throne are also nourished from the splendor of the *Shechinah*.[37]

In this passage, the angelic creatures holding the Deity's seat are said to be nurtured by the presence of the divine form situated on the Merkabah. *Exodus Rabbah* 47:5 thus points to a connection between the supernatural nourishment and the angelic state of the great prophet. Furthermore, elsewhere, *Exodus Rabbah* 47:5 makes the conceptual link even more explicit by stating that the prophet's supernatural sustenance emulates the condition of the celestial citizens.[38]

It has already been mentioned that, in early Jewish accounts, the angelic food often serves as an eschatological marker, which signals the seer's transition to the original prelapsarian condition of the protoplast. Rabbinic materials too have often interpreted the heavenly nourishment not only as the habitual means for sustenance of the angelic being[39] but also as the means of nourishment for the protological and eschatological humankind.[40] Thus, *b. Ber.* 17a reads:

> A favorite saying of Rab was: [The future world is not like this world.] In the future world there is no eating nor drinking nor propagation nor business nor jealousy nor hatred nor competition, but the righteous sit with their crowns on their heads feasting on the brightness of the divine presence, as it says, And they beheld God, and did eat and drink.[41]

It is possible that these midrashic testimonies do not represent merely a later rabbinic invention but Jewish lore with very ancient roots, possibly predating the *Apocalypse of Abraham*. The account of Abraham's unconventional nourishment found in the Slavonic apocalypse seems to point to these ancient roots of Moses' feeding on the *Shechinah*, since, in the Slavonic apocalypse, the theme of Abraham's sustenance on Yahoel is situated within a cluster of distinctive Mosaic motifs. Other studies have noted the "Mosaic" flavor of the celestial feeding in the *Apocalypse of Abraham*, suggesting that the authors of the Slavonic apocalypse must draw on such traditions. David Halperin, for example, reflecting on the tradition of the heavenly provision found in *Apocalypse of Abraham*, suggested that, like Abraham,

> Moses also discovered that the divine presence is itself nourishment enough. That is why Exodus 24:11 says that Moses and his companions beheld God, and ate and drank. This means, one rabbi explained, that the sight of God was food and drink to them; for Scripture also says, In the light of the King's face there is life. . . . We may assume that the author of the *Apocalypse of Abraham* had such midrashim

in mind when he wrote that "my food was to see the angel who was with me, and his speech—that was my drink."[42]

It is also evident that the Mosaic tradition of celestial nourishment has a priority over the Abrahamic developments, as this motif is deeply rooted in early biblical and extrabiblical Mosaic testimonies. For instance, Exodus 24:11 testifies that Moses and his associates "beheld God, and they ate and drank." Such nourishment did not involve conventional human sustenance, as Deuteronomy 9:9 and 9:18 state that the prophet did not eat bread or drink water. Moreover, the prophet's forty-day ordeal, when he was sustained by the food of the angels, has been set in parallel by early Jewish interpreters to another account of the supernatural feeding, namely, the story of the Israelites' forty years' wandering in the Egyptian desert, during which the people of God were nourished on the food of angels—manna.[43] The LXX version of Psalm 77(78):25 makes this connection explicit, identifying the manna of the wilderness as the bread of angels.[44] Further, the *Wisdom of Solomon* 16:20 also attests to a similar tradition. In Pseudo-Philo's *Biblical Antiquities*, moreover, Moses himself tells the Israelites that they have eaten the bread of angels for forty years.[45] Later rabbinic sources also understand manna as the angels' provision.[46]

The tradition that Moses was fed through the *vision* of the divine form betrays very ancient conceptual roots. Already, in the formative Genesis account, the protoplasts' feeding on the fruit of the Tree of the Knowledge of Good and Evil coincides with the motif of their eyes being opened.[47] Scholars have noted[48] that Philo, also, in his *Quaestiones et Solutiones in Exodum*, is cognizant of the visual nature of Moses' celestial nourishment, calling his vision the food of souls. *Quaestiones et Solutiones in Exodum*, then, depicts Moses' visionary experience in the following way:

> What is the meaning of the words, "they appeared to God in the place and they ate and drank?" Having attained to the face of the father, they do not remain in any mortal place at all, for all such places are profane and polluted, but they send and make a migration to a holy and divine place, which is called by another name, logos. Being in this place, through the steward, they see the master in a lofty

> and clear manner, envisioning God with the keen-sighted eyes of the mind. But this vision is the food of souls, and true partaking is the cause of a life of immortality. Wherefore, indeed, it is said, "they ate and drank." For those who are indeed very hungry and thirsty did not fail to see God become clearly visible, but like those who, being famished, find an abundance of food, they satisfied their great desire.[49]

Andrea Lieber has proposed that in this Philonic passage Moses' encounter on Mount Sinai is spiritualized in such a way that "the vision of the divine presence satiates, like the sacrificial meal."[50] Further, Lieber suggests that

> Philo appears influenced by the tradition, witnessed also in rabbinic, patristic and pseudepigraphic literature, that there is no "eating" in heaven; angelic beings do not require food like humans, yet their "bodies" are nonetheless sustained by divine means.[51]

It appears that, like later rabbinic testimonies, the *Apocalypse of Abraham* is drawing on this cluster of early Mosaic motifs. A panoply of distinctive Mosaic markers found in the Slavonic pseudepigraphon, including Abraham's forty-day fast and his travel to the mountain Horeb point to such a possibility. Previous studies have convincingly demonstrated the paramount importance of Mosaic traditions for the authors of the *Apocalypse of Abraham*, a writing in which many details of the patriarch's journey become patterned after the visionary portfolio of the son of Amram.[52]

In this respect, it is noteworthy that these Mosaic motifs loom especially large in and around the verses that tell about Abraham's celestial nourishment. In fact, the next verse that follows the theme of spiritual nourishment (*Apoc. Ab.* 11:3) tells about the seer and his angelic companion's arrival to Horeb, the mountain where Moses received his revelation; it reads: "And I ate no bread and drank no water, because [my] food was to see the angel who was with me, and his speech with me was my drink. And we came to the glorious God's mountain—Horeb."[53]

It is also noteworthy that, both in the Mosaic tradition and in the *Apocalypse of Abraham*, one can find references to the themes of both eating *and* drinking. David Halperin suggests that the Mosaic trend might draw on the passage from Exodus 24:11 that states that Moses and his companions "beheld God, and ate and drank."[54] Both Mosaic and Abrahamic passages make reference to the forty-day abstinence from human food during which the celestial nourishment occurs. Such parallels again point to the formative Mosaic blueprint that stands behind the traditions of celestial nourishment present in the Slavonic apocalypse.

Fiery Provisions

Later rabbinic testimonies about Moses' angelic feeding often mention the luminous form of the Deity—the portentous source of substance on Mount Sinai. This feature is indicative of the importance of anthropomorphic tenets in the Mosaic narratives. In the Book of Exodus, the prophet's encounter at Sinai became one of the crucial nexuses of the anthropomorphic ideologies in which one can find not only developed *Kavod* terminology but also the imagery of God's countenance—the Deity's *Panim* (another crucial tenet of the priestly anthropomorphic paradigm).

Yet, in the *Apocalypse of Abraham*, in which the divine body traditions become challenged and reshaped by the rival audial paradigms, the motif of nourishment on the divine form received a novel polemical reformulation.[55] Scholars have suggested that one such polemical clash takes place in the story of Bar-Eshath, an infamous idol of Abraham's father that perishes in flames, serving as fuel for Terah's meal. In *Apocalypse of Abraham* 5:9–12, the young hero of the faith relates the following encounter:

> And it came to pass, after I had put the splinters on the fire, in order to cook food for my father. . . . When I came back again I found Bar-Eshath fallen backwards, his feet enveloped in fire and terribly burned. Laughing greatly to myself, I said, "Bar-Eshath, you certainly are able to kindle fire and cook food!" And it came to pass, while I was speaking laughingly, that he was gradually burned up by

> the fire and became ashes. And I brought the food to my father, [and] he ate.[56]

I have argued elsewhere that Bar-Eshath's story reveals the polemics against the divine body traditions. Bar-Eshath's depiction attempts to deconstruct the familiar imagery of the anthropomorphic divine Form, which is often depicted in Jewish and Christian accounts with the feet/lower body enveloped in fire.[57] For our study, it is important that the account of the idol's fiery demise is connected with the motif of nourishment. Moreover, it seems to point to the fact that, in the *Apocalypse of Abraham*, the reader encounters several traditions of "nourishment" on anthropomorphic forms, authentic as well as idolatrous.

Thus, while in *Apocalypse of Abraham* 5:14–17 the false divine representation, embodied by the idol Bar-Eshath, assists in the nourishment of the idolater Terah,[58] later in the text the true divine form represented by the Angel of the Tetragrammaton becomes the authentic source for the seer's provision.

The polemics against the divine body traditions in our apocalypse appear to be unfolded in the midst of a dialectical mix of demotion and exaltation. As one remembers, the anthropomorphic body of Terah's idol undergoes a fiery ordeal and perishes. As the apocalypse's story unfolds, Abraham too is drawn into an array of fiery tests laden with the possibility of catastrophic demise. Yet, unlike Bar-Eshath, Abraham endures and survives the test of the heavenly furnace. While the idol becomes the means of nourishment, the patriarch escapes such a destiny. This comparison of Bar-Eshath to Abraham is not farfetched. The aforementioned speech of Azazel, from chapter 13, clearly envisions such a connection. In it, the fallen angel warns the patriarch that he can, during his celestial journey, perish in the heavenly fire, becoming heavenly food.[59]

In this respect, it is intriguing that later rabbinic testimonies about Moses' ordeal on Mount Sinai associate spiritual nourishment with the visionary's demise in heavenly fire by juxtaposing the story of the prophet's feeding on the splendor of the *Shechinah* with the story of the death of Nadab and Abihu—Aaron's sons who were said to have perished in the fire of the Holy of Holies. Thus, *Leviticus Rabbah* 20:10, a passage that deals with the mysterious death of the two sons of Aaron, describes the following tradition:

> R. Joshua of Siknin in the name of R. Levi observed: Moses did not feed his eyes on the *Shechinah* and derived benefit from the *Shechinah*. . . . Nadab and Abihu, however, fed their eyes on the *Shechinah* and did not derive benefit therefrom, as may be inferred from the following: And Nadab and Abihu died before the Lord.[60]

Exodus Rabbah 3:1 attests to a similar tradition:

> R. Hoshaia the Elder said: Moses did well in hiding his face, for God said to him: Since thou didst show me respect and hide thy face when I would show Myself to thee, I assure thee that thou wilt be near Me on the mountain for forty days and forty nights. Thou wilt not eat nor drink, but wilt feast on the splendor of the *Shechinah*, as it is said: and Moses knew not that the skin of his face sent forth beams (Ex. XXXIV, 29). But Nadab and Abihu uncovered their heads and fed their eyes on the lustre of the *Shechinah*, as it is said: And upon the nobles of the children of Israel He laid not His hand; and they beheld God, and did eat and drink (ib. XXIV, 11). Did they not receive [the penalty of death] for what they had done?[61]

These rabbinic passages again draw attention to the question of how the celestial citizens are fed on the luster of the divine form. We briefly explored this enigmatic praxis earlier in our study, during our analysis of *2 Enoch* 56, in which the angelic body of the seventh antediluvian hero was "nourished" by the splendor of the divine Face. It is possible that the rabbinic passages about the fiery demise of Nadab and Abihu, unfolded in the midst of the story of Moses' supernatural feeding, might also be related to this practice of celestial nourishment. The corporealities of Aaron's sons, however, unlike the transformed bodies of Moses and Enoch, were not able to sustain the terror of the divine light, being annihilated by its fatal splendor.

The rabbinic interpretation of the fiery demise of Nadab and Abihu also brings to mind both the Bar-Eshath episode, in which the idol perishes in the flames, and Abraham's own trials in the Slavonic apocalypse, in which he is depicted as passing the dangerous fiery thresholds. In this respect, it is possible that the patriarch's fiery trials on his way to the divine presence themselves represent his supernatural nourishment. Jewish apocalyptic and mystical traditions often depict the angelic hosts bathing in the rivers of fire.[62] For example, Daniel 7:10 describes a stream of fire flowing from the presence of the Deity. The imagery of the celestial rivers of fire is also found in the *Songs of the Sabbath Sacrifice* (*Song 10*, *4Q405* 15ii–16 2).[63] Similarly, *Hekhalot Zutarti* (*Synopse* §390) reads:

> One *hayyah* rises above the seraphim and descends upon the tabernacle of the youth whose name is Metatron, and speaks with a loud voice. A voice of sheer silence. . . . Suddenly the angels fall silent. The watchers and holy ones become quiet. They are silent, and are pushed into the river of fire.[64]

Sefer Haqomah 155–164 also attests to this tradition:

> And (the) angels who are with him come and encircle the Throne of Glory. They are on one side and the (celestial) creatures are on the other side, and the *Shechinah* is on the Throne of Glory in the center. And one creature goes up over the seraphim and descends on the tabernacle of the lad whose name is Metatron and says in a great voice, a thin voice of silence, "The Throne of Glory is glistening!" Immediately, the angels fall silent and the *irin* and the *qadushin* are still. *They hurry and hasten into the river of fire.*[65]

In some rabbinic passages, the angels are bathing in the rivers of fire after their trips to the lower regions in order to purify themselves and restore their celestial form.[66] These enigmatic rituals of bathing in the fiery rivers streaming from the throne of the Deity seem to pertain to the daily nourishing routines of the celestial citizens.

Previous studies have often suggested that the symbolism of the divine furnace is mirrored in the dualistic framework of the *Apocalypse of Abraham*, most notably in the imagery of the furnace of Azazel.[67] The fiery nature of the heavenly abode is mentioned multiple times in the text. Moreover, it is notable that Abraham's journey into the heavenly realm is depicted as a movement into a realm of fire. Also, the realm of the antagonist is depicted with similar imagery. In Yahoel's speech, for instance, found in chapter 14, which reveals the true location of the chief antagonist, the arch-demon's abode is designated as the furnace of the earth. Azazel himself, moreover, is depicted as the "burning coal" or the "firebrand" of this infernal kiln.

This imagery of the furnace is explicitly brought to bear on the notion of nourishment in the Slavonic apocalypse in *Apocalypse of Abraham* 13:36.[68] Azazel's warning to the patriarch in this passage about becoming "food" for celestial beings perishing in the fire of the upper abode becomes paradoxically invoked later in the text when the Deity himself designates some human beings as the "food" for another, in this case demonic, furnace, namely, "the fire of hell." Thus, in *Apocalypse of Abraham* 31:3–5, we read:

> Since I have destined them to be food for the fire of hell, and ceaseless soaring in the air of the underground depths, the contents of a worm's belly. For those who do justice, who have chosen my will and clearly kept my commandments, will see them. And they will rejoice with joy at the destruction of the abandoned. And those who followed after the idols and after their murders will rot in the womb of the Evil One—the belly of Azazel, and they will be burned by the fire of Azazel's tongue.

Interestingly, this passage identifies the fiery tongue of Azazel with the fire of hell—that is to say, the very reality by which the sinners will be destroyed. In the aural conceptual framework of the Slavonic apocalypse in which the divine Voice is revealed in the midst of fire, Azazel's fiery manifestation also appears to be surrounded with distinctive aural connotations.

Transformation through Celestial Nourishment

Other studies have noted the distinctive soteriological dimension that accompanies the motif of spiritual nourishment.[69] Through their feeding on the luster of the *Shechinah*, exalted patriarchs and prophets have proleptically foreshadowed the eschatological condition of humankind, in which earthly creatures will be once again sustained like the angels, by the divine presence. It is important here that both in the Mosaic tradition and in the *Apocalypse of Abraham* celestial nourishment occurs during the ascetic practices of the visionaries, namely, during their forty-day fasts. Thus, in *Apocalypse of Abraham* 9:7, the seer is commanded by God that he must "for forty days abstain from every food which issues from fire, and from the drinking of wine, and from anointing [yourself] with oil."[70] As noted above, the patriarch's abstinence from human food mimics the biblical fast of the son of Amram.

Similar motifs, in which the tradition of celestial nourishment unfolds in the midst of ascetic practices, are also found in another Jewish pseudepigraphical account, namely, *Joseph and Aseneth*. Like Moses and Abraham, the protagonist of the story, an Egyptian maiden, fasts and is then nourished by the angelic being.[71]

The celestial initiation stories of Abraham and Aseneth, as we see, are strikingly similar. As in the *Apocalypse of Abraham*, in *Joseph and Aseneth* we can find a paradoxical mix of visual and aural imagery in the portrayals of angelic food.[72] Such a mixture is especially evident in the depiction of the chief angelic characters of each narrative, namely, the celestial agents responsible for initiations of the respective seers. Scholars have noted the "aural" characteristics of the figure of Yahoel, the central symbol of the audial ideology of the *Apocalypse of Abraham*. In particular, the Slavonic pseudepigraphon defines him as the mediation of "my [God's] ineffable name (*неизрекомаго имени моего*)."[73] Even apart from the explanation of the guide's office, the peculiar designation "Yahoel" (Slav. *Иаоилъ*) itself unequivocally denotes the angel as the embodiment of the divine Name. Thus Abraham is not merely sustained by seeing and hearing an angelic being but is nourished on the representation of the divine Name.

Similarly, as in the Abrahamic pseudepigraphon, *Joseph and Aseneth* depicts the human seer as being fed by the Angel of the Name. With respect to this, Ross Kraemer suggests that "the designation of the angelic double of Joseph . . . [is] probably closely associated, if not to be identified, with the Name-Bearing Angel."[74] Yet, while both angelic entities might be connected with the aural *Shem* theology, the corporeal thrust of the visual paradigm is not entirely absent in either account, as both angelic "feeders" are portrayed as anthropomorphic embodiments of the divine Name.

The aural aspect of both accounts is manifested also in the fact that supernatural nourishment comes from the *mouths* of the angels. In the *Apocalypse of Abraham* the patriarch receives his unconventional provision from the mouth of Yahoel when the speech of the great angel serves as Abraham's drink. The aural aspect of nourishment is also present in *Joseph and Aseneth*, specifically through Aseneth's repeated affirmations about the provenance of the honeycomb from the mouth of the celestial being.[75] *Joseph and Aseneth* 16:8–10, for instance, reads:

And the comb was big and white as snow and full of honey. And that honey was like dew from heaven and its exhalation like breath of life. And Aseneth wondered and said in herself, Did then this comb come out of the man's mouth, because its exhalation is like the breath of this man's mouth?[76]

Also, *Joseph and Aseneth* 16:11 provides a similar affirmation of the aural source of the angelic food; it reads:

> And Aseneth was afraid and said, "Lord, I did not have a honeycomb in my storeroom at any time, but you spoke and it came into being. Surely this came out of your mouth, because its exhalation is like breath of your mouth."[77]

Other scholars suggest that the provenance of the angelic food in *Joseph and Aseneth* coming from the mouth of the celestial being has roots in the biblical manna traditions. Andrea Lieber observes:

> [T]he association of the honeycomb with mannah is explicit: it was like dew from heaven, white like snow, containing the breath of life. Indeed the honeycomb, like mannah, is identified with the 'word' of the angel—the *anthropos* spoke and the comb came from his angelic mouth.[78]

In the Book of Deuteronomy, the manna tradition has been reformulated in terms of the aural paradigm when the symbolism of heavenly nourishment was juxtaposed with imagery of the word coming from the Deity's mouth. Thus, in Deuteronomy 8:3, we find the following tradition:

> He humbled you by letting you hunger, then by feeding you with manna, with which neither you nor your ancestors were acquainted, in order to make you understand that one does not live by bread alone, but by every word that comes from the mouth of the Lord. (NRSV)[79]

Given that the Book of Deuteronomy first initiated polemics against the visual anthropomorphic paradigm present in Ezekiel and the Priestly Source, the fact that such a striking aural reformulation comes from this biblical text is not coincidental.[80]

It appears that the peculiar transformations of the Egyptian maiden and the Jewish patriarch found in *Joseph and Aseneth* and the *Apocalypse of Abraham*, respectively, are profoundly affected by the aural *Shem* ideologies. In fact, one can understand the natures of both visionaries as literally reconstituted by their ingestion of the divine Name. It is not coincidental, moreover, that the transformation is executed aurally—that is to say, from the mouth of the angel of the Name to the mouth of an earthly creature. In the *Apocalypse of Abraham*, the patriarch drinks the words coming forth from the mouth of Yahoel, and is fed by the sight of this hypostatic representation of the divine Name. In *Joseph and Aseneth*, similarly, the heavenly man, who bears some characteristics of the Angel of the Name, puts the angelic food that originated from his mouth into the mouth of the female seer.

Moreover, if, in both pseudepigraphons, the human seers are indeed transformed by means of their ingestions of the divine Name, such initiatory practices point to an important ancient trajectory. Other scholars have noted, for example, that Aseneth's partaking of the celestial food is reminiscent of certain ritual practices, through which cultic images are given life by placing the divine Name in their mouths.[81] These rituals are rooted in ancient Mesopotamian and Egyptian animation ceremonies of cultic statues known as the rite of the "washing of the mouth" (*mīs pî*) and the "opening of the mouth" (*pīt pî*).[82] Some scholars have argued that these trends exercised a formative influence on some later Hermetic[83] traditions and Kabbalistic stories about the creation of the artificial humanoid.[84]

Returning again to the pseudepigraphical accounts of Abraham and Aseneth, we see that the peculiar metamorphoses effected through the mouth of the celestial beings are replete with protological symbolism. These transformational accounts appear to replicate, here, the paradigmatic event of the creation of humankind when the spirit of life was blown from the mouth of the Deity into the mouth of the lifeless human body molded from the dust of earth.[85] Such protological connections are more distinctive in *Joseph and Aseneth*, in which the angelic food, the honeycomb, is compared with the spirit of life. Through the ingestion of the divine Name, then, the seers of both the *Apocalypse of Abraham* and *Joseph and Aseneth* become "new Protoplast," returning to the prelapsarian condition of humanity.[86] Such "vivifications" of the seers bring to mind later Jewish Golem legends in which the lifeless body of the artificial humanoid is "vivified" when God's name is inserted into his mouth.[87] The theme of vivification of human "idols" brings us again to the theme of idolatry, so prominent in both pseudepigraphical texts.

It has already been noted in our study that in the *Apocalypse of Abraham* the stand against the divine body tradition and reaffirmation of the aural paradigm often takes the form of polemics against idols. In this respect it is intriguing that in *Joseph and Aseneth*, as in the Slavonic apocalypse, the theme of celestial nourishment appears in the midst of a fight with idolatry. Interestingly, both protagonists are initially portrayed as idolaters. In the beginning of the Slavonic apocalypse, for instance, Abraham manufactures idols and participates in idolatrous worship. Similarly, Aseneth is portrayed as an idol worshiper at the beginning of the narrative. *Joseph and Aseneth* 8, in this regard, states that Aseneth's lips were defiled because she "blesses with her mouth dead and dumb idols."[88] Later, however, she, like Abraham, destroys her idols.[89]

This peculiar fight against idolatry, furthermore, seems to betray some polemical developments that lay behind both texts. As noted above, both accounts are permeated with the dialectical mix of visual and aural imagery. Both heroes, for example, are not simply fed, like Moses, on the celestial form alone, but are also nourished by the divine Name. Scholars have noted that the imagery of the divine Name looms especially large in the longer version of *Joseph and Aseneth*.[90] It is important to our study that in Aseneth's hymn of repentance (*Jos. Asen.* 11:17), the divine Name is mentioned in the context of the opening of the seer's mouth.[91] Ross Kraemer notes that "in the longer version, Aseneth blesses not only 'the Lord, your God' but also the name of angel."[92] Later, Pentephres's daughter will ingest the heavenly food coming from the mouth of the Angel of the Name. Kraemer argues that "it is particularly in the longer text that the angelic figure is more closely aligned with the figure developed in other sources as the Name-Bearing Angel—the virtual double of God."[93] In the *Apocalypse of Abraham*, too, the patriarch will be nourished on the hypostatic Name of God.

A further important aural marker present in both texts is that both pseudepigraphons portray the seers' involvement in the aural praxis of praise. The significance of the patriarch's hymns to the overall conceptual framework of the *Apocalypse of Abraham* has been recognized in previous studies.[94] More specifically, in the Slavonic apocalypse, Abraham gains access to the highest heavenly realm through means of a hymn.[95] Scholars have noted that the patriarch's praise is reminiscent of later Hekhalot hymns.[96] Similar suggestions have been made concerning Aseneth's practices as well. Kraemer, for instance, argues:

> Aseneth wishes not only to glorify the figure (of the angel), language that might be imported from Judges 13, but to sing hymns. . . . This perpetual glorification and singing of hymns is precisely the activity envisioned for the angels in heaven in so many hekhalot and mystical-visionary texts. Taken together with other passages, particularly in the longer version, it points to Aseneth's own desire not only to become like the angels in heaven but also to do so in accordance with a particular understanding of angelic identity and activity.[97]

Interestingly, both in the *Apocalypse of Abraham* and in *Joseph and Aseneth,* the chief angelic protagonists prevent the seers from worshipping them. Yahoel brings Abraham up from his knees, and, in *Joseph and Aseneth*, the angel refuses to accept the seer's worship.[98] These traditions again point to the subtle polemics against celestial corporeal representations in both the Slavonic apocalypse and *Joseph and Aseneth.*

The Nourishment of Azazel

The theme of food coming from a spiritual creature receives its further inverse appropriation in chapter 23 of the *Apocalypse of Abraham*, in which the seer beholds the fallen angel Azazel nourishing Adam and Eve. *Apocalypse of Abraham* 23:6–11 reads:

> And they were standing under a tree of Eden, and the fruit of the tree was like the appearance of a bunch of grapes of vine. And behind the tree was standing, as it were, a serpent in form, but having hands and feet like a man, and wings on its shoulders: six on the right side and six on the left. And he was holding in his hands the grapes of the tree

> and feeding the two whom I saw entwined with each other. And I said, "Who are these two entwined with each other, or who is this between them, or what is the fruit which they are eating, Mighty Eternal One?" And he said, "This is the reason of men, this is Adam, and this is their desire on earth, this is Eve. And he who is between them is the Impiety of their pursuits for destruction, Azazel himself."[99]

This depiction of the protological couple entwined with the demonic spiritual agent is laden with an array of transformational motifs. It is not coincidental that, like Abraham's metamorphosis, the negative transformation of the protoplasts is also conveyed through the metaphor of sustenance. Yet the nature of sustenance is significantly different. Unlike the patriarch, who was nourished by the contemplation of the celestial being,[100] the protoplasts are in this case fed not through the vision or speech of the spiritual being but by "physical food," in the form of grapes. This reliance on the conventional human provisions brings to mind the aforementioned cluster of motifs reflected in the *Primary Adam Books*, in which the protoplasts, after their expulsion from Paradise, transition to the "food of beasts."[101]

Note here that the protoplasts' eating habits inversely mirror the nourishing mode of the patriarch. While Abraham transitions to the celestial prelapsarian condition of humanity, renouncing conventional nourishment, Adam and Eve head in the opposite direction through consumption of earthly food. If the metaphors of nourishment indeed have this transformational significance in our text, one finds here a negative mirroring of the patriarch's metamorphosis, an inverse dualistic strategy prominent in other parts of the *Apocalypse of Abraham* as well.

It is important to note that Azazel's feeding of the protoplasts is a rare motif in Jewish lore. The appearance of such a depiction in the *Apocalypse of Abraham*, then, is not likely simply coincidental. Rather, it is a meaningful portrayal that nicely corroborates other feeding episodes found throughout the text. As suggested, this depiction of the negative spiritual agent feeding the protological humans is posited in the text as the conceptual counterpart to the nourishment performed by another prominent spiritual agent of the story, namely, the angel Yahoel. Other scholars have noted the inverse symmetrical correspondences between Yahoel and Azazel. These figures are two pivotal characters of the story who stand in striking opposition to each other, specifically in the central sacerdotal rite of the apocalypse—the Yom Kippur ceremony. During this ceremony, one spiritual agent represents the celestial high priest, while the other represents the celestial scapegoat.

Yet, while in some portions of the Slavonic apocalypse Azazel indeed is depicted as the proverbial scapegoat, the demoted creature stripped of his celestial "attire," in the account of the protoplasts' feeding, the depiction of Azazel hints at his former heavenly state by reference to his twelve wings upon his shoulders.

Furthermore, the antagonist's stance near the Tree of the Knowledge of Good and Evil also deserves our close attention. One can discern here a certain parallelism in the infamous tree and Azazel. Not surprisingly, then, the depiction of both entities utilizes similar symbolism. For instance, as the tree holds grapes on its branches, Azazel holds grapes in his hands. In view of such correspondences, it is possible to envision the antagonist as the arboreal symbol. Further, the motif that the demon is entwined with the protoplasts is reminiscent not only of the classic attributes of the serpent but also the entwined branches of the tree themselves. Thus the entwined Azazel can be understood as the tree, or branches, from which the humans are nourished by the forbidden fruit. We can see, then, the parallelism in the two symbols of corruption: the Tree of the Knowledge of Good and Evil and Azazel, both entities laden with forbidden fruits. This portrayal of the antagonistic mediator as the paradisal tree brings to mind other apocalyptic accounts in which the heavenly mediators, like an exalted Jacob or Christ, are portrayed as the paradisal arboreal symbol—that is to say, the Tree of Life.

Feeding with the Whole Extent?

It is also intriguing that, in *Apocalypse of Abraham* 23, the motif of Azazel's feeding coincides with the imagery of his being intertwined with the subjects of his nourishment. The peculiarity of his feeding brings to mind the aforementioned apocalyptic testimonies in which human seers are nourished by the whole extent of the Deity or its representation in the form of the Angel of the Name. Azazel, like the Angel of the Name, though in the inverse, provides nourishment not only through the mouths of the protoplasts but also through his physical presence, namely, the whole extent of his body. Interestingly, as in *2 Enoch* 22, in which the luminous body of the seventh antediluvian hero "reflects" the shining form of the Deity, here, too, the intertwined bodies of the first humans mirror the serpentine form of their seducer.

Next let us consider the imagery of the protoplasts' entwining with the fallen Azazel. Other scholars discern in such entwining a kind of erotic symbolism, arguing that it represents a sexual union reminiscent of a *ménage à trois*.[102] Other Jewish accounts also closely link the motifs of nourishment and sexual union. For example, in *Joseph and Aseneth*, the erotic imagery of a kiss appears along with the symbolism of nourishment. Thus, in *Joseph and Aseneth* 8, Joseph, who is fed on the bread of life, refuses to kiss Aseneth, whose lips are defiled by the food of idols.[103] Later, after partaking of the angelic food offered by the heavenly counterpart of Joseph, Aseneth is kissed by his celestial guest. In *Joseph and Aseneth* 19:11, the erotic imagery of a kiss again coincides with the symbolism of nourishment:

> And Joseph kissed Aseneth and gave her spirit of life, and he kissed her the second time and gave her spirit of wisdom, and he kissed her the third time and gave her spirit of truth.[104]

The important detail of this passage from *Joseph and Aseneth*, which most clearly connects the motifs of nourishment and erotic encounter, is that Joseph's kiss gives Aseneth the spirit of life. Joseph's kiss evokes the description of the angelic food found in chapter 16,[105] in which Joseph's heavenly counterpart, represented by the Angel of the Lord, gives the female visionary the honeycomb: "And the comb was big and white as snow and full of honey. And that honey was like dew from heaven and its exhalation like breath of life."[106]

In light of such parallels it appears that the link between nourishment and erotic imagery in *Apocalypse of Abraham* 23 is not coincidental, as it reveals an inverse appropriation of the familiar conceptual constellations found in Jewish apocalyptic accounts.

Feeding on Azazel

The presence of Azazel in the midst of the protoplasts points to another important transformational aspect of our text, namely, that the demon's nature somehow becomes part of the protoplasts' nature. Such demonic in-dwelling represents an inverse type of the positive transformation of Abraham during his journey into the heavenly realm. As mentioned above, the tradition of the seer's nourishment on the Angel of the Name, reflected both in the *Apocalypse of Abraham* and *Joseph and Aseneth*, is connected with the ritual of "vivification" of the protoplast (and Golem) by means of the divine Name. In the case of Abraham and Aseneth, the transformation brought by nourishment signals their return to the condition of the prelapsarian humanity. In his investigation of the vivification of Golem/Adam by the powers of the Tetragrammaton, Gershom Scholem notes another cluster of traditions in which the idols or antagonistic figures are brought to life by being vivified not by the divine Name but, inversely, by the devil's entrance.[107] Thus, for example, according to one legend, Samael speaks from the mouth of the Golden Calf.[108] A similar tradition is found in the *Primary Adam Books* in which the serpent becomes a lyre for Satan during his deception of the protoplasts. Satan's assumption of a serpentine form, moreover, might represent the "anti-paradigm" of transformation, namely, the antagonist's transition from an upper (angelic) to a lower (animal) form, which inversely mirrors the glorious metamorphosis of the apocalyptic visionary, who undergoes a transition from garments of skin to garments of light. The Armenian version of the *Primary Adam Books* describes just such a negative transformation of Satan.[109] The Adversary's animal manifestation is not merely a phantom—he inhabits the actual living creature. The serpent is possessed by Satan.[110]

In view of the aforementioned accounts, it is possible that two alternative traditions of sustenance depicted in the *Apocalypse of Abraham*—one angelic and the other demonic—stand in a conceptual opposition to each other. While Abraham (and Aseneth) became nourished on the Angel of the Name's presence, Adam and Eve are fed on Azazel's presence.[111]

Conclusion

Our study demonstrates that the symbolism of nourishment found in the Slavonic apocalypse plays an important conceptual role in the dualistic framework of this enigmatic Jewish work. Such imagery helps elucidate the transformations of the main characters of the apocalyptic narrative—the metamorphoses that shepherd them to their protological or eschatological conditions. In this respect, the theme of nourishment appears to serve as an important conceptual bridge that connects protological and eschatological events. It promises that the corruption of the first human pair, who ate the forbidden fruit in the Garden Eden, will be reversed, in the end, through a parallel act of sustenance that will return humankind to its original angelic state. Various eschatological meals, found both in Jewish and Christian accounts, from the Eucharist to rabbinic stories about the righteous feasting on the body of the Leviathan, point to the restorative significance of the final nourishments of the elected humans who will, in the *eschaton*, undo the consequences of the protological fall.

Another important aspect is that the accounts of nourishment, attested to in the Slavonic apocalypse, occur in the midst of polemics between aural and visual conceptual currents. Such polemics affect the depiction of both those who are fed and those who are feeding. Yet it is not always possible to clearly disentangle the respective conceptual streams. In this respect, interestingly, in the crucial nourishing episode of the apocalypse, which portrays Abraham's feeding on Yahoel, both visual *and* aural markers play a pivotal role. Here the human seer is sustained both on the vision of the form of the great angel *and* on the voice of the celestial creature. Such complex imagery found in the *Apocalypse of Abraham* clearly points to the existence of a conceptual mixture in which features of the novel aural paradigm are unfolded in the midst of the visionary realities of the formative Mosaic traditions.

Thus the imagery of nourishment in the Slavonic apocalypse reveals a paradoxical mix of the *Kavod* and *Shem* conceptual developments in which the promulgation of the theology of the divine Name and its portentous role in the transformation of the seer is linked with the theophanic imagery of the visual paradigm. The influence of this polemical encounter between two important revelatory trends has had lasting consequences for later Jewish and Christian developments.

The Messianic Scapegoat in the *Apocalypse of Abraham*

> . . . for there is no light except that which issues from darkness, for when that "Other Side" is subdued the Holy One is exalted in glory. In fact, there can be no true worship except that which comes from darkness, and there is no good except that which comes from evil.
>
> —*Zohar* II.184a

Introduction

In the *Apocalypse of Abraham* 29, the Deity reveals to the seer one of the most profound eschatological mysteries. The revelation deals with the appearance of a future messianic leader of humankind, an ambiguous character depicted in very obscure terms. *Apocalypse of Abraham* 29:4–13 reads:

> <And I looked> and saw a man going out from the left side of the heathen. Men and women and children, great crowds, went out from the side of the heathen and they worshiped him. <And> while I was still looking, those on the right side went out, and some shamed this man, and some struck him, and some worshiped him. <And> I saw that as they worshiped him, Azazel ran and worshiped, and having kissed his face he turned and stood behind him. And I said, "Eternal Mighty One! Who is this shamed and struck man, worshiped by the heathen with Azazel?" And

> he answered and said, "Hear, Abraham, the man whom you saw shamed and struck and again worshiped is the laxity of the heathen for the people who will come from you in the last days, in this twelfth hour of the age of impiety. And in the [same] twelfth period of the close of my age I shall set up the man from your seed which you saw. Everyone from my people will [finally] admit him, while the sayings of him who was as if called by me will be neglected in their minds. And that you saw going out from the left side of the picture and those worshiping him, this [means that] many of the heathen will hope in him. <And> those of your seed you saw on the right side, some shaming and striking him, and some worshiping him, many of them will be misled on his account. And he will tempt those of your seed who have worshiped him.[1]

This depiction has been viewed by experts as the most puzzling passage of the entire apocalypse.[2] Numerous interpretations have been offered that discern in these passages either a later Christian interpolation[3] or the original conceptual layer.[4] The vague portrayal of the main characters has also provoked impassioned debates about whether they display features of Jewish or Christian messiahs. These traditional polemics, however, have not often adequately considered the overall conceptual universe of the text, especially its cultic framework. More specifically, such interpretations have overlooked several features of the passage, including references to Azazel and his worship of the messianic figure, that hint to sacerdotal traditions.

Recent studies on the *Apocalypse of Abraham*, however, point to the importance of cultic motifs in the text. Some scholars have even suggested that a sacerdotal vision permeates the whole fabric of the text; Daniel Harlow, for example, argues that priestly concerns affect the entire conceptual framework of the apocalypse.[5] His research shows that all the main characters of the story appear to be endowed with priestly credentials, and this includes not only positive figures, such as Yahoel and Abraham, but also negative ones, including Azazel, Terah, and Nahor, who are depicted as corrupted sacerdotal servants causing pollution of heavenly and earthly sanctuaries.

Many scholars agree that the sacerdotal features of the text appear to be connected with the Yom Kippur ordinance, the central atoning rite in the Jewish tradition, which culminated in two portentous cultic events: the procession of the high priestly figure into the Holy of Holies and the banishment of the scapegoat to the wilderness. Scholars have noted that the peculiar movements of the main characters of the Slavonic apocalypse resemble the aforementioned sacerdotal events. While Yahoel and Abraham ascend to the celestial Holy of Holies, the main antagonist of the story, the fallen angel Azazel, is banished into a supernal wilderness. In this sacerdotal depiction, the main angelic protagonist of the story, the angel Yahoel, appears to be understood as the heavenly high priest, while the main antagonist of the text, the fallen angel Azazel, as the eschatological scapegoat. Further, scholars have noted that in chapters 13 and 14 of the *Apocalypse of Abraham* Yahoel appears to be performing the climactic action of the Yom Kippur atoning ceremony—namely, the enigmatic scapegoat ritual through which impurity was transferred onto a goat named Azazel and then, through the medium of this animal, dispatched into the wilderness.

This connection with the main atoning rite of the Jewish tradition and its chief sacerdotal vehicle, the scapegoat Azazel, is important for our study of the messianic passage found in *Apocalypse of Abraham* 29. In that text Azazel appears to be playing a distinctive role in the course of his interaction with the messianic character whom he kisses and even worships. The sudden appearance of Azazel, the chief cultic agent of the Yom Kippur ceremony, might not be coincidental in our passage, as the sacerdotal dynamics of the atoning rite appear to be profoundly affecting the messianic characters depicted in chapter 29 of the Slavonic apocalypse.

In view of these traditions it is necessary to explore the meaning of the messianic passage in chapter 29 in the broader sacerdotal framework of the entire text and, more specifically, in its relation to the Yom Kippur motifs. Some peculiar details in the depiction of the messianic character point to his connection with the scapegoat ritual in which he himself appears to be envisioned as a messianic scapegoat.

I. Messianic Reinterpretation of the Scapegoat Imagery in Second- and Third-Century Christian Authors

Many scholars note how the messianic figure in chapter 29 is depicted in terms reminiscent of Christian motifs, specifically the traditions about the passion of Jesus and his betrayal by Judas.[6] For instance, in the *Apocalypse of Abraham*, the messianic figure is described as being shamed and stricken and also as being kissed by Azazel. The abuses the messianic figure endures in *Apocalypse of Abraham* 29 have often been construed as allusions to Jesus' suffering, and Azazel's kiss to the infamous kiss of Judas in the Garden of Gethsemane.[7] While the allusions in the Gospels accounts of the betrayal and passion of Christ have been much discussed, insufficient attention has been given to certain connections between the messianic passage and later Christian interpretations. Yet, in the second century CE, when the *Apocalypse of Abraham* was likely composed, several Christian authors sought to interpret Jesus' passion and betrayal against the background of the scapegoat rite. In these Christian reappraisals, Jesus was viewed as the scapegoat of the atoning rite who, through his suffering and humiliation, took upon himself the sins of the world. Although scholars often note the similarities in the depictions of the messiah in *Apocalypse of Abraham* 29 and some biblical Jesus traditions, they are often reluctant to address these second-century developments in which the Christian messiah's suffering and humiliation received a striking sacerdotal significance. Given the permeating influence of the Yom Kippur sacerdotal imagery on the Slavonic apocalypse, we need to explore more closely these postbiblical Christian elaborations.

One of the earliest remaining witnesses to the tradition of the Christian messiah as the scapegoat[8] can be found in the *Epistle of Barnabas*, a text scholars usually date to the end of the first century or the beginning of the second century CE,[9] which is the time when the *Apocalypse of Abraham* was likely composed. *Epistle of Barnabas* 7:6–11 reads:

> Pay attention to what he commands: "Take two fine goats who alike and offer them as a sacrifice; and let the priest take one of them as a whole burnt offering for sins." But what will they do with the other? "The other," he says, "is cursed." Pay attention to how the type of Jesus is revealed. "And all of you shall spit on it and pierce it and wrap a piece of scarlet wool around its head, and so let it be cast into the wilderness." When this happens, the one who takes the goat leads it into the wilderness and removes the wool, and

> places it on a blackberry bush, whose buds we are accustomed to eat when we find it in the countryside. (Thus the fruit of the blackberry bush alone is sweet.) And so, what does this mean? Pay attention: "The one they take to the altar, but the other is cursed," and the one that is cursed is crowned. For then they will see him in that day wearing a long scarlet robe around his flesh, and they will say, "Is this not the one we once crucified, despising, piercing, and spitting on him? Truly this is the one who was saying at the time that he was himself the Son of God." For how is he like that one? This is why "the goats are alike, fine, and equal," that when they see him coming at that time, they may be amazed at how much he is like the goat. See then the type of Jesus who was about to suffer. But why do they place the wool in the midst of the thorns? This is a type of Jesus established for the church, because whoever wishes to remove the scarlet wool must suffer greatly, since the thorn is a fearful thing, and a person can retrieve the wool only by experiencing pain. And so he says: those who wish to see me and touch my kingdom must take hold of me through pain and suffering.[10]

In this passage the suffering of Christ is compared with the treatment of the scapegoat on Yom Kippur.[11] It is important for our study that the *Epistle of Barnabas* depicts the scapegoat alongside another important animal of the atoning rite: the sacrificial goat of YHWH.[12] *Barnabas* underlines the fact of similarity, or even twinship, of the goats who shall be "alike, fine, and equal." As we will see later, this dual typology might be present in *Apocalypse of Abraham* 29, which appears to describe not one but two messianic figures, one of whom proceeds from the left side of the Gentiles and the other from the right lot of Abraham.

Another important feature of the passage from the *Epistle of Barnabas* is its depiction of the scapegoat's exaltation—that is to say, the depiction in which he is crowned and dressed in a long scarlet robe.[13] This motif of the scapegoat's exaltation is also present in the *Apocalypse of Abraham*, in which the messianic scapegoat is repeatedly venerated by worshipers from both lots and by Azazel.

In light of the sacerdotal dimension of the messianic passage from chapter 29, where the cultic veneration of the messianic figure is couched in Yom Kippur symbolism, we should also note that the *Epistle of Barnabas* gives sacerdotal significance to the scarlet wool placed on the scapegoat by portraying it as the high priestly robe of Christ at his second coming.[14] In this regard, the *Epistle of Barnabas* is not a unique extrabiblical testimony to early Christian understanding of Jesus as the scapegoat. A close analysis of the Christian literature of the second and third centuries CE shows that this interpretation was quite popular among principal Christian sources of the period. For example, in chapter 40 of his *Dialogue with Trypho*, a text written in the middle of the second century CE, Justin Martyr compares Jesus with the scapegoat. In this text, he conveys the following tradition:

> Likewise, the two identical goats which had to be offered during the fast (one of which was to be the scapegoat, and the other the sacrificial goat) were an announcement of the two comings of Christ: Of the first coming, in which your priests and elders send him away as a scapegoat, seizing him and putting him to death; of the second coming, because in that same place of Jerusalem you shall recognize him whom you had subjected to shame, and who was a sacrificial offering for all sinners who are willing to repent and to comply with that fast which Isaiah prescribed when he said, *loosing the strangle of violent contracts*, (διασπῶντες στραγγαλιὰς βιαίων συναλλαγμάτων)[15] and to observe likewise all the other precepts laid down by him (precepts which I have already mentioned and which all believers in Christ fulfill). You also know very well that the offering of the two goats, which had to take place during the fast, could not take place anywhere else except in Jerusalem.[16]

Although Justin's text seems to be written later than the *Epistle of Barnabas*, it is not a reworking of *Barnabas*'s traditions but instead represents independent attestation to a traditional typology.[17] John Dominic Crossan observes:

> [T]here are significant differences between the application in *Barnabas* 7 and *Dialogue* 40 that indicate that Justin is

> not dependent on Barnabas. The main one is the divergent ways in which each explains how two goats can represent the (two comings of) the one Christ. For *Barnabas* 7 the two goats must be alike. For *Dialogue* 40 the two goats and the two comings are both connected to Jerusalem. They represent, therefore, two independent versions of a traditional typology foretelling a dual advent of Jesus, one for Passion and death, the other for *parousia* and judgment.[18]

Further, in his understanding of the scapegoat ritual, Justin reveals striking similarities with the interpretation of the Yom Kippur imagery in extrabiblical Jewish materials.[19] It points to a possibility that early Christian interpretations were developed in dialogue with contemporaneous Jewish traditions. Examining this dialogue can be important for understanding not only early Christian accounts of the messianic scapegoat but also Jewish messianic reinterpretations, similar to those found in the *Apocalypse of Abraham* where messianic speculations were conflated with the scapegoat symbolism.

Justin also makes several interesting appropriations of the biblical traditions that the *Epistle of Barnabas* does not make. One of them is his usage of the tradition from Isaiah 58:6 to elaborate the symbolism of the messianic scapegoat. Daniel Stökl Ben Ezra notes that this appropriation represents the first instance when this passage from Isaiah is viewed in the context of the Yom Kippur imagery.[20] The Septuagint version of this passage from Isaiah uses the language of "loosing,"[21] which is similar to some formulae from the *Apocalypse of Abraham*, to which we will return later in our study.

In Tertullian's *Against Marcion* 3:7 and *Against the Jews* 14:9, both works written in the beginning of the third century CE, one can again see a messianic reinterpretation of the scapegoat imagery.[22] *Against Marcion* 3:7 reads:

> If also I am to submit an interpretation of the two goats which were offered at the Fast, are not these also figures of Christ's two activities? They are indeed of the same age and appearance because the Lord's is one and the same aspect: because he will return in no other form, seeing he has to be recognized by those of whom he has suffered injury. One of them however, surrounded with scarlet, cursed

> and spit upon and pulled about and pierced, was by the people driven out of the city into perdition, marked with manifest tokens of our Lord's passion: while the other, made an offering for sins, and given as food to the priests of the temple, marked the tokens of his second manifestation, at which, when all sins have been done away, the priests of the spiritual temple, which is the Church, were to enjoy as it were a feast of our Lord's grace, while the rest remain without a taste of salvation.[23]

In his testimonies to the messianic scapegoat, Tertullian appears to rely on the traditions conveyed by *Barnabas* and Justin.[24] His knowledge of the original typology remains uncertain.

As we conclude this section, let us again underline the similarities in the aforementioned Christian reinterpretations of the scapegoat ritual and the messianic passage in *Apocalypse of Abraham* 29. First, all the Christian testimonies considered here combine the imagery of the two goats chosen during the Yom Kippur ceremony, sometimes even emphasizing their equality. This fact might be a curious parallel to the *Apocalypse of Abraham* 29 in which one can possibly detect the depiction of not one but two intertwining messianic figures—one positive and the other negative.

Second, it is intriguing that in *Barnabas*, as in the Slavonic apocalypse, the Messiah's humiliation is paradoxically linked with his exaltation. The curses coincide with the crown. Such exaltation, both in Christian interpretations and in the *Apocalypse of Abraham,* is laced with significant cultic features, including the motifs of the worship and transference to the messianic character of attributes of the various characters involved in the Yom Kippur ceremony. In these peculiar reinterpretations, which take place both in the Christian texts and in the Jewish apocalypse, one can see elaborate cultic dynamics that attempt to bring corresponding messianic characters into the complex world of the Yom Kippur rite. One of the most important nexuses of this sacerdotal process is without doubt the identification of this messianic character with the scapegoat figure.

Another important similarity is that the aforementioned Christian authors depict the two emblematic animals of the Yom Kippur ceremony as two manifestations of Christ—one in suffering and another in victory. Justin effectively summarizes this idea when he suggests, in the beginning of his passage, that "likewise, the two identical goats which had to be offered during the fast (one of which was to be the scapegoat, and the other the sacrificial goat) were an announcement of the two comings of Christ."[25] This is a striking parallel to the traditions in *Apocalypse of Abraham* 29 in which the messianic figure appears to proceed initially from the left lot, associated with Azazel, and later from the right lot, tied to Abraham.[26]

Having examined these Christian interpretations of the messianic scapegoat, let us now proceed to a closer investigation of similar developments in the *Apocalypse of Abraham.*

II. Messianic Reinterpretation of the Yom Kippur Imagery in the Apocalypse of Abraham

Initial Procession of the Messianic Figure from the Left Side

The enigmatic revelation given to the seer in chapter 29 of the *Apocalypse of Abraham* begins with the appearance of a human figure emerging from the left side: "And I looked and saw a man going out from the left side of the heathen."[27] This tradition of the messianic figure's procession from the left side, the side associated in the text with the lot of Gentiles, was often taken to be puzzling, since the well-known Jewish and Christian candidates for the messianic office, including Jesus himself, were, at least historically, closely linked with the lot of Israel. This tradition, however, may have more than a merely historical significance but rather a cultic and eschatological significance as well. Moreover, this tradition cannot be fully understood unless we examine the meaning and the role of the two eschatological lots in the overall conceptual framework of the Slavonic apocalypse.

Graphic depictions of the two lots, one associated with the nation of Israel and the other with the heathen, are widely dispersed throughout the second, apocalyptic, part of the pseudepigraphon. It was noted that these portrayals are reminiscent not only of the eschatological portions of humanity found in the Qumran materials[28] that associate these entities with the heathen and Israel but also of the imagery of sacrificial lots prominent in the Yom Kippur ritual. Indeed, the word "lot" (Slav. часть) in the Slavonic text appears to be connected to the Hebrew גורל, a term prominent in cultic descriptions of the atoning rite found in biblical and rabbinic accounts,[29] as well as the eschatological developments in the Qumran materials.[30] Yet, in the Slavonic pseudepigraphon, these cultic entities, known from classic depictions of the Yom Kippur ordinance, receive a new apocalyptic and eschatological significance. In this respect, the *Apocalypse of Abraham* shares much with the Qumran materials. For instance, as in Qumran materials, in which the lots are often linked to fallen angelic figures or translated heroes (like Belial or Melchizedek), in the Slavonic apocalypse, the portions of humanity are now tied to the main characters of the story, namely, the fallen angel Azazel[31] and the translated patriarch Abraham.[32] The association of the left lot with the infamous fallen angel bearing the name of the scapegoat solidifies the close link of the cultic and eschatological dimensions of the Slavonic apocalypse. In this context, the procession of the messianic figure from the left side, which is unambiguously associated in the *Apocalypse of Abraham* with Azazel, emphasizes the close connections of the messianic figure with the portion of the scapegoat.

Another feature that strengthens the messianic character's association with the left lot is that immediately after his emergence from the left side, in the beginning of the passage, the crowds who worshipped this leader also came from the left side: "Men and women and children, great crowds, went out from the side of the heathen and they worshiped him."[33] In this description, the left lot is again viewed as an abode of the Gentiles. The left side is thus associated not only with the provenance and procession of the messianic figure but also with his initial cultic veneration and exaltation.

The Maltreatment of the Messiah

The second important conceptual nexus concerns details about the treatment of the messianic figure in *Apocalypse of Abraham* 29, who is portrayed as being shamed and stricken. Often this humiliation and abuse has been interpreted as allusions to the suffering that Jesus endured before his crucifixion. Yet other important symbolic markers in the text, such as the association with the left lot and the messiah's interaction with the celestial scapegoat of the story of the fallen angel Azazel, suggest that the messianic figure is also connected with the Yom Kippur cultic settings. If there is such a connection, then abuses endured by the messianic character may reflect the Yom Kippur ceremony in which the infamous cultic animal was maltreated and shamed in a ritual fashion by his handlers and by the people.[34] *M. Yoma* 6:4 recounts the ritual humiliation and abuse visited upon the scapegoat:

> . . . And they made a causeway for it because of the Babylonians who used to pull its hair, crying to it, "Bear [our sins] and be gone! Bear [our sins] and be gone!" Certain of the eminent folk of Jerusalem used to go with him to the first booth. There were ten booths from Jerusalem to the ravine [which was at a distance of] ninety ris (which measure seven and a half to the mile).[35]

Further, *m. Yoma* 6:6 notes that the scapegoat was pushed from behind by his handlers into the ravine and its body was broken in pieces; it reads:

> What did he do? He divided the thread of crimson wool and tied one half to the rock and the other half between its horns, and he pushed it from behind; and it went rolling down, and before it reaches half the way down the hill it was broken in pieces.[36]

It is clear that the aforementioned Christian interpreters of the second and third centuries CE, who tried to link Jesus' suffering with the Yom Kippur imagery, were aware of the Jewish cultic traditions of the scapegoat's mistreatment. For instance, *Epistle of Barnabas* mentions the abuses endured by the scapegoat, including prodding and spitting; it reads: "And all of you shall spit on it and pierce it and wrap a piece of scarlet wool around its head, and so let it be cast into the wilderness."[37]

Similarly, in passages dealing with the scapegoat traditions, Tertullian describes the maltreatment of the cultic animal as follows:

> One of them however, surrounded with scarlet, cursed and spit upon and pulled about and pierced, was by the people driven out of the city into perdition, marked with manifest tokens of our Lord's passion. . . .[38]

> One of them, however, which was surrounded with scarlet, cursed and spat upon and perforated and punctured, was driven outside the city by the people to ruin. . . .[39]

Some scholars have also suggested that the crimson thread attached to the head of the scapegoat might symbolize the suffering and torture of the scapegoat.[40] In Christian interpretations, the crimson band was often connected with Jesus' crown of thorns.

Some passages in the *Apocalypse of Abraham* also seem cognizant of traditions concerning ritual humiliation in their portrayals of the celestial scapegoat, namely, the fallen angel Azazel. Chapters 13 and 14 offer an eschatological version of the scapegoat ritual in which the heavenly priest Yahoel and his apprentice patriarch Abraham appear as sacerdotal servants who impose ritual curses on the fallen angel bearing the name of the scapegoat. This motif is found, for example, in *Apocalypse of Abraham* 13:7–14 in which an enigmatic interaction occurs between the high priest Yahoel and the scapegoat Azazel:

> Reproach is on you, Azazel! Since Abraham's portion is in heaven, and yours is on earth. Since you have chosen it and desired it to be the dwelling place of your impurity. Therefore the Eternal Lord, the Mighty One, has made you a dweller on earth. And because of you [there is] the wholly-evil spirit of the lie, and because of you [there are] wrath and trials on the generations of impious men. Since the Eternal Mighty God did not *send* the righteous, in their bodies, to be in your hand, in order to affirm through them the righteous life and the destruction of impiety. . . . Hear, adviser! Be shamed by me, since you have been appointed to tempt not to all the righteous! Depart from this man! You cannot deceive him, because he is the enemy of you and of those who follow you and who love what you desire. For behold, the garment which in heaven was formerly yours has been set aside for him, and the corruption which was on him has gone over to you.[41]

It has been previously observed that Yahoel's address to the scapegoat here has a ritual significance, as it bears resemblance to several actions of the high priest and handlers of the scapegoat on Yom

Kippur. Reproaching and shaming of Azazel in *Apocalypse of Abraham* 13:7 and 13:11 are reminiscent of such ritual curses pronounced upon the scapegoat.[42]

If the depiction of the humiliated messiah in chapter 29 is seen in the light of the aforementioned traditions, it is possible that the authors of the text may have tried to establish there a subtle connection between the humiliation of Azazel and the messianic figure, so as to reinforce the link between the two ambiguous characters and posit the messianic figure as an earthly envoy of Azazel and maybe even an earthly version of the heavenly scapegoat.

The Messiah and Azazel

The messianic narrative in chapter 29 reaches an important conceptual crux in the messiah's reception by Azazel. Here we observe one of the most puzzling encounters in the Slavonic apocalypse, an enigmatic interaction between the celestial scapegoat and its human counterpart. The providential ties between the two eschatological characters are then sealed through the mysterious kiss of the arch-demon: "And I saw that as they worshiped him, Azazel ran and worshiped, and having kissed his face he turned and stood behind him."[43]

This perplexing scene appears to further solidify the connections between the messianic imagery and the cultic scapegoat traditions. While portrayals of the eschatological characters' mistreatment and even death are common in Jewish and Christian accounts, Azazel's sudden appearance in the eschatological narrative in chapter 29 is distinctive and may indicate that the messianic tradition in the *Apocalypse of Abraham* is closely connected with the Yom Kippur rite. Further, certain details of the messianic character's reception by Azazel seem to have here a pronounced cultic meaning.[44] That Azazel embraces him is especially significant. The scapegoat offering on the Day of Atonement was often understood in the Jewish tradition as a gift *to* Azazel, with the demon envisioned as a recipient of the ominous sacrificial portion. This notion is already imbedded in the earliest form of the atoning rite, finding its confirmation first in the conspicuous designations of the goats, one designated as the goat for the Lord and the other for Azazel,[45] and second in the peculiar spatial dynamics of the Yom Kippur ceremony, according to which the sacerdotal animal's expulsion into the wilderness coincided with the human celebrant's entrance into the Holy of Holies. In this inverse cultic symmetry, the demonic and divine realms are depicted as mirroring one another, as both characters enter into their respective domains, each ruled by an antagonistic power.

The celebrants' entrance into their respective realms also had a striking theophanic significance. Although this dimension was conspicuous in the symbolism of the high priest's entrance into the Holy of Holies, by which he was breaching the threshold of the divine Presence, it was also reflected negatively, in a deconstructed form, in the portrayals of the scapegoat as he was breaching the boundaries of the netherworld. Their respective entrances into the new realms affected the ontological condition of the characters, which was manifested in their wardrobes. Similar to the garment of the high priest, which was depicted as a copy of the macrocosm and decorated with the divine Name[46] and attributes, the scapegoat's attire was decorated with curses and sins, symbolized by the red color of its crimson band. And like the high priest's cultic garments, which went through notable changes on his path toward the divine presence, the crimson "garment" of the scapegoat was also miraculously transformed into color on its way to Azazel's realm.[47]

In view of these cultic developments, the figure of the scapegoat appears overlaid with theophanic features in the *Apocalypse of Abraham*. Indeed, scholars have noted that the fallen angel Azazel, conceived in the *Apocalypse of Abraham* as a celestial scapegoat, is portrayed as an imitator of the most exalted theophanic attributes, including the attribute of the divine Glory, *Kavod*.[48] Considering this unusual adaptation of traditional theophanic imagery in the portrayals of demonic characters, one might wonder whether the interaction between Azazel and the messianic character in chapter 29 contains similar traditions, and thus might too represent one of the epiphanies of the arch-demon, whose manifestations are widely dispersed in the Slavonic apocalypse.

This consideration draws our attention again to one of the most notable features of the interaction between the fallen angel and the ambiguous messiah in chapter 29, namely, the infamous kiss of the demon. This encounter might be viewed as a specimen of erotic imagery, a kind of symbolism that plays quite a prominent role in the Slavonic apocalypse.[49] Such symbolism can point to a theophanic dimension, as some Jewish apocalyptic and mystical accounts often imbue eroticism with theophanic meaning.[50] This erotic theophanic facet is often present in apocalyptic and mystical *imaginaires* of Yom Kippur rite[51] in which human seers enter into the celestial Holy of Holies, where they often are embraced and even kissed by the Deity. We see this, for instance, in *2 Enoch*, in which the seer reports that, after his ascent into the highest heaven, the Deity embraced him with his hand.[52] The reference to the embracing or helping hand of God is found also in the *Exagoge* of Ezekiel the Tragedian.[53] The early roots of this tradition can be traced to the biblical Exodus account that has Moses appearing to be closely guarded and protected by the hand of the Deity.

Some later Jewish mystical accounts offer even more salient erotic interactions between the Deity and a seer, depicting human visionaries kissed by God.[54] One thinks of *Hekhalot Rabbati* (*Synopse* §163), which portrays God's kiss of the heavenly image of the patriarch Jacob; it reads:

> And testify to them. What testimony? You see Me—what I do to the visage of the face of Jacob your father which is engraved for Me upon the throne of My glory. For in the hour that you say before Me "Holy," I kneel on it and embrace it and kiss it and hug it and My hands are on its arms three times, corresponding to the three times that you say before Me, "Holy," according to the word that is said, Holy, holy, holy (Isaiah 6:3).[55]

In view of these accounts of the divine embrace and kiss, which constitute the theophanic apex of Jewish mystical lore, might we suggest that Azazel's kiss in *Apocalypse of Abraham* 29 also has a theophanic meaning?[56] If so, this nicely interplays with other deconstructive "epiphanies" of the arch-demon in the Slavonic apocalypse that are laden with erotic overtones, including Azazel's appearance in the midst of the primordial pair of the protoplasts[57] in *Apocalypse of Abraham* 23:4–11.[58]

The peculiar imagery of the "face" is another important detail that links the kiss of Azazel in the messianic passage with theophanic imagery in the aforementioned apocalyptic and mystical accounts in which seers are embraced or kissed by the Deity. Both *2 Enoch* and *Hekhalot Rabbati* make a connection between God's face and the visionary's face. In these accounts, the visionary's identity is engraved on the Deity's face and serves as a kind of screen or *façade* for the divine countenance. In *Apocalypse of Abraham* 29 the countenance imagery plays a pivotal conceptual role in being applied not only to God and the righteous but also Azazel and his elect: "Azazel ran and worshiped, and having kissed his face he turned and stood behind him."[59] Here, as in the aforementioned visionary accounts in which seers often become servants or even representations of the divine Face, the messianic character kissed by Azazel becomes the earthly *façade* of his demonic presence. It is then no surprise that in *Apocalypse of Abraham* 29:7 the messianic man "was worshiped by the heathen with Azazel." The phrase "worshiped with Azazel" might indicate that the eschatological character has become a kind of "icon" of Azazel through which one can worship the demon.[60]

The Messianic Idol

Azazel's kiss appears also to be closely linked with the Slavonic apocalypse's distinctive stance against idolatry. Before we explore more closely this important aspect of the text, we should underline the unique nature of Azazel's embrace and kiss of the messianic scapegoat, as Jewish lore does not provide us with any other clear textual testimonies in which the scapegoat was embraced or kissed. Yet, another embrace or kiss is attested to several times, with respect to another animal sacrificial symbol of Jewish tradition, namely, the Golden Calf. Several rabbinic passages, including *b. Yoma* 66b, include the theme of kissing and embracing the Golden Calf:

> One said: Whosoever sacrificed and burned incense died by the sword; whosoever embraced and kissed [the calf] died the death [at the hands of Heaven]; whosoever rejoiced in his heart died of dropsy. The other said: He who had sinned before witnesses and after receiving warning, died by the sword; he who sinned before witnesses but without previous warning, by death; and he who sinned without witnesses and without previous warning, died of dropsy.[61]

The motif of embracing and kissing the Golden Calf is also attested in the Hekhalot literature,[62] and its roots can be traced to certain biblical accounts.[63] Its presence in these traditions is instructive for our study because they frame the motif in a cultic setting in which the kiss is understood as an act of worship. This cultic connection is an important parallel to Azazel's kiss in *Apocalypse of Abraham* 29 in which the celestial scapegoat's kiss has a sacerdotal significance communicated through conspicuous use of the formulae of "worship" in connection with the erotic event.[64] The language of "worship" is very strong in the immediate context of the messianic passage, stronger than anywhere else in the text. In the very beginning of the passage, in verse 4, readers learn that the great crowds will worship the messianic man. Verse 5 says that the man will go through humiliation and abuses, but he will still be worshipped. In verse 6, Azazel is worshipping him. In verse 7, Abraham asks the Deity about worship offered to the eschatological man and God's answer confirms the terminology. Finally, verses 11 through 13 also mention worship offered to this eschatological character.

References to worshipping objects other than God are closely tied, in the *Apocalypse of Abraham*, with the theme of idolatry.[65] In chapter 3, Terah worships his idols.[66] In chapter 25, Abraham sees the idol of jealousy in the Temple, and a man worshipping it.[67] The pervasive symbolism of worship in the messianic passage indicates that the eschatological character in chapter 29 is envisioned as an idol. Along such lines, Robert Hall has argued that in *Apocalypse of Abraham* 29 "Azazel sets up another idol, a human being."[68] He further remarks that "in *Apoc. Abr.* [the] vision of the man who is worshiped continues the theme of idolatry connected with Azazel. Not only does the figure encourage the heathen to worship him, but it deceives many Jews as well."[69]

In view of these intense polemics against idols in various parts of the Slavonic apocalypse, we should return to the paradigmatic case of idolatry in Jewish lore, namely, the Golden Calf episode, and clarify its connection with the scapegoat tradition. Moreover, in order to better grasp the conceptual links between these two sacrificial animals of the Jewish tradition, which in later Jewish lore were often connected with the revelation received by Moses on Mount Sinai, we must now explore more closely the mold of the Mosaic traditions in the Slavonic apocalypse.

As in later rabbinic materials, Yom Kippur imagery in the *Apocalypse of Abraham* appears to be connected with Mosaic lore.[70] Later

Jewish traditions closely link the etiology of the Yom Kippur ordinance with Moses' fight against the idolatry of the Golden Calf. In these later rabbinic interpretations, Moses' struggle with the infamous idol, his forty-day fast, his vision of the Deity, and his reception of the portentous revelation on Sinai were understood as a chain of formative events linked to the establishment of the Yom Kippur festival. Some of these traditions viewed Moses' visionary ordeals as a cosmic prototype of the symbolic actions that, while the Temple still stood, were to be reenacted annually by the high priest in the Holy of Holies. In this new sacerdotal context of the atoning rite, the fight against the Golden Calf has a new cultic meaning.

It is intriguing that in the *Apocalypse of Abraham*, as in the Exodus account, the forty-day fast follows the hero's fight against idolatry. The stories of the two visionaries parallel each other. Moses burns the Golden Calf in Exodus 32 and fasts in chapter 34. Abraham, too, burns the idol of his father, which bears the name Bar-Eshath, and then enters a ritual fast. This parallelism might indicate the authors' intention to refashion the story of Abraham along the lines of the Mosaic typology. As in later rabbinic and mystical accounts, the atoning rite may have been given a new Mosaic reinterpretation, which now closely connects the Yom Kippur ordinance with the Golden Calf story.

In later rabbinic texts, the Golden Calf idolatry is linked with the assignment of a sacrificial portion to the left side, which was often identified with the offering of the scapegoat to Azazel on Yom Kippur.[71] The scapegoat ritual may also be seen as a symbolic reenactment of the Golden Calf episode. For example, Tamara Prosic argues that

> . . . the ritual for Azazel repeats the golden calf episode in that it reinforces Yahweh as the only cultic figure through ceremonial expulsion of the other god. The whole ritual actually resembles a performance of a banishing act. . . . Azazel's goat is left alive and driven into the wilderness. In symbolic language, the old god begins as an equal to Yahweh and is acknowledged at the beginning of the ritual as one who is also partaking in the sacrificial cult, but after the lottery, only one god is honored between the two who are waiting for their respective sacrifice. Only Yahweh's goat is ritually killed and presented on the altar thus becoming a proper sacrifice. The same cultic status and the inherent honour of being a

> god's offering is denied to Azazel's animal; it is left alive and banished into the wilderness, the symbol of non-habitable spaces, where there are no altars and no worshippers and where it can never become a sacrifice. Azazel, although admitted initially by bringing his would-be sacrifice within the sacred space, is denied proper worship, the allegiance to him is abjured, and he is step by step removed from the cult and pushed into a symbolic void.[72]

This reflection on the scapegoat as an idol that must be banished through ceremonial expulsion helps us to better grasp the link between the tradition of the scapegoat in the Slavonic apocalypse and the theme of idolatry found in the text. It also elucidates the function of the messianic scapegoat in the apocalyptic version of the atoning rite taking place in the Slavonic apocalypse, as this eschatological character appears to be understood as a sort of gatherer of the impurity who is predestined to attract the idolaters, not only from the portion of the Gentiles but also from the lot of Abraham, leading both into the hands of Azazel.[73]

The Messianic Dyad

As noted earlier, second- and third-century Christian interpretations include messianic depictions that often encompass the imagery of both goats used during the Yom Kippur festival: the scapegoat and the goat for YHWH. Such interpretations often combine the functions and attributes of the two goats and apply the conceptual amalgam to Jesus. It is possible that the *Apocalypse of Abraham* is employing a similar interpretive strategy in which the scapegoat imagery is enhanced with features of the immolated goat. Moreover, given our hypothesis that the scapegoat's symbolism takes on distinctive messianic overtones, the two emblematic animals of the atoning rite might receive there the form of the messianic dyad.

A close reading of chapter 29 shows that its narrative is portraying not one but two messianic figures, the features of which represent a puzzling mix. In verses 4–8 we are told that the messiah will come from the side of the Gentiles, while verses 9 and 10 speak of the messiah as coming from the seed of Abraham.[74] In view of this apparent contradiction, scholars have suggested that the text may speak about not one but two messianic characters—the first coming from the left lot, the portion associated with the Gentiles, and the second from the right, the portion of Abraham and God. Alexander Kulik proposes that "the eschatological scenario of *Apoc. Ab.* 29 might have the well-known Jewish eschatological duo-messianic structure[75] (in this case: anti-Messiah vs. true Messiah)."[76] There is no textual contradiction if we assume that 29:4–8 speaks of an anti-Messiah who is "going out from the left side of the heathen" and "worshiped by the heathen with Azazel."[77] This hypothesis is promising for resolving textual puzzles in chapter 29. The tradition of the messianic pair, in which each agent has distinctive eschatological roles and functions, is a recurrent motif in Jewish lore.[78] An early example is found in the Dead Sea Scrolls materials in which the messiahs of Aaron and Israel[79] fulfill unique eschatological functions, one cultic and the other royal.[80] Later Jewish materials are also cognizant of the concept of the two messiahs, one suffering and dying and the other victorious. For example, later Jewish sources often speak of the Messiah, the son of Joseph (or Ephraim),[81] who will endure suffering to atone for the sins of the Israelites, as well as the Messiah, the son of David,[82] who is predestined to be a glorious ruler.[83]

It is significant that one member of the messianic duo, like the eschatological figure from *Apocalypse of Abraham* 29, will experience maltreatment and suffering.[84] What is also important for our study is that in the second century CE, when the *Apocalypse of Abraham* was composed, we find, under the influence of the political situation and Christian messianic developments, highly elaborate reflection on the concept of the true versus false messiah.[85] Scholars trace the development of the true/false messianic pair to the Bar Kokhba uprising. Harris Lenowitz suggests:

> [T]he events of the Bar Kosiba uprising displayed the new doctrine of two messiahs—if they did not actually create the doctrine—in its most pernicious form. . . . In peculiar countermeasure to the two-messiah doctrine, the idea of the false messiah was soon developed as well; it also arose in close interaction with Christian views. During the Galilean rebellions, the term "false" was first applied to a prophet in a messianic context, paving the way for the explicit application of the term to messiahs. But it was the Christian texts

> that coined the term *pseudochristoi* (Greek for "false messiahs"); Matthew 24:4, 6, 24; Mark 13:5, 21–22; and Luke 21:3 all use the term *pseudochristos* to refer to messianic pretenders. The Jewish tradition follows the Christian; the Greek term is borrowed and translated in the much later Hebrew term *mashiah sheker*, which reshapes and alters the previous Hebrew usage of the term "lying" (*sheker*), in connection with the witness and prophet, so that it means "false witness, false prophecy."[86]

It has been noted that these conceptual developments "have no need for two authentic messiahs, the first of whom is doomed to die. Instead the false messiah identifies the true one by contrast."[87]

If Kulik is right that the *Apocalypse of Abraham* 29 presumes two messiahs, the second messianic figure, like the first, can be associated with the Yom Kippur context. This view may be supported by the idea that the second messianic figure, also like the first, is identified with a distinctive eschatological allotment: the right portion, which is often identified in the text as the lot of Abraham and God. Such identification is important for discerning possible links with the Yom Kippur ceremony in which the right lot, associated with God, is also identified with the goat for YHWH.

Another important detail of the messianic passage is that the portrayals of two messianic figures are not clearly demarcated, but rather are confused. Such confusion has been taken by many students of the Slavonic apocalypse as proof that the entire messianic passage represents an interpolation. Yet, in the light of aforementioned Christian accounts, in which the characteristics of the two "messianic goats" were also often paradoxically mixed and not clearly distinguished,[88] it is possible that the mixing of the features of the positive and negative messianic characters represents a deliberate strategy of the authors of the Slavonic apocalypse.

Yet, while features of the two messianic figures often appear intertwined and sometimes confused, their respective eschatological functions are nevertheless clearly delineated in the program outlined by the authors. Thus, the first, mistreated messiah appears to be endowed with a rather misleading, yet purifying function, and, as the scapegoat of the atoning rite, can be understood as a gatherer and remover of the impurity associated with the Gentiles and idolatrous Hebrews. In contrast, the second messianic character appears to be playing the more traditional messianic role, the role reiterated in *Apocalypse of Abraham* 31:1, which depicts the *parousia* of the victorious messiah who will come with the sound of the trumpet and power in order to gather the elect.[89]

Distraction for the Heathen

The ambiguous, misleading role of the mistreated messiah, who comes at the apex of impiety, cannot be fully grasped without a proper understanding of the multifaceted nature of the scapegoat's place in the Yom Kippur ordinance.

Later Jewish interpreters often stress that one of the essential functions of the scapegoat was to distract or weaken the power of the Other Side during the most important atoning feast of the Jewish liturgical year. For example, in the *Book of Zohar*, the scapegoat "weakens" the power of the left side by serving as a distraction. *Zohar* I.113b–114b transmits the following tradition:

> Come and see: Similarly, on the day that judgment appears in the world and the blessed Holy One sits on the Throne of Judgment, Satan appears, accusing and seducing above and below, to destroy the world and seize souls. . . . On Yom Kippur one must pacify and appease him with that goat offered to him, and then he turns into an advocate for Israel. . . .[90]

Isaiah Tishby offers interesting remarks on the famous parable in the *Book of Zohar* in which a king makes special arrangements for a celebratory feast with his son and friends. He orders a separate meal for ill-wishers and quarrelers so their presence would not spoil the happy occasion.[91] Tishby notes that "according to this parable the purpose of sending a goat to Azazel is to remove *sitra ahra* from the 'family circle' of Israel and the Holy One, blessed be He, on the Day of Atonement."[92]

In view of these traditions, it is possible that in the *Apocalypse of Abraham* the scapegoat-messiah also serves as a distraction or decoy; he is sent to mislead and weaken the heathen of the left lot and to prepare the safe arrival of the true (second) messiah who will arise from the right lot. One of the crucial pieces of evidence here is that he is openly labeled in the text as the "weakening" of the Gentiles[93] (Slav. *ослаба*).[94] As in the later Jewish reinterpretation of the atoning rite, the messianic scapegoat is depicted here as an eschatological instrument for weakening and distracting *sitra ahra*, represented by the heathen. The passage has several affirmations of this messianic role, noting "many of the heathen will have hope in him," that some people from the right lot "will be misled on his account," and that "he will tempt those of your [Abraham's] seed who have worshiped him."[95]

Since, according to the text, the false messiah will mislead not only Gentiles but also sinful Hebrews, it is possible that the Slavonic term *oslaba* has an additional meaning of "liberation," which would refer to the cathartic purifying release of Israel's sins to the realm of the Other Side associated with Gentiles.[96] The messianic figure thus will take with him the idolatrous portion of Israel. In this respect, the text specifically mentions that the messianic figure will appear at the apex of the impiety, defined as the "twelfth hour of the age of impiety," and that he will release it to the left side represented by Azazel.[97] This context underlines the principal "elimination" aspect of the scapegoat ritual whereby impurity must be removed from the human *oikoumene* into an uninhabitable realm.

Conclusion

Although many scholars have suggested that the messianic passage in chapter 29 of the *Apocalypse of Abraham* is a later Christian interpolation, this study revisited some details in this enigmatic eschatological account that may provide new evidence for its belonging to the original layer of the text. Our analysis suggests that the messianic narrative shares a number of crucial ideological tenets with the original conceptual core of the Slavonic apocalypse, including its peculiar polemic against idolatry and veneration of anthropomorphic images, which are repeatedly portrayed in the *Apocalypse of Abraham* as objects of worship. It also appears that the messianic passage might play an important, if not central, role in the sacerdotal framework of the text, which is thoroughly steeped in cultic traditions. As in Christian sacerdotal reinterpretations of messianic imagery in *Barnabas* and Justin the Martyr, the Slavonic apocalypse authors are also refashioning their messianic traditions through the prism of the Yom Kippur ordinance.

In light of these Christian developments, the possibility that authors of the *Apocalypse of Abraham* had some knowledge of contemporaneous Christian messianic currents should not be completely excluded. Some scholars have suggested that the early Christian concepts of the false messiah(s) often exercised a formative influence on similar Jewish developments in the second century CE.[98] If the authors of the *Apocalypse of Abraham* tried to appropriate Jesus traditions in their depiction of the messiah in chapter 29, as has been suggested by several scholars, it is possible that their appropriation was not solely based on the Gospel accounts but also drew from more extended contemporaneous cultic reinterpretations of Jesus' passion in which the Christian Messiah was identified with the proverbial scapegoat of the Yom Kippur ritual.

PART II

Studies in *2 Enoch*

Adoil Outside the Cosmos

God Before and After Creation in the Enochic Tradition

> [V]essels shattered and collapsed, for they were not able to contain the light expanding and emanating from within them . . . the saints in their death transform these sparks of holiness. . . .
>
> —Chaim Vital, *Etz Chaim*

Introduction

Unlike other early Enochic writings, the *2 (Slavonic) Apocalypse of Enoch* depicts a unique story of primordial creation, revealing an elaborate course of events that preceded the visible creation of the world.[1] The importance of this mystical account is underlined by the fact that it was delivered to the seventh antediluvian hero by God himself. Chapter 25 of *2 Enoch* recounts how, at the end of the patriarch's celestial tour to the throne of Glory, the Deity unveils to the seer that prior to the visible creation he had called out from nothing the luminous aeon Adoil to become the foundation of the upper things. The account describes the enigmatic event of Adoil's disintegration during the course of which the aeon becomes the cornerstone of the visible creation upon which the Deity establishes his throne. Here, like the depictions found in the Lurianic Kabbalah, the bursting of the primordial vessel of light is depicted as the first creative act of the Deity that gives life to the visible order of everything. Even more striking is that this primordial act of establishing the visible reality is then paralleled in the later chapters of the Slavonic apocalypse that focus on the eschatological demise.

In light of this, scholars have noted that the protological account in chapter 25, dealing with the establishment of the created order, appears to correspond with the order of eschatological events in chapter 65 in which, during his short visit to earth, Enoch conveys to his children the mystery of the last times.[2] The patriarch reveals that, after the final judgment, time will collapse and all the righteous of the world will be incorporated into the luminous aeon of the righteous. The description of this final aeon betrays some striking similarities to the primordial aeon Adoil depicted in chapter 25. The revelation also seems to suggest that the righteous Enoch, translated to heaven and transformed into a luminous celestial creature, represents the first fruit of this eschatological aeon that will eventually gather all the righteous into a single entity.

The purpose of this chapter is to explore these traditions about the primordial aeon Adoil in the Slavonic apocalypse, as well as the role of Enoch in its eschatological restoration.

The Aeon before Creation

The Upper Foundation

The Slavonic apocalypse underlines the portentous nature of the primordial cosmogonic account by stressing that this special knowledge has never been revealed to any other creatures, including the angels. This supraangelic disclosure, given to the visionary after his celestial metamorphosis, can be seen as the pinnacle of the esoteric instruction the seventh antediluvian hero acquired in the upper realm. An extensive description of this revelation is provided by both the shorter and the longer recensions of the Slavonic text. The shorter recension[3] of *2 Enoch* 25 offers the following account:

> And I commanded the lowest things: "Let one of the invisible things come out visibly!" And Adail descended, extremely large. And I looked at him, and, behold, in his belly he had a great age. And I said to him, "Disintegrate yourself, Adail, and let what is disintegrated from you become visible." And

> he disintegrated himself, and there came out from him the great age. And thus it carried all the creation which I had wished to create. And I saw how good it was. And I placed for myself a throne, and I sat down on it. To the light I spoke: "You go up higher and be solidified and become the foundation for the highest things." And there is nothing higher than the light, except nothing itself. And I spoke, I straightened myself upward from my throne.[4]

The central character of the story is the aeon Adoil ("Adail" in the shorter recension)[5] who is depicted in the text as the chief cosmogonic agent responsible for the "revelation" of the visible creation. Further, this enigmatic entity is depicted as both the mother and the midwife of creation, someone that conceives and then releases the whole creation from its cosmic belly. The text emphasizes the enormous size of Adoil, defining him as "extremely large." He is portrayed as pregnant with creation by containing a great aeon in his stomach. Also, Adoil's disintegration provides the beginning for all visible reality and serves as the foundation on which God is able to establish the first visible manifestation of the created order, namely, his throne. It is noteworthy that in both recensions the Deity commands Adoil to become the foundation of the highest things.[6] This terminological identification of Adoil with the concept of foundation is important for our study.[7]

Another significant feature, for our purposes, is the portrayal of Adoil, in the longer recension, as the revealer.[8] His disintegration is understood in the text as the revelation of the created order: "And the great age came out, and it revealed all the creation which I had thought up to create."

Finally, another notable detail in the depiction of Adoil is the repeated references to his luminous nature. The emphasis on the luminosity of the primordial aeon is even more apparent in the longer recension, which emphasizes not only the outer shining nature of the protological agent but also his internal luminous state, depicted there as a pregnancy with great light.[9]

Inverse Symmetry of Light and Darkness

The disintegration of the vessel of light at the beginning of creation will be reversed by the eschatological restoration at the end of time, when the final aeon of the righteous will gather the dispersed particles of light in the souls of the elect into a new luminous gathering. This symmetry of the primordial and eschatological vessels once again illustrates the symmetrical principle of *Urzeit* and *Endzeit* often found in Jewish apocalyptic accounts.[10]

The Slavonic apocalypse appears cognizant not only of the temporal symmetry of the beginning and the end but also of another, spatial mirroring of the lower and the upper realms, expressed through the symbolism of light and darkness. Light and darkness are set in striking opposition, especially in the creational account of *2 Enoch*.

Immediately after the description of the luminous aeon Adoil, the text describes another preexistent entity, namely, the aeon of darkness—that is to say, the second paradoxical helper of the Deity at creation, personified under the name Arukhas (Arkhas in the longer recension). The shorter recension of *2 Enoch* 26:13 unveils the following depiction of Arukhas:

> And I called out a second time into the lowest things, and I said, "Let one of the invisible things come out solid and visible." There came out Arukhas, solid and heavy and very black. And I saw how suitable he was. And I said to him, "Come down low and become solid! And become the foundation of the lowest things!" And he came down and became solid. And he became the foundation of the lowest things. And there is nothing lower than the darkness, except nothing itself.[11]

One of the intriguing features of this account is that the darkness is not a mere created thing, as in the biblical creational account, but is instead a preexistent demiurgic entity that is summoned by the Deity from the order of realities that preceded creation. It is equal and symmetrical to the divine light, as both Adoil and Arukhas are brought from the same order of "the lower things"—a possible designation of the preexistent divine Pleroma. Further, the processions of Arukhas are reminiscent of earlier descriptions of Adoil's processions. In both instances, after summoning the aeons, the Deity orders their disintegration. His command to Arukhas—"Open yourself up . . . and let what is born from you become visible!"—can be compared to the almost identical command given to Adoil, namely, "Disintegrate yourself, Adail, and let what is disintegrated from you become visible." In response to this divine order, both Arukhas and Adoil give birth to their respective aeons, or ages of creation: "[Arukhas] disintegrated himself. There came out an age, dark, very large, carrying the creation of all lower things;" and "[Adoil] disintegrated himself, and there came out from him the great age."

Despite such parallels between the actions of Adoil and Arukhas, we are dealing here with an inverse symmetry that utilizes the dichotomies of light and darkness, upper and lower. Adoil's disintegration produces the luminous aeon, while the disintegration of Arukhas produces its dark counterpart. Furthermore, in comparison with Adoil's disintegration, which provides "the foundation of the upper things," Arukhas's opening lays "the foundation of the lower things."

Portrayed as the demiurgic faculty equal to the divine light, the divine darkness provides a unique glimpse into the dynamics of the divine "Left Side," demonstrating the complexity of the creational imagery found in the Slavonic apocalypse, in which the divine light was dispersed not due to the fall of the primordial human but through a command of the Deity. As the primordial vessel of light bursts forth by virtue of the Deity's command, so too does the primordial darkness arise from the very essence of the Godhead, becoming the chief mediatorial agent of the creator.

The Cosmogony of 2 Enoch: Light inside of Light

Scholars have noted several parallels between the creational narrative found in the Slavonic apocalypse and certain hermetic and gnostic cosmogonies. These scholars often understand *2 Enoch*'s account as an important early testimony to the Jewish matrix of these later cosmogonic speculations.[12] In light of these similarities, others have speculated that Adoil's imagery may be connected with the myth of the Heavenly Man. Such imagery becomes prominent in the later hermetic and gnostic texts and collections,[13] including the *Corpus Hermeticum* in which the Anthropos inherits the luminosity of the Father[14] and becomes the blueprint for the created order and humankind by disintegrating himself into the physical realm. This motif is also conveyed in the *Poimandres*,[15] through the erotic metaphor of Anthropos falling in love with Nature.[16] In commenting on the features of the Heavenly Man myth in the story of Adoil, Jarl Fossum draws attention to the peculiar symbolism of light conveyed in the longer recension of the Slavonic pseudepigraphon through the expression "light out of light." He proposes that this imagery of light—possibly rendered in the Greek *Vorlage* of *2 Enoch* through the term φῶς, as in many other accounts that contain the Heavenly Man ideology—might have an anthropomorphic significance.[17] It is well known that the heavenly Anthropos traditions often play on the ambiguity of the φως terminology, which can designate either φώς "a man" or φῶς "light," both pointing to the luminous and anthropomorphic nature of the Celestial Human.[18] In view of these conceptual developments, Adoil can be understood in the Slavonic apocalypse as an anthropomorphic entity that is predestined to serve not only as the pattern of the visible creation but also as the blueprint of humanity. The possible "human" form of Adoil seems reaffirmed in both recensions through references to his belly.

The anthropomorphic dimension of the φως symbolism was also evident in the hermetic and gnostic cosmologies that often play on the ambiguity of this terminology in their depiction of the Heavenly Man. In this respect it is intriguing that some gnostic anthropogonies use expressions very similar to *2 Enoch* by describing the Heavenly Man "Adamas" as "a light which radiated from the light."[19]

The Anthropogony of 2 Enoch: Sophia and Seven

The enigmatic unfolding of the cosmogonic process in the Slavonic apocalypse receives further conceptual development in the account of the creation of Adam that follows this narration. The cosmogonic account of Adoil's disintegration in chapters 25 through 27 and the anthropogonic account of Adam's creation found in chapter 30 appear to be closely connected with each other, as some of Adam's qualities resemble some peculiar features of the great aeon. One of the prominent features here is a parallel in the luminosity of Adoil and the luminosity of Adam. Thus, according to *2 Enoch* 30:12, the prelapsarian Adam was a very special celestial being. The Slavonic apocalypse defines him as a second angel who was great and glorious.[20]

The designation of Adam as a "second angel" is also intriguing in light of previous scholarly suggestions that Adoil too appears to be envisioned in the text as an angel.[21] In view of the possible angelic nature of the first aeon, Adam's designation as the second angel may have been conceived as a subtle link between the two characters by placing the patriarch in parallel with the Heavenly Man. Additional imagery found in the text seems to corroborate this connection. In this respect it is noteworthy that the account of Adam's creation ends with an arcane hymn about the two "substances" of humanity—invisible and visible:

> From invisible and visible substances I created man.
> From both his natures come both death and life.
> And (as my) image he knows the word like (no) other creature.
> But even at his greatest he is small,
> And again at his smallest he is great.[22]

In light of this juxtaposition of the invisible and the visible, it is worth noting that the descent of Adoil in both recensions of *2 Enoch* 25:1 is rendered, similarly, as transition from an invisible into a visible condition: "And I commanded the lowest things: 'Let one of the invisible things descend visibly!' And Adoil descended, extremely large."[23]

Moreover, the aforementioned hymn makes an enigmatic juxtaposition between the invisible and visible substances of the protoplast and the conditions of death and life, which possibly signify here the states of mortality and immortality: "From invisible and visible substances I created man. From both his natures come both death and life." It is striking that the *Poimandres* 15 offers a similar cluster of traditions about the twofold nature of humankind, in which the immortal part is linked with the Heavenly Man; it reads: "Because of this, unlike any other living thing on earth, mankind is twofold—in the body mortal but immortal in the essential man."[24]

All these parallels help to clarify the subtle correlations between Adoil and Adam, providing further insight into the relationships between *2 Enoch*'s cosmogony and anthropogony.

The unity of the cosmological and anthropological developments in the Slavonic apocalypse is also evident in the tradition about the sevenfold nature of humanity. The longer recension of *2 Enoch* 30:8–9 recounts that Adam was created from seven "components"[25] and endowed with seven "properties/faculties":[26]

> And on the sixth day I commanded my wisdom to create man out of the seven components:

His flesh from earth;
His blood from dew and from the sun;
His eyes from bottomless sea;
His bones from stone;
His reason from the mobility of angels and from clouds;
His sinews and hair from grass of the earth;
His spirit from my spirit and from wind.
And I gave him 7 properties:[27]
Hearing to the flesh;
Sight to the eyes;
Smell to the spirit;
Touch to the sinews;
Taste to the blood;
To the bones—endurance;
To the reason—sweetness.[28]

Such accounts of the creation of Adam, from seven substances, are important for our study. They are again reminiscent of the hermetic and gnostic developments in which the sevenfold anthropogonic pattern is intertwined with the sevenfold cosmogony. For example, in *Poimandres* 16–17, the following cryptic tradition can be found:

> Poimandres said: "This is the mystery that has been kept hidden until this very day. When nature made love with the man, she bore a wonder most wondrous. In him he had the nature of the cosmic framework of the seven, who are made of fire and spirit, as I told you, and without delay nature at once gave birth to seven men, androgyne and exalted, whose nature were like those of the seven governors . . .
>
> As I said, then, the birth of the seven was as follows. <Earth> was the female. Water did the fertilizing. Fire was the maturing force. Nature took spirit from the ether and brought forth bodies in the shape of the man. From life and light the man became soul and mind; from life came soul, from light came mind, and all things in cosmos of the senses remained thus until a cycle ended <and> kinds of things began to be."[29]

As we see, here, humanity's origin is traced to the seven spirits[30] who are responsible for "giving birth" to the seven androgynous humans.[31] It is also intriguing that in *Poimandres* 16–17 the sevenfold anthropogony corresponds to the sevenfold cosmology (wherein the seven proto-humans are correlated to the seven celestial governors-planets called "administrators") and also to the "senses" or elements of nature and the human body. We find this account in *Poimandres* 9; it reads:

> The mind who is god, being androgyne and existing as life and light, by speaking gave birth to a second mind, a craftsman, who, as god of fire and spirit, crafted seven governors; they encompass the sensible world in circles (ἐν κύκλοὶς),[32] and their government is called faith.[33]

The symbolism of the planetary "circles" in this passage is reminiscent of the imagery in the Slavonic apocalypse. A tradition found in the longer recension of *2 Enoch* 27:3–4 speaks of God creating seven great "circles" in the "foundation of light":

> And I made a foundation of light around the water. And I created seven great circles inside it, and I gave them an appearance of crystal, wet and dry, that is to say glass and ice, and to be the circuit for water and the other elements. And I pointed out to each one of them his route, to the seven stars, each one of them in his own heaven, so that they might travel accordingly. And I saw how good it was. And I made a division between the light and between the darkness, that is to say, in the middle of the waters, this way and that way. And I said to the light that it should be day, and to the darkness I commanded that it should be night. And evening came, and again morning came, that is the first day.[34]

In this passage, the creation of the seven planetary circles and seven stars appears to be connected, as in the *Corpus Hermeticum*, with the sevenfold nature of primordial humanity. Our study will later show that in the account of Adam's creation in *2 Enoch* 30, the list of the seven planets is given immediately before the account of the protoplast's creation from the seven components. Here, as in the hermetic literature, the seven "governors" of the heavens are depicted as the defining cosmological pattern that precedes the sevenfold nature of primordial humanity.

We see a similar correspondence between the sevenfold cosmology and the sevenfold anthropogony in several gnostic texts, including the *Apocryphon of John*, in which the seven components of Adam's body correspond to the seven anthropogonic agents associated with planetary spheres and responsible for the fashioning of the first human's body.[35] Thus, the passages from *Apocryphon of John* (NHC, II, 11, 23–35 and 15, 1–29) unveil the identities of seven rulers and their role in the creation of the psychic body of Adam; they read:

> And the rulers created seven powers for (each of) them, and the powers created for themselves six angels for each one until they became 365 angels. And these are the bodies belonging with the names: the first <is> Athoth, he has a sheep's face; the second is Eloaiou, he has a donkey's face; the third is Astaphaios, he has a [hyena's] face; the fourth is Yao, he has a [serpent's] face with seven heads; the fifth is Sabaoth, he has a serpent's face; the sixth is Adonin, he had a monkey's face; the seventh is Sabbede, he has a shining fire-face. This is the sevenness of the week (NHC, II, 11, 23–35).[36]

> And he said to the authorities which attend him, "Come, let us create a man according to the image of God and according to our likeness, that his image may become a light for us." And they created through their respective powers in correspondence with the characteristics which were given. And each authority supplied a characteristic by means of the form of the image which he had seen in its psychic (form). He created a being according to the likeness of the first, perfect Man. And they said, "Let us call him Adam, that his name may become a power of light for us." And the powers began (to create): the first one, Goodness, created a bone-soul; and the second, Providence, created a sinew-soul; the third, Divinity, created a flesh-soul; and the fourth, the Lordship, created a marrow-soul; the fifth, Kingdom, created a blood-soul; the sixth, Envy, created a skin-soul; the seventh, Understanding, created a hair-soul. And the multitude of the angels attended him, and they received from the authorities the seven substances of the

soul in order to create the proportions of the limbs and the proportions of the trunk and the proper working together of each of the parts (NHC, II, 15, 1–29).[37]

Here, as in the aforementioned hermetic materials, the correspondence between the Heavenly Man and his "material" counterpart is mediated by the anthropogonic sevenfold pattern. Several other gnostic texts also attest to this tradition of the seven androgynous anthropogonic "mediators." For example, *On the Origin of the World* (NHC, II, 101–102) reads:

> Seven appeared in chaos, androgynous. They have their masculine names and their feminine names. . . . These are the [seven] forces of the seven heavens of [chaos]. And they were born androgynous, consistent with the immortal pattern that existed before them, according to the wish of Pistis.[38]

Here again, as in the aforementioned passages from the *Poimandres,* the connection is made between the seven androgynes and the sevenfold pattern according to which they were "born."

While the list of the corresponding celestial governing planets is not explicitly outlined in the versions of the *Apocryphon of John,* their authors knew these astral correlations.[39] Roelof van den Broek summarizes the correspondences found in the several versions of the *Apocryphon of John* by offering the following juxtaposition of archons, powers, planets, and soul substances:[40]

Iaoth	Pronoia	Moon	Marrow
Eloaios	Divinity	Mercury	Bones
Astaphaios	Goodness	Venus	Sinews
Iao	Fire	Sun	Flesh
Sabaoth	Kingship	Mars	Blood
Adoni	Synesis	Jupiter	Skin
Sabbataios	Sophia	Saturn	Hair[41]

These correlations are thought provoking, as they show close similarities with the planetary list given in the creational narrative of the Slavonic apocalypse. It is also intriguing that in *2 Enoch* this planetary list precedes almost immediately the rosters of the seven components and properties of Adam. Thus the longer recension of *2 Enoch* 30:2–3 reads:

> And on the fourth day I commanded: "Let there be great lamps on the heavenly circles."
>
> On the first, the highest circle, I placed the star Kronos;
> On the 2nd <lower down, I placed> Afridit;
> On the 3rd Arris;
> On the 4th the sun;
> On the 5th Zeous;
> On the 6th Ermis;
> And on the 7th, the lowest the moon.[42]

Although some Greek names on this planetary list appear to have been corrupted during the long transmission history of the Slavonic apocalypse,[43] it is not difficult to restore their original forms; they read:[44]

> 1st circle—Saturn (Kronos)
> 2nd circle—Venus (Aphrodite)
> 3rd circle—Mars (Ares)
> 4th circle—the sun
> 5th circle—Jupiter (Zeus)
> 6th circle—Mercury (Hermes)
> 7th circle—the moon

This list is reminiscent of the planetary list of the Archons provided by van den Broek, although it misplaces Jupiter and Venus,[45] and reverses the order of planets, starting with Saturn (Kronos) and concluding with the moon. Van den Broek notes[46] that, according to Origen's *Contra Celsum* VI:31, this reversal of the planetary order was part of the Ophites' cosmological system.[47]

The cluster of traditions surrounding the creation of the protoplast in the Slavonic apocalypse, like the gnostic and hermetic materials, points to the unity of the cosmological and anthropogonic speculations, which are tied together through the distinctive sevenfold patterns. Although the applications of the sevenfold patterns in relation to humanity have been known in various Hellenistic milieux from the most ancient times, the peculiar nature of these developments in the Slavonic apocalypse appears to draw them closer to the variants found in later hermetic and gnostic texts. In this respect, another even more striking parallel in the account of creation in *2 Enoch* 30 and the gnostic materials should be noted. In the longer recension[48] of *2 Enoch* 30:8, the Deity commanded his Wisdom[49] to create man out of the seven components.[50] Scholars have noted the parallels between this role of Wisdom (Gk. *Sophia*) in the creation of the first human in the Slavonic apocalypse and the gnostic texts.[51] Some have suggested that the Sophia tradition in *2 Enoch* 30 might be an early Jewish prototype of the later gnostic developments.[52]

Although, in *Poimandres's* version of the anthropogonic myth, Nature is responsible for the creation of the seven androgynous beings, in some Nag Hammadi materials it is Sophia ("Wisdom")[53] that generates the immortal sevenfold pattern, the portentous blueprint later imitated in the seven androgynous archons.[54] She is also one of the seven "powers"—that is to say, the entity corresponding to the name of archon Sabbataios on the lists of rulers in the *Apocryphon of John*. It is intriguing that, as in the Slavonic apocalypse, in which Wisdom is in charge of the sevenfold pattern, in gnostic and some other related materials Sophia takes charge of the seven entities responsible for the creation of the first human. Thus, *On the Origin of the World* (NHC, II, 101, 23–102, 7) reads:

> Seven appeared in chaos, androgynous . . . And they were born androgynous, consistent with the immortal pattern that existed before them, according to the wish of Pistis (Sophia): so that the likeness of what had existed since the beginning might reign to the end.[55]

Here, Wisdom (Sophia) is put in charge of the "immortal" sevenfold pattern according to which the seven androgynous archons are brought into existence. The *Hypostasis of the Archons* (NHC, II, 87, 4–14) offers a similar tradition that puts Sophia in charge of the sevenfold pattern that lays the basis for the creation of humankind.[56]

The Sophia tradition found in the Slavonic apocalypse may indeed be one of the most veiled conceptual developments in the text. The true extent of this enigmatic demiurgic entity assisting the

Deity in his creation remains shrouded in mystery. It is possible that in *2 Enoch* Sophia is linked not only with fashioning the sevenfold human body but also with generating the seven celestial "governors." It is intriguing that in chapter 48 Enoch, while outlining the process of the creation of celestial bodies, mentions that they were "fixed" by God's own wisdom.[57]

In concluding this section dealing with protological developments, we should again highlight the prominence of the sevenfold patterns in the text's cosmological and anthropological developments. While many sevenfold lists found in the Slavonic apocalypse appear to have been irreparably corrupted during the text's long journey through various religious and linguistic milieux, these sevenfold patterns represent the paramount link connecting the protological narrative with its eschatological counterpart, in which the sevenfold blueprint will again play a vital role.

The Aeon after Creation

The Final Aeon as the Reverse Anthropogony

It is time to return to the tradition of the primordial aeon in the Slavonic apocalypse. The aforementioned primeval account of creation, narrated by God in chapters 25 and 26 of the Slavonic pseudepigraphon, is invoked in abbreviated form in the subsequent chapters of the text in which Enoch unveils to his sons the knowledge he received during his celestial trip. There the reader also encounters some additional cosmological details pertaining not only to the beginning of creation but also its final destiny.

Chapter 65 of *2 Enoch* deals with the final instructions related by the translated hero of the faith to humanity immediately before his second and final departure to heaven. The final place of this revelation, among the other mysteries conveyed by Enoch to humankind during his short visit, underlines the significance of this disclosure. In many ways, it appears to be set in parallel with the account of the Lord's own instructions about the secrets of creation, which Enoch also received from the Deity at the end of his heavenly trip, after the preliminary revelations conveyed to him by his psychopomps and angel Vereveil.

This enigmatic revelation is intriguing, not only in the *format* of its delivery, which parallels the secrets of creation revealed by the Lord in chapters 25 and 26, but also in its peculiar *content*, which in many ways mirrors the familiar conceptual framework of the protological revelation. The shorter recension of *2 Enoch* 65:1–11 reads:

> "Listen, my children! Before all things existed, (and) before all creation came about, the Lord established the age of creation, and after that he created all his creation, visible and invisible. . . . When the whole creation which the Lord has created, shall come to an end, and when each person will go to the Lord's great judgment, then the time periods will perish, and there will be neither years nor months nor days, and hours will no longer be counted; But they will constitute a single age.[58] And all the righteous, who escape from the Lord's great judgment, will be collected together with the great age. And <the age> at the same time will unite with the righteous, and they will be eternal. And there will be among them neither weariness nor suffering nor affliction nor expectation of violence nor the pain of the night nor darkness. But they will have a great light for eternity, <and> an indestructible wall, and they will have a great paradise, the shelter of an eternal residence. How happy are the righteous who will escape the Lord's great judgment, for their faces will shine forth like the sun."[59]

The patriarch begins his narration with references to the familiar theme of the primeval aeon already encountered in chapter 25. These protological events are then set in parallel with the chain of eschatological actions that, according to the authors of the apocalypse, will reintegrate the remnant of the creation—an elite group of humans—into a single aeon which will collect all the righteous of the world.[60] The final consummation of all creation into a single aeon recalls the initial protological disintegration of Adoil, who once gave birth to the multiplicity of created forms.[61] In comparison with the cosmogonic character of the primeval aeon, the last aeon has distinctive anthropogonic features. In this respect it seems that the reverse cosmogonesis of the last days also presupposes the reversal of the anthropogonic process in the course of which the righteous of the world and their exemplar, the seventh antediluvian hero, inherit some qualities of the prelapsarial Adam and some distinctive features of his cosmogonic blueprint, the primordial aeon Adoil. Here, in contrast to many other Jewish accounts of the last days, the eschatological humanity does not simply regain the original state of the protoplast, instead returning to the condition of the immaterial Anthropos—that is to say, the anthropomorphic primordial aeon, Adoil.

The Beloved Seventh

It has already been noted that chapter 65 of the Slavonic apocalypse provides a striking description of the final age. Yet some details about the eschatological entity can also be found in the longer recension of the following chapter of *2 Enoch* (chapter 66) in which the seventh antediluvian patriarch tells his children about the sevenfold nature of the final aeon.

2 Enoch 66:6–8 reads:

> Walk my children in long-suffering . . . having love for one another, until you go out from this age of suffering, so that you may become inheritors of the never-ending age. How happy are the righteous who shall escape the Lord's great judgment; for they will be made to shine seven times brighter than the sun. For in that age everything is estimated sevenfold—light and darkness and food and enjoyment and misery and paradise and tortures. . . .[62]

This tradition about the sevenfold nature of the final age is intriguing in that it recalls the familiar cluster of the sevenfold patterns permeating the anthropogony of the Slavonic apocalypse, namely, the feature discussed in detail in the first part of our investigation.

In light of the anthropogonic nature of the final age—described in the Slavonic apocalypse as the final abode of perfected humanity, the gathering place of the righteous—invocation of the details of the protoplast's creation does not seem entirely inappropriate. Unlike some gnostic texts in which the seven elements of Adam's corporeality are linked to the seven infamous anthropogonic agents responsible for fashioning Adam's psychic body, in the Slavonic apocalypse Wisdom creates, out of seven properties, the perfect human being whom the text describes as the great and glorious celestial creature.

The sevenfold nature of the final age inhabited by perfected humanity thus calls to mind the perfect sevenfold nature of the protoplast before his fall. This connection is further strengthened in the initial verses of chapter 65 in which Enoch relates to his children the mystery of the final aeon. There some peculiar details of the protoplast's creation are invoked, including the elements of the sevenfold pattern of his "properties." Thus, in *2 Enoch* 65:1–2 the patriarch says the following:

> Listen, my children! Before ever anything existed, and before ever any created thing was created, the Lord created the whole of his creation, visible and invisible. And however much time there was went by. Understand how, on account of this, he constituted man in his own form, in accordance with a similarity. And he gave him
>
> eyes to see,
> and ears to hear,
> and heart to think,
> and reason to argue.
>
> And the Lord set everything forth for the sake of man, and he created the whole of creation for his sake.[63]

It is interesting that in this passage the details of the primordial cosmogony and anthropogony are closely linked.

The seventh antediluvian hero's peculiarly selective memory, which strives to bring together the account of the great aeon Adoil and the story of the protoplast's creation, points to the importance of this conceptual correlation for understanding the mystery of the sevenfold final aeon, which is predestined to shelter transformed humanity, which is now returning to its original condition. Further, it appears that the connection of the *seventh* antediluvian hero with this *sevenfold* pattern of the final age is not coincidental either. It is possible that, here, as in many other Enochic texts, the seventh human being is envisioned as the first fruit of perfected humanity, predestined to return to its original prelapsarian condition. The proleptic account of this portentous return is described in detail in chapter 22 of the Slavonic apocalypse in which the seventh antediluvian hero undergoes a dramatic metamorphosis that transforms him into a glorious celestial being, a creature identical in its luminous nature to the protoplast.

Thus it does not seem coincidental that the return to the original state of humankind, once endowed with the sevenfold pattern of "components" and "properties," is executed through the seventh human being. The portentous place of the seventh human, overshadowed by his unique role in restoring the condition of the first human, is known in many ancient interpretive traditions. In this respect, it is noteworthy that in the story of the seventh antediluvian hero one encounters another even more ancient Mesopotamian version of the sevenfold anthropogony, viz., the primordial myth about seven proto-humans, known in Mesopotamian pantheons as *apkallu*.[64] The *apkallu*[65] are envisioned as agents responsible for bringing humanity to perfection through education and transmission of celestial knowledge. In a way, these seven *apkallu* might be seen as the spiritual entities standing behind the seven antediluvian heroes. Scholars have noted the connections between the *apkallu* traditions and the Sumerian King List—that is, the roster in which a prototype of Enoch, the seventh antediluvian king Enmeduranki, plays an important role.[66] This tradition about the special place of the seventh human as the chosen vessel of the upper realm was not lost or forgotten during the long theological history of the seventh antediluvian hero.

Enoch as the Righteous One

It does not seem coincidental that the portentous revelation about the final aeon of the righteous comes from the mouth of the seventh antediluvian patriarch, the hero known in Jewish lore for his exemplary righteousness. In light of this connection, the motif of Enoch's righteousness should be examined further. The epithet "righteous man" becomes an important designation of the seventh antediluvian hero already in the beginning of his story, in which his righteousness is juxtaposed with the wickedness of the antediluvian generation and the transgressions of the Watchers.

In the very first verses of one of the earliest Enochic booklets, the *Book of the Watchers* (*1 Enoch* 1:2), the patriarch is defined as a righteous man. In *1 Enoch* 15:1 the same designation comes, now from the mouth of the Deity himself; it reads: "And he answered me and said to me with his voice: Hear! Do not be afraid, Enoch, (you) righteous man and scribe of righteousness."[67] Besides the patriarch's exemplary behavior, which allowed him to become the paragon of righteousness for future generations, this passage also points to another important office of the seventh antediluvian hero as the teacher of righteousness, an office in which he was desperately attempting to rescue and sustain the moral and cosmological order of the antediluvian world by delivering oracles of doom and calls to repentance that he received from God and the angels.[68] Early Enochic materials (*1 Enoch* 12:4 and 15:1) thus repeatedly define him as the scribe of righteousness.

Moreover, it is quite possible that Enoch's connection with the eschatological destiny of the righteous may be already ascertained in the early Enochic writings. According to *1 Enoch,* the patriarch travels to the enigmatic location called "the paradise of righteousness," which might represent here another designation for the eschatological gathering of the righteous.

Enoch-Metatron as the Foundation

It has already been noted that in the protological account dealing with the creation of the world Adoil is depicted as the foundation of visible things, both earthly and heavenly, including the very seat of the Deity, his throne. In view of the aforementioned parallelism between the descriptions of the first and last aeons, it appears that the "eschatological age" is also connected with the idea of the foundation. Although the description of the eschatological gathering of the righteous does not directly refer to this entity as the foundation, the idea is evident in the text through several implicit details.

In commenting on the identification of the final aeon with the righteous, Moshe Idel notes that in Jewish mysticism the righteous are often portrayed as the cosmological foundation of the world.[69] He points, for instance, to the tradition found in *b. Hag.* 12b, in which the righteous are depicted as the cosmological foundation of the world:[70]

> It is taught: R. Jose says: Alas for people that they see but know not what they see, they stand but know not on what they stand. What does the earth rest on? On the pillars, for it is said: Who shaketh the earth out of her place, and the

> pillars thereof tremble. . . . But the Sages say: [The world] rests on twelve pillars, for it is said: He set the borders to the peoples according to the number [of the tribes] of the children of Israel. And some say seven pillars, for it is said; she hath hewn out her seven pillars.[71] R. Eleazar b. Shammua says: [It rests] on one pillar, and its name is "Righteous," for it is said: But "Righteous" is the foundation of the world.[72]

It seems, then, no coincidence that the "revealer" and the "first fruit" of the eschatological aeon—the righteous Enoch—also appears to be conceived in some pseudepigraphical and rabbinic accounts as the pillar or foundation of the world.

As noted, early Enochic booklets highlight the contrast between the righteousness of Enoch and the unrighteousness of the antediluvian generation, in which the Watchers' interference causes moral and cosmological collapse, leading the cosmos and the human race into catastrophe. In the protological mishap leading to the annihilation of the earth's inhabitants, in the waters of the Flood, one might see a proleptic reenactment of the eschatological collapse of the last days during which the seventh antediluvian hero is also predestined to play an important role. In this catastrophic chain of events affecting the whole fabric of creation, Enoch can be seen as the righteous one who attempts to sustain the created order, in many ways serving as the pillar of the antediluvian world. This important role of the seventh antediluvian hero, as the sustainer and protector of creation, is reaffirmed in the *Book of Jubilees*, which depicts the patriarch as the cosmic dam against the waters of the Flood.[73]

Enoch's role in sustaining the world was not forgotten in later Jewish materials. Idel's research identifies an important tradition, preserved in later Jewish mysticism, which portrays the seventh antediluvian hero as the foundation that sustains the world; he states, "[T]he righteous is the foundation of the world. For [the sake of] one [single] righteous the world is maintained and it is Enoch the son of Yared."[74] The author(s) of this tradition, which might stem from the early Enochic literature, appear to be informed by the extrabiblical roles and actions of the seventh patriarch, who served there as the pillar sustaining creation's moral and cosmological order in the turmoil of the antediluvian generation.

This understanding of Enoch as the foundation of the world is not atypical in Jewish mystical lore in which the patriarch's heavenly counterpart, the supreme angel Metatron, was traditionally understood as the force sustaining the world. These cosmological functions were exhibited first in Metatron's role as the governor or the prince of the world,[75] an office already discernible in *2 Enoch*[76] and further developed in the Hekhalot mysticism, including traditions found in *Sefer Hekhalot*.[77] It is intriguing that Enoch-Metatron's governance of the world includes not only administrative functions but also the duty of conserving the world. Moshe Idel refers to the treatise *The Seventy Names of Metatron* in which the angel and God seize the world in their hands.[78] This motif of the Deity and his vice-regent grasping the universe in their cosmic hands evokes the conceptual developments found in the *Shi*ᶜ*ur Qomah* and Hekhalot materials, in which Enoch-Metatron possesses a cosmic corporeality comparable to the physique of the Deity and is depicted as the measurement of the divine Body.[79]

In light of these traditions, it seems possible that, already, in the Slavonic apocalypse, Enoch is portrayed as the eschatological foundation of the world[80] who participates in the final aeon of the righteous, and can thus be seen as the first fruit of this eschatological gathering. In this respect, like Adoil who anticipates the protological aeon that gives all creation its beginning, Enoch too anticipates the future eschatological aeon when the creation will collapse and all the righteous will be united together. Both Adoil and Enoch can thus be seen as outstanding exemplars preordained to manifest the protological and eschatological states through their ontological conditions, thus serving as "personifications" of these aeons. Both heroes are also united by the quality of their luminosity that serves as an important sign of the beginning and end of time. Here, as in the Lurianic Kabbalah, the primordial divine light, dispersed during Adoil's disintegration and then the fall of the protoplast, must be restored through the efforts of the righteous who will become a new eschatological vessel of the uncreated light.

Enoch as the Vessel of Light

2 Enoch 66:11 describes the condition of the righteous in the final aeon, depicting them as luminous beings; it reads, "How happy are the righteous who will escape the Lord's great judgment, for their faces will shine forth like the sun."[81] This tradition about righteous humans emitting light seems to be tied implicitly in the text to the story of its revealer, namely, the seventh antediluvian patriarch, who himself underwent a dramatic luminous transformation. The passage seems to suggest that Enoch—depicted in chapter 22 as undergoing a luminous metamorphosis before the Face of God,[82] which turns him into a shining celestial creature—becomes the very first fruit of this future aeon in which all righteous persons will eventually regain the condition of luminosity. The eschatological luminosity here points to the protological condition of Adoil and, more important, to the incorruptible luminous state of the protoplast, a condition humanity lost after Adam's fall.[83]

Here the righteous of the world are depicted as the gatherers of divine light, viz., those who repair both cosmogonic and anthropogonic vessels of the primordial light by turning themselves into the luminous vessel of the last days.[84] One might see in this mysterious aeonic gathering of the transformed humans the eschatological refashioning of the luminosity of the Heavenly Man,[85] who is restored through the efforts of righteous souls now able to reconstitute the particles of divine light into a single aeon.[86]

The Demiurgic Role of Enoch

Although the Slavonic apocalypse insists on the Deity's role as the sovereign[87] Creator of the universe, scholars have[88] noted that this emphasis on the sovereignty of the Deity in creation is not entirely monolithic in the Slavonic text, *if* one considers the Deity's decision to share the secrets of creation[89] that He did not explain even to the angels.

Thus here one can discern a delegation of the demiurgic function to God's vice-regent, a motif that will play an important role in the Metatron traditions in *Sefer Hekhalot* and the *Zohar*. In these texts, the letters on the crown given to Metatron attest to his partaking in the works of creation. Some scholars note that the link between Metatron and the "secrets of creation" manifested in the Hekhalot tradition may witness to his role as a demiurge, or at least to his participation in the work of creation.[90] Jarl Fossum draws attention to the tradition attested in *Genesis Rabbah* 5:4 on Genesis 1:9, according to which "the voice of the Lord became a guide (מטטרון) to the waters, as it is written: 'The voice of the Lord is over the waters.' "[91] Fossum proposes that this passage might refer to the Metatron's demiurgic role.[92] He also suggests that while the depiction of Metatron in *Sefer Hekhalot* is not demiurgic, it points to the matrix of ideas out of which the Gnostic concept of the demiurge possibly arose.[93] The beginning of the tendency towards Enoch-Metatron's demiurgic profile might already be detected in *2 Enoch*, a text that puts great emphasis on Enoch's knowledge of the secrets of creation and which sometimes describes Enoch as if he were a divine being.[94]

In this respect, Enoch's demiurgic function—which is hinted at by his access to the esoteric knowledge of the final aeon and his revelation of this knowledge to the people of the earth—might be set in parallel to the demiurgic function of Adoil, who is depicted as the revealer of the primordial aeon.

Conclusion

In later Metatron lore, Enoch-Metatron is portrayed as the perfector of human souls who, like Abatur in the Mandaean tradition, is responsible for the progress of human souls to their final destiny.[95] Both the Babylonian Talmud[96] and Hekhalot literature[97] hint at this mysterious office of Metatron by depicting him as the teacher of Torah to the souls of deceased children.[98]

In view of our previous investigation, it appears that this later account of Metatron's role, as the "captain" of souls,[99] might already be hinted at in *2 Enoch* via the translated hero's enigmatic participation in the economy of the eschatological gathering of human souls in the final aeon of the righteous.[100]

This promise of the final gathering of righteous souls into a single luminous entity gives us hope that the aeonic vessels of primordial light, shattered in the beginning, will be eventually restored at the end of time.

The Veneration Motif in the Temptation Narrative of the Gospel of Matthew

Lessons from the Enochic Tradition

> Hence the perfection of all things is attained when good and evil are first of all commingled, and then become all good, for there is no good so perfect as that which issues out of evil.
>
> —*Zohar* II.184a

Introduction

The story of Jesus' temptation in the wilderness found in the synoptic gospels baffles the reader with a plethora of apocalyptic motifs.[1] Some features in Matthew's version of Jesus' encounter with Satan in the desert seem to contain more explicit references to apocalyptic traditions than do Mark and Luke.[2] Mark and Luke, who take the forty-day period to encompass the whole process of temptation,[3] seem to use the traditional allusion to the forty years of the Israelites' ordeal in the wilderness. Yet Matthew's emphasis on the initiatory forty-day fasting that is followed by the appearance of Satan might suggest that the fast serves here as a tool for inducing a visionary experience.[4] The canonical stories of two famous visionaries of the Hebrew Bible, Moses and Elijah, contain passages referring specifically to the period of forty days. Exodus 24:18 tells of Moses abiding forty days and forty nights at the top of Mount Sinai.[5] 1 Kings 19:8 refers to the story of Elijah's being sustained by angels for forty days[6] during his journey to Mount Horeb.[7] In both accounts, as in Matthew, the motif of the forty-day fast appears along with the theme of the encounter on a mountain, signifying a visionary experience on high.

If we accept the transformational value of fasting in Matthew's account, the fast may have served to induce the vision not of God, but of Satan.[8] The depiction could have a polemical flavor in attempting to challenge or deconstruct traditional apocalyptic settings.

The apocalyptic thrust in Matthew's version of the temptation story has been noted by scholars.[9] I have even suggested in earlier work that the narrative mimics or even offers a polemic against the apocalyptic ascent and vision trends.[10] Many details of the account also reveal a connection to the protological typologies prominent in Jewish apocalyptic accounts. The aim of this study is to explore more closely the connections in Matthew's version of the temptation narrative with extrabiblical apocalyptic traditions, especially those found in the Enochic materials.

Adamic Traditions and the Temptation Narrative

It has been long recognized by scholars that the story of Jesus' temptation in the synoptic Gospels seems to be influenced by an Adamic typology.[11] Some studies suggested that the chain of pivotal Adamic themes known from biblical and extrabiblical accounts is already introduced in the terse narration of Jesus' temptation in the Gospel of Mark.[12] For example, Joachim Jeremias draws attention to the phrase in Mark 1:12 that Jesus "was with the wild beasts" (ἦν μετὰ τῶν θηρίων). In Jeremias's opinion, this phrase is reminiscent of the protoplast who lived among wild animals in paradise according to Genesis 2:19. Jeremias suggests that Jesus might be envisioned, in the Gospel of Mark, as an eschatological Adam who restores peace between humans and animals.[13] He proposes that Mark's account sets forth a belief that "paradise is restored, the time of salvation is dawning; that is what ἦν μετὰ τῶν θηρίων means. Because the temptation has been overcome and Satan has been vanquished, the gate to paradise is again opened."[14] Jeremias also discerns the Adamic typology in the saying that the angels did Jesus "table service" (διηκόνουν αὐτῷ). In his view, "this feature, too, is part of the idea of paradise and can only be understood in that light. Just as, according to the Midrash, Adam lived on angels' food in paradise, so the angels give Jesus nourishment. The table-service of angels is a symbol of the restored communion between man and God."[15] Richard Bauckham also sees a cluster of Adamic motifs in Mark's version of the temptation story and argues that it envisions Jesus "as the eschatological Adam who, having resisted Satan, instead of succumbing to temptation as Adam did, then restores paradise: he is at peace with the animals and the angels serve him."[16] From this perspective, Jesus' temptation by Satan plays a pivotal role in the unfolding of the Adamic typological appropriations.[17] Dale Allison draws attention to another possible connection with the protoplast story by wondering whether Mark's "forty days" is also part of his Adamic typology. He notices that, according to *Jubilees* 3:9, Adam was placed in Eden forty days after he was created, and in the *Primary Adam Books,* Adam does penance for forty days.[18]

In Matthew and Luke, the Adamic typology hinted at in Mark receives further conceptual development. Moreover, not only the temptation narrative but other parts of Matthew and Luke become affected by the panoply of Adamic motifs. It has been suggested, for example, that "perhaps Luke prefaced his temptation account with a genealogy that concludes with Adam (Luke 3:38) because the evangelist viewed Jesus' victory over temptation as a reversal of Adam's failure."[19] Similarly, Matthew's Gospel continues the appropriation and development of the Adamic typology in the unfolding story of Jesus' temptations. It appears that the most concentrated presence of Adamic motifs can be found in the third temptation in which Satan asks Jesus to prostrate himself before him. This cultic motif of worship appears to be reaffirmed at the end of the temptation narrative, which tells that angels approached Jesus and served him.

In the search for the conceptual roots of this veneration motif, scholars have often turned to the account of Adam's elevation and veneration by angels, found in various versions of the so-called *Primary Adam Books.* Although known macroforms of the *Primary Adam Books* survive only in their later medieval versions, these later Christian compilations undoubtedly contain early Jewish conceptual seeds that might also stand behind the veneration motif in the gospels' temptation story.

One particular theme found in the *Primary Adam Books* deserves special attention, namely, the account of the protoplast's creation and his introduction into the angelic community. During this initiation, Adam is ordered to venerate the Deity, and then God commands the angelic hosts to venerate the protoplast. Further, although some angels agree to venerate Adam, Satan refuses to bow down before the first human. This cluster of motifs is intriguing as it recalls that which is found in Matthew. In the gospel, the tempter asks Jesus to prostrate himself, suggesting literally that he will "fall down" (πεσὼν) before Satan. Matthew seems to hew, here, more closely to the Adamic blueprint than Luke, as in Luke πεσὼν is missing. Here one again encounters an example of Matthean Adamic Christology that depicts Jesus as the last Adam. The presence of such conceptualization in Matthew is not unusual as implicit and explicit comparisons of Adam and Jesus are already made in the earliest Christian materials, including the Pauline epistles and the Gospel of Mark. Thus scholars have suggested that the understanding of Jesus as the last Adam can be found as early as Romans 5, which predates Matthew. Moreover, some studies propose that the Pauline material might constitute the conceptual basis for the Adamic typology found in the synoptic gospels. Thus, for example, Dale Allison argues,

> [I]f the Jesus of Mark 1:12–13 undoes the work of Adam, then one is inevitably reminded of Paul's Christology, in which Adam's disobedience and its attendant effects are contrasted with Jesus' obedience and its attendant effects (Rom 5:12–21; 1Cor 15:21–23, 45–49). Indeed, one wonders, given the other intriguing connections between Mark and Paul, whether Mark 1:12–13 was composed under Paul's influence.[20]

Satan's request for veneration also can be a part of the evangelists' Adam Christology: Satan, who lost his celestial status by refusing to venerate the first Adam, is now attempting to reverse the situation by asking the last Adam to bow down.

Although the tradition of Satan's request for worship is also found in Luke, Matthew appears to reinforce this veneration theme further by adding the peculiar terminology of prostration and by concluding his temptation story with the appearance of servicing angels. It is possible that these embellishments are intended to affirm the traditions of devotion to and exaltation of the last Adam that are constructed both negatively and positively by invoking the memory of the first Adam's veneration.[21] Scholars have noted wide usage of the formulae of worship and veneration in the Gospel of Matthew that appears to be more consistent than in the other synoptic gospels.[22] In view of this tendency, the Adamic tradition of veneration of humanity might also be perceived in other parts of Matthew, including the magi story narrated earlier in the gospel. It is noteworthy that both the temptation and the magi narratives contain identical terminology of worship. First, in the magi story one can see repeated usage of the verb προσκυνέω (cf. Matt. 2:2; 2:8; 2:11), which is also prominent in the temptation story (Matt. 4:9; 4:10). In both accounts this terminology appears to have a cultic significance.[23] Also, both in the magi story and in the third Matthean temptation of Jesus one can find a distinctive juxtaposition of the expression "falling down" (πεσόντες/πεσὼν) with the formulae of worship (προσεκύνησαν/προσκυνήσῃς).[24]

The story of the magi speaks of mysterious visitors from the East who came to pay homage to the newborn king of the Jews. Some details of the account suggest that one might have here not simply the story of veneration by foreign guests but, possibly, the theme of angelic reverence. Some scholars have pointed to the angelological details of the narrative. For example, it has been observed that the mysterious star, which assists the magi in their journey to the messiah, appears to be an angel, more specifically a guiding angel whose function is to lead the foreign visitors to Jesus.[25] Other features of the story are also intriguing, as they, like the details of the temptation narrative, seem to betray some traces of apocalyptic traditions. It is also possible that here, as in the temptation story, one can see a cluster of Adamic motifs. The baby Jesus, for instance, might be depicted as an eschatological counterpart of the first human, and, just as in the creation of the protoplast, which in the *Primary Adam Books* is marked by angelic veneration, the entrance of the last Adam into the world is also celebrated by a similar ritual of obeisance.

Let us now explore more closely other possible Adamic allusions in the story of the magi. First, the origin of the magi from the East (ἀπὸ ἀνατολῶν) might show a possible connection with Eden, a garden which according to biblical testimonies was planted in the East.[26] Gifts of the magi, including frankincense and myrrh, which were traditionally used in antiquity as ingredients of incense,[27] bring to mind Adam's sacrifices, which according to Jewish extrabiblical lore the protoplast was offering in the Garden of Eden in fulfillment of his sacerdotal duties. Such sacrifices are mentioned in *Jubilees* 3:27, a passage that depicts Adam as a protological high priest[28] who burns incense in Paradise.[29] In view of the possible cultic flavor of the magi story, Jesus might be understood there not simply as the last Adam but as a priestly eschatological Adam in a fashion reminiscent of the *Book of Jubilees*. In the context of these traditions, the magi could be understood as visitors, possibly even angelic visitors, from the Garden of Eden, once planted in the East, who are bringing to a new priest the sacerdotal tools used in the distant past by Adam.[30] This exegetical connection is not implausible given that some later Christian materials, including the *Cave of Treasures*, often associate the gifts of the magi with Adam's sacrifices.[31]

Moreover, it appears that other details of the magi narrative, including the peculiar juxtaposition of its antagonistic figure with the theme of worship, again bring to mind the protoplast story reflected in various versions of the *Primary Adam Books*, with its motifs of angelic veneration and Satan's refusal to worship the first human. Recall that Matthew connects the main antagonist of the magi story, Herod, with the theme of veneration by telling that the evil king promised to worship the messianic child.[32]

The magi narrative demonstrates that the veneration motifs play an important role in the overarching theological framework of Matthew's gospel. The cultic significance of the veneration motif can be further illustrated in Matthew's transfiguration story in chapter seventeen.[33] There, at the end of Jesus' transfiguration on the mountain, the already familiar veneration motif is evoked, again, when the disciples, overwhelmed with the vision, throw themselves down with their faces to the ground.[34] It is noteworthy that this depiction of the disciples' prostration at Jesus' transfiguration is strikingly absent in both Mark and Luke. In Matthew this motif seems to fit nicely in the chain of previous veneration occurrences, thus evoking the memory of both the falling down of the magi and Satan's quest for prostration—traditions likewise absent from other synoptic accounts.[35]

Enochic Traditions and the Temptation Narrative

Although previous studies have investigated the cluster of Adamic allusions in the synoptic versions of the temptation narrative, they have often been reluctant to explore the formative influences of the Enochic tradition. It is possible that the motif of angelic veneration of humanity reflected in the Gospel of Matthew has its true origins not in the

Adamic tradition but in early Enochic lore, a portentous mediatorial trend in which the early Jewish angelology received its most profound symbolic expression. So, in *2 Enoch,* which is often viewed by scholars as being contemporary with or possibly even earlier than the Gospel of Matthew,[36] one can find a cluster of intriguing conceptual developments connected with the theme of angelic veneration. The first part of this Jewish apocalypse depicts Enoch's ascent to heaven. *2 Enoch* 21–22 narrates the final stage of the patriarch's celestial journey during which the seventh antediluvian hero is brought by his angelic guides to the edge of the seventh heaven. At the Deity's command, the archangel Gabriel invites the patriarch to be a permanent servant of God. Enoch agrees, and the archangel carries him to the glorious face of God, where the patriarch does obeisance to the Deity. God then personally repeats the invitation to Enoch to stand before him forever. After this invitation, another archangel, Michael, brings the patriarch to the front of the face of the Lord. The Lord then tells his angels, sounding them out: "Let Enoch join in and stand in front of my face forever!" In response to the Deity's command the angels do obeisance to Enoch.[37]

Scholars have noted that *2 Enoch* 21–22 is reminiscent of the account of Adam's elevation and his veneration by angels found in Armenian, Georgian, and Latin versions of the *Primary Adam Books,* in which the archangel Michael is depicted as bringing the first human being into the divine presence, forcing him to bow down before God.[38] In the *Primary Adam Books*, the Deity then commands all the angels to bow down to the protoplast.[39] The results of this order are mixed. Some angels agreed to venerate Adam, while others, including Satan, refuse to do obeisance.[40] Michael Stone notes that, along with the motifs of Adam's elevation and his veneration by angels, the author of *2 Enoch* also appears to be aware of the motif of angelic disobedience and refusal to venerate the first human. Stone draws attention to the phrase "sounding them out," found in *2 Enoch* 22:6, which another translator of the Slavonic text rendered as "making a trial of them."[41] Stone suggests that the expressions "sounding them out" or "making a trial of them" imply here that it is the angels' obedience that is being tested.[42] Stone concludes that *2 Enoch* 21–22 is reminiscent of the traditions found in Armenian, Georgian, and Latin versions of the *Primary Adam Books.*[43]

Scholars have also observed striking structural similarities in the veneration accounts in *2 Enoch* and those in Armenian, Georgian, and Latin versions of the *Primary Adam Books*. The accounts include three chief events:

A. Installation on high (in the *Primary Adam Books* Adam is created and situated in heaven; in *2 Enoch* the seventh antediluvian patriarch is brought to heaven).

B. Veneration of the Deity (in the *Primary Adam Books* Adam does obeisance to God; in *2 Enoch* the seventh antediluvian hero does obeisance to the Deity).

C. Initiation into the celestial community: angelic veneration of the protagonist and Satan's refusal to bow down (in the *Primary Adam Books* God commands the angels to bow down. All the angels do obeisance. Satan and his angels disobey. In *2 Enoch* the angelic rebellion is assumed. God tests whether this time the angels will obey).[44]

It is noteworthy that both *2 Enoch* and the *Primary Adam Books* operate with the double veneration: first, the human protagonists, Enoch and Adam, are asked to bow down before the Deity, and second, they are themselves venerated by the angels, an event that signifies their acceptance into the community of celestial citizens.

Keeping in mind these conceptual developments, we now turn our attention to the temptation narrative in the Gospel of Matthew. Here one can discern the already familiar patterns manifested in *2 Enoch* and the *Primary Adam Books*. Like Enoch and Adam, Jesus first is brought to the elevated place represented by the divine mountain. He is then asked to venerate Satan, an idolatrous pseudo-representation of the Deity. Finally, the Matthean version of the temptation narrative portrays Jesus' initiation into the community of angels who came to offer their services. In view of these similarities, it is possible that the tradition of veneration reflected in *2 Enoch*, which is believed by some scholars to be written before the destruction of the Second Jerusalem Temple, and therefore before the composition of the Gospel of Matthew, might exercise formative influence not only on the protoplasts stories in the *Primary Adam Books* but also on the story of Jesus' temptation in Matthew.[45]

Apocalyptic Features of the Temptation Narrative

If the author of the Gospel of Matthew was indeed cognizant of the apocalyptic traditions similar to those found in *2 Enoch*, it is apparent that the Christian authors were not just blindly appropriating these currents; rather, they attempted to deconstruct these themes by assigning some familiar attributes and duties of the angels and the Deity to the ominous mediator Satan. We should now direct our attention to these paradoxical reformulations of the apocalyptic motifs.

Satan as Jesus' Psychopomp and Angelus Interpres

Jewish apocalyptic accounts often depict the transportation of human visionaries into the upper realms with the help of angelic guides. In view of these apocalyptic currents, it is striking that, in the temptation narrative, Satan serves as a psychopomp of Jesus and transports him to high, possibly even the highest, places.[46] In apocalyptic literature, angels or archangels often serve as visionaries' psychopomps. For example, in *2 Enoch*, the seventh antediluvian patriarch is taken to heaven by two angels. In the same apocalyptic account, Melchizedek is transported on the wings of Gabriel to the Garden of Eden.[47] In the temptation narrative, Satan seems to be fulfilling similar functions of a transporting angel.[48] It is important that in both cases Satan is transporting Jesus not to hell, but to "high places," first to the top of the Temple in the Holy City and then to the highest mountain. Some scholars believe that the mountain here represents the place of divine abode, as in some other apocalyptic texts. Satan's apocalyptic roles are puzzling, and might represent an attempt to deconstruct familiar apocalyptic motifs.

It is also noteworthy that in both Matthew and Luke, Satan serves not merely as a psychopomp but also as an *angelus interpres* who literally "leads up" (ἀναγαγὼν αὐτὸν) the visionary and "shows him" (δείκνυσιν αὐτῷ/ἔδειξεν αὐτῷ) the visionary reality, thus fulfilling the traditional functions of the interpreting angels in Jewish apocalyptic and mystical accounts. The interaction between the seer and his demonic guide also reveals influences of the Mosaic typology. Scholars have noted terminological similarities in the temptation narrative and Deuteronomy 34:1–4,[49] in which God serves as an *angelus interpres* during Moses' vision on Mount Nebo, showing (ἔδειξεν) the prophet the Promised Land and giving him an explanation of it.[50] Yet, the *angelus interpres* traditions found in Matthew attempt to transcend the "Mosaic" biblical makeup by enhancing the story with details of extrabiblical apocalyptic accounts.

The Progression to the Highest Place

It has been observed that, in comparison with Luke, Matthew's order of Jesus' temptations attests to the seer's upward gradual progression as he goes from the lower places to higher places, from the desert to a pinnacle in the Temple and finally to a sacred mountain.[51] This dynamic is reminiscent of heavenly journeys that depict visionaries' progress from lower to higher heavens.[52] Often these visionary accounts portray the seer's initiation, occurring at the highest point of his journey. It is noteworthy, then, that it is in the third and final temptation in Matthew that the cluster of veneration motifs is introduced at the highest point. It again brings to mind the seventh antediluvian patriarch's journey in *2 Enoch,* in which the seer's arrival to the highest heaven is peaked by angelic veneration. The third Matthean temptation takes place on a mountain. Several scholars have remarked that the mountain might allude to the place of divine presence and dominion. Here, however, strangely enough, it becomes the exalted place from which Satan asks Jesus to venerate him. In the Enochic and Mosaic traditions, the high mountain often serves as one of the technical designations of the *Kavod*. For example, *1 Enoch* 25:3 identifies the high mountain as a location of the throne of God.[53] In the *Exagoge* of Ezekiel the Tragedian, Moses is identified with the *Kavod* on the mountain.[54] If indeed Matthew has in mind the mountain of the *Kavod*, Satan's ability to show Jesus all the kingdoms of the world and their splendor might be a reference to the celestial curtain *Pargod*, the sacred veil of the divine presence, which in *3 Enoch* 45 is described as an entity that literally "shows" all generations and all kingdoms at the same time.[55] As has been already demonstrated in our previous chapter on the cosmological temple, these revelatory functions of the *Pargod* are also reflected in the *Apocalypse of Abraham,* in which the horizontal heavenly curtain associated with the firmament unveils to Abraham the whole course of human history.[56] Scholars have noted striking similarities in the presentation of revelations in the *Apocalypse of Abraham* and the temptation narrative.[57] Although some attestations to the *Pargod* symbolism are found in later rabbinic and Hekhalot accounts, the early roots of these developments can be traced to the apocalyptic imagery of the heavenly tablets in Mesopotamian and early Enochic materials. Several Second Temple Jewish materials testify that these media of revelation, as in the later *Pargod* tradition, are able to communicate to the seer the totality of historical and physical reality.[58]

The Transformation of the Seer

It has already been demonstrated that in the temptation story Satan fulfills several functions traditionally ascribed to angelic figures, such as offices of the psychopomp and the *angelus interpres*. Yet the elusive adversary is able to mimic not only the duties of angelic figures but also the Deity himself. It is thus possible that, in the Matthean account, Satan is portrayed as an idolatrous negative replica of the divine *Kavod*.

Previous studies have often missed the transformational thrust of the veneration themes found in the temptation story. Nevertheless, in *2 Enoch* and in the story of Adam's veneration in the *Primary Adam Books*, in which the human seers are ordered to bow down to the Deity, the hero's veneration of God appears to coincide with his transition into a new ontological state. Satan's request for veneration has affinities with this cluster of transformational motifs. What is important here is that Satan requests veneration while standing on the mountain, the location interpreted by scholars as a reference to the place of the divine presence. Satan's presence on the mountain appears to be envisioned in the temptation narrative as a counterpart of divine habitation. Is it possible, then, that Satan positions himself here as the negative counterpart of *Kavod*?

In Jewish apocalyptic accounts, the ritual of prostration before the divine *Kavod* often plays a pivotal role in the transformation of a seer into a celestial being, or even his identification with the divine form.[59] In the course of this initiation, a visionary often acquires the nature of the object of his veneration, including the luminosity that signals his identification with the radiant manifestation of the Deity.

In the light of these traditions, it is possible to detect a similar transformational motif in the temptation narrative. One encounters here an example of negative transformational mysticism; by forcing Jesus to bow down, the tempter wants the seer to become identified with Satan's form, in opposition to the visionaries of Jewish apocalyptic writings who, through their prostration before the divine Face, become identified with the divine *Kavod*.

The Standing One

The transformation of human seers in the apocalyptic accounts often leads to their inclusion into the celestial retinue. This new office presumes unceasing service, uninterrupted with rest. In the rabbinic tradition, the citizens of heaven are predestined to stand forever, as there is no sitting in heaven.[60] Apocalyptic and mystical accounts, therefore, often identify an angelic state with a standing posture. Thus, in the aforementioned account of Enoch's transformation into an angelic being in *2 Enoch* 21–22, one can find repeated references to the seer's standing position. Moreover, both the angels and the Deity promise to the seventh antediluvian hero that he will be standing before God's presence forever. Scholars believe that these promises represent the first known attestations that hint at the future office of Enoch-Metatron as the *sar happanim*—the prince of divine presence, a special angelic servant whose role is to stand forever in front of the Deity.[61] It is noteworthy that not only Matthew but also Luke contains references to Jesus' standing and installation to this position by his angelic psychopomp, Satan.[62] This tradition is reminiscent of Enoch's installation in the Slavonic apocalypse, in which he was also placed in this standing position by his angelic guide.

It appears that both in *2 Enoch* and in the temptation story the installation of the seer as a "standing one" might be connected with the Mosaic typology.[63] The tradition of Moses' standing plays an important role already in the biblical materials. Thus, in Exodus 33, the Lord commands Moses to stand near him: "There is a place by me where you shall stand on the rock." A similar command also is found in Deuteronomy 5:31, in which God, again, orders Moses to stand with him: "But you, stand here by me, and I will tell you all the commandments, the statutes and the ordinances, that you shall teach them." The motif of standing also plays a significant part in extrabiblical Mosaic accounts, including the *Exagoge* of Ezekiel the Tragedian, in which Moses is portrayed as standing before the divine throne.[64]

In view of the aforementioned developments in *2 Enoch* and the *Exagoge*, it is possible that Jesus' standing position on high reflects a cluster of apocalyptic motifs. Yet, in the synoptic accounts of Jesus' temptation, this tradition receives a new polemical meaning because the seer's installation is performed by the main antagonist of the story, Satan.

As we conclude this section of our study, let us draw attention to the structure of the second Matthean temptation in which Satan asks Jesus to throw himself down, and in which the motif of the seer's installation to the standing position occurs. It has been noted that the third temptation appears to reflect three events found also in *2 Enoch* and in the *Primary Adam Books*: first, the installation of the seer by his psychopomp; second, the seer's veneration of the Deity; and third, angelic veneration of the seer. In *2 Enoch,* after the seventh antediluvian hero is brought by his psychopomp to the highest place, he first bows down before the Deity and then is exalted by the angels through their veneration. The same pattern is present in the *Primary Adam Books* in which the archangel Michael first "presents" Adam before the Deity,[65] then Adam bows down before God,[66] followed by his exaltation through angelic obeisance.[67] In light of these developments, it is intriguing that the structure of the second Matthean (and the third Lukan) temptation might reflect a similar structure. The seer is first installed to the high place by his psychopomp.[68] Then he is asked to throw himself down.[69] Then his psychopomp cites scriptures to assure the seer that he will be elevated by the angels.[70] As this story unfolds, one can see three narrative steps, which involve first installation, second denigration, and finally angelic exaltation. In view of these correspondences, it is possible that the second temptation anticipates the events of the third temptation by foreshadowing its threefold structure.

Conclusion

The polemical nature of Matthew's appropriations of the apocalyptic traditions in the temptation story remains one of the enigmas of this biblical text. At the same time, this overwhelming deconstructive thrust helps illuminate the puzzling form of the veneration motifs in this portion of Matthew's gospel. Like other apocalyptic themes, the veneration themes are also deconstructed: the exalted human protagonist refuses to venerate a pseudo-representation of the Deity, and the angelic hosts in their turn do not explicitly bow down to the hero. This striking reworking brings us again to the function of the veneration motifs not only in the temptation story but the whole gospel. Although scholars have argued that the veneration motifs in the temptation story, and especially Jesus' refusal to venerate Satan, are closely connected with the theme of idolatry, it appears that some other even more important conceptual ramifications might also be at play. Thus both in *2 Enoch* and the *Primary Adam Books*, the angelic veneration plays a portentous role in the construction of a unique upper identity of the apocalyptic heroes, often revealing the process of their deification.[71] In these texts, angelic veneration shepherds the human protagonists into their new supraangelic ontology when they become depicted as "icons" or "faces" of the Deity, the conditions often established both via angelic obeisance and the seers' own venerations of the Deity. Yet, in the temptation story, the divinity of the human protagonist is affirmed in a new paradoxical way, not through the veneration motifs, but through their deconstruction. This new way of establishing the hero's upper identity appears to be novel, yet one is able to detect similar developments in the later Jewish "two powers in heaven" debates, with their emphasis on the deconstruction of the veneration motifs. Although in the *Primary Adam Books* it is Satan who opposes veneration of humanity, in the later "two powers in heaven" developments this function of opposition is often transferred to the Deity himself. In these later accounts, it is God who opposes veneration of the newly created protoplast and shows to angelic hosts that his beloved creature does not deserve the obeisance reserved now solely for the Creator.[72] Yet, in the midst of these debates, which might be interpreted as attempts to limit the possibility for *theosis*, one can find one of the most profound exaltations of humanity ever recorded in Jewish lore—a tradition that portrays the seventh antediluvian patriarch as יהוה הקטן, a lesser representation of the Deity.[73] Here, as in the temptation narrative of Matthew's gospel, a deconstruction of the veneration motifs opens new paradoxical horizons for the deification of humankind.

Primordial Lights

The Logos and Adoil in the Johannine Prologue and *2 Enoch*

Introduction

The Gospel of John begins with the Prologue, which is a hymn containing complex and unique protological imagery. In contrast to the opening chapters of Genesis, which center on the creation of the world and humankind, the Prologue unveils the realities that preceded the beginning of the creational process. This emphasis on preexistent realities is very rare in early Jewish lore and found only in a few extrabiblical apocalyptic accounts. Despite the uniqueness of such imagery, not all of these apocalyptic writings have received proper attention from scholars of the Fourth Gospel. As Christopher Rowland notes, "[L]ittle attempt has been made to relate the gospel to the earlier apocalyptic texts of Judaism which either antedate the gospel or are roughly contemporary with it."[1]

One early Jewish text that deals with preexistent matters but has been consistently ignored by Johannine scholars is *2 (Slavonic) Enoch*. This text is a Jewish pseudepigraphon written in the first century CE before the destruction of the Second Jerusalem Temple, just a few years earlier than the Fourth Gospel. Like the Johannine Prologue, this Jewish writing unveils the state of affairs that preceded the creation of the world by depicting an enigmatic character—the luminous aeon Adoil—as the Deity's helper at creation. Despite some striking parallels with the Prologue's imagery, however, this Jewish apocalypse has been routinely neglected by major commentators and students of the Fourth Gospel. The lack of interest is striking since most Jewish narratives contemporary to the Johannine Prologue rarely speak about preexistent mediators assisting the Deity at creation.

The aim of this chapter, then, is to explore more closely the protological developments found in *2 Enoch* and their similarities with the imagery of the Prologue of the Gospel of John.

2 Enoch

Protological descriptions, including the details of the creation of the world and humankind, represent one of the main conceptual centers found in Jewish apocalyptic accounts, as protology is so closely connected with eschatology. Many of these elaborations continue the narrative trajectory implicit already in the formative stories found in the initial chapters of the Book of Genesis. Some of these accounts, such as the Johannine Prologue, attempt to go beyond the boundaries of conventional biblical imagery and initiate their readers into the details of the reality that preceded the visible creation.

2 Enoch belongs to this unique group of early Jewish texts that divulges the realities that preceded the genesis of the world. In chapters 24–25 of *2 Enoch*, the Deity reveals to the patriarch Enoch, the translated antediluvian hero, some unique details in the mysteries of creation found neither in earlier Enochic booklets nor in any other Second Temple Jewish materials. One noteworthy aspect of this revelation concerns the order of events before the visible creation. The Deity tells the seer that prior to visible creation he summoned the luminous aeon Adoil from nonbeing, ordering him to become the foundation of all created things. It describes Adoil's transmutation into the cornerstone of creation on which the Deity establishes his throne. Both shorter and longer recensions of *2 Enoch* provide an extensive description of this revelation. In the longer recension of *2 Enoch* 24–25, the account has the following form:

> Before anything existed at all, from the very beginning, whatever exists I created from the non-existent, and from the invisible the visible. Listen, Enoch, and pay attention to these words of mine! For not even to my angels have I explained my secrets, nor related to them their origin, nor my endlessness (and inconceivableness), as I devise the creatures, as I am making them known to you today. For,

> before any visible things had come into existence, I, the one, moved around in the invisible things, like the sun, from east to west and from west to east. But the sun has rest in himself; yet I did not find rest, because everything was not yet created. And I thought up the idea of establishing a foundation, to create a visible creation. And I commanded the lowest things: "Let one of the invisible things descend visibly!" And Adoil descended, extremely large. And I looked at him, and, behold, in his belly he had a great light. And I said to him, "Disintegrate yourself, Adoil, and let what is born from you become visible." And he disintegrated himself, and there came out a very great light. And I was in the midst of the [great] light. And light out of light is carried thus. And the great age came out, and it revealed all the creation which I had thought up to create. And I saw how good it was. And I placed for myself a throne, and I sat down on it. And then to the light I spoke: "You go up higher (than the throne), and be solidified [much higher than the throne], and become the foundation of the higher things." And there is nothing higher than the light, except nothing itself. And again I bowed (?) myself and looked upward from my throne.[2]

The shorter recension of *2 Enoch* 24–25 provides a slightly different description:

> Before anything existed at all, from the very beginning, whatever is I created from non-being into being, and from the invisible things into the visible. And not even to my angels have I explained my secrets, nor related to them their composition, nor my endless and inconceivable creation which I conceived, as I am making them known to you today. Before any visible things had come into existence, and the light had not yet opened up, I, in the midst of the light, moved around in the invisible things, like one of them, as the sun moves around from east to west and from west to east. But the sun has rest; yet I did not find rest, because everything was not yet created. And I thought up the idea of establishing a foundation, to create a visible creation. And

> I commanded the lowest things: "Let one of the invisible things come out visibly!" And Adail descended, extremely large. And I looked at him, and, behold, in his belly he had a great age. And I said to him, "Disintegrate yourself, Adail, and let what is disintegrated from you become visible." And he disintegrated himself, and there came out from him the great age. And thus it carried all the creation which I had wished to create. And I saw how good it was. And I placed for myself a throne, and I sat down on it. To the light I spoke: "You go up higher and be solidified and become the foundation for the highest things." And there is nothing higher than the light, except nothing itself. And I spoke, I straightened myself upward from my throne.[3]

Adoil, a luminous aeon, and here the central character of the story, is depicted as God's helper who brings the whole creation into existence.[4] In the Slavonic apocalypse, Adoil is not merely a created entity but rather an agent of creation.[5] The portrayal of the whole creation emerging from Adoil's body further affirms the role of this character as the generating force of creation.[6] He belongs to the class of the "invisible things" that existed before creation. He thus does not appear during the process of creation but is "summoned" by the Deity from the circle of "invisible things," a feature that provides an additional indication of his preexistence. Instead of the familiar biblical "let there be," postulating creation *ex nihilo*, the readers of the Slavonic apocalypse hear quite different formulae, such as "Let one of the invisible things come out visibly!" The text's emphasis on the "descent" of Adoil before his participation in God's project might serve as an indication of his initial exalted status, the state that is also implied at the end of the narrative in which God orders the light of Adoil to go higher than the Deity's throne. Adoil's exact status remains shrouded in mystery. Although he is portrayed as one of the "invisible things," it is unclear if the text understands him as an angelic or a divine being or as a part of the divine Pleroma. A suggestion of the divine nature of Adoil comes from the shorter recension of *2 Enoch* 24, which places God in the midst of the invisible preexistent things; it reads: "Before any visible things had come into existence, and the light had not yet opened up, I, in the midst of the light, moved around in the invisible things, *like one of them*, as the sun moves around from east to west and from west to east."[7] This depiction of the Deity "moving around" like the sun in the "invisible things" is reminiscent of a solar system in which God is envisioned as a chief luminary and the "invisible things" possibly as planets. Such a depiction might denote the divine nature of the "invisible things" as "lesser deities" or circles of the divine Pleroma.

In the unfolding drama of creation, Adoil is portrayed as God's servant, obediently executing the Deity's commands and acting strictly according to the wishes of his master: "And thus it carried all the creation which I had wished to create." The account leaves the impression that Adoil might be understood here as a demiurgic hand of the Deity. Regarding the etymology of Adoil's name, Robert Henry Charles has proposed that it might derive from the Hebrew יד אל, translated as the "Hand of God."[8] Jarl Fossum offers additional insights into the demiurgic connotation of Adoil's name by noting that "it was a Jewish doctrine that God had created the world and man with his very hand(s), and the creative Hand of God even seems to have been hypostasized."[9] This tradition of the demiurgic extremities of the Deity received prominent development in the later Jewish lore where Enoch-Metatron is often understood as the Deity's hypostatic hand or his hypostatic finger.[10]

It is noteworthy that, in contrast to Genesis 1, where the Deity fashions the visible world and his creatures by his direct commands, in the Slavonic apocalypse, God chooses to act via a preexistent mediator, who is envisioned in the text as an anthropomorphic figure. The anthropomorphic qualities of Adoil are hinted at in the text in a reference to his belly. He is depicted as one who nurses the whole creation inside his preexistent body, and then, like a mother, gives birth to the created order. All of creation literally emerges from his broken body, depicted in *2 Enoch* as a disintegration of the primordial anthropomorphic vessel that gives birth to everything.[11]

Another important feature of Adoil is his association with light. The shorter recension suggests that the hidden preexistent light was concealed in Adoil's belly.[12] The luminous nature of the primordial aeon is especially evident in the longer recension, as it portrays the Deity bathing in the light produced from Adoil's disintegration.

Similar to the demiurgic light, darkness in *2 Enoch* is also depicted as a preexistent and demiurgic entity,[13] and has its own personified agent—Arkhas or Arukhas, who is portrayed as the foundation of the "lowest things." The shorter recension of *2 Enoch* 26:13 provides the following portrayal of Arukhas:

> And I called out a second time into the lowest things, and I said, "Let one of the invisible things come out solid and visible." There came out Arukhas, solid and heavy and very black. And I saw how suitable he was. And I said to him, "Come down low and become solid! And become the foundation of the lowest things!" And he came down and became solid. And he became the foundation of the lowest things. And there is nothing lower than the darkness, except nothing itself.[14]

In this account, Arukhas is depicted much like Adoil, although, in this case, he is depicted as an aeonic demiurgic "vessel" of darkness who gives birth to all lower things. Like the aeon of light, Arukhas belongs to the class of the preexistent "invisible things," and is likewise not created but "summoned." The aeonic creational processions are similar in both cases, as Arukhas also gives birth by "opening himself up." It is possible that Adoil and Arukhas are understood as the personifications of the preexistent light and darkness that paradoxically reflect each other. Despite such mirroring, the Deity clearly prefers the realm of Adoil. Disintegration of Adoil provides the foundation (Slav. *основание*) upon which God establishes the first visible manifestation of the created order, namely, his throne.

Another significant feature of this account of creation is Adoil's designation as a "revealer" found in the longer recension. His revelations are understood as "ontological," rather than verbal, disclosures; this account reads: "And the great age came out, and it revealed all the creation which I had thought up to create."

The traditions of Adoil and Arukhas, two personified primordial helpers assisting the Deity in bringing the world into existence, invite some consideration of the mediatorial proclivities of *2 Enoch*. It appears that the Deity's aids in creation in the Slavonic apocalypse are not exhausted by the figures of Adoil and Arukhas but include others. Although scholars have noted that the epilogue of the creational account emphasizes that God is the sole creator and does not have an adviser or successor to his creation, the epilogue does not deny the demiurgic assistants. Other studies have noticed that, in *2 Enoch*'s creational account, God's wisdom and his word[15] are also mentioned as the agents of creation.[16] Indeed, in both recensions[17] of *2 Enoch* 30:8, the Deity commands his wisdom to create man. Like Adoil and

Arukhas at the very beginning of creation, another demiurgic mediator, Sophia, is commissioned to help the Deity with the later stages of the creational process by assisting him in the creation of humankind. Scholars often see the Sophia traditions as the formative bedrock for later Jewish mediatorial developments, including the Johannine Prologue.[18]

A reference to Sophia as God's helper in *2 Enoch* 30 is important to our study because it points to the complex creational universe of the Slavonic apocalypse, which is a Jewish text that strives to accommodate several mediatorial trends. It is intriguing that in both cases (Adoil and Sophia) the demiurgic agents act as the Deity's servants who fulfill the "commands" of their master. In *2 Enoch* 30:8, the Deity narrates to the seer that he "commanded" his wisdom to create man. This expression recalls the account of Adoil in which the luminous aeon also receives a "command" from God; it reads: "And I commanded (повелѣх) the lowest things: 'Let one of the invisible things descend visibly!' And Adoil descended, extremely large." Both passages use identical Slavonic terminology (Slav. повелѣх). The reference to the divine word, which is mentioned along with Sophia[19] as a demiurgic agent in *2 Enoch* 33:4,[20] also demonstrates that the authors of the Slavonic apocalypse are cognizant not only of early traditions of the demiurgic wisdom but also of later Jewish and Christian conceptual currents similar to those found in the Prologue of John, in which the wisdom traditions were conflated with the tradition of the divine Name.

The Johannine Prologue

Before proceeding to an analysis of conceptual parallels between the Logos and Adoil in the Fourth Gospel and *2 Enoch,* one general similarity between the two accounts deserves our attention. It appears that, despite their uniqueness, both accounts are deeply affected by the imagery found in Genesis 1 in which one finds the familiar oppositions of visible and invisible, darkness and light, categories that also play a paramount role in the Johannine and Enochic accounts. The opening phrase of the Johannine hymn, "in the beginning" (ἐν ἀρχῇ), is also present in *2 Enoch's* creational account,[21] evoking the Genesis story. Although in Genesis the expression "in the beginning" pertains to the creation of the world, the phrase, both in *2 Enoch* and in the

Prologue, is related to precreational realities. Regarding the Johannine Prologue, Raymond Brown notes that "the opening words of verse one are similar to Genesis 1:1. While the author of Genesis is referring to creation, the author of the Fourth Gospel is speaking of eternity. There is no indication that the Word is a part of God's created order."[22]

God's Helpers in Creation

It appears that, like *2 Enoch*, the Prologue understands the Logos not as an independent "creator" but rather as a creational agent whose task is to execute God's thoughts, plans, and wishes. As demonstrated earlier, in *2 Enoch*, the Deity himself affirms the "executive" nature of Adoil by saying that the luminous aeon carried all the creation that he "had wished to create." The same pattern is discernible in the Fourth Gospel, in which the Logos is depicted not as a demiurge but rather as the helper of the Father. Scholars have noted that the Prologue makes it quite clear that "God is the Creator; his Word is the agent."[23] Raymond Brown suggests that "in saying that it is through the Word that all things came into being, the Prologue is at distance from Gnostic thought whereby a demiurge, and not God, was responsible for material creation, which is evil. Since the Word is related to the Father and the Word creates, the Father may be said to create through the Word. Thus, the material world has been created by God and is good."[24] Personifying both Adoil and the Logos further highlights the distance between the Deity and his "helpers."[25] At the same time, both accounts stress that their preexistent mediators are active creative participants, not simply inert tools of the Deity. Brown observes that "the role of the Word is not a passive, but an active one. The Logos functions."[26] Similarly, in *2 Enoch*, Adoil's active participation is hinted at by his depiction as the "mother" of all creation, a caregiver that "nurses" the whole creation in the preexistent time and then gives birth to it.

Preexistent Beings

Another common feature of the two creation accounts is that both the existence of the Logos and Adoil precedes the act of creation; neither "helper" is made during its process. The exact origin of the mediators is unknown. Although both protological accounts start with the phrase "in the beginning," the phrase does not signify the starting point of creation as it does in Genesis 1. Instead, it brings the reader into the midst of preexistent divine reality. Both the Logos and Adoil are thus understood as a part of the divine realm. Brown rightly points out that the presence of the Logos "in the beginning," unlike in Genesis, "refers to the period before creation and is a designation, more qualitative than temporal, of the sphere of God."[27]

Concealed Entities

In both accounts, the revelations of Adoil and the Logos are wrapped in language of concealment and understood as the utmost divine mysteries. The Deity in *2 Enoch* tells the seventh antediluvian hero that even his angels lack access to this revelation.[28] Here, the mediatorial agents who helped the Deity to bring the world into existence remain hidden from creation, which includes even celestial creatures. In the Prologue, a similar idea can be found, that the one through whom the world came into being remained hidden from the world.[29] It also appears that in both accounts the esoteric knowledge about preexistent realities eventually becomes revealed to the elect human beings—in *2 Enoch* to the seventh antediluvian hero and his adepts, and in the Prologue to those who believe in Christ. In both cases, the revelation of the preexistent realities has a soteriological value that provides the key to the mystery of salvation.[30] It is thus not coincidental that in *2 Enoch* the disclosure about Adoil is conceptually tied to the revelation about the final "age," an entity that mirrors the primordial aeon of light.

Personified Demiurgic Lights

Also, both accounts associate their chief creational agents with preexistent light. It has been already demonstrated in our study that in *2 Enoch* Adoil is understood not merely as a luminous entity but as a bearer of the preexistent demiurgic light. He, like the Logos in the Prologue, is himself a source of light. The fact that both light and "all creation" are situated in the belly of Adoil further elucidates that the light of the primordial aeon is indeed the demiurgic light.

In the Prologue of John, similar developments can be discerned in which the Logos is portrayed as the personification of the divine light.[31] Scholars have remarked that "the equivocal equivalence of the

Word and the Light systems is established in the Prologue, where both are identified as agents of creation (1:3, 10), both enter the world (1:4, 9–10, 14) and, implicitly, both are the objects of 'receiving,' 'knowing,' and 'believing.' "[32] Such depiction of the light as an agent of creation indicates that we are dealing here, as in *2 Enoch*, with the concept of the demiurgic light.

Moreover, it is noteworthy that, like the Logos, who is understood as the source of both preexistent and "material" light, the "light of the world," Adoil is also associated with both luminous entities, expressed in the longer recension of the Slavonic apocalypse as "carrying light out of light." In John 1:5, the symbolism of light is conflated with the imagery of darkness, as in Genesis 1. Yet such juxtaposition of the light and darkness is reminiscent not only of the imagery found in the first chapter of the Hebrew Bible but also the imagery of *2 Enoch*, in which the light of Adoil is juxtaposed with the darkness of another primordial aeon, namely, Arukhas, which is clearly separated from its luminous counterpart.

Ontological Revealers

It appears, also, that both Adoil and the Logos are understood as revealers. Rudolph Bultmann suggested that "the hymn that forms the basis of the Prologue praises the Logos as the Revealer."[33] Indeed, in the case of the Logos, the revelatory potentials are already manifested even in the title of this divine agent, namely, the Word of God.[34] The "revelations" of the Word are ontological disclosures, as well as "verbal" ones. As Raymond Brown notes, "the fact that the Word creates means that creation is an act of revelation. All creation bears the stamp of God's Word."[35] The entire creative process is understood, within this conceptual framework, as a continuous revelation of the Deity. The same concept is encountered in the Slavonic apocalypse in which Adoil's activity at creation is depicted as the ontological revelation of God. The longer recension of *2 Enoch* designates Adoil as the revealer. His revelations, as with the Logos, represent ontological disclosures in his creative work. Adoil's disintegration is identified in the text as the revelation of the created order: "And the great age came out, and it revealed all the creation which I had thought up to create."

The ontological revelations of Adoil and the Logos seem to be present in the peculiar metamorphoses of both characters, during which their preexistent forms become shepherded into the realities of the material world. Adoil's transformation is manifested through his disintegration, when this vessel of light bursts, giving life to all creation, while the Logos' incarnation, expressed in the Prologue as the Word becoming flesh, demonstrates his transformation.

Sources of All Creation

Another notable feature of these accounts is that both underscore the comprehensiveness of the creational efforts of their preexistent mediators. John 1:3 states that through the divine Logos "all things came into being . . . and without him not one thing came into being." The expression "all things" (πάντα) found in this passage is often understood by the interpreters as a reference to "all the creation."[36] Brown notes that beginning with the second century, the phrase " 'all things came into being' has been taken as a reference to creation. . . . The verb 'came into being' is ἐγένετο, used consistently to describe creation in the LXX of Gen 1."[37]

The tradition found in John 1:3 can be compared with the testimony about Adoil found in both recensions of *2 Enoch* 25, which tell that Adoil "carried *all the creation* (Slav. всю тварь) which I had wished to create."[38] This statement is rather puzzling since a few verses later Arukhas is also depicted as the one who brings the "lower things" into existence. Such discrepancies might reflect the creational narrative's composite nature, as it attempts to reconcile several demiurgic mediatorial trends.

It is also noteworthy that both accounts depict their respective creational agents as the demiurgic "vessels" that conceal the whole creation inside of them. In Adoil's case, the whole creation is said to be contained in the belly of the primordial aeon. A similar conceptual development might also be present in the Fourth Gospel. Some scholars have proposed that the Prologue indicates that creation was initially hidden in the Logos.[39] If the Prologue indeed portrays the Logos, like Adoil, as the primordial vessel of all created things, it points to a similar conceptual development in which the Deity creates the world by emptying his preexistent demiurgic vessels.[40]

Heavenly Men

Both accounts also hint at the anthropomorphic nature of their respective demiurgic agents, depicting them as the Heavenly Men. As suggested in our study, the Slavonic apocalypse unveils the anthropomorphic nature of Adoil through the portrayal of his light-filled belly. Several studies suggest that Adoil is envisioned in *2 Enoch* as the Heavenly Man. April DeConick argues that "the creative activity of the heavenly Man is highlighted in . . . the story of Adoil found in *2 Enoch*. . . . where . . . a man-like figure, descends with a great light in his stomach."[41] The anthropomorphic nature of Adoil appears to be implied, in *2 Enoch* 65, in which the final aeon, accommodating the remnant of humankind, is depicted as an eschatological replica of Adoil. Such eschatological gathering is reminiscent of the sculpturing of the "Last Statue" in the Manichaean tradition in which the righteous remnant is predestined to reconstitute the anthropomorphic form of the Heavenly Man at the end of the world.[42]

Similar to Adoil's imagery found in the Slavonic apocalypse, the Logos is also depicted as an anthropomorphic entity and, more precisely, as the Heavenly Man. This understanding of the Logos as an anthropomorphic figure is a pre-Christian development, clearly documented already in Philo's writings in which the Logos is portrayed as the Heavenly Man. Analyzing the Logos' speculations found in Philo's *De Confusione Linguarum*,[43] Thomas Tobin argues that, in these passages, "the Logos has been identified with the figure of the 'heavenly man.' "[44] Tobin suggests that this important conceptual development "has taken place in the Hellenistic Jewish interpretation of the Logos in connection with interpretations of texts from Genesis 1–3."[45] Tobin concludes that "this assimilation in Hellenistic Judaism of the Logos to the figure of the heavenly man may have served as an important step in the kind of reflection that led to the identification of the Logos with a particular human being, Jesus of Nazareth, in the hymn in the Prologue of John."[46]

Demarcations of Light and Darkness

The symbolism of the opposition of light and darkness plays an equally important role both in *2 Enoch* and the Prologue of John. Much ink has been spilled about the antithetical relation between light and darkness in the Johannine hymn.[47] Thomas Tobin, among others, notes that "a second element in the hymn that moves beyond the viewpoints found in Jewish wisdom literature is the stark contrast between light and darkness . . . found in John 1:4–5."[48] The Prologue insists that the darkness has not been able to overcome the light. Such strict delineation between light and darkness once again brings to mind *2 Enoch*, in which darkness is not only clearly separated from light but even has its own personification in the figure of Arukhas.

It seems, then, that both in *2 Enoch* and the Prologue, Adoil and the Logos serve not only the personifications of the light but also the demarcations or the "walls" whose functions are to prevent the mixing of the light and the darkness. When the shorter recension of *2 Enoch* 65 speaks of the luminosity of the final eschatological aeon that mirrors Adoil, this imagery is conflated with the symbolism of the wall; it reads: "But they will have a great light for eternity, <and> an indestructible wall."[49]

Conclusion

It has been long recognized that the Prologue of John was influenced by the wisdom traditions. However, the complex question about the exact mold of the sapiential currents that influenced the author of the hymn remains unanswered. John Ashton notes that "we do not need to ask from what source the author of the hymn derived his ideas, for both the general theme and the specific details are abundantly illustrated in wisdom tradition. Rather we have to ask what there was in the tradition which could have stimulated his own imaginative response: what precisely did he take from it?"[50]

The same can be asked of *2 Enoch*'s own appropriation of the wisdom traditions. It appears that while the tradition of the demiurgic wisdom is hidden within the Logos speculation in the Prologue, the Slavonic apocalypse clearly separates it from Adoil's deeds by invoking the actions of Sophia in the creation of humankind later in the text. This postulation of several demiurgic mediators points to the composite nature of the creational account of *2 Enoch*, in which various mediatorial streams are forced to interact. Another important feature of *2 Enoch*'s creational account is its peculiar mediatorial pairs; in the beginning Adoil is coupled with Arukhas, and in the conclusion Wisdom is paired with the Word. The last pair is especially noteworthy because it evokes the Johannine account in which the Jewish wisdom traditions are conflated with the imagery of the divine Word. It has been noted that the Prologue seems to be influenced by a particular mold of the sapiential tradition that emphasizes the aural revelation of the Deity; Nicola Frances Denzey, for instance, argues that the Prologue remains a representative example of not simply a Wisdom tradition, "but rather of a distinct 'Word tradition' which shared sapiental literature's dependency on Genesis yet interpreted it rather differently. This tradition attributed a creative force not to God's hypostasized forethought or Wisdom, but to his Voice or Word."[51] While the Prologue, like Philo, conflates the aural tradition of the divine Word with the anthropomorphic ideology of the Heavenly Man, it appears that, in *2 Enoch*, these two conceptual streams remain clearly separated.[52] Moreover, in the Slavonic apocalypse the Deity uses a plethora of various demiurgic "instruments," aural as well as anthropomorphic. While in the beginning he forcefully creates with his luminous form by bursting the anthropomorphic vessel of the primordial light, which gives birth to everything, he later chooses to mold humankind with another helper—his Wisdom, the mediator who is paired in *2 Enoch* with the divine Word but, unlike in the Prologue, not entirely fused with it. These intriguing interactions provide a unique glimpse into the complex world of Jewish mediatorial debates of the late Second Temple period and the conceptual developments that played a formative role in both the Slavonic apocalypse and the Johannine hymn.

Conclusion

> R. Isaac said: The Torah was given as black fire upon white fire in order to contain the right in the left, so that the left would be restored to the right. . . .
>
> —*Zohar* II.84a

The *Apocalypse of Abraham* and *2 Enoch* are often envisioned by distinguished students of early Jewish mysticism as crucial formative witnesses anticipating later Jewish mystical concepts and imagery. One of the first experts to explore the connections between later Kabbalistic traditions and the mystical imagery found in the Slavonic pseudepigrapha was the great Gershom Scholem, "the founding father of the academic discipline of Jewish mysticism."[1] His hypotheses concerning the links among various strands of Jewish mysticism were recently subjected to critical exploration, revealing some of the deficiencies of his approach.[2] Yet his intuitions about the formative roots of some apocalyptic imagery found in Jewish pseudepigrapha remain valuable, exercising an influence on those who continue to search for the seedbed of early Jewish mysticism in the Second Temple environment.

Not being a Jewish pseudepigrapha or apocalyptic literature scholar himself, which did not allow him to systematically explore these early apocalyptic traditions, Scholem nevertheless repeatedly drew attention to these early Jewish documents in search of their possible influence on later Jewish mystical developments.[3] Among the great variety of textual evidence Scholem explored, his attention was drawn to two pseudepigraphons—*2 Enoch* and the *Apocalypse of Abraham*—two enigmatic Jewish documents with uncertain provenance and history of transmission, which survive only in their Slavonic translations. In his seminal work *Major Trends in Jewish Mysticism* and other writings, Scholem viewed *2 Enoch* and the *Apocalypse of Abraham* as two important witnesses to the development of Jewish mystical concepts and imagery in the pseudepigrapha.[4] Scholem, and other scholars after him, often drew attention especially to the angelological developments found in the *Apocalypse of Abraham* and *2 Enoch*, noting that the traditions of Yahoel or the translated Enoch appear to shape the future profile of the great angel Metatron. In Scholem's opinion the development of various trends of the Metatron tradition was greatly indebted both to the conceptual streams similar to the Yahoel tradition found in the *Apocalypse of Abraham* and to the exalted Enoch tradition found in *2 Enoch*.[5] While the angelological developments found in *2 Enoch* and the *Apocalypse of Abraham* have received some attention from the scholars of Jewish mysticism, the demonological developments found in these documents have been often left in shadow. Yet, as demonstrated in this volume, both documents offer readers not only the novel angelological traditions but also unique demonological material as well. Despite the striking intensity of the demonological symbolism, the imagery of the spiritual antagonists of the Slavonic pseudepigrapha has never been explored systematically in connection with later Jewish mystical developments. This collection of studies represents one of the first attempts to approach these demonological traditions, and to provide a glimpse into the influential nature of these conceptual developments.

As mentioned in our introduction to this volume, the dualistic patterns of the demonic imitation of the divine found in the Slavonic pseudepigrapha appear to be anticipating some later Jewish mystical developments, especially reflected in the Castilian Kabbalah and the Zoharic tradition, with their tendency of "positing of a demonic realm morphologically paralleling the realm of the divine."[6] Thus, Isaiah Tishby has argued that the Zoharic understanding of the demonic realm or the Other Side "is constructed on the pattern of the divine emanatory system of ten *sefirot*."[7] Moreover, he suggests that "the parallelism between 'the Other Side' and 'the Divine Side' is so complete that by contemplating the *sefirot* of 'the Other Side,'[8] it is possible to gain knowledge and understanding of the divine sefirotic system."[9] The "architecture" of the demonic side thus provides theological insight into the mysteries of its divine counterpart. We learn from this study that the demonic and divine/angelic counterparts portrayed in the

Slavonic pseudepigrapha also stand in striking mirroring-opposition, when the demonic counterpart tries to inversely imitate the divine and angelic attributes. In such mirroring, the demonology is posing as the negative reaffirmation of the angelological and theophanic settings. The symbolism of the demonic realm thus serves an important conceptual function—an apophatic reaffirmation of the divine. The same function of the mutual theological reaffirmation is found in later Jewish mysticism with its tendency to portray the sefirotic system of the Other Side as the mirroring image of the divine *sefirot*.

Association of the Other Side, *sitra ahra*, with the left side in later Jewish mysticism[10] and its imitation of the divine right side is also reminiscent of some developments found in the Slavonic pseudepigrapha, especially the *Apocalypse of Abraham* in which the right lot associated with Abraham and God is often put in the patriarch's disclosures in visual parallelism with the left lot of Azazel.[11]

Another important lesson that the Slavonic pseudepigrapha appears to be holding for the later Jewish mysticism is its unique erotic symbolism of the spiritual unions. The eroticizing overtones in the depiction of the encounters between visionaries and various divine and angelic manifestations are not uncommon in early Jewish apocalyptic accounts in which the seers are routinely embraced or even kissed by the Deity or his various anthropomorphic representations during the visionaries' initiations or upon their arrivals to God's abode. As our study has demonstrated, the *Exagoge* of the Ezekiel Tragedian, *2 Enoch*, and *Joseph and Aseneth* provide striking examples of such erotic symbolism. Yet, in the *Apocalypse of Abraham*, this eroticizing dimension of the spiritual encounters has also been extended to the demonic side. Such peculiar eroticizing tendencies found, for example, in the *Apocalypse of Abraham*'s depiction of Azazel's seduction of the protoplast or his interaction with the false messiah appear formative for the later Jewish "erotisation" of the activities of the Other Side in later Jewish mysticism.[12] In this respect it is intriguing that both the *Apocalypse of Abraham* and the *Zohar* depict their antagonists in the midst of the erotic union of the protoplasts in the Garden of Eden.[13]

It has been noted in our study that the antagonism of the divine and demonic sides, which unfolds in the *Apocalypse of Abraham* in several conceptual dimensions, including the messianic and sacerdotal, is not entirely novel, as it has certain affinities with the early Jewish developments reflected in some Qumran materials. Yet the unique mold of this messianic and sacerdotal imagery appears to stand conceptually closer to later mystical traditions than to its earlier apocalyptic counterparts.[14] One striking similarity here is the peculiar emphasis on the preexistent roots of the relationships between the demonic and the divine, and entertaining the idea that evil has its origins in the very essence of the divine realm. Such ideas are expressed in the Slavonic pseudepigraphical texts by the imagery of two primordial aeons—light and darkness, reflected, for instance, in *2 Enoch*'s account of Adoil and Arukhas as well as in the *Apocalypse of Abraham's* depiction of the Leviathan.

The striking portrayal of the preexistent darkness summoned by the Maker from the depths of the divine *Pleroma* during the process of creation, when the darkness mirrors the divine light, brings to mind some later Jewish mystical concepts in which the dark demonic forces are said to be derived from the Deity.[15] In this respect, Eitan Fishbane reminds us that "the notion that evil derives from, and is even located within, the Deity[16] is a startling conception in the history of Jewish thought. This was one of the signature ideas of Castilian Kabbalah in general and of the *Zohar* in particular."[17]

2 Enoch's depiction of Adoil as the vessel of light, disintegrated in beginning of creation, and then restored by the righteous gatherers of light at the end of time, again constitutes a striking parallel to later Jewish mystical developments. More specifically, it brings to mind certain concepts found in the Lurianic Kabbalah, with its imagery of disintegration of the primordial vessels of light and their final restoration through the efforts of the righteous of the world.

The protological imagery of Leviathan, depicted as the primordial sacred foundation in the *Apocalypse of Abraham*, is also instructive in invoking some later Jewish mystical parallels in which the symbolism of the sea monster, conflated with the imagery of light and darkness, points to the primordial roots of the conflict between the divine and the demonic. In this respect, scholars have noted that in the Zoharic mythology "the war between holiness and uncleanness had begun before the world was created."[18] This primordial battle is exemplified by "the great monster, the head of *sitra ahra*, who lays over the great deep, and the rays of divine light were not able to penetrate the darkness of the deep[19] and set in motion the work of creation."[20] As one can see, in the *Zohar*, as well as in the Slavonic apocalypse, the great monster serves as the paradoxical *Axis Mundi*.[21] Such a crucial role in the architecture of the entire created order explains why the imagery of the great monster became emblematic of the mysteries of God's creation in the later Jewish mysticism, to the point that later interpreters often refer to the secrets of the *Maᶜase Bereshit* as the mysteries of Leviathan and Behemoth.[22]

Later Jewish mystical developments accentuate the power of the Other Side and the difficulties conquering it in an open battle.[23] Later Zoharic traditions often emphasize that "it is better . . . to placate 'the Other Side' and bribe it with gifts, in order to avoid a direct confrontation."[24] The idea of appeasing the Other Side through "peaceful" means, including the conventional sacerdotal instruments,[25] frequently occurs in the *Zohar*.[26]

This tendency of placating the demonic side through the sacerdotal means brings us to another important lesson that the Slavonic pseudepigrapha, especially the *Apocalypse of Abraham*, holds for the later Jewish mysticism, namely, the emphasis on the sacerdotal dimension of the demonic realm. This development constitutes a formative conceptual shift that endows the "Other Side" with forceful cultic significance, placing it in the heart of Jewish sacerdotal life exemplified by, for example, the Yom Kippur ritual, during which the infamous scapegoat becomes a spiritual agent of the Other Side. In this respect, the Slavonic pseudepigrapha develops some earlier traditions found in other apocalyptic writings, such as the *Book of the Watchers* and the *Animal Apocalypse*, in which the chief antagonist of the Enochic tradition, the fallen angel Asael, is depicted as the cosmic scapegoat. As our study has demonstrated, the further eschatological reformulation of the scapegoat ritual found in the Slavonic apocalypse will play a formative role for the later Jewish mystical developments in which the Yom Kippur rite is often understood as an allotment of a special portion of sacrifices to the demonic realm. Such appeasing through sacrifice does not, however, diminish the antagonistic stand between the demonic and the divine sides. On the contrary, as our analysis of the mirroring dualistic features of the high priest and the scapegoat has also demonstrated, a hint of dualism is sometimes more obvious in the sacerdotal appeasing of the Other Side than in description of direct warfare between the divine and the demonic.[27]

The unusual intensity of demonological symbolism found in the *Apocalypse of Abraham* might itself stem from the peculiarities of the book's sacerdotal outlook, which attempts to find answers to the catastrophic loss of the terrestrial sanctuary. Here, the ineffectiveness of the polluted sanctuary strengthens the powers of the Other Side. The correspondence between the increasing power of the demonic Side and pollution or destruction of the terrestrial sanctuary can be found in later Jewish mystical developments, including Zoharic mythology, with its understanding that "when the Temple was destroyed the rule of the *Shekhinah* was shattered and 'the Other Side' become dominant."[28]

Yet, like the Slavonic pseudepigraphical texts, with their vision of the eschatological sanctuary, the Zoharic tradition too anticipates future subjugation of the Other Side by the sacerdotal means.[29] As Tishby observes, "[I]n the future, the fortunes of the *Shekhinah* will be restored, and 'the Other Side' will be humiliated and destroyed."[30]

These striking parallels between the Slavonic pseudepigraphical texts and later Jewish mystical traditions raise the question of possible channels of transmission and influence. Yet, this question has proven to be the most difficult challenge for students of early Jewish mysticism (also encountered by Gershom Scholem), who experience great difficulties demonstrating historical links between the apocalyptic traditions and later molds of the Jewish mystical tradition, including Hekhalot literature and the Zoharic tradition. Peter Schäfer has reflected on Scholem's challenges, noting that "he does not make an attempt to prove the historical connection between the alleged Merkavah speculations of the 'old apocalyptics' and the Mishnah teachers of rabbinic Judaism or the Merkavah mystics presented in the Hekhalot literature."[31]

The question of transmission of early apocalyptic traditions into the later rabbinic mileux is even more challenging in the case of the Slavonic pseudepigrapha, considering the enigmatic origins and vague transmission history of this corpus, which has left no traces or allusions, even in the Byzantine environment, in the traditional literary pool for the majority of religious documents circulated in Slavonic milieux. Yet one recent discovery pertaining to the Slavonic pseudepigraphical texts provides some hope regarding the issues of the origins and transmission of this important evidence for the history of early Jewish mysticism. In 2006, the Dutch scholar Joost Hagen, while doing research on Coptic manuscripts from Qasr Ibrim in Egyptian Nubia, identified photographs of four small Coptic parchment fragments as portions of *2 Enoch* 36–42.[32] These Coptic fragments, whose preliminary date is, according to Hagen, between the 8th and 10th centuries CE, became the earliest fragments of *2 Enoch* known to the scholarly community. These newly identified Coptic witnesses point to a possible Egyptian provenance for some Slavonic pseudepigrapha, a hypothesis entertained by scholars long before the identification of the Qasr Ibrim's fragments of *2 Enoch*.[33]

There is a certain providential irony in the fact that some Slavonic pseudepigraphical texts dealing with the unique mythology of evil came from Egypt, the geographical location often depicted in later Jewish mysticism as the domain of the demonic side.[34] Scholars are now forced to "descend" to these Jewish documents from Egypt in order to better understand the origins of Jewish mysticism. In doing so, they are destined to emulate prominent ancient seekers of secrets, the exalted patriarchs and prophets of the biblical stories, who once were privileged, according to later Jewish lore, to "descend" to Egypt in order to be initiated into the utmost mysteries of the Other Side.[35] In this respect, it is not coincidental that the profound knowledge about the demonic side become revealed in the *Apocalypse of Abraham* through the story of Abraham, a patriarch who once too underwent a journey into Egypt. From the most famous Jewish mystical compendium, one learns about Abraham's "descent" into the mysteries of the Other Side symbolically represented by his journey into Egypt: " 'And Abram went down to Egypt' . . . This verse hints at wisdom and the levels down below, to the depths of which Abraham descended. He knew them but did not become attached."[36]

Notes

Introduction

1. On this conceptual development see J. Dan, "Samael, Lilith, and the Concept of Evil in Early Kabbalah," *AJSR* 5 (1980) 17–40; M. Idel, "The Evil Thought of the Deity," *Tarbiz* 49 (1980) 356–364 [Hebrew]; G. Scholem, "The Kabbalah of R. Jacob and R. Isaac, the Sons of R. Jacob ha-Kohen," *Maddaᶜei ha-Yahadut* 2 (1927) 165–293 [Hebrew]; idem, "Sitra Ahra: Good and Evil in the Kabbalah," in: *On the Mystical Shape of the Godhead: Basic Concepts in the Kabbalah* (New York: Schocken, 1991) 56–87; I. Tishby, *The Doctrine of Evil and the "Kelippah" in Lurianic Kabbalism* (Jerusalem: Magnes, 1984) [Hebrew]; idem, *The Wisdom of the Zohar: An Anthology of Texts* (3 vols.; London: The Littman Library of Jewish Civilization, 1989); E. R. Wolfson, "Left Contained in the Right: A Study in Zoharic Hermeneutics," *AJSR* 11 (1986) 27–52; idem, "Light through Darkness: The Ideal of Human Perfection in the Zohar," *HTR* 81 (1988) 73–95.

The Curses of Azazel

1. The general scholarly consensus holds that the apocalypse was composed after 70 CE and before the end of the second century CE. The depiction of the destruction of the Temple in chapter 27 and the peculiar interest in the idea of the celestial sanctuary represented by the divine Chariot hint at the fact that the earthly sanctuary was no longer standing. Another significant chronological marker is established by the second century work—the *Clementine Recognitiones* 32–33 which provides one of the earliest external references for the dating of the *Apocalypse of Abraham*. On the date of the *Apocalypse of Abraham*, see G.H. Box and J.I. Landsman, *The Apocalypse of Abraham. Edited, with a Translation from the Slavonic Text and Notes* (TED, 1.10; London, New York: The Macmillan Company, 1918) xv–xix; B. Philonenko-Sayar and

M. Philonenko, *L'Apocalypse d'Abraham. Introduction, texte slave, traduction et notes* (Semitica, 31; Paris: Librairie Adrien-Maisonneuve, 1981) 34–35; R. Rubinkiewicz, "Apocalypse of Abraham," *The Old Testament Pseudepigrapha* (2 vols.; ed. J.H. Charlesworth; New York: Doubleday, 1983–1985) 1.681–705 at 683; idem, *L'Apocalypse d'Abraham en vieux slave. Introduction, texte critique, traduction et commentaire* (ŹM, 129; Lublin: Towarzystwo Naukowe Katolickiego Uniwersytetu Lubelskiego, 1987) 70–73; A. Kulik, "К датировке 'Откровения Авраама,'" *In Memoriam of Ja. S. Lur'e* (eds. N.M. Botvinnik and Je.I. Vaneeva; St. Petersburg: Fenix, 1997) 189–195; idem, *Retroverting Slavonic Pseudepigrapha: Toward the Original of the Apocalypse of Abraham* (TCS, 3; Atlanta: Scholars, 2004) 2–3.

2. Cf. C. Fletcher-Louis, "The Revelation of the Sacral Son of Man," in: *Auferstehung-Resurrection* (eds. F. Avemarie and H. Lichtenberger; Tübingen: Mohr/Siebeck, 2001) 282; A.A. Orlov, "Eschatological Yom Kippur in the *Apocalypse of Abraham*. Part I. The Scapegoat Ritual," in *Symbola Caelestis. Le symbolisme liturgique et paraliturgique dans le monde chrétien* (Scrinium 5; eds. A. Orlov and B. Lourié; Piscataway: Gorgias Press, 2009) 79–111.

3. With respect to the Yom Kippur traditions in the *Apocalypse of Abraham*, see L.L. Grabbe, "The Scapegoat Tradition: A Study in Early Jewish Interpretation," *JSJ* 18 (1987) 165–179 at 157; R. Helm, "Azazel in Early Jewish Literature," *AUSS* 32 (1994) 217–226 at 223; B. Lourié, "Propitiatorium in the Apocalypse of Abraham," in *The Old Testament Apocrypha in the Slavonic Tradition: Continuity and Diversity* (eds. L. DiTommaso and C. Böttrich; TSAJ, 140; Tübingen: Mohr/Siebeck, 2011) 267–277; D. Stökl Ben Ezra, "Yom Kippur in the Apocalyptic Imaginaire and the Roots of Jesus' High Priesthood," in *Transformations of the Inner Self in Ancient Religions* (eds. J. Assmann and G. Stroumsa; Leiden: Brill, 1999) 349–366; idem, "The Biblical Yom Kippur, the Jewish Fast of the Day of Atonement and the Church Fathers," *SP* 34 (2002) 493–502; idem, *The Impact of Yom Kippur on Early Christianity: The Day of Atonement from Second Temple Judaism to the Fifth Century* (WUNT, 163; Tübingen: Mohr/Siebeck, 2003) 94.

4. Regarding heavenly Temple/heavenly priesthood traditions, see J.L. Angel, *Otherworldly and Eschatological Priesthood in the Dead Sea Scrolls* (STDJ, 86; Leiden: Brill, 2010); V. Aptowitzer, "The Celestial Temple as Viewed in the Aggadah," in *Binah: Studies in Jewish Thought* (ed. J. Dan; Binah: Studies in Jewish History, Thought, and Culture, 2; New York: Praeger, 1989) 1–29; M. Barker, *The Gate of Heaven: The History and Symbolism of the Temple in Jerusalem* (London: SPCK, 1991); J.J. Collins, "A Throne in the Heavens: Apotheosis in Pre-Christian Judaism," in *Death, Ecstasy, and Other Worldly Journeys* (eds. J.J. Collins and M. Fishbane; New York: State University of New York Press, 1995) 43–57; B. Ego, *"Im Himmel wie auf Erden"* (WUNT, 2.34; Tübingen: Mohr/Siebeck, 1989); R. Elior, "From Earthly Temple to Heavenly

Shrines: Prayer and Sacred Song in the Hekhalot Literature and its Relation to Temple Traditions," *JSQ* 4 (1997): 217–267; D.N. Freedman, "Temple Without Hands," in *Temples and High Places in Biblical Times: Proceedings of the Colloquium in Honor of the Centennial of Hebrew Union College-Jewish Institute of Religion, Jerusalem, 14–16 March 1977* (ed. A. Biran; Jerusalem: Hebrew Union College-Jewish Institute of Religion, 1981) 21–30; I. Gruenwald, *Apocalyptic and Merkavah Mysticism* (AGAJU, 14; Leiden: Brill 1980); D. Halperin, *The Faces of the Chariot: Early Jewish Response to Ezekiel's Vision* (TSAJ, 16; Tübingen: Mohr/Siebeck, 1988); idem, "Heavenly Ascension in Ancient Judaism: The Nature of the Experience," *SBLSP* 26 (1987) 218–231; R.G. Hamerton-Kelly, "The Temple and the Origins of Jewish Apocalyptic," *VT* 20 (1970) 1–15; M. Himmelfarb, "From Prophecy to Apocalypse: The Book of the Watchers and Tours of Heaven," in *Jewish Spirituality: From the Bible Through the Middle Ages* (ed. A. Green; New York: Crossroad, 1986) 145–165; idem, "Apocalyptic Ascent and the Heavenly Temple," *SBLSP* 26 (1987) 210–217; idem, *Ascent to Heaven in Jewish and Christian Apocalypses* (New York/Oxford: Oxford University Press, 1993); idem, "The Practice of Ascent in the Ancient Mediterranean World," in *Death, Ecstasy, and Other Worldly Journeys* (eds. J.J. Collins and M. Fishbane; Albany: SUNY Press, 1995) 123–137; C.R. Koester, *The Dwelling of God: The Tabernacle in the Old Testament, Intertestamental Jewish Literature and the New Testament* (CBQMS, 22; Washington, DC: Catholic Biblical Association of America, 1989); J.D. Levenson, "The Temple and the World," *JR* 64 (1984) 275–298; idem, "The Jerusalem Temple in Devotional and Visionary Experience," in *Jewish Spirituality: From the Bible Through the Middle Ages* (ed. A. Green; New York: Crossroad, 1987) 32–59; A.J. McNicol, "The Heavenly Sanctuary in Judaism: A Model for Tracing the Origin of the Apocalypse," *JRS* 13 (1987) 66–94; C.R.A. Morray-Jones, "Transformational Mysticism in the Apocalyptic-Merkabah Tradition," *JJS* 43 (1992) 1–31; idem, "The Temple Within: The Embodied Divine Image and its Worship in the Dead Sea Scrolls and Other Jewish and Christian Sources," *SBLSP* 37 (1998) 400–431; C. Newsom "'He Has Established for Himself Priests': Human and Angelic Priesthood in the Qumran Sabbath Shirot," in *Archaeology and History in the Dead Sea Scrolls: The New York University Conference in Memory of Yigael Yadin* (ed. L.H. Schiffman; JSPSS, 8; Sheffield: JSOT Press, 1990) 101–120; G.W.E. Nickelsburg, "The Apocalyptic Construction of Reality in 1 Enoch," in *Mysteries and Revelations: Apocalyptic Studies since the Uppsala Colloquium* (ed. J.J. Collins; JSPSS, 9; Sheffield: JSOT Press, 1991) 51–64; R. Patai, *Man and Temple in Ancient Jewish Myth and Ritual* (New York: KTAV, 1967); C. Rowland, "The Visions of God in Apocalyptic Literature," *JSJ* 10 (1979) 137–154; idem, *The Open Heaven: A Study of Apocalyptic in Judaism and Early Christianity* (London: SPCK, 1982); A.F. Segal, "Heavenly Ascent in Hellenistic Judaism, Early

Christianity and Their Environment," *ANRW* 2.23.2 (1980) 1333–1394; M.S. Smith, "Biblical and Canaanite Notes to the Songs of the Sabbath Sacrifice from Qumran," *RevQ* 12 (1987) 585–588.

5. Scholars have previously noted the sacerdotal significance of this angelic figure who appears to be dressed as a high priest. Thus Martha Himmelfarb argues that Yahoel's wardrobe has strong priestly associations. For instance, the linen band around his head recalls Aaron's headdress of fine linen (Exod 28:39), the purple coloring of the angel's robe invites comparisons to one of the colors of the high-priestly garments of Exodus 28, while his golden staff seems similar to Aaron's rod that miraculously sprouted in the wilderness after Korah's rebellion "to indicate the choice of Aaron and his descendants as priests (Num 17:16–26)." Himmelfarb, *Ascent to Heaven in Jewish and Christian Apocalypses,* 62. Himmelfarb also draws attention to the rainbow-like appearance of Yahoel's turban, which, in her opinion, "brings together the two central color schemes employed elsewhere in the description of God as high priest, namely, whiteness and the multicolored glow." Himmelfarb, *Ascent to Heaven in Jewish and Christian Apocalypses,* 62. Yahoel's role as a heavenly high priest also appears later in the text (*Apoc. Ab.* 10:9) through his liturgical office as choirmaster of the Living Creatures, which is reminiscent of the liturgical office of Enoch-Metatron in the Merkabah tradition. Regarding this tradition, see A. Orlov, "Celestial Choir-Master: The Liturgical Role of Enoch-Metatron in *2 Enoch* and the Merkabah Tradition," *JSP* 14.1 (2004) 3–24.

6. Concerning the Azazel traditions, see J. Blair, *De-Demonising the Old Testament: An Investigation of Azazel, Lilith, Deber, Qeteb and Reshef in the Hebrew Bible* (FAT, 2.37; Tübingen: Mohr/Siebeck, 2009) 55–63; J. De Roo, "Was the Goat for Azazel destined for the Wrath of God?" *Bib* 81 (2000) 233–241; W. Fauth, "Auf den Spuren des biblischen Azazel (Lev 16): Einige Residuen der Gestalt oder des Namens in jüdisch-aramäischen, griechischen, koptischen, äthiopischen, syrischen und mandäischen Texten," *ZAW* 110 (1998) 514–534; C.L. Feinberg, "The Scapegoat of Leviticus Sixteen," *BSac* 115 (1958) 320–331; M. Görg, "Beobachtungen zum sogenannten Azazel-Ritus," *BN* 33 (1986) 10–16; Grabbe, "The Scapegoat Tradition: A Study in Early Jewish Interpretation," 165–179; Helm, "Azazel in Early Jewish Literature," 217–226; B. Janowski, *Sühne als Heilsgeschehen: Studien zur Sühnetheologie der Priesterschrift und zur Wurzel KPR im Alten Orient und im Alten Testament* (WMANT, 55; Neukirchen-Vluyn: Neukirchener Verlag, 1982); idem, "Azazel," in *Dictionary of Deities and Demons in the Bible* (eds. K. van der Toorn et al.; Leiden: Brill, 1995) 240–248. B. Jürgens, *Heiligkeit und Versöhnung: Levitikus 16 in seinem literarischen Kontext* (New York: Herder, 2001); H.M. Kümmel, "Ersatzkönig und Sündenbock," *ZAW* 80 (1986) 289–318; R.D. Levy, *The Symbolism of the Azazel Goat* (Bethesda: International Scholars Publication, 1998); O. Loretz, *Leberschau, Sündenbock,*

Asasel in Ugarit und Israel: Leberschau und Jahwestatue in Psalm 27, Leberschau in Psalm 74 (UBL, 3; Altenberge: CIS-Verlag, 1985); J. Maclean, "Barabbas, the Scapegoat Ritual, and the Development of the Passion Narrative," *HTR* 100 (2007) 309–334; C. Molenberg, "A Study of the Roles of Shemihaza and Asael in 1 Enoch 6–11," *JJS* 35 (1984) 136–146; J. Milgrom, *Studies in Cultic Theology and Terminology* (SJLA, 36; Leiden: Brill, 1983); D. Rudman, "A Note on the Azazel-goat Ritual," *ZAW* 116 (2004) 396–401; W.H. Shea, "Azazel in the Pseudepigrapha," *JATS* 13 (2002) 1–9; Stökl Ben Ezra, "Yom Kippur in the Apocalyptic Imaginaire and the Roots of Jesus' High Priesthood," 349–366; idem, "The Biblical Yom Kippur, the Jewish Fast of the Day of Atonement and the Church Fathers," 493–502; idem, *The Impact of Yom Kippur on Early Christianity*; A. Strobel, "Das jerusalemische Sündenbock-ritual. Topographische und landeskundische Erwägungen zur Überlieferungsgeschichte von Lev. 16,10,21f," *ZDPV* 103 (1987) 141–168; H. Tawil, "ʿAzazel the Prince of the Steppe: A Comparative Study," *ZAW* 92 (1980) 43–59; M. Weinfeld, "Social and Cultic Institutions in the Priestly Source against Their ANE Background," in *Proceedings of the Eighth World Congress of Jewish Studies* (Jerusalem: Magness Press, 1983) 95–129; A. Wright, *The Origin of the Evil Spirits: The Reception of Genesis 6.1–4 in Early Jewish Literature* (WUNT, 2.198; Tübingen: Mohr/ Siebeck, 2005) 104–117; D.P. Wright, *The Disposal of Impurity: Elimination Rites in the Bible and in Hittite and Mesopotamian Literature* (SBLDS, 101; Atlanta: Scholars, 1987).

7. The phrase "dwelling place of your impurity" here alludes to the purgative function of the scapegoat ceremony, the rite centered on removing the impurity heaped on the sacrificial animal to the dwelling place of the demon in the wilderness. As Jacob Milgrom observes ". . . the goat is simply the vehicle to dispatch Israel's impurities and sins to the wilderness/ netherworld." Milgrom, *Leviticus 1–16*, 1021.

8. Kulik, *Retroverting Slavonic Pseudepigrapha*, 20.

9. Thus Daniel Stökl Ben Ezra notes the terminology of "sending" things to Azazel in *Apoc. Ab.* 13:10, which Alexander Kulik traces to the Greek term ἀποστέλλω or Hebrew שלח. Kulik, *Apocalypse of Abraham: Towards the Lost Original*, 90. Stökl Ben Ezra proposes that this terminology "might allude to the sending out of the scapegoat." Stökl Ben Ezra, *The Impact of Yom Kippur on Early Christianity*, 94.

10. For instance, Crispin Fletcher-Louis notes a possible connection between this command found in *Apoc. Ab.* 13:12 and the dispatching formula given to the scapegoat in *m. Yoma* 6:4: "Take our sins and go forth." Fletcher-Louis, "The Revelation of the Sacral Son of Man," 282.

11. H. Danby, *The Mishnah* (Oxford: Oxford University Press, 1992) 169.

12. One can see that the cursing formula appears to reflect the earlier biblical form found in Lev 16:21, in which the imposition of sins on the head

of the scapegoat is followed by his departure into the wilderness: ". . . and Aaron shall lay both his hands upon the head of the live goat, and confess over him all the iniquities of the people of Israel, and all their transgressions, all their sins; and he shall put them upon the head of the goat, and send him away into the wilderness by the hand of a man who is in readiness."

13. It is clear that the high priest Yahoel is performing here the so-called "transference function"—the crucial part of the scapegoat ritual—wherein the high priest conveys the sins of Israel onto the head of the goat through confession and the laying-on of hands. On the "transference" function, see also Milgrom, *Leviticus 1–16,* 1041. Clarifying the conceptual background of this ritual, Stephen Finlan notes that "curse-transmission is one of the key moments in expulsion rituals." S. Finlan, *Problems with Atonement: The Origins of, and Controversy About, the Atonement Doctrine* (Collegeville, MN: Liturgical Press, 2005) 45. It should be noted that the transference of Abraham's sins to Azazel here has been traditionally interpreted by scholars in the context of Yom Kippur. Thus Robert Helm notes that "the transference of Abraham's corruption to Azazel may be a veiled reference to the scapegoat rite. . . ." Helm, "Azazel in Early Jewish Tradition," 223. Similarly, Lester Grabbe argues that the phrasing in the statement that "Abraham's corruption has 'gone over to' Azazel suggest[s] an act of atonement." Grabbe, "The Scapegoat Tradition: A Study in Early Jewish Interpretation," 157.

14. "Reproach is on you, Azazel!" Kulik, *Retroverting Slavonic Pseudepigrapha*, 20.

15. "Be shamed by me . . ." Kulik, *Retroverting Slavonic Pseudepigrapha*, 20.

16. For instance, see D. Harlow, "Idolatry and Alterity: Israel and the Nations in the *Apocalypse of Abraham*," in *The "Other" in Second Temple Judaism. Essays in Honor of John J. Collins* (eds. D.C. Harlow, M. Goff, K.M. Hogan and J.S. Kaminsky; Grand Rapids: Eerdmans, 2011) 302–330 at 314.

17. Harlow observes that "in chap. 12 Yahoel acts like a senior priest showing a junior priest the ropes; he instructs Abraham: 'Slaughter and cut all this, putting together the two halves, one against the other. But do not cut the birds.' " Harlow, "Idolatry and Alterity: Israel and the Nations in the *Apocalypse of Abraham*," 314.

18. Kulik, *Retroverting Slavonic Pseudepigrapha*, 21.

19. Philonenko-Sayar and Philonenko, *L'Apocalypse d'Abraham*, 68.

20. Philonenko-Sayar and Philonenko, *L'Apocalypse d'Abraham*, 68.

21. Danby, *The Mishnah,* 166.

22. Philonenko-Sayar and Philonenko, *L'Apocalypse d'Abraham*, 68.

23. Lev 16:22: "The goat shall bear on itself all their iniquities to a barren region; and the goat shall be set free in the wilderness." Cf. also *Zohar* II.184b: "That Other Side is the central point of the desolate world, for he

rules over all desolation and ruin. And the central point of all habitation is the side of Holiness; thus Jerusalem stands in the center of the whole inhabited world." Matt, *The Zohar: Pritzker Edition*, 6.36.

24. Milgrom, *Leviticus 1 16*, 1045.

25. Cf. *b. Yoma* 67b: "Our Rabbis taught: Azazel—it should be hard and rough. One might have assumed that it is to be in inhabited land, therefore the text reads: 'In the wilderness.'" I. Epstein, *The Babylonian Talmud. Yoma* (London: Soncino, 1935–1952) 67b.

26. Colson, *Philo*, 7.207. These traditions point to the so-called "elimination" aspect of the scapegoat ritual. In such traditions, impurity must be removed from the inhabitable world into an uninhabitable (or, in the language of the *Apocalypse of Abraham*, "untrodden") realm. In this regard, Stökl Ben Ezra suggests that the language of "untrodden parts of the earth" is reminiscent of the Septuagint version's translation of Leviticus 16:22 (εἰς γῆν ἄβατον). See Stökl Ben Ezra, *The Impact of Yom Kippur on Early Christianity*, 94.

27. Along these lines, Daniel Harlow notes that "Yahoel teaches Abraham a kind of exorcistic spell to drive Azazel away." Harlow, "Idolatry and Alterity: Israel and the Nations in the *Apocalypse of Abraham*," 315.

28. This imagery, however, is not entirely novel, and can be traced to the early Enochic writings in which the scapegoat Azazel was refashioned into the fallen angel Asael. This transition will be explored in detail later in this study.

29. Regarding the clothing metaphors within the scapegoat rite, see A. Dorman, "'Commit Injustice and Shed Innocent Blood.' Motives behind the Institution of the Day of Atonement in the Book of Jubilees," in *The Day of Atonement: Its Interpretation in Early Jewish and Christian Traditions* (eds. T. Hieke and T. Nicklas; TBN, 15; Leiden: Brill, 2012) 57.

30. For possible Mesopotamian antecedents of the scapegoat's band, see I. Zatelli, "The Origin of the Biblical Scapegoat Ritual: The Evidence of Two Eblaite Texts," *VT* 48 (1998) 254–263. In some Eblaite texts a goat wears a silver bracelet hanging from its neck. Ida Zatelli argues that "the bracelet hanging from the neck signifies an offering, almost a payment for the purgation." Zatelli, "The Origin of the Biblical Scapegoat Ritual," 257.

31. Cf. G. Stemberger, "Yom Kippur in Mishnah Yoma," in *The Day of Atonement: Its Interpretation in Early Jewish and Christian Traditions* (eds. T. Hieke and T. Nicklas; TBN, 15; Leiden: Brill, 2012) 133.

32. Stökl Ben Ezra notes that although the "Mishnah does not explicitly refer to the whitening of the scapegoat ribbon, this seems to be assumed." Stökl Ben Ezra, *The Impact of Yom Kippur on Early Christianity*, 131.

33. Stemberger, "Yom Kippur in Mishnah Yoma," 133.

34. Cf. also *m. Shekalim* 4:2: "The [Red] Heifer and the scapegoat and the crimson thread were bought with the *Terumah* from the Shekel-chamber."

Danby, *The Mishnah*, 155; *m. Shabbat* 9:3: "Whence do we learn that they tie a strip of crimson on the head of the scapegoat? Because it is written, Though your sins be as scarlet they shall be as white as snow." Danby, *The Mishnah*, 108.

35. Danby, *The Mishnah*, 166.

36. Danby, *The Mishnah*, 170.

37. Danby, *The Mishnah*, 170.

38. For a comparative analysis of Barnabas's account and the mishnaic testimonies about the crimson band, see O. Skarsaune, *The Proof from Prophecy: A Study in Justin Martyr's Proof-Text Tradition: Text-Type, Provenance, Theological Profile* (NovTSup, 56; Leiden: Brill, 1987) 308.

39. *The Apostolic Fathers* (ed. B.D. Ehrman; LCL 24–25; 2 vols.; Cambridge, Massachusetts: Harvard University Press, 2003) 2.37–41.

40. Ehrman, *The Apostolic Fathers*, 2.39.

41. See Stökl Ben Ezra, *The Impact of Yom Kippur on Early Christianity*, 157. This motif of binding with the scarlet band represents a curious parallel to the binding of Azazel in *1 Enoch*, in which the demon is bound as a sacrificial animal and thrown into the abyss. Later rabbinic traditions are also cognizant of the binding of the demon. Thus, for example, *Zohar* III.208a reads: "Now when God saw that these fallen angels were seducing the world, He bound them in chains of iron to a mountain of darkness. Uzza He bound at the bottom of the mountain and covered his face with darkness because he struggled and resisted, but Azael, who did not resist, He set by the side of the mountain where a little light penetrated. . . . Now Uzza and Azael used to tell those men who came to them some of the notable things which they knew in former times when they were on high, and to speak about the holy world in which they used to be. Hence Balaam said of himself: 'He saith, which heareth the words of God'—not the voice of God, but those things which he was told by those who had been in the assembly of the Holy King. He went on: 'And knoweth the knowledge of the Most High,' meaning that he knew the hour when punishment impended over the world and could determine it with his enchantments. 'Which seeth the vision of the Almighty': this vision consisted of the 'fallen and the open of eyes,' that is Uzza, who is called 'fallen' because he was placed in the darkest depth, since after falling from heaven he fell a second time, and Azael, who is called 'open of eye' because he was not enveloped in complete darkness." H. Sperling and M. Simon, *The Zohar* (5 vols.; London and New York: Soncino, 1933) 5.312.

42. *Tertullian. Adversus Marcionem* (ed. E. Evans; 2 vols; Oxford, Clarendon Press, 1972) 1.191. Similar testimony appears in *Against the Jews* 14:9: "In fact, thus also let me make an interpretation of the two goats that were offered at the fast. Do these not also show the two conditions of the Christ who is already come? They are indeed of the same age and appearance on

account of the one and the same aspect of the Lord, because he will return in no other form, seeing that he has to be recognized by those from whom he has suffered injury. One of them, however, which was surrounded with scarlet, cursed and spat upon and perforated and punctured, was driven outside the city by the people to ruin, marked with obvious emblems of the suffering of Christ, who, having been surrounded with a scarlet garment, spat upon and knocked about with every physical violence, was crucified outside the city. The other, however, made an offering for offences, and given as food only to the priests of the temple, is marked with the proof of his second manifestation, because when all offences have been done away, the priests of the spiritual temple—that is, the church—were to enjoy as it were a feast of our Lord's grace, while the rest remain without a taste of salvation." G.D. Dunn, *Tertullian* (London: Routledge, 2004) 103.

43. Stökl Ben Ezra, *The Impact of Yom Kippur on Early Christianity,* 158; M. Richard, "Les fragments du commentaire de S. Hippolyte sur les Proverbes de Solomon," *Le Muséon* 79 (1966) 65–94 at 94.

44. Kulik, *Retroverting Slavonic Pseudepigrapha*, 20.

45. Orlov, "The Eschatological Yom Kippur in the *Apocalypse of Abraham*," 98–100.

46. Orlov, "The Eschatological Yom Kippur in the *Apocalypse of Abraham*," 99.

47. For a discussion about whether both goats were decorated with ribbons, see Stemberger, "Yom Kippur in Mishnah Yoma," 126. *B. Yoma* 41b offers a discussion on this subject as well.

48. *m. Yoma* 6:6 reads: "He divided the thread of crimson wool and tied one half to the rock and the other half between its horns, and he pushed it from behind." Danby, *The Mishnah*, 170; *Barnabas* 7 reads: "When this happens, the one who takes the goat leads it into the wilderness and removes the wool, and places it on a blackberry bush, whose buds we are accustomed to eat when we find it in the countryside." Ehrman, *The Apostolic Fathers*, 2.39.

49. *m. Yoma* 6:8: "R. Ishmael says: Had they not another sign also?—a thread of crimson wool was tied to the door of the Sanctuary and when the he-goat reached the wilderness the thread turned white: for it is written, Though your sins be as scarlet they shall be as white as snow." Danby, *The Mishnah,* 170.

50. *m. Shabbat* 9:3: "Whence do we learn that they tie a strip of crimson on the head of the scapegoat? Because it is written, Though your sins be as scarlet they shall be as white as snow." Danby, *The Mishnah,* 108.

51. "The traditional text adds a third solution, not to be found in the best manuscripts Kaufmann and Parma: a crimson thread tied to the door of the sanctuary would turn white as soon as the goat had reached the wilderness, thus fulfilling Isa 1:18: "though your sins are like scarlet, they shall be

like snow; though they are red like crimson, they shall become like wool." Stemberger, "Yom Kippur in Mishnah Yoma," 133.

52. Cf. *b. Yoma* 39a: "Our Rabbis taught: Throughout the forty years that Simeon the Righteous ministered, the lot ['For the Lord'] would always come up in the right hand; from that time on, it would come up now in the right hand, now in the left. And [during the same time] the crimson-colored strap would become white. From that time on it would at times become white, at others not." Epstein, *The Babylonian Talmud. Yoma*, 39a; *b. Yoma* 39b: "Our Rabbis taught: During the last forty years before the destruction of the Temple the lot ['For the Lord'] did not come up in the right hand; nor did the crimson-coloured strap become white." Epstein, *The Babylonian Talmud. Yoma*, 39b.

53. Cf. *b. Yoma* 67a: "But let him tie the whole [thread] to the rock?—Since it is his duty [to complete his work with] the he-goat, perhaps the thread might become fast white, and he would be satisfied. But let him tie the whole thread between its horns?—At times its head [in falling] is bent and he would not pay attention. Our Rabbis taught: In the beginning they would tie the thread of crimson wool on the entrance of the Ulam without: if it became white they rejoiced; if it did not become white, they were sad and ashamed. Thereupon they arranged to tie it to the entrance of the Ulam within. But they were still peeping through and if it became white, they rejoiced, whereas, if it did not become white, they grew sad and ashamed. Thereupon they arranged to tie one half to the rock and the other half between its horns. R. Nahum b. Papa said in the name of R. Eleazar ha-Kappar: Originally they used to tie the thread of crimson wool to the entrance of the Ulam within, and as soon as the he-goat reached the wilderness, it turned white. Then they knew that the commandment concerning it had been fulfilled, as it is said: If your sins be as scarlet, they shall be as white wool." Epstein, *The Babylonian Talmud. Yoma*, 67a.

54. Cf. also *m. Shabbat* 9:3: "Whence do we learn that they tie a strip of crimson on the head of the scapegoat? Because it is written, Though your sins be as scarlet they shall be as white as snow." Danby, *The Mishnah*, 108.

55. Cf. Fletcher-Louis, "Revelation of the Sacral Son of Man," 284; J.A. Emerton, "Binding and Loosing—Forgiving and Retaining," *JTS* 13 (1962) 325–331 at 329–330.

56. Lev 16:21: "[A]nd Aaron shall lay both his hands upon the head of the live goat, and confess over him all the iniquities of the people of Israel, and all their transgressions, all their sins; and he shall put them upon the head of the goat, and send him away into the wilderness by the hand of a man who is in readiness."

57. Milgrom, *Leviticus 1–16*, 1041.

58. Wright, *The Disposal of Impurity: Elimination Rites in the Bible and in Hittite and Mesopotamian Literature*, 17.

59. It is intriguing that in the *Book of Jubilees* the scapegoat imagery is juxtaposed with the clothing metaphors when their authors connect the scapegoat imagery with the symbolism of Joseph's garments. Thus, *Jubilees* 34:12–19 reads: "Jacob's sons slaughtered a he-goat, stained Joseph's clothing by dipping it in its blood, and sent (it) to their father Jacob on the tenth of the seventh month. He mourned all that night because they had brought it to him in the evening. He became feverish through mourning his death and said that a wild animal had eaten Joseph. That day all the people of his household mourned with him. They continued to be distressed and to mourn with him all that day. His sons and daughter set about consoling him, but he was inconsolable for his son. That day Bilhah heard that Joseph had perished. While she was mourning for him, she died. She had been living in Qafratefa. His daughter Dinah, too, died after Joseph had perished. These three (reasons for) mourning came to Israel in one month. They buried Bilhah opposite Rachel's grave, and they buried his daughter Dinah there as well. He continued mourning Joseph for one year and was not comforted but said: 'May I go down to the grave mourning for my son.' For this reason, it has been ordained regarding the Israelites that they should be distressed on the tenth of the seventh month—on the day when (the news) which made (him) lament Joseph reached his father Jacob—in order to make atonement for themselves on it with a kid—on the tenth of the seventh month, once a year—for their sins. For they had saddened their father's (feelings of) affection for his son Joseph. This day has been ordained so that they may be saddened on it for their sins, all their transgressions, and all their errors; so that they may purify themselves on this day once a year." J. VanderKam, *The Book of Jubilees* (2 vols.; CSCO, 510–511; Scriptores Aethiopici, 87–88; Leuven: Peeters, 1989), 2.228–229. With respect to this tradition, see also J.P. Scullion, *A Traditio-historical Study of the Day of Atonement* (Ph.D. diss.; Catholic University of America, 1991) 125–131; C. Carmichael, "The Origin of the Scapegoat Ritual," *VT* 50 (2000) 167–182.

60. Danby, *The Mishnah,* 170.

61. Cf. *b. Yoma* 67b: "And he that letteth go the goat for Azazel shall wash his clothes, i.e., he flings it down headlong and his garments become then unclean." Epstein, *The Babylonian Talmud. Yoma*, 67b.

62. Cf. Lev 16:26: "And he who lets the goat go to Azazel shall wash his clothes and bathe his body in water, and afterward he may come into the camp."

63. For an understanding of the expression "The Lord rebuke you, O Satan" as a cursing formula, see A. Caquot, "גער" in *Theological Dictionary of the Old Testament* (eds. G.J. Botterweck and H. Ringgren, Grand Rapids, MI: Eerdmans, 1979) 3.52.

64. See R. Hanhart, *Sacharja* (BKAT, 14/7; Neukirchen: Neukirchener Verlag, 1990) 166–240; H. Blocher, "Zacharie 3. Josué et le Grand Jour des

Expiations," *ETR* 54 (1979) 264–270; Stökl Ben Ezra, *The Impact of Yom Kippur on Early Christianity*, 80–81.

65. Lev 16:23–24a. See also Stökl Ben Ezra, *The Impact of Yom Kippur on Early Christianity*, 31.

66. *1 Enoch* 10 reads: "And throw on him jagged and sharp stones, and cover him with darkness; and let him stay there forever, and cover his face, that he may not see light, and that on the great day of judgment he may be hurled into the fire." M. Knibb, *The Ethiopic Book of Enoch: A New Edition in the Light of the Aramaic Dead Sea Fragments* (2 vols.; Oxford: Clarendon Press, 1978) 2.87–88. The *Book of Zohar* III.208a conveys a similar tradition about the covering of rebellious angels with darkness; it reads: "Now when God saw that these fallen angels were seducing the world, He bound them in chains of iron to a mountain of darkness. Uzza He bound at the bottom of the mountain and covered his face with darkness because he struggled and resisted, but Azael, who did not resist, He set by the side of the mountain where a little light penetrated." Sperling and Simon, *The Zohar*, 5.312.

67. Grabbe, "The Scapegoat Tradition: A Study in Early Jewish Interpretation," 165–179; Stökl Ben Ezra, "Yom Kippur in the Apocalyptic *Imaginaire* and the Roots of Jesus' High Priesthood," 349–366; idem, *The Impact of Yom Kippur on Early Christianity*, 85–88.

68. The formulae of binding found in *1 Enoch* 10 are also significant since they may be related to the ritual of binding the scapegoat with the band, a procedure that looms large in mishnaic and early Christian accounts of the Yom Kippur ritual.

69. It is possible that even some early Christian authors were already cognizant of such identification. For instance, Daniel Stökl Ben Ezra observes, "Matthew 27:28 changes Mark's term for the red cloak the soldiers put around Jesus, from πορφύρα (purple) to κοκκίνη (scarlet), the equivalent of the biblical שני or the mishnaic הזהורית (לשון) also appearing in *Barnabas* 7. The expression χλαμύς κοκκίνη is an exceptional combination of words appearing only in Matthew 27:28 and its commentaries." D. Stökl Ben Ezra, "Fasting with Jews, Thinking with Scapegoats: Some Remarks on Yom Kippur in Early Judaism and Christianity, in Particular *4Q541*, Barnabas 7, Matthew 27 and Acts 27," *The Day of Atonement. Its Interpretations in Early Jewish and Christian Traditions* (eds. T. Hieke and T. Nicklas; TBN, 18; Leiden: Brill, 2011), 165–188 at 183.

70. Stökl Ben Ezra, *The Impact of Yom Kippur on Early Christianity*, 154.

71. "For then they will see him in that day wearing a long scarlet robe around his flesh, and they will say, 'Is this not the one we once crucified, despising, piercing, and spitting on him?' " Ehrman, *The Apostolic Fathers*, 2.39.

72. Cf. *b. Zebahim* 88b: "R. 'Inyani b. Sason also said: Why are the sections on sacrifices and the priestly vestments close together? To teach you:

as sacrifices make atonement, so do the priestly vestments make atonement. The coat atones for bloodshed, for it is said, And they killed a he-goat, and dipped the coat in the blood." Epstein, *The Babylonian Talmud. Zebahim*, 88b.

73. Stökl Ben Ezra, "The Biblical Yom Kippur, the Jewish Fast of the Day of Atonement and the Church Fathers," 494.

74. *Targum Pseudo-Jonathan* to Lev 16:4: "He shall put on the holy tunic of fine linen, and he shall have breeches of fine linen on his body, he shall gird himself with a sash of fine linen, and he shall bind the turban of fine linen on his head. They are sacred vestments." M. McNamara et al., *Targum Neofiti 1: Leviticus, Targum Pseudo-Jonathan: Leviticus* (ArBib, 3; Collegeville: Liturgical Press, 1994) 166.

75. Exod 39:30–31: "They made the rosette of the holy diadem of pure gold, and wrote on it an inscription, like the engraving of a signet, 'Holy to the Lord.' They tied to it a blue cord, to fasten it on the turban above. . . ."

76. C.N.R. Hayward, *The Jewish Temple: A Non-Biblical Sourcebook* (London: Routledge, 1996) 41–42.

77. P. Alexander, "3 (Hebrew Apocalypse of) Enoch," in *The Old Testament Pseudepigrapha* (2 vols.; ed. J.H. Charlesworth; New York: Doubleday, 1983–1985) 1.223–315 at 265–266.

78. It is interesting that in *b. Yoma* 37a, when the lot of the divine Name is compared with the lot of Azazel, the passage mentions the front-plate of the high priest: "Our Rabbis taught: And Aaron shall cast lots upon the two goats—'lots,' i.e., made of any material. One might have assumed that he should cast two lots on the head of each, therefore [Scripture repeats]: One lot for the Lord and the other lot for Azazel, i.e., there is but one lot 'for the Lord,' and there is but one lot 'for Azazel'—One might have assumed that he shall give upon the head of each a lot each 'for the Lord' and 'for Azazel,' therefore Scripture says: 'One lot for the Lord,' i.e., there is but one lot 'for the Lord' and but one lot 'for Azazel'—Why then does Scripture say: [he shall cast] 'lots'? [That means to say] that they must be alike: he must not make one of gold and the other of silver, one large, the other small; 'lots' [means they may be made] of any material. But that is self-evident?—No, it is necessary [to state that], as it was taught: Since we find that the [high priest's] front-plate had the name of the Lord inscribed thereon and was made of gold, I might have assumed that this too must be made of gold, hence it says [twice] 'lot' . . . 'lot,' to include [permission to make it of] olive-wood, nut-wood or box-wood." Epstein, *The Babylonian Talmud. Yoma*, 37a.

79. Cf. *m. Yoma* 6:2: "He bound a thread of crimson wool on the head of the scapegoat. . . ."; *m. Yoma* 6:6 "He divided the thread of crimson wool and tied one half to the rock and the other half between its horns. . . ."

80. ". . . and wrap a piece of scarlet wool around its head. . . ." Ehrman, *The Apostolic Fathers*, 2.39.

81. Matt, *The Zohar: Pritzker Edition*, 6.240–241.

82. *Targum Neofiti 1, Leviticus; Targum Pseudo-Jonathan, Leviticus*, 169. Hanson argues that "Pseudo-Jonathan is a targum which bears close affinities with 1 Enoch." Hanson, "Rebellion in Heaven, Azazel, and Euhemeristic Heroes in 1 Enoch 6–11," 223.

83. Clothing with curses represents a curious parallel to clothing with the Name found in the traditions about Moses' investiture with the divine Name during his Sinai experience and Jesus' investiture with the divine Name at his baptism. For the detailed discussion of these traditions, see J. Fossum, *The Name of God and the Angel of the Lord: Samaritan and Jewish Mediation Concepts and the Origin of Gnosticism* (WUNT, 36; Tübingen: Mohr/Siebeck, 1985) 76–112.

84. Slav. *неизрекомаго имени моего*. Kulik, *Retroverting the Slavonic Pseudepigrapha*, 17; Rubinkiewicz, *L'Apocalypse d'Abraham en vieux slave*, 128; Philonenko-Sayar and Philonenko, *L'Apocalypse d'Abraham. Introduction, texte slave, traduction et notes*, 58.

85. For Christian reinterpretations of the curse of the scapegoat and its application to the mission of Christ in Gal 3:13–14, see D.R. Schwartz, "Two Pauline Allusions to the Redemptive Mechanism of the Crucifixion," *JBL* 102 (1983) 259–283; Stökl Ben Ezra, "Fasting with Jews, Thinking with Scapegoats: Some Remarks on Yom Kippur in Early Judaism and Christianity, in Particular 4Q541, Barnabas 7, Matthew 27 and Acts 27," 176.

86. Knibb, *The Ethiopic Book of Enoch*, 2.87–88.

87. R.H. Charles, *The Book of Enoch* (Oxford: Clarendon, 1893); D. Dimant, *The Fallen Angels in the Dead Sea Scrolls and the Related Apocrypha and Pseudepigrapha* (Ph.D. diss.; The Hebrew University of Jerusalem, 1974) [Hebrew]; idem, "*1 Enoch* 6–11: A Methodological Perspective," *SBLSP* (1978) 323–339; C.H.T. Fletcher-Louis, "The Aqedah and the Book of Watchers (*1 Enoch* 1–36)," in: *Studies in Jewish Prayer* (eds. R. Hayward and B. Embry; JSSS, 17; Oxford: Oxford University Press, 2005) 1–33 at 24; A. Geiger, "Einige Worte über das Buch Henoch," *JZWL* 3 (1864) 196–204 at 200; Grabbe, "The Scapegoat Tradition: A Study in Early Jewish Interpretation," 165–179; P. Hanson, "Rebellion in Heaven, Azazel, and Euhemeristic Heroes in *1 Enoch 6–11*," *JBL* 96 (1977) 195–233; Helm, "Azazel in Early Jewish Literature," 217–226; G. Nickelsburg, "Apocalyptic and Myth in 1 Enoch 6–11," *JBL* 96 (1977) 383–405; D.C. Olson, "1 Enoch," in: *Eerdmans Commentary on the Bible* (eds. J.D.G. Dunn and J.W. Rogerson; Grand Rapids: Eerdmans, 2003) 904–941 at 910; Rubinkiewicz, *Die Eschatologie von Henoch 9–11 und das Neue Testament*, 88–89; Stökl Ben Ezra, "Yom Kippur in the Apocalyptic Imaginaire and the Roots of Jesus' High Priesthood," 349–366; idem, *The Impact of Yom Kippur on Early Christianity*, 85–88.

88. Concerning the term "Hermon" as a play on the verb חרם—"to ban, or consecrate on oath," see Charles, *The Book of Enoch*, 63; E. Isaac,

"1 (Ethiopic Apocalypse of) Enoch," in *The Old Testament Pseudepigrapha* (2 vols.; ed. J. H. Charlesworth; Garden City, NY: Doubleday, 1983–1985) 1.15, footnote k; R. Adelman, *The Return of the Repressed: Pirqe De-Rabbi Eliezer and the Pseudepigrapha* (JSJSS, 140; Leiden: Brill, 2009) 119; G.W.E. Nickelsburg, *1 Enoch 1: A Commentary on the Book of 1 Enoch: Chapters 1–36; 81–108* (Hermeneia; Fortress, 2001) 177; K.A. Morland, *The Rhetoric of Curse in Galatians: Paul Confronts Another Gospel* (Atlanta: Scholars, 1995) 89. Nickelsburg, for instance, observes that "the mutual anathematizing of the watchers . . . explains the name of the mountain on which it took place (חרמון)." Nickelsburg, *1 Enoch 1*, 177.

89. Knibb, *The Ethiopic Book of Enoch*, 2.67–69.

90. It is also intriguing that in some traditions it is Enoch who binds the Watchers with a curse on Mount Hermon. Regarding this tradition, see J.T. Milik, *The Books of Enoch: Aramaic Fragments of Qumrân Cave 4* (Oxford: Clarendon, 1976) 336–337.

91. Nickelsburg observes that "these verses are tied together by the theme of oath and anathema and the triple occurrence of the pair of verbs denoting these. Having decided to execute the deed, the watchers formalize the conspiracy with an oath that is sealed with sanctions against anyone who reneges. . . . Different from the usual formulation, the oath here does not require some form of abstinence; indeed, it seals the intention for sexual activity. There is perhaps an intended irony in the idea of the watchers binding themselves with a curse. By avoiding that curse (i.e., by carrying out the deed), they fall under the terrible curse of God's eternal punishment. With the taking of the oath, the watchers have agreed to a deliberate act of rebellion against God, and our text has moved far beyond its biblical prototype." Nickelsburg, *1 Enoch 1*, 177.

92. Cf. *1 Enoch* 6:4: "Let us all swear an oath, and bind one another with curses. . . ."; *1 Enoch* 6:5 "Then they all swore together and all bound one another with curses to it."; *1 Enoch* 6:6: "And they called the mountain Hermon, because on it they swore and bound one another with curses." Knibb, *The Ethiopic Book of Enoch*, 2.68–69.

93. Dimant, "1 Enoch 6–11: A Methodological Perspective," 325; A.Y. Reed, *Fallen Angels and the History of Judaism and Christianity: The Reception of Enochic Literature* (Cambridge: Cambridge University Press, 2005) 254.

94. Olson suggests that " 'holy ones' to whom Kasbeel revealed the *Beqa* oath are the very angels who later became the fallen Watchers of *1 Enoch* 6–7." Olson, *Enoch. A New Translation*, 271.

95. Commenting on this portion of the text, George Nickelsburg suggests that Kesbeel "used some sort of cunning to extract from Michael some sort of secret information about the divine name and an oath, which he then passed on to the other rebel angels who transmitted heavenly secrets

to humanity." G.W.E. Nickelsburg and J.C. VanderKam, *1 Enoch 2: A Commentary on the Book of 1 Enoch: Chapters 37–82* (Hermeneia; Minneapolis: Fortress, 2012) 305.

96. Knibb, *The Ethiopic Book of Enoch*, 2.159–164.

97. Olson observes that the angelic list found in *1 Enoch* 69:2 "is simply copied from the one at 6:2, but with many corruptions." Olson, *Enoch. A New Translation*, 126.

98. Nickelsburg sees a connection between the oath of Kesbeel and the oath which was sworn by the fallen angels in *1 Enoch* 6. He suggests that Kesbeel "is the 'chief of the oath' that was sworn by the rebel angels as they conspired to descend to earth (see 6:4–5). Thus in his role as 'chief of the oath' Kesbeel corresponds roughly to Shemihazah in chap. 6." Nickelsburg and VanderKam, *1 Enoch 2*, 306.

99. C. Kaplan, "The Hidden Name," *JSOR* 13 (1929) 181–184. With respect to the oath imagery in *1 Enoch* 69 Olson notes that "it is common place in mystical Judaism that the Name of God is the force which binds and orders all things in creation, and a word that binds is by definition an oath. The idea is certainly old enough to appear in the 'Parables.' " Olson, *Enoch. A New Translation*, 271.

100. See *1 Enoch* 41:5: "And I saw the chambers of the sun and the moon, whence they go out and whither they return, and their glorious return, and how one is more honoured than the other, and their magnificent course, and (how) they do not leave the course, neither adding (anything) to, nor omitting (anything) from, their course, and (how) they keep faith with one another, observing (their) oath." Knibb, *The Ethiopic Book of Enoch*, 2.129.

101. See *Jubilees* 36:7: "Now I will make you swear with the great oath—because there is no oath which is greater than it, by the praiseworthy, illustrious, and great, splendid, marvelous, powerful, and great name which made the heavens and the earth and everything together—that you will continue to fear and worship him. . . ." VanderKam, *The Book of Jubilees*, 2.238.

102. Regarding the association of the demiurgic name with the oath, see S.M. McDonough, *YHWH at Patmos: Rev. 1:4 in Its Hellenistic and Early Jewish Setting* (WUNT, 2.107; Tübingen: Mohr/Siebeck, 1999) 128–130; Fossum, *Name of God*, 257ff.

103. In this respect, it is intriguing that some rabbinic texts describe the process of cursing using the divine Name. One such tradition, for example, can be found in *Mekhilta de-Rabbi Ishmael*, which speaks of cursing using the Tetragrammaton: "[C]urse it means by using the divine name, so also when it says do not curse it means not to curse by using the divine name." *Mekhilta de-Rabbi Ishmael: A Critical Edition on the Basis of the Manuscripts and Early Editions with an English Translation, Introduction and Notes* (2 vols; ed. J.Z. Lauterbach; Philadelphia: The Jewish Publication Society, 2004) 2.388.

Jonathan Ben-Dov notes that ". . . oaths and the great name as elements of creation appear again in later Jewish literature such as Hekhalot and late midrash." J. Ben-Dov, "Exegetical Notes on Cosmology in the Parables of Enoch," in: *Enoch and the Messiah Son of Man: Revisiting the Book of Parables* (ed. G. Boccaccini; Grand Rapids: Eerdmans, 2007) 143–150 at 149.

104. The demiurgic powers of the divine Name are also unfolded in the aforementioned passage from *3 Enoch* 12:1–2: "R. Ishmael said: The angel Metatron, Prince of the Divine Presence, the glory of highest heaven, said to me: Out of the abundant love and great compassion wherewith the Holy One, blessed be he, loved and cherished me more than all the denizens of the heights, he wrote with his finger, as with a pen of flame, upon the crown which was on my head, the letters by which heaven and earth were created; the letters by which seas and rivers were created; the letters by which mountains and hills were created; the letters by which stars and constellations, lightning and wind, thunder and thunderclaps, snow and hail, hurricane and tempest were created; the letters by which all the necessities of the world and all the orders of creation were created. Each letter flashed time after time like lightnings, time after time like torches, time after time like flames, time after time like the rising of the sun, moon, and stars." Alexander, "3 Enoch," 265–266. This demiurgic list is reminiscent to the list given in *1 Enoch* 69. Cf. also *3 Enoch* 41:1–3: "R. Ishmael said: Metatron said to me: Come and I will show you the letters by which heaven and earth were created; the letters by which seas and rivers were created; the letters by which mountains and hills were created; the letters by which trees and grasses were created; the letters by which stars and constellations were created; the letters by which the orb of the moon and the disk of the sun, Orion and the Pleiades, and all the various luminaries of Raqia were created; the letters by which the ministering angels were created; the letters by which the seraphim and the creatures were created; the letters by which the throne of glory and the wheels of the chariot were created; the letters by which the necessities of the world were created; the letters by which wisdom and understanding, knowledge and intelligence, humility and rectitude were created, by which the whole world is sustained. I went with him and he took me by his hand, bore me up on his wings, and showed me those letters, engraved with a pen of flame upon the throne of glory, and sparks and lightnings shoot from them and cover all the chambers of Arabot." Alexander, "3 Enoch," 1.292.

105. Cf. *Gen. Rab.* 12:10: "R. Berekiah said in the name of R. Judah b. R. Simeon: Not with labour or wearying toil did the Holy One, blessed be He, create the world, but: 'By the Word of the Lord, and the heavens were already made.' By means of heh, He created them." *Midrash Rabbah* (eds. H. Freedman and M. Simon; 10 vols; London: Soncino, 1961) 1.95; *Gen. Rab.* 12:10: "R. Abbahu said in R. Johanan's name: He created them with the

letter heh. All letters demand an effort to pronounce them, whereas the heh demands no effort; similarly, not with labour or wearying toil did the Holy One, blessed be He, create His world." Freedman and Simon, *Midrash Rabbah*, 1.95; *Gen. Rab.* 12:10: ". . . with a heh created He them,' it follows that this world was created by means of a heh. Now the heh is closed on all sides and open underneath: that is an indication that all the dead descend into she'ol; its upper hook is an indication that they are destined to ascend thence; the opening at the side is a hint to penitents. The next world was created with a yod: as the yod has a bent [curved] back, so are the wicked: their erectness shall be bent and their faces blackened [with shame] in the Messianic future, as it is written, And the loftiness of man shall be bowed down." Freedman and Simon, *Midrash Rabbah*, 1.95; *b. Men.* 29b: "it refers to the two worlds which the Holy One, blessed be He, created, one with the letter he and the other with the letter yod. Yet I do not know whether the future world was created with the yod and this world with the he or this world with the yod and the future world with the he; but since it is written, These are the generations of the heaven and of the earth when they were created." Epstein, *The Babylonian Talmud. Menahoth*, 29b. Cf. also *3 Enoch* 15B:5 Metatron reveals to Moses the letters of the divine Name which is understood there as an oath: "But Moses said to him, 'Not so! lest I incur guilt.' Metatron said to him, 'Receive the letters of an oath which cannot be broken!' " Alexander, "3 Enoch," 1.304.

106. Concerning these traditions, see Fossum, *The Name of God*, 253–256.

107. In the Palestinian targumic tradition (*Targ. Neof.*, *Frag. Targ.*) the divine command יהי uttered by God during the creation of the world is identified with the Tetragrammaton. For a detailed discussion of this tradition, see Fossum, *The Name of God*, 80. Thus, *Targum Neofiti* reads: "He who spoke, and the world was there from the beginning, and is to say to it: יהי, and it will be there,—He it is who has sent me to you." *Fragmentary Targum* attests to a similar tradition: " 'He who said to the world from the beginning: יהי, and it was there, and is to say to it: יהי, and it will be there.' And He said: Thus you shall say to the Israelites: 'He has sent me to you.' " The connection between the divine command and the divine Name has very ancient roots and is found in the *Prayer of Manasseh* (2nd century BCE–1st century CE), in which the divine "Word of Command" and God's Name are put in parallelism. *Prayer of Manasseh* 1–3 reads: "O Lord, God of our fathers, God of Abraham, Isaac, Jacob, and their righteous offspring; He who made the heaven and the earth with all their beauty; He who bound the sea and established it by the command of his word, He who closed the bottomless pit and sealed it by his powerful and glorious name. . . ." J.H. Charlesworth, "Prayer of Manasseh," in: *The Old Testament Pseudepigrapha* (2 vols.; ed. J. H. Charlesworth; New York: Doubleday, 1983–1985) 2.625–637 at 634. Regarding the same tradition,

see also *Samaritan Liturgy* 445.2: "It was created by a word, [namely, by] יהי; and, in a flash, it was made new."

108. In later Jewish accounts fallen angels are portrayed as bound with the divine Name. Thus, Moshe Idel brings attention to a late 15th century anonymous diary of revelations called the *Book of the Answering Angel*, in which the fallen angels are bound with the divine Name: "I shall come and bind them [i.e. Samael and Ammon No] with iron cables and cords of love [made] of the mighty name [of God] so that they will not be able to move to and fro. . . ." M. Idel, "The Origin of Alchemy According to Zosimos and a Hebrew Parallel," *REJ* 145 (1986) 117–124 at 120.

109. It is also intriguing that in *1 Enoch* 5, immediately before the story of the fallen angels binding themselves with the curses and the oath, the readers of the *Book of the Watchers* hear that the name will be changed into the curse. Thus, *1 Enoch* 5:6 reads: "In those days you will transform your name into an eternal curse to all the righteous, and they will curse you sinners for ever—you together with the sinners." Knibb, *The Ethiopic Book of Enoch*, 2.66.

110. This angelic name שמיחזה is often translated by scholars as "my Name has seen," "the Name sees," or "he sees the Name." Cf. Milik, *The Books of Enoch*, 152; Knibb, *The Ethiopic Book of Enoch*, 2.67–68; S. Uhlig, *Das äthiopische Henochbuch* (JSHRZ, 5.6; Gütersloh: Gütersloher Verlaghaus, 1984) 516; Black, *The Book of Enoch*, 119; Nickelsburg, *1 Enoch 1*, 179; M. Sokoloff, "Notes on the Aramaic Fragments of Enoch from Qumran Cave 4," *Maarav* 1 (1978–1979) 197–224 at 207; D. Olson, *Enoch. A New Translation: The Ethiopic Book of Enoch, or 1 Enoch* (North Richland Hills: Bibal Press, 2004) 32; Wright, *The Origin of Evil Spirits*, 120–121; S. Bhayro, *The Shemihazah and Asael Narrative of 1 Enoch 6–11: Introduction, Text, Translation and Commentary with Reference to Ancient Near Eastern and Biblical Antecedents* (AOAT, 322; Münster: Ugarit-Verlag, 2005) 233–235; idem, "Noah's Library: Sources for 1 Enoch 6:11," *JSP* 15 (2006) 163–177 at 172–177. Scholars often interpret it as a reference to the divine Name. For example, Nickelsburg suggests that "the reference is to the name of 'my' God." Nickelsburg, *1 Enoch 1*, 179. Fossum proposes that "in the original myth, then, Shemyaza, whose name may mean 'He sees the Name' (שמיחזה), can have been described as successful in his attempt at capturing 'the Hidden Name' from Michael." Fossum, *The Name of God*, 258.

111. Cf. G.A. Barton, "The Origin of the Names of Angels and Demons in the Extra-Canonical Apocalyptic Literature to 100 A.D.," *JBL* 31 (1912) 156–167 at 163; Milik, *The Books of Enoch*, 153; Knibb, *The Ethiopic Book of Enoch*, 2.73; Uhlig, *Das äthiopische Henochbuch*, 518; Black, *The Book of Enoch*, 121; Olson, *Enoch. A New Translation*, 32. Nickelsburg also underlines the demiurgic aspect of the angelic name by noting that "this name, which occurs several times in the Hebrew Bible for other persons, designates God's

creative activity. In 8:3, it may refer to the angel's function as fabricator." Nickelsburg, *1 Enoch 1*, 180.

112. Milik notes that "several scholars have conjectured that the roles of two chief angels are paralleled in the model of the Babylonian antediluvian kings and sages; Shemihazah is a king and Asa'el is a sage." See Milik, *The Books of Enoch*, 29. Milik equates these two figures with the human figures Noah (king) and Enoch (sage). Regarding this, see also Wright, *The Origin of Evil Spirits*, 119. This again points to the inverse parallelism of protagonists and antagonists of the apocalyptic accounts noted above.

113. These later rabbinic materials give additional knowledge about the demiurgic powers of the Watchers who are able to refashion radically the earthly realm. *3 Enoch* 5:7–9 reads: "What did the men of Enosh's generation do? They roamed the world from end to end, and each of them amassed silver, gold, precious stones, and pearls in mountainous heaps and piles. In the four quarters of the world they fashioned them into idols, and in each quarter they set up idols about 1,000 parasangs in height. They brought down the sun, the moon, the stars and the constellations and stationed them before the idols, to their right and to their left, to serve them in the way they served the Holy One, blessed be he, as it is written, 'All the array of heaven stood in his presence, to his right and to his left.' How was it that they had the strength to bring them down? It was only because Uzzah, Azzah, and Aza'el taught them sorceries that they brought them down and employed them, for otherwise they would not have been able to bring them down." Alexander, "3 Enoch," 1.260.

114. The Watchers' illicit revelations inversely mirror the Deity's disclosures unveiled to the seventh antediluvian hero.

115. Knibb observes that ". . . it may be noted that in [*1 Enoch*] 8.3 the names of the angels correspond to their functions." Knibb, *The Ethiopic Book of Enoch*, 2.69. Cf. also Wright, *The Origin of Evil Spirits*, 121.

116. The transmission of the illicit knowledge of the divine Name to humans might be hinted at in the *Book of the Similitudes*. Thus, commenting on *1 Enoch* 69:14, George Nickelsburg suggests that Kesbeel "tricked Michael into revealing the secrets of the divine name. Kesbeel, in turn, revealed the name to his angelic colleagues, who used it in the oath that they swore as they conspired to rebel against God. Verse 14 may also imply that they revealed the divine name to humanity ('those who showed the sons of men everything that was in secret')." Nickelsburg and VanderKam, *1 Enoch 2*, 307.

117. Milik, *The Books of Enoch*, 327. The fallen angels traditions found in the *Tafsirs* and other Islamic interpretations convey similar beliefs. For the fallen angels traditions found in the interpretations of Sura 2:96, see B. Heller "La chute des anges: Shemhazai, Ouzza et Azaël," *REJ* 60 (1910) 202–212; E. Littmann, "Harut und Marut," in: *Festschrift Friedrich Carl Andreas* (Leipzig:

Harrassowitz, 1916) 70–87; L. Jung, *Fallen Angels in Jewish, Christian, and Mohammedan Literature* (Philadelphia: Dropsie College for Hebrew and Cognate Learning, 1926) 124–139; P.J. de Menasce, "Une légende indo-iranienne dans l'angélologie judéomusulmane: à propos de Hârût et Mârût," *EA* 1 (1947) 10–18; B.J. Bamberger, *Fallen Angels: Soldiers of Satan's Realm* (Philadelphia: Jewish Publication Society, 1952) 114–117; G. Vajda, "Harut wa-Marut," in: *Encyclopaedia of Islam* (ed. B. Lewis et al.; Leiden: Brill, 1971) 3.236b–237; T. Fahd, "Anges, démons et djinns en Islam," in: *Génies, anges et démons* (SO, 8; Paris: Seuil, 1971) 173–174; J. Reeves, *Jewish Lore in Manichaean Cosmogony: Studies in the Book of Giants Traditions* (Cincinnati: Hebrew Union College Press, 1992) 144–145; F. Abdullaeva, *Персидская кораническая экзегетика: Тексты, переводы, комментарии* (С.-Петербург: Петербургское Востоковедение, 2000); P. Crone, "The Book of the Watchers in the Qur'an," in: *Exchange and Transmission Across Cultural Boundaries: Philosophy, Mysticism and Science in the Mediterranean World* (eds. H. Ben-Shammai, S. Shaked, and S. Stroumsa; Jerusalem: The Israel Academy of Sciences and Humanities, 2013) 16–51.

118. Abdullaeva, *Персидская кораническая экзегетика*, 31.

119. The *Apocalypse of Abraham* defines him as the mediation of "my [God] ineffable name (Slav. неизрекомаго имени моего)." Even apart from this explanation of the guide's spectacular office, the peculiar designation Yahoel (Slav. Иаоиль) in itself reveals unequivocally the angelic creature as the representation of the divine Name. It is no coincidence that in the text, which exhibits similarities with the Deuteronomic *Shem* theology, the angelic guide of the protagonist is introduced as the Angel of the Name. Some studies have noted the formative role of the figure of the Angel of the Name (or the Angel of YHWH) in the conceptual framework of the deuteronomic and deuteronomistic *Shem* ideologies. According to one of the hypotheses, the figure of the Angel of the LORD (or the Angel of the divine Name) found in the Book of Exodus constituted one of the conceptual roots of the *Shem* theology. It is interesting that the aural praxis of the great angel is not confined solely to the imposition of curses on Azazel. In fact, the angel's interaction with all characters of the story takes the form of such aural practices. In this respect, it is not coincidental that the text defines him as the Singer of the Eternal One (*Apoc. Ab.* 12:4). He is exceptional both as a practitioner and as an instructor of this "aural mysticism," conveying the teachings of the praxis to various types of God's creatures, earthly as well as celestial. In *Apoc. Ab.* 10:8–9 he is described as the celestial choirmaster of the *Hayyot:* "I am a power in the midst of the Ineffable who put together his names in me. I am appointed according to his commandment to reconcile the rivalries of the Living Creatures of the Cherubim against one another, and teach those who bear him [to sing] the song in the middle of man's night, at the seventh hour"

(*Apoc. Ab.* 10:8–9). This role can again be compared to the future office of Metatron who often functions in the Hekhalot and *Shi*ᶜ*ur Qomah* accounts as the celestial choirmaster conducting the liturgies of the Living Creatures. Yahoel's expertise in heavenly praise does not seem to be limited to heavenly matters. In the apocalypse he is also depicted as the one who initiates a human visionary, the patriarch Abraham, into this mystical praxis of praising the Deity that serves here as an alternative practice to the vision mysticism.

The Cosmological Temple in the Apocalypse of Abraham

1. With respect to the temple and creation, see: M. Barker, *Creation: A Biblical Vision for the Environment* (London: T&T Clark, 2010) 42–49; G.K. Beale, *The Temple and the Church's Mission: A Biblical Theology of the Dwelling Place of God* (New Studies in Biblical Theology, 17; Downers Grove, IL: Apollos, 2004); U. Cassuto, *A Commentary on the Book of Genesis* (Jerusalem: Magnes, 1989) 122–123; B. Janowski "Die heilige Wohnung des Höchsten. Kosmologische Implikationen der Jerusalemer Tempeltheologie," in: *Gottesstadt und Gottesgarten. Zu Geschichte und Theologie des Jerusalemer Tempels* (eds. O. Keel and E. Zenger; QD, 191; Freiburg: Herder, 2002) 24–68; idem, "Der Tempel als Kosmos—Zur kosmologischen Bedeutung des Tempels in der Umwelt Israels," in: *Egypt—Temple of the Whole World—Ägypten—Tempel der Gesamten Welt. Studies in Honour of Jan Assmann* (ed. S. Meyer; Leiden: Brill, 2003) 163–186; M. Metzger, "Keruben und Palmetten als Dekoration im Jerusalemer Heiligtum und Jahwe, 'der Nahrung gibt allem Fleisch,'" in: *Zion—Ort der Begegnung. FS L. Klein* (ed. F. Hahn; BBB, 90; Bodenheim, 1993) 503–529; S. Schroer, *In Israel gab es Bilder. Nachrichten von darstellender Kunst im Alten Testament* (OBO, 74; Freiburg: Universitätsverlag; Gottingen: Vandenhoeck & Ruprecht, 1987) 47–122; J. Strange "The Idea of Afterlife in Ancient Israel: Some Remarks on the Iconography in Solomon's Temple," *PEQ* 117 (1985) 35–40; J. van Seters, "Solomon's Temple: Fact and Ideology in Biblical and Near Eastern Historiography," *CBQ* 59 (1997) 45–57; H. Weippert, "Die Kesselwagen Salomos," *ZDPV* 108 (1992) 8–41; W. Zwickel, *Der salomonische Tempel* (Kulturgeschichte der antiken Welt, 83; Mainz: Von Zabern, 1999); H. Weippert, "Die Kesselwagen Salomos," *ZDPV* 108 (1992) 8–41.

2. *Apoc. Ab.* 19:1–4: "And a voice came to me out of the midst of the fire, saying, 'Abraham, Abraham!' And I said, 'Here am I!' And he said, 'Look at the levels which are under the expanse on which you are brought and see that on no single level is there any other but the one whom you have searched for or who has loved you.' And while he was still speaking, and behold, the levels opened, and there are the heavens under me. . . ." Kulik, *Retroverting Slavonic Pseudepigrapha*, 24–25.

3. *Apoc. Ab.* 21:1–2: "And he said to me, 'Look now beneath your feet at the expanse and contemplate the creation which was previously covered over. On this level there is the creation and those who inhabit it and the age that has been prepared to follow it.' And I looked beneath the expanse at my feet and I saw the likeness of heaven and what was therein." Kulik, *Retroverting Slavonic Pseudepigrapha*, 26.

4. Kulik, *Retroverting Slavonic Pseudepigrapha*, 26.

5. Janowski, "Der Tempel als Kosmos—Zur kosmologischen Bedeutung des Tempels in der Umwelt Israels," 165–175.

6. Janowski, "Der Tempel als Kosmos—Zur kosmologischen Bedeutung des Tempels in der Umwelt Israels," 175–184.

7. Cf. *Jub.* 8:19: "He knew that the Garden of Eden is the holy of holies and is the residence of the Lord." VanderKam, *The Book of Jubilees*, 2.53. Regarding this tradition, Jacques van Ruiten notes that in *Jubilees*, "[T]he Garden of Eden is seen as a Temple, or, more precisely as a part of the Temple: the room which is in the rear of the Temple, where the ark of the covenant of the Lord is placed, and which is often called 'Holy of Holies.' " J. van Ruiten, "Eden and the Temple: The Rewriting of Genesis 2:4–3:24 in the Book of Jubilees," in: *Paradise Interpreted: Representations of Biblical Paradise in Judaism and Christianity* (ed. G.P. Luttikhuizen; TBN, 2; Leiden: Brill, 1999) 76.

8. Understanding Eden as the temple presupposes the protoplast's role as a sacerdotal servant. Van Ruiten suggests that the author of *Jubilees* sees Adam acting as a prototypical priest who burns incense at the gate of the Garden of Eden. He draws a parallel between this description and a tradition found in Exodus: "[T]he incense is burned in front of the Holy of Holies. The burning of incense is a privilege given to the priests, namely the sons of Aaron." Van Ruiten also calls attention to another important detail related to the function of Adam as priest, namely, the covering of nakedness. He reminds us that covering one's nakedness is a condition for offering since the priests are explicitly bidden to cover their nakedness. The author of *Jubilees* likewise lays emphasis on covering nakedness. Van Ruiten, "Eden and the Temple," 77–78. On sacerdotal Edenic traditions, see also J.R. Davila, "The Hodayot Hymnist and the Four Who Entered Paradise," *RevQ* 17/65-68 (1996) 457–478; F. García Martínez, "Man and Woman: Halakhah Based upon Eden in the Dead Sea Scrolls," in: *Paradise Interpreted: Representations of Biblical Paradise in Judaism and Christianity* (ed. G. Luttikhuizen; TBN, 2; Leiden: Brill, 1999) 95–115 at 112–113; E. Noort, "Gan-Eden in the Context of the Mythology of the Hebrew Bible," in: *Paradise Interpreted: Representations of Biblical Paradise in Judaism and Christianity* (ed. G. Luttikhuizen; TBN, 2; Leiden: Brill, 1999) 25; D.W. Parry, "Garden of Eden: Prototype Sanctuary," in *Temples of the Ancient World: Ritual and Symbolism* (ed. D.W. Parry; Provo: Desecret, 1994) 126–151; J. van Ruiten, "Visions of the Temple in the

Book of Jubilees," in: *Gemeinde ohne Tempel/Community without Temple: Zur Substituierung und Transformation des Jerusalemer Tempels und seines Kults im Alten Testament, antiken Judentum und frühen Christentum* (eds. B. Ego et al.; WUNT, 118; Tübingen: Mohr/Siebeck, 1999) 215–228; G.J. Wenham, "Sanctuary Symbolism in the Garden of Eden Story," in: *Proceedings of the Ninth World Congress of Jewish Studies, Division A: The Period of the Bible* (Jerusalem: World Union of Jewish Studies, 1986) 19–25 at 21–22; M. Wise, "4QFlorilegium and the Temple of Adam," *RevQ* 15/57–58 (1991) 103–132.

9. Beale notes that "Ezekiel 32 explicitly calls Eden the first sanctuary, which substantiates that Eden is described as a temple because it is the first temple, albeit a 'garden-temple.'" Beale, *The Temple and the Church's Mission*, 80. Some scholars argue that Solomon's temple was an intentional replication of the Garden of Eden, especially in its arboreal likeness. For this, see Beale, *The Temple and the Church's Mission*, 72; L.E. Stager, "Jerusalem and the Garden of Eden," in *Festschrift for F.M. Cross* (Eretz Israel, 26; Jerusalem: Israel Exploration Society, 1999) 183–193; idem, "Jerusalem as Eden," *BAR* 26 (2000) 36–47.

10. Kulik, *Retroverting Slavonic Pseudepigrapha*, 26.

11. ". . . His offering was one silver dish, etc. The dish was in allusion to the court which encompassed the Tabernacle as the sea encompasses the world." Freedman and Simon, *Midrash Rabbah*, 6.546. Concerning a similar tradition in *Midrash Tadshe*, see G. MacRae, *Some Elements of Jewish Apocalyptic and Mystical Tradition and Their Relation to Gnostic Literature* (2 vols.; Ph.D. diss.; University of Cambridge, 1966) 55.

12. ". . . The reference is to the building of Herod. Of what did he build it?—Rabbah replied, Of yellow and white marble. Some there are who say, With yellow, blue and white marble. The building rose in tiers in order to provide a hold for the plaster. He intended at first to overlay it with gold, but the Rabbis told him, Leave it alone for it is more beautiful as it is, since it has the appearance of the waves of the sea." Epstein, *The Babylonian Talmud. Sukkah* 51b.

13. 1 Kgs 7:23–25 reads: "Then he made the molten sea; it was round, ten cubits from brim to brim, and five cubits high, and a line of thirty cubits measured its circumference. Under its brim were gourds, for thirty cubits, compassing the sea round about; the gourds were in two rows, cast with it when it was cast. It stood upon twelve oxen, three facing north, three facing west, three facing south, and three facing east; the sea was set upon them, and all their hinder parts were inward" (NRSV). See also 2 Kgs 16:17; 2 Kgs 25:13; 1 Chr 18:8; 2 Chr 4:2; Jer 52:17.

14. Elizabeth Bloch-Smith observes that "the exaggerated size of the structures of the Solomonic Temple courtyard would suggest that they were not intended for human use, but belonged to the realm of the divine." E.

Bloch-Smith "'Who is the King of Glory?' Solomon's Temple and Its Symbolism," in: *Scripture and Other Artifacts. Essays on the Bible and Archeology in Honor of Philip J. King* (eds. M. Coogan et al; Louisville: Westminster, 1994) 19–31 at 21.

15. Bloch-Smith "'Who is the King of Glory?' Solomon's Temple and Its Symbolism," 20. See also C.L. Meyers, "Sea, Molten," in *Anchor Bible Dictionary* (ed. D.N. Freedman; New York: Doubleday, 1992) 5.1061–1062.

16. V. Hurowitz, "Inside Solomon's Temple," *Bible Review* 10:2 (1994) 24–36.

17. *Apoc. Ab.*21:5: "I saw there the rivers and their overflows, and their circles;" Ezek 47:1: "water was flowing from below the threshold of the temple."

18. Regarding this biblical passage, Wenham observes that "the brief account of the geography of the garden in 2:10–14 also makes many links with later sanctuary design. 'A river flows out of Eden to water the garden' . . . Ps 46:5 speaks of 'a river whose streams make glad the city of God' and Ezekiel 47 describes a great river flowing out of the new Jerusalem temple to sweeten the Dead Sea." Wenham, "Sanctuary Symbolism in the Garden of Eden Story," 22.

19. "A river flows out of Eden to water the garden, and from there it divides and becomes four branches" (NRSV). Regarding the rivers of paradise, see also *2 Enoch* 8; *1QH 14* and 16.

20. Beale, *The Temple and the Church's Mission*, 72.

21. "They feast on the abundance of your house, and you give them drink from the river of your delights. For with you is the fountain of life; in your light we see light" (NRSV).

22. Beale, *The Temple and the Church's Mission*, 74.

23. "There is an uninterrupted supply not only of water, just as if there were a plentiful spring rising naturally from within, but also of indescribably wonderful underground reservoirs, which within a radius of five stades from the foundation of the Temple revealed innumerable channels for each of them, the streams joining together on each side. All these were covered with lead down to the foundation of the wall; on top of them a thick layer of pitch, all done very effectively. There were many mouths at the base, which were completely invisible except for those responsible for the ministry, so that the large amounts of blood which collected from the sacrifices were all cleansed by the downward pressure and momentum. Being personally convinced, I will describe the building plan of the reservoirs just as I understood it. They conducted me more than four stades outside the city, and told me to bend down at a certain spot and listen to the noise at the meeting of the waters. The result was that the size of the conduits became clear to me, as has been demonstrated." R.J.H. Shutt, "Letter of Aristeas," *The Old Testament*

Pseudepigrapha (2 vols.; ed. J. H. Charlesworth; New York: Doubleday, 1983–1985) 2.7–34 at 18–19.

24. A similar image of the overflowing water surrounding the Temple courtyard is found also in *Joseph and Aseneth* 2:17–20: "And there was in the court, on the right hand, a spring of abundant living water. . . ." Scholars have noted that "detailed description of [Aseneth's] garden clearly echoes Ezekiel's account of what he saw in his celebrated temple-vision (Ezek. 40–8)." G. Bohak, *Joseph and Aseneth and the Jewish Temple in Heliopolis* (Atlanta: Scholars, 1996) 68.

25. "Then the angel showed me the river of the water of life, bright as crystal, flowing from the throne of God and of the Lamb through the middle of the street of the city" (NRSV).

26. The motif of resting is also noteworthy. Rest imagery is often laden with sacerdotal connotations. Some studies point, more specifically, to a connection between the motif of rest and temple imagery. With respect to this connection, see Beale, *The Temple and the Church's Mission*, 60–62; J.H. Walton, *Genesis* (NIVAC, Grand Rapids: Zondervan, 2001) 149–155; M. Weinfeld, "Sabbath, Temple and the Enthronement of the Lord—The Problem of the Sitz im Leben of Genesis 1:1–2:3," in: *Mélanges bibliques et orientaux en l'honneur de M. Henri Cazelles* (eds. A. Caquot and M. Delcor; Kevelaer: Butzon & Bercker, 1981) 501–512 at 501–502.

27. Such a peculiar constellation of subjects—turbulent rivers, trees, and paradisal imagery—is also found in the Leviathan passage from *Zohar* II.34a-b: "This verse has been established, but *God created the sea serpents*—as we have established: This is Leviathan and his mate. *Tanninim, Sea serpents*—spelled deficiently, because the blessed Holy One slew the female, preserving her for the righteous, as has been established. *The great sea serpent* (Ezek 29:3)—there are nine rivers in which he sprawls, and one river whose waters are calm, into which pour blessings of the waters of the Garden three times a year. When twice, that river is blessed, but not greatly; when once, not so. The sea serpent enters that river, gathering strength, swimming along—entering the sea, swallowing fish of many kinds, gaining dominion, and returning to that river. These nine rivers flow and rise, banked by numerous trees and grasses of various kinds." Matt, *The Zohar: Pritzker Edition*, 4.150–1.

28. Concerning this, see Beale, *The Temple and the Church's Mission*, 78.

29. With respect to the *Apocalypse of Abraham*'s use of the Ezekelian traditions, see: Rubinkiewicz, "Apocalypse of Abraham," 685.

30. Patai, *Man and Temple in Ancient Jewish Myth and Ritual*, 108–109.

31. Regarding the tripartite structure of the entire creation in the Jewish tradition, see L.J. Stadelman, *The Hebrew Conception of the World—A Philological and Literary Study* (Rome: Biblical Institute, 1970) 9.

32. *Josephus* (10 vols.; LCL; trs. H. S. J. Thackeray and R. Markus; Cambridge: Harvard University Press, 1926–65) 4.373–375.

33. Thackeray and Markus, *Josephus*, 4.403.

34. *De Specialibus Legibus* 1.66 reads: "The highest, and in the truest sense the holy, temple of God is, as we must believe, the whole universe, having for its sanctuary the most sacred part of all existence, even heaven. . . ." *Philo* (10 vols.; LCL; trs. F.H. Colson and G.H. Whitaker; Cambridge, Massachusetts: Harvard University Press, 1929–1964) 7.137. *Zohar* II.149a conveys a similar tradition: "Said R. Isaac: 'We are aware that the structure of the Tabernacle corresponds to the structure of heaven and earth.'" Sperling and Simon, *The Zohar*, 4.22. Cf. also *Zohar* II.231a: "Now, the Tabernacle below was likewise made after the pattern of the supernal Tabernacle in all its details. For the Tabernacle in all its works embraced all the works and achievements of the upper world and the lower, whereby the Shechinah was made to abide in the world, both in the higher spheres and the lower. Similarly, the Lower Paradise is made after the pattern of the Upper Paradise, and the latter contains all the varieties of forms and images to be found in the former. Hence the work of the Tabernacle, and that of heaven and earth, come under one and the same mystery." Sperling and Simon, *The Zohar*, 4.289; *Zohar* II.235b: "Now, the lower and earthly Tabernacle was the counterpart of the upper Tabernacle, whilst the latter in its turn is the counterpart of a higher Tabernacle, the most high of all. All of them, however, are implied within each other and form one complete whole, as it says: 'that the tabernacle may be one whole' (Ex. XXVI, 6). The Tabernacle was erected by Moses, he alone being allowed to raise it up, as only a husband may raise up his wife. With the erection of the lower Tabernacle there was erected another Tabernacle on high. This is indicated in the words 'the tabernacle was reared up (*hukam*)' (Ex. XL, 17), reared up, that is, by the hand of no man, but as out of the supernal undisclosed mystery in response to the mystical force indwelling in Moses that it might be perfected with him." Sperling and Simon, *The Zohar*, 4.303.

35. M. Weinfeld, "Sabbath, Temple and the Enthronement of the Lord—The Problem of the Sitz im Leben of Genesis 1:1–2:3," 503. See also S.E. Balentine, *The Torah's Vision of Worship* (Minneapolis: Fortress Press, 1999) 67–68; Beale, *The Temple and the Church's Mission*, 60–61; M. Buber, *Die Schrift und ihre Verdeutschung* (Berlin: Schocken, 1936) 39ff; M. Fishbane, *Text and Texture* (New York: Schocken, 1979) 12; P. J. Kearney, "Creation and Liturgy: The P Redaction of Ex 25–40," *Zeitschrift für die alttestamentliche Wissenschaft* 89.3 (1977) 375–378 at 375; J. D. Levenson, *Sinai and Zion: An Entry into the Jewish Bible* (Minneapolis: Winston Press, 1985) 143; idem, *Creation and the Persistence of Evil: The Jewish Drama of Divine Omnipotence* (San Francisco: Harper & Row, 1988) 85–86; Walton, *Genesis*, 149; Wenham, "Sanctuary Symbolism in the Garden of Eden Story," 19–25.

36. Concerning the *Pargod* traditions, see: Alexander, "3 Enoch," 1.296; D. Arbel, *Beholders of Divine Secrets: Mysticism and Myth in the Hekhalot and Merkavah Literature* (Albany: SUNY Press, 2003) 39, 100; H. Bietenhard, *Die*

himmlische Welt im Urchristentum und Spätjudentum (WUNT, 2; Tübingen: Mohr/Siebeck, 1951) 73ff.; F.T. Fallon, *The Enthronment of Sabaoth* (NHMS, 10; Leiden: Brill, 1978) 55; D. Halperin, *The Merkabah in Rabbinic Literature* (New Haven, American Oriental Society, 1980) 169, note 99; O. Hofius, *Der Vorhang vor dem Thron Gottes* (WUNT, 14; Tübingen: Mohr/Siebeck, 1972) 17ff.; MacRae, *Some Elements of Jewish Apocalyptic and Mystical Tradition and Their Relation to Gnostic Literature*, 1.49–78; C.R.A. Morray-Jones, *A Transparent Illusion: The Dangerous Vision of Water in Hekhalot Mysticism: A Source-critical and Tradition-historical Inquiry* (JSJSS, 59; Leiden: Brill, 2002) 164ff; H. Odeberg, *3 Enoch or the Hebrew Book of Enoch* (New York: KTAV, 1973) 141; C. Rowland and C. Morray-Jones, *The Mystery of God: Early Jewish Mysticism and the New Testament* (CRINT, 12; Leiden: Brill, 2009) 372; S. Shaked, *Dualism in Transformation: Varieties of Religion in Sasanian Iran* (London: School of Oriental and African Studies, 1994) 5.

37. Cf. M.E. Stone, "Apocalyptic Literature," in: *Jewish Writings of the Second Temple Period: Apocrypha, Pseudepigrapha, Qumran Sectarian Writings, Philo, Josephus* (ed. M.E. Stone; CRINT, 2.2; Assen: Van Gorcum, 1984) 417, n. 190. B. Philonenko-Sayar and M. Philonenko, "Apocalypse d'Abraham," in *La Bible. Écrits intertestamentaires* (eds. A. Dupont-Sommer et al.; La Bibliothèque de la Pléiade; Paris, 1987) 1691–1730, esp. 1720, n. 9.

38. The disclosure of the curtain to R. Ishmael in *3 Enoch* is not a unique rabbinic tradition. Other rabbinic materials make reference to visionaries who were privileged to behold the *Pargod*. According to the Babylonian Talmud and the *Book of Zohar*, the protoplast was the first human being who received a vision of every generation and its leaders. *B. Sanh.* 38b reads: "And that is what Resh Lakish meant when he said: What is the meaning of the verse, This is the book of the generations of Adam? It is to intimate that the Holy One, blessed be He, showed him [Adam] every generation and its thinkers, every generation and its sages. When he came to the generation of Rabbi Akiba, he [Adam] rejoiced at his learning but was grieved at his death, and said: How weighty are Thy friends to me, O God." Epstein, *The Babylonian Talmud. Sanhedrin* 38b. In the *Alphabet of R. Akiba,* the famous tanna receives the revelation of the future sages of Israel on the curtain. Cf. A. Jellinek, *Beth ha-Midrash* (6 vols.; Jerusalem: Wahrmann, 1967) 3.44.

39. For the *Pargod* traditions in rabbinic literature, see also; *b. Yoma* 77a; *b. Ber.* 18b; *b. Hag.* 15a-b; *b. Sanh.* 89b; *b. Sotah* 49a; *Pirke de Rabbi Eliezer* 4:6; *Zohar* I.47a; II.149b–150a; *Maseket Hekhalot* 7. According to *b. Sanh.* 38b. a similar vision was given to Adam when the first human was shown every generation and its most stellar man. Odeberg compares this tradition to the revelation of the *Pargod* to R. Ishmael. See H. Odeberg, *3 Enoch or the Hebrew Book of Enoch* (New York: KTAV, 1973) 141

40. *3 Enoch* 45:1–6 reads: "R. Ishmael said: Metatron said to me: Come and I will show you the curtain of the Omnipresent One, which is spread

before the Holy One, blessed be he, and on which are printed all the generations of the world and all their deeds, whether done or to be done, till the last generation. I went and he showed them to me with his fingers, like father teaching his son the letters of the Torah; and I saw: each generation and its potentates; each generation and its heads; each generation and its shepherds; each generation and its keepers. . . . And I saw: Adam and his generation, their deeds and their thoughts . . . The Messiah the son of Joseph and his generation, and all that they will do to the gentiles. . . ." Alexander, "3 Enoch," 1.296–299. Jewish mystical lore attempts to explicate how the omniscient historical and physical reality can be constantly present before the eyes of the creator. In *Zohar* I.90b–91b, this tradition takes the following form: "Come and see: Rabbi Shim'on said, '*This is the book of the generations of Adam* (Genesis 5:1). Was there really a book? Rather they have established that the blessed Holy One showed Adam every generation with its expounders. . . . 'How did He reveal them? You might say he saw through the Holy Spirit that they were destined to enter the world, like someone forseeing the future through wisdom. Not so! Rather he saw them all with his very eyes, witnessing the image in which all were destined to abide in the world. How could that be? Because since the day the world was created, all those souls destined to abide in human beings stand in the presence of the blessed Holy One in the actual image they are destined to assume in the world. Similarly, after all the righteous depart from this world, their souls all ascend; and the blessed Holy One prepares for them another image in which to be clothed, resembling how they were in this world. So they all stand in His presence, and Adam saw them with his own eyes. . . . When the blessed Holy One showed Adam all those generations of the world, he saw each and every one, each and every generation standing in the Garden of Eden in the image they were destined to assume in this world." Matt, *The Zohar: Pritzker Edition*, 2.71–75. As we can see, the revelation to Adam has very similar content as the revelation given to R. Ishmael in *Sefer Hekhalot*. The first human too sees each generation and "its students."

41. Thackeray and Markus, *Josephus*, 3.265.

42. Thackeray and Markus, *Josephus*, 5.405.

43. Kulik, *Retroverting Slavonic Pseudepigrapha*, 26.

44. Philonenko-Sayar and Philonenko, *L'Apocalypse d'Abraham. Introduction, texte slave, traduction et notes*, 84. The Slavonic term простертие can mean "spreading." It is reminiscent of the already-mentioned passage from *3 Enoch* 45 in which the heavenly curtain is spread before the Deity: "which is spread before the Holy One." The other Slavonic term used for the description of the medium of revelation is образование or образ—an image, a picture.

45. MacRae makes an important distinction between the two orientations of celestial veil. In his opinion, "two types of veil emerge: the Wilon or curtain dividing heaven from earth (or noetic world from sense-perceptible),

and the *Pargod* or curtain before the divine throne in heaven." MacRae, *Some Elements of Jewish Apocalyptic and Mystical Tradition and Their Relation to Gnostic Literature*, 68.

46. The term is derived from Lat. *velum*. Alexander, "3 Enoch," 1.269.

47. MacRae, *Some Elements of Jewish Apocalyptic and Mystical Tradition and Their Relation to Gnostic Literature*, 49.

48. Epstein, *The Babylonian Talmud. Hagiga* 12b.

49. Sometimes all the firmaments are understood as "curtains." *Zohar* II.164b speaks of the following tradition: "Rabbi Ḥiyya opened, *Wrapped in light as in a garment, spreading the heavens like a curtain* (Psalms 104:2). This verse has been established, for when the blessed Holy One created the world, He enwrapped Himself in that primordial light, and with it created the heavens. Come and see: Light and dark were as one, light on the right, darkness on the left. What did the blessed Holy One do? He combined them and from the created the heavens. What is *shamayim*, heavens? *Esh*, fire, and *mayim*, water. They were joined as one, and from them He created *shamayim*, heavens, making peace between them. When they were combined as one, He stretched them *like a curtain*, stretching them and making them into a letter *vav*, and this is called *a curtain*. *Curtains* (Exodus 26:1)—for look, from this letter spread a radiancc, becoming *curtains*! Seven expanses are stretched, concealed in a supernal treasury, as has been established, with one expanse lying above them. That expanse has no color, has no revealed place to be contemplated, though it is susceptible to discernment. This expanse is concealed and illumines all of them, impelling them on their journeys, every single one fittingly. From this expanse and beyond, no one can know or perceive, and one should shut his mouth, neither speaking nor contemplating in discernment. Whoever contemplates recoils, for no one can know. There are *ten curtains*, which are ten expanses. And who are they? The curtains of the Dwelling, which are ten and are susceptible to knowing by the wise of heart." Matt, *The Zohar: Pritzker Edition*, 5.451–453. Cf. *Zohar* II.209a: "However, here one should contemplate, for there are *heavens*, and then there are *heavens*! Heavens below and earth beneath them; heavens above and earth beneath them. All rungs, higher and lower, correspond to this pattern, these resembling those. Heavens below are *ten curtains*, as is said: *Spreading the heavens like a curtain* (Psalms 104:2)" Matt, *The Zohar: Pritzker Edition*, 6.192.

50. Cf. MacRae, *Some Elements of Jewish Apocalyptic and Mystical Tradition and Their Relation to Gnostic Literature*, 50. Philip Alexander observes, "It would seem, then, that the first heaven is regarded as a sort of veil or curtain which either conceals the heavenly world from human eyes, or which, by being opened and shut, is the cause of daylight and darkness." Alexander, "3 Enoch," 1.269.

51. Hofius, *Der Vorhang vor dem Thron Gottes*, 21.

52. Regarding similar traditions about Wilon in *Midrash Konen* and other rabbinic materials, see Hofius, *Der Vorhang vor dem Thron Gottes*, 20–21; MacRae, *Some Elements of Jewish Apocalyptic and Mystical Tradition and Their Relation to Gnostic Literature*, 50.

53. Kulik, *Retroverting Slavonic Pseudepigrapha*, 26; Philonenko-Sayar and Philonenko, *L'Apocalypse d'Abraham. Introduction, texte slave, traduction et notes*, 82–84. With respect to this passage William Whitney rightly observes that "Abraham remains in the seventh heaven and gazes down through the successive veils of the heavenly firmaments." K.W. Whitney, Jr., *Two Strange Beasts: Leviathan and Behemoth in Second Temple and Early Rabbinic Judaism* (HSM, 63; Winona Lake, Ind.: Eisenbrauns, 2006) 68.

54. *Midrash Bereshit Rabbati* (ed. Ch. Albeck; Jerusalem: Mekitse Nirdamim, 1940) 32.

55. Freedman and Simon, *Midrash Rabbah*, 5.483.

56. Matt, *The Zohar: Pritzker Edition*, 1.202. Christian interpreters were also cognizant of the tradition of firmament as a sacred veil. In his *Christian Topography* 2:35, Cosmas Indicopleustes writes about the following tradition: "Now the divine Apostle in the epistle to the Hebrews, in explaining the inner Tabernacle, or that which was within the veil, declares that it was a pattern of the heavenly—that is, of the kingdom of the heavens or the future state, taking the veil which divides the one Tabernacle into two for the firmament; just as the firmament placed in the middle, between the heaven and the earth. . . ." *The Christian Topography of Cosmas, an Egyptian Monk. Translated from the Greek, and Edited with Notes and Introduction* (ed. J.W. McCrindle; Cambridge: Cambridge University Press, 2010) 42–43.

57. *Nag Hammadi Codex II, 2-7* (2 vols.; eds. B. Layton et al.; NHS, 20; Leiden: Brill, 1989) 1.253

58. *Nag Hammadi Codex II, 2-7*, 1.255.

59. *Nag Hammadi Codex II, 2-7*, 2.31.

60. These lower "sacerdotal" chambers also contain some cultic settings including the aforementioned theophany of Azazel.

61. Concerning the concept of the Foundation Stone, see L. Ginzberg, *Legends of the Jews* (7 vols.; Baltimore: The John Hopkins University Press, 1998) 5.15; E. Burrows, "Some Cosmological Patterns in Babylonian Religion," in: *The Labyrinth* (ed. S.H. Hooke; London: SPCK; New York: Macmillan, 1935) 45–70; Patai, *Man and Temple in Ancient Jewish Myth and Ritual*, 54–58; P. Schäfer, "Tempel und Schöpfung. Zur Interpretation einiger Heiligtumstraditionen in der rabbinischen Literatur," *Studien zur Geschichte und Theologie des rabbinischen Judentums* (AGJU, 15; Leiden: Brill, 1978) 122–133; Fossum, *The Name of God*, 250ff.; J. D. Levenson, *Sinai and Zion: An Entry into the Jewish Bible* (San Francisco: Harper & Row, 1985) 133ff; Fletcher-Louis, "The Revelation of the Sacral Son of Man," 272ff.

62. Scholars note that the sealing of the abyss with the Foundation Stone can be traced to the Mesopotamian traditions. See Burrows, "Some Cosmological Patterns in Babylonian Religion," 55; Fossum, *The Name of God*, 250.

63. Thus, the *Book of Zohar* I.231a depicts the Foundation Stone as cosmological foundation: "The world was not created until He took a certain stone—a stone called *even shetiyyah*, Foundation Stone. The blessed Holy One took it and cast it into the abyss, and it became lodged from above to below. . . . It is the central point of the whole world, and on this point stands the Holy of Holies, as is written: *or who laid her cornerstone?* (Job 38:6). *Her cornerstone*—as is written: *a tested stone, precious cornerstone* (Isaiah 28:16), and similarly: *It has become the cornerstone* (Psalms 118:22). Come and see: This stone was created from water, fire, and air, crystallizing from them all, becoming a single stone. That stone stands over the abyss; sometimes waters flow from it, filling the abyss. This stone stands as a sign in the middle of the world." Matt, *The Zohar: Pritzker Edition*, 3.396–397. See also *y. Yoma* 5:4: "Rebbi Johanan said, why is it called Foundation Stone? Because on it the world is based. Rebbi Hiyya stated: Why is it called Foundation Stone? Because on it the world is based." *The Jerusalem Talmud. Tractates Pesahim and Yoma. Edition, Translation and Commentary* (ed. H.W. Guggenheimer; SJ, 74; Berlin: De Gruyter, 2013) 525; *Numbers Rabbah* 12:4: ". . . the building of the world commenced from the spot on which the Temple was to stand. R. Jose b. Ilalafta said: Why was it called Foundation Stone? Because thereon began the foundation of the world." Freedman and Simon, *Midrash Rabbah*, 5.457.

64. Cf. *Zohar* I.72a: "Rabbi Yehudah opened, saying, 'This stone that I have set up as a pillar will become the house of God (Genesis 28:22). This is the Foundation Stone, upon which the world was planted, upon which the Temple was built.'" Matt, *The Zohar: Pritzker Edition*, 1.424.

65. The shorter recension of *2 Enoch* 25 reads: "And I commanded the lowest things: 'Let one of the invisible things come out visibly!' And Adail descended, extremely large. And I looked at him, and, behold, in his belly he had a great age. And I said to him, 'Disintegrate yourself, Adail, and let what is disintegrated from you become visible.' And he disintegrated himself, and there came out from him the great age. And thus it carried all the creation which I had wished to create. And I saw how good it was. And I placed for myself a throne, and I sat down on it." F. Andersen, "2 (Slavonic Apocalypse of) Enoch," *The Old Testament Pseudepigrapha* (2 vols.; ed. J.H. Charlesworth; New York: Doubleday, 1983–1985) 1.145.

66. Cf. *Zohar* I.71b: "'Above the expanse over their heads—an appearance of sapphire stone' (Ezek 1.26). This is the Foundation Stone, centric point of the entire universe, upon which stands the Holy of Holies." Matt, *The Zohar: Pritzker Edition*, 1.423

67. Danby, *The Mishnah*, 167. Cf. also *Leviticus Rabbah* 20:4: "After the disappearance of the ark there was a foundation stone in its place. Why was it so called? R. Jose son of R. Halafta said it was because from it the foundation of the world was constructed." Freedman and Simon, *Midrash Rabbah*, 4.256.

68. Charlesworth, "Prayer of Manasseh," 634.

69. Cf. also *Targ.* Eccl. 3.11.

70. *b. Sukkoth* 53b; *b. Makkoth* 11a; *y. Sanhedrin* 29a.

71. Regarding this, see Fossum, *The Name of God*, 250.

72. *Targum Pseudo-Jonathan* to Exod 28:30 speaks of the rock of foundation with which God sealed the mouth of the great abyss in the beginning.

73. M.A. Fishbane, *Biblical Myth and Rabbinic Mythmaking* (Oxford: Oxford University Press, 2003) 210.

74. This function of the monster is widely recognized by scholars. William Whitney, for instance, observes that "in *Apoc. Ab.* 10:8–12 the place of Leviathan as the cosmic axis is more closely defined. There, though he lies at the foundation of the world, he also resides above the underworld." Whitney, *Two Strange Beasts*, 123. Leviathan's function is also affirmed in later Jewish lore; Whitney notes that in the *Midrash on the Length of the World*, Leviathan is envisioned as the foundation of the world. Whitney, *Two Strange Beasts*, 115–116.

75. Thus, Yehuda Liebes reflects on rabbinic understanding of the fin of Leviathan as the foundation of the world. He notes that in *Zohar* II.34a-b the fin of the Leviathan is construed as the cosmological pillar, similar to R. Simeon. Y. Liebes, *Studies in the Zohar* (trs. A. Schwartz et al.; Albany: SUNY Press, 1993) 72. In *Pirke de Rabbi Eliezer* 9 the whole world is supported by the fins of Leviathan: ". . . the Leviathan, the flying serpent, and its dwelling is in the lowest waters; and between its fins rests the middle bar of the earth." *Pirke de Rabbi Eliezer* (ed. G. Friedlander; 2nd ed.; New York: Hermon Press, 1965) 63–64.

76. *1 Enoch* 60:7 portrays Leviathan above springs of water.

77. *Pesikta Rabbati* 48:3 reads: "I intended Leviathan to be sustenance for thee in the time-to-come. But if it were necessary for thee to feed him, thou wouldst be unable to provide for him. So huge is he, our Masters taught, that were he not lying upon the deep and pressing down upon it, the deep would come up and destroy the world by flooding it." Braude, *Pesikta Rabbati*, 2. 824.

78. M.A. Fishbane, *Biblical Myth and Rabbinic Mythmaking* (Oxford: Oxford University Press, 2003) 208. Some Jewish texts depict Leviathan swallowing the chaotic waters, a tradition found in *3 Baruch* 4. Cf. also *b. Baba Bathra* 74b: "Rab Judah further stated in the name of Rab: The Jordan issues from the cavern of Paneas. It has been taught likewise: The Jordan issues from the cavern of Paneas and passes through the Lake of Sibkay and the Lake

of Tiberias and rolls down into the great sea from whence it rolls on until it rushes into the mouth of Leviathan; for it is said: He is confident because the Jordan rushes forth to his mouth." With respect to this tradition, see Whitney, *Two Strange Beasts*, 112–113; A. Kulik, "The Mysteries of Behemoth and Leviathan and the Celestial Bestiary of 3 Baruch," *Le Muséon* 122 (2009) 291–329 at 306–309. Alexander Kulik notes that "regulating the world water system by swallowing superfluous waters is known as a function of primeval sea monsters." Kulik, "The Mysteries of Behemoth and Leviathan," 307.

79. Thus, in relation to the Foundation Stone, Fishbane observes that "the image conveys the sense that the stone serves as a plug against its upsurge. . . ." Fishbane, *Biblical Myth and Rabbinic Mythmaking*, 126–127.

80. Fishbane, *Biblical Myth and Rabbinic Mythmaking*, 210.

81. Whitney, *Two Strange Beasts*, 117.

82. *Zohar* II.222a: "When the Holy One, blessed be He, was about to create the world, He detached one precious stone from underneath his throne of Glory and plunged it into the Abyss, one end of it remaining fastened therein whilst the other end stood out above; and this other and superior head constituted the nucleus of the world, the point out of which the world started, spreading itself to right and left and into all directions, and by which it is sustained. That nucleus, that stone, is called *shethyiah* (foundation), as it was the starting-point of the world. The name *shethyiah*, furthermore, is a compound of *shath* (founded) and *Yah* (God), signifying that the Holy One, blessed be He, made it the foundation and starting-point of the world and all that is therein." Sperling and Simon, *The Zohar*, 4.258–259.

83. *1 Enoch* 60:9: "And I asked that other angel to show me the power of those monsters, how they were separated on one day and thrown, one into the depths of the sea, and the other on to the dry ground of the desert." Knibb, *The Ethiopic Book of Enoch*, 2.144.

84. *Apoc. Ab.* 10:9–10: "I am appointed according to his commandment to reconcile the rivalries of the Living Creatures of the Cherubim against one another, and teach those who bear him [to sing] the Song in the middle of man's night, at the seventh hour. I am made in order to rule over the Leviathans, since the attack and the threat of every reptile are subjugated to me." Kulik, *Retroverting Slavonic Pseudepigrapha*, 18. The parallelism between angels and monsters might also be reflected in *Zohar* II.20a: "All were created in one moment. And He made this world corresponding to the world above, and everything which is above has its counterpart here below, and everything here below has its counterpart in the sea; and yet all constitute a unity. He created angels in the upper worlds, human beings in this world, and the Leviathan in the sea."

85. The pairing of the Leviathans and the Chariot is also found in *Midrash Rabbah* on the Song of Songs 1:28 wherein the revelation of the

secrets of the Chariot is conflated with the revelation of the secrets of Behemoth and Leviathan. *Song of Songs Rabbah* 1:28 reads: "For whence was Elihu the son of Barachel the Buzite to know how to reveal to Israel the secrets of Behemoth and Leviathan, and whence was Ezekiel to know how to reveal to them the secrets of the Chariot. Hence it is written: The King hath brought me into his [secret] chambers." Freedman and Simon, *Midrash Rabbah*, 9.47–48.

86. Whitney, *Two Strange Beasts*, 65.

87. Whitney, *Two Strange Beasts*, 66.

88. Whitney, *Two Strange Beasts*, 118. The origins of Leviathan as "*Circuitus Mundi*" is found in early Christian materials. Concerning this, see Whitney, *Two Strange Beasts*, 121; Kulik, "The Mysteries of Behemoth and Leviathan," 299.

89. Epstein, *The Babylonian Talmud. Baba Bathra*, 75a.

90. Philip Alexander notes that the concept of the celestial Temple was appropriated in varieties of ways in Jewish lore. He suggests that "the doctrine of the celestial sanctuary and the angelic liturgy is ambivalent and can be exploited in a number of different ways. It can be used to validate the terrestrial cult: if the earthly cult is in alignment with the heavenly, then it is efficacious. This, we suggested, was the meaning of the doctrine in the original priestly theology of Second Temple Judaism. It can also be used to substitute for the terrestrial cult. This is how it actually functioned at Qumran, and in priestly circles after 70. But in both these cases this substitution would have been deemed as only temporary, pending the restoration of the temple in Jerusalem. The idea of the celestial cult could also be used to replace and in effect negate the terrestrial cult." P. Alexander, *The Mystical Texts: Songs of the Sabbath Sacrifice and Related Manuscripts* (LSTS, 61; London: T&T Clark, 2005) 133.

91. See A. Orlov, "'The Likeness of Heaven': Kavod of Azazel in the Apocalypse of Abraham," in *With Letters of Light: Studies in the Dead Sea Scrolls, Early Jewish Apocalypticism, Magic and Mysticism* (Ekstasis, 2; eds. D. Arbel and A. Orlov; Berlin; N.Y.: de Gruyter, 2010) 232–253.

The Demise of the Antagonist in the Apocalyptic Scapegoat Tradition

1. Orlov, "The Eschatological Yom Kippur in the Apocalypse of Abraham: Part I: The Scapegoat Ritual," 79–111.

2. With respect to the question of the rivalry between various priestly clans in the Second Temple period, see G. Boccaccini, *Middle Judaism. Jewish Thought, 300 B.C.E. to 200 C.E.* (Minneapolis: Fortress, 1991); idem, *Roots of Rabbinic Judaism* (Grand Rapids: Eerdmans, 2002).

3. Danby, *The Mishnah,* 170.

4. *m. Yoma* 4:2 attests to the initial "clothing" of two goats of the Yom Kippur ritual in which one crimson band is tied around the horns of the scapegoat, while the other around the neck of the immolated goat; it reads: "He bound a thread of crimson wool on the head of the scapegoat and he turned it towards the way by which it was to be sent out; and on the he-goat that was to be slaughtered [he bound a thread] about its throat." Danby, *The Mishnah,* 166.

5. The tradition of the scarlet band is also reflected in *m. Shekalim* 4:2: "The [Red] Heifer and the scapegoat and the crimson thread were bought with the *Terumah* from the Shekel-chamber." Danby, *The Mishnah,* 155; *m. Shabbat* 9:3: "Whence do we learn that they tie a strip of crimson on the head of the scapegoat? Because it is written, though your sins be as scarlet they shall be as white as snow." Danby, *The Mishnah,* 108.

6. Cf. R. Hiers, " 'Binding and Loosing': The Matthean Authorizations," *JBL* 104 (1985) 233–250 at 233. It also can be understood as a release from the oath placed on the cultic animal by the high priest. Some studies suggest that the meaning can be understood in terms of later rabbinic usage, namely, the authority to absolve or release a person from some sort of vow. Hiers, "Binding and Loosing," 233.

7. Some studies point to the semantic overlap between terminology of loosing and forgiving in Semitic languages. Cf. Fletcher-Louis, "Revelation of the Sacral Son of Man," 284; Emerton, "Binding and Loosing—Forgiving and Retaining," 329–30.

8. Stökl Ben Ezra, *The Impact of Yom Kippur on Early Christianity,* 31, footnote 71.

9. *St. Justin Martyr. Dialogue with Trypho* (trs. T.F. Falls and T.P. Halton; ed. M. Slusser; Washington, DC: Catholic University of America Press, 2003) 62.

10. *Barnabas* 7:6–11 reads: "Pay attention to what he commands: 'Take two fine goats who alike and offer them as a sacrifice; and let the priest take one of them as a whole burnt offering for sins.' But what will they do with the other? 'The other,' he says, 'is cursed.' Pay attention to how the type of Jesus is revealed. 'And all of you shall spit on it and pierce it and wrap a piece of scarlet wool around its head, and so let it be cast into the wilderness.' When this happens, the one who takes the goat leads it into the wilderness and removes the wool, and places it on a blackberry bush, whose buds we are accustomed to eat when we find it in the countryside. (Thus the fruit of the blackberry bush alone is sweet.) And so, what does this mean? Pay attention: 'The one they take to the altar, but the other is cursed,' and the one that is cursed is crowned. For then they will see him in that day wearing a long scarlet robe around his flesh, and they will say, 'Is this not the one we once

crucified, despising, piercing, and spitting on him? Truly this is the one who was saying at the time that he was himself the Son of God.' For how is he like that one? This is why 'the goats are alike, fine, and equal,' that when they see him coming at that time, they may be amazed at how much he is like the goat. See then the type of Jesus who was about to suffer. But why do they place the wool in the midst of the thorns? This is a type of Jesus established for the church, because whoever wishes to remove the scarlet wool must suffer greatly, since the thorn is a fearful thing, and a person can retrieve the wool only by experiencing pain. And so he says: those who wish to see me and touch my kingdom must take hold of me through pain and suffering." Ehrman, *The Apostolic Fathers*, 2.37–41.

11. Cf. also *y. Yoma* 6:5: "Originally they were tying it to their windows; some of them were turning white and some turning red; these were ashamed in front of the others. They changed and tied it to the door of the Sanctuary. Some years it was turning white, in others turning red. They changed and tied it to the rock." *The Jerusalem Talmud. Tractates Pesahim and Yoma. Edition, Translation and Commentary* (ed. H.W. Guggenheimer; SJ, 74; Berlin: De Gruyter, 2013) 566.

12. Among early sources, Zok is mentioned in both *m. Yoma* 6:4–6 and *Targum Pseudo-Jonathan* on Lev 16:10. Isidore Epstein suggests that "Zok means a mountain peak; it may be the special name of the mountain whence the he-goat was flung down." Epstein, *The Babylonian Talmud. Seder Mo'ed*, 3.316.

13. See also: *b. Yoma* 67b: "Raba said: The view of him who says they are permitted is more reasonable, for the Torah did not say 'Send away' to create [possibility of] offence. Our Rabbis taught: Azazel—it should be hard and rough. One might have assumed that it is to be in inhabited land, therefore the text reads: 'In the wilderness.' But whence do we know that it [is to be in] a Zok?—therefore the text reads: 'Cut off.'" Epstein, *The Babylonian Talmud. Yoma*, 67b; *b. Yoma* 67b: "R. Simeon says: And he that letteth go the goat for Azazel shall wash his clothes, i.e., he flings it down headlong and his garments become then unclean." Epstein, *The Babylonian Talmud. Yoma*, 67b; *b. Yoma* 71a: "Raba said, Scripture says: [But the goat . . . for Azazel] shall be set alive. How long must it needs be set alive? Until the time of Atonement—Now when is the time of Atonement? At the time when the blood is sprinkled, not beyond it." Epstein, *The Babylonian Talmud. Yoma*, 71a. The tradition of pushing the scapegoat off a mountain maybe also reflected in the tradition of naming the mountain as Azazel. Regarding this, cf. *b. Yoma* 67b: "Another [Baraitha] taught: Azazel, i.e., the hardest of mountains. . . ." Epstein, *The Babylonian Talmud. Yoma*, 67b.

14. *The Jerusalem Talmud. Tractates Pesahim and Yoma. Edition, Translation and Commentary* (ed. H.W. Guggenheimer; SJ, 74; Berlin: De Gruyter,

2013) 559. Cf. also *y. Yoma* 6:5: "What did he do? He split the shiny strip; half of it he bound on the rock and half of it he bound between its horns. Then he pushed it backwards, it rolled descending. It did not reach half of the declivity before it dissolved into limbs." *The Jerusalem Talmud. Tractates Pesahim and Yoma. Edition, Translation and Commentary* (ed. H.W. Guggenheimer; SJ, 74; Berlin: De Gruyter, 2013) 565.

15. McNamara et al., *Targum Neofiti 1, Leviticus; Targum Pseudo-Jonathan, Leviticus*, 169.

16. Grabbe, "The Scapegoat Tradition," 159.

17. See *Apoc. Ab. 14:5*: "May you be the fire brand of the furnace of the earth! Go, Azazel, into the untrodden parts of the earth." Kulik, *Retroverting Slavonic Pseudepigrapha*, 21.

18. Kulik, *Retroverting Slavonic Pseudepigrapha*, 20.

19. Knibb, *The Ethiopic Book of Enoch*, 2.87–88.

20. Olson, *Enoch. A New Translation*, 34.

21. Stökl Ben Ezra, *The Impact of Yom Kippur on Early Christianity*, 87; Olson, *Enoch. A New Translation*, 38.

22. Geiger, "Einige Worte über das Buch Henoch," 200.

23. Cf. *Targum Pseudo-Jonathan* to Lev 16:10: "The goat on which the lot of Azazel fell shall be set alive before the Lord to make atonement for the sinfulness of the people of the house of Soq, that is Beth Haduri." McNamara et al., *Targum Neofiti 1, Leviticus; Targum Pseudo-Jonathan, Leviticus*, 167; *Targum Pseudo-Jonathan* to Lev 16:22: "The goat shall carry on himself all their sins to a desolate place; and the man shall let the goat go into the desert of Soq, and the goat shall go up on the mountains of Beth Haduri, and the blast of wind from before the Lord will thrust him down and he will die." McNamara et al., *Targum Neofiti 1, Leviticus; Targum Pseudo-Jonathan, Leviticus*, 169.

24. Cf. *1 Enoch* 10:11: "And the Lord said to Michael: 'Go, inform Semyaza and the others with him who have associated with the women to corrupt themselves with them in all their uncleanness." *1 Enoch* 10:14; "And then he (Semyaza) will be burnt and from then on destroyed with them; together they will be bound until the end of all generations." Knibb, *The Ethiopic Book of Enoch*, 2.89–90.

25. Cf. *1 Enoch* 10:8: "And the whole earth has been ruined by the teaching of the works of Azazel, *and against him write down all sin*." Knibb, *The Ethiopic Book of Enoch*, 2.88.

26. Concerning the theme of pollution caused by the fallen angels' actions, see Dimant, "1 Enoch 6–11: A Methodological Perspective," 325; M. Douglas, *Purity and Danger: An Analysis of Concepts of Pollution and Taboo* (London: Praeger, 1969) 41–57; Molenberg, "A Study of the Roles of Shemihaza and Asael in 1 Enoch 6–11," 139.

27. In his comments on *4Q203*, Milik suggests that "Azazel appears here in his expiatory role (Lev. 16:8, 10, 26), for he seems to be punished for the sins of the giants." Milik, *The Books of Enoch*, 313

28. *The Dead Sea Scrolls Study Edition* (eds. F. García Martínez and E. Tigchelaar; 2 vols.; Leiden: Brill, 1997) 411.

29. *4Q180* 1:1–10 reads: "Interpretation concerning the ages which God has made: An age to conclude [all that there is] and all that will be. Before creating them he determined [their] operations [according to the precise sequence of the ages,] one age after another age. And this is engraved on the [heavenly] tablets [for the sons of men,] [for] /[a]ll/ the ages of their dominion. This is the sequence of the son[s of Noah, from Shem to Abraham,] [unt]il he sired Isaac; the ten [generations . . .] [. . .] Blank [. . .] [And] interpretation concerning 'Azaz'el and the angels wh[o came to the daughters of man] [and s]ired themselves giants. And concerning 'Azaz'el [is written . . .] [to love] injustice and to let him inherit evil for all [his] ag[e . . .] [. . .] (of the) judgments and the judgment of the council of [. . .]." García Martínez and Tigchelaar, *The Dead Sea Scrolls Study Edition*, 371–373. Concerning similar traditions, see also *4Q181*.

30. Later rabbinic materials also link the sacrificial animal known from the scapegoat ritual to the story of the angelic rebels. *b. Yoma* 67b, for example, records the following tradition: "The School of R. Ishmael taught: Azazel—[it was so called] because it obtains atonement for the affair of Uza and Aza'el." Epstein, *The Babylonian Talmud. Yoma,* 67b.

31. In relation to this tradition, Patrick Tiller cautiously suggests that "the temporary rocky prison of Asael may be somehow related to the offering of a live goat, which bears the sins of Israel, to Azazel on the Day of Atonement (Leviticus 16)." P.A. Tiller, *A Commentary on the Animal Apocalypse of 1 Enoch* (EJL, 4; Atlanta: Scholars, 1993) 371.

32. See also in *1 Enoch* 10:4–7; 12–14; 88:3; and *Jub.* 5:6.

33. Daniel Olson argues that "the Book of Enoch must be credited with playing a major role in forming the terrible picture of Hell as the fiery pit into which the wicked will be thrown to perish forever. Such a place is foreshadowed in Isa 66:24, but the specific idea that Gehenna is a bottomless pit of fire originally intended for the devil and his angels, taken for granted in the New Testament, is first met in these pages." Olson, *Enoch. A New Translation*, 38.

34. Knibb, *The Ethiopic Book of Enoch*, 2.89–90. The biblical roots of the motif of the incarceration of heavenly beings in the subterranean realm can be found in Isa 24:21–22: "On that day the Lord will punish the host of heaven, in heaven, and on earth the kings of the earth. They will be gathered together like prisoners in a pit; they will be shut up in a prison, and after many days they will be punished." Regarding this tradition, see D. Aune, *Revelation 17–22* (WBC, 52C; Nashville: Nelson, 1998) 1078.

35. Eibert Tigchelaar suggests that "most scholars agree that the text really consists of several tales or traditional elements that have been merged into a not completely uniform story." E.J.C. Tigchelaar, *Prophets of Old and the Day of the End: Zechariah, the Book of Watchers and Apocalyptic* (OS, 35; Leiden: Brill, 1996) 166.

36. Some scholars see more than two distinctive narrative strands in *1 Enoch 6–11*. Cf. C.A. Newsom, "The Development of 1 Enoch 6–19: Cosmology and Judgment," *CBQ* 42 (1980) 310–329 at 313–314; Bhayro, *The Shemihazah and Asael Narrative of 1 Enoch 6–11*, 11–20.

37. Cf. R.H. Charles, *The Apocrypha and Pseudepigrapha of the Old Testament* (2 vols.; Oxford: Clarendon, 1913) 2.191; G.W.E. Nickelsburg, "Apocalyptic and Myth in *1 Enoch* 6–11," *JBL* 96 (1977) 383–405; P. Hanson, "Rebellion in Heaven, Azazel, and Euhemeristic Heroes in *1 Enoch* 6–11," *JBL* 96 (1977) 195–233; J. Collins, "Methodological Issues in the Study of *1 Enoch*," *SBLSP* 13.1 (1978) 315–322; Dimant, "1 Enoch 6–11: A Methodological Perspective," 323–339; Newsom, "The Development of *1 Enoch* 6–19," 310–29; Molenberg, "A Study of the Roles of Shemihaza and Asael in *1 Enoch* 6–11," 136–146; J. VanderKam, *Enoch and the Growth of An Apocalyptic Tradition* (CBQMS, 16; Washington, DC: The Catholic Biblical Association of America, 1984) 122–130; Tigchelaar, *Prophets of Old and the Day of the End: Zechariah, the Book of Watchers and Apocalyptic*, 166–167; Nickelsburg, *1 Enoch*, 165–173; D. Dimant, "*1 Enoch* 6–11: A Fragment of a Parabiblical Work," *JJS* 53 (2002) 223–237; Bhayro, *The Shemihazah and Asael Narrative of 1 Enoch 6–11*, 1–20.

38. Tigchelaar summarizes the scholarly consensus by saying that "nowadays most scholars tend to regard the Semhazah material as the first layer of the text, to which additions belonging to an Asael cycle have been added." Tigchelaar, *Prophets of Old and the Day of the End: Zechariah, the Book of Watchers and Apocalyptic*, 167.

39. With respect to the conflation of two separate tradition-cycles in *1 Enoch 6–11*, see Nickelsburg, *1 Enoch*, 165–173.

40. Nickelsburg, *1 Enoch*, 171. Nickelsburg suggests that this myth "was modeled after something very close to the Prometheus myth." Nickelsburg, *1 Enoch*, 171.

41. Hanson, "Rebellion in Heaven, Azazel, and Euhemeristic Heroes in *1 Enoch* 6–11," 222. For criticism of Hanson's position, see Dimant, "*1 Enoch* 6–11: A Methodological Perspective," 336; Grabbe, "The Scapegoat Tradition," 153–155; H. Drawnel, "The Punishment of Asael (1 En 10:4–8) and Mesopotamian Anti-Witchcraft Literature," *RevQ* 25 (2012) 369–394 at 370–371.

42. Scholars note that the complex nature of the angelic imprisonment's imagery in these early Enochic materials operates with various types of subterranean/desert prisons, temporary as well as permanent. Sometimes these

separate entities are combined into a single prison. With respect to this, Patrick Tiller observes that "in both the *Book of the Watchers* and the *Animal Apocalypse*, there are two prisons into which the Watchers will be cast. The first, a temporary prison, is described as two separate places in 10.4–5 (=88.1) and 10.12 (=88.3). In 18.12–16 and 21.1–6 these two places are combined into a single prison for both the wandering and the fallen angels. In the later part of the Book of the Watchers (18.12–16; 21.1–6), this prison is not an abyss at all but a dark, desert wasteland. In chapters 6–12, it is not clear whether the temporary prisons are abysses or not. The permanent prison, the abyss of fire, is described in 10.6, 13; 18.9–11; and 21.7–10 in the *Book of the Watchers* and in 90.24–25 in the *Animal Apocalypse*. The abyss described by Jude seems to be a composite of all of these prisons: it is dark (10.4–5; 88.1); it is reserved for the wandering stars (18.12–16; 21.1–6); and it is eternal (10.6, 13; 21.7–10)." Tiller, *A Commentary on the Animal Apocalypse of 1 Enoch*, 252–254.

43. Regarding traditions of the fallen angels' imprisonment in the *Book of Watchers* and the *Animal Apocalypse*, see Tiller, *A Commentary on the Animal Apocalypse of 1 Enoch*, 253.

44. Knibb, *The Ethiopic Book of Enoch*, 2.215.

45. "And I saw one of those four who had come out first, how he took hold of that first star which had fallen from heaven, and bound it by its hands and its feet, and threw it into an abyss; and that abyss was narrow, and deep, and horrible, and dark." Knibb, *The Ethiopic Book of Enoch*, 2.198.

46. It constitutes a curious parallel to a tradition of the fallen angels found in *2 Enoch*. The longer recension of *2 Enoch* 18 speaks of the imprisonment of the fallen Watchers in darkness; it reads: "And similar to them are those who went down as prisoners in their train, who are in the second heaven, imprisoned in great darkness."

47. The motif of the fallen angels' imprisonment in the abyss also appears in later Enochic traditions and the Christian witnesses to this Enochic theme. *2 Enoch* speaks of the imprisonment of the fallen angels under the earth: "And I said to the Grigori, 'I have seen your brothers and their deeds and their torments and their great prayers; and I have prayed for them. But the Lord has sentenced them *under the earth* until heaven and earth are ended forever'" (*2 Enoch* 18:7). 2 Pet 2:4, similarly, speaks of the imprisonment of the fallen angels beneath the earth: "For if God did not spare the angels when they sinned, but cast them into hell and committed them to chains of deepest darkness to be kept until the judgment. . . ." (NRSV).

48. VanderKam, *The Book of Jubilees*, 2.33.

49. VanderKam, *The Book of Jubilees*, 2.33.

50. VanderKam, *The Book of Jubilees*, 2.229.

51. Carmichael, "The Origins of the Scapegoat Ritual," 167–181. For criticism of Carmichael's hypothesis, see, among others, Blair, *De-Demonising*

the Old Testament: An Investigation of Azazel, Lilith, Deber, Qeteb and Reshef in the Hebrew Bible, 22.

52. Gen 37:19–25 reads: "They said to one another, 'Here comes this dreamer. Come now, let us kill him and throw him into one of the pits; then we shall say that a wild animal has devoured him, and we shall see what will become of his dreams.' But when Reuben heard it, he delivered him out of their hands, saying, 'Let us not take his life.' Reuben said to them, 'Shed no blood; throw him into this pit here in the wilderness, but lay no hand on him'—that he might rescue him out of their hand and restore him to his father. So when Joseph came to his brothers, they stripped him of his robe, the long robe with sleeves that he wore; and they took him and threw him into a pit. The pit was empty; there was no water in it. Then they sat down to eat; and looking up they saw a caravan of Ishmaelites coming from Gilead, with their camels carrying gum, balm, and resin, on their way to carry it down to Egypt."

53. Philo, in *De Plantatione*, 60–61, writes: "Mark how he has again given the name of 'portion' and 'lot' of God to the character that has eyes to see Him and accords Him genuine devotion, while he says that the children of earth, whom he entitles sons of Adam, have been dispersed and broken up and no more gathered together but are become a mob incapable of following the guidance of right reason. For virtue is in very deed the cause of harmony and unity, whereas the contrary disposition brings about dissolution and dismemberment. An illustration of what has been said is afforded by that which is done year by year on the day called the 'Day of Atonement.' It is enjoined on that day to assign by lot two goats, one for the Lord, and one for separation (Lev. xvi. 8), a twofold description, one for God and one for created things. That which exalts the First Cause shall be allotted to Him, while that which exalts creation shall be banished, driven from the most holy places, *to find itself amid rocky chasms in trackless and unhallowed regions*." Colson and Whitaker, *Philo*, 3.243–5, emphasis mine.

54. Stokl, *The Impact of Yom Kippur on Early Christianity*, 88.

55. "Then I saw an angel coming down from heaven, holding in his hand the key to the bottomless pit and a great chain. He seized the dragon, that ancient serpent, who is the Devil and Satan, and bound him for a thousand years, and threw him into the pit, and locked and sealed it over him, so that he would deceive the nations no more, until the thousand years were ended. After that he must be let out for a little while" (NRSV).

56. For example, Lester Grabbe notes that "although there is no explicit reference to the scapegoat ceremony, Rev. 20, 1–3.10 has clear connections with *1 Enoch* 10, 4–5. Note the common features: Asael is bound prior to the judgment just as is Satan. This binding seems to include chains, according to *1 Enoch* 54, 3–5, though the exact date of the Parables is disputed. Just as

Satan is cast into the abyss, so are Asael and others according to Syncellus's version of *1 Enoch* 9, 4: 'Then the Most High commanded the holy archangels, and they bound their leaders [sc. of the fallen angels] and threw them into the abyss until the judgement.' In the final judgement, just as Satan is cast into a 'lake of fire' . . . so Asael and his companions are cast into an 'abyss of fire' . . . Thus, the punishment of Satan has been assimilated to the Asael tradition of 1 Enoch." Grabbe, "The Scapegoat Tradition," 160–161.

57. David Aune analyzes the similarities between Rev 20:1–3 and *1 Enoch* 10:4–6, noting the following parallels: "Rev 20:1–3, 7–10: (1) An angel descends from heaven with a key and a chain (v. 1). (2) The angel seizes and binds Satan (v. 2a). (3) Satan will be imprisoned one thousand years (v. 2b). (4) Satan is cast into a pit that is locked and sealed (v. 3). (5) Satan is released for an unspecified period (vv. 3b, 7–9). (6) Satan and his associates are cast into the lake of fire for eternal torment (v 10). *1 Enoch* 10:4–6 contains the following motifs: (1) God sends an angel (Raphael). (2) Azazel (an alias for Satan) is bound by the angel. (3) Azazel is thrown into darkness and imprisoned "forever." (4) The time of imprisonment, however, will actually end at the great day of judgment. (5) On the great day of judgment Azazel is thrown into the fire. A similar sequence is evident in *1 Enoch* 10:11–13: (1) God sends an angel (Michael). (2) The angel binds Semyaza (another alias for Satan) and his associates. (3) They are imprisoned under the earth. (4) The period of imprisonment is limited to seventy generations. (5) On the day of judgment they are thrown into the abyss of fire." D. Aune, *Revelation 17–22* (WBC, 52C; Nashville: Nelson, 1998) 1078. Aune concludes his comparative analysis with the following: "Since the narrative pattern found twice in Rev 20:1–10 (i.e., in vv. 1–3 and 7–10) also occurs twice in *1 Enoch*, it seems likely that both authors are dependent on a traditional eschatological scenario. The enumeration of motifs found in these three passages exhibits a striking similarity, though John has introduced the innovation of the temporary release of Satan." Aune, *Revelation 17–22*, 1078–1079.

58. Cf., for example, the Armenian version of the *Life of Adam and Eve* 12:1–16:2, which tells about the expulsion of the infamous rebel, reads: "Satan also wept loudly and said to Adam. 'All my arrogance and sorrow came to pass because of you; for, because of you I went forth from my dwelling; and because of you I was alienated from the throne of the cherubs who, having spread out a shelter, used to enclose me; because of you my feet have trodden the earth. . . . Thereupon, God became angry with me and commanded to expel us from our dwelling and to cast me and my angels, who were in agreement with me, to the earth; and you were at the same time in the Garden. When I realized that because of you I had gone forth from the dwelling of light and was in sorrows and pains. . . .'" *A Synopsis of the Books of Adam and Eve. Second Revised Edition* (eds. G.A. Anderson, M.E. Stone; EJL, 17; Atlanta: Scholars, 1999) 15E–18E.

59. In the Latin version of the aforementioned text (12.1–16:2), the adversary describes his lost condition with the language of glory: "O Adam, all my enmity, jealousy, and resentment is towards you, since on account of you I was expelled and alienated from my glory, which I had in heaven in the midst of the angels. Then the Lord God grew angry with me and sent me forth with my angels from our glory. On account of you we were expelled from our dwelling into this world and cast out upon the earth. Immediately we were in grief, since we had been despoiled of so much glory, and we grieved to see you in such a great happiness of delights." Anderson and Stone, *A Synopsis of the Books of Adam and Eve*, 15–18E.

60. The tradition of Satan's metamorphosis into the living form of the serpent is also present in the Georgian version: "And the serpent told him, 'How can we have them excluded?' The devil replied and told the serpent, 'Be a sheath for me and I will speak to the woman through your mouth a word by which we will trick (them).' And the two of them came together and they allowed their heads to hang on the wall of the paradise at the time where the angels had ascended to bow down to God. Then the devil changed himself into the image of an angel; he praised the praises of the angels. And I was gazing in the direction of the enclosure to hear the praises. I stared and I saw him like an angel and at once he became invisible for he had gone forth to bring the serpent. And he told him, 'Arise and come and I will be with you and I will speak through your mouth that which it is proper for you to say.' He took on the form of the serpent (to go) close to the wall of paradise and the devil slipped inside the serpent and he allowed his head to hang on the wall of paradise. He cried out and said, 'Shame on you, woman, you who are in the paradise of Delight (and) who are blind! Come to me and I will tell you a certain secret word.'" Anderson and Stone, *A Synopsis of the Books of Adam and Eve*, 50E–52E.

61. Andersen, "2 Enoch," 1.148. *2 Enoch* 7 tells about the suspended "hanging" position of the fallen angels during their punishment: "And there I perceived prisoners under guard, hanging up, waiting for the measureless judgment." Andersen, "2 Enoch," 1.112.

62. Isa 14:12–15 reads: "How you are fallen from heaven, O Day Star, son of Dawn! How you are cut down to the ground, you who laid the nations low! You said in your heart, 'I will ascend to heaven; I will raise my throne above the stars of God; I will sit on the mount of assembly on the heights of Zaphon; I will ascend to the tops of the clouds, I will make myself like the Most High.' But you are brought down to Sheol, to the depths of the Pit" (NRSV). The importance of this formative passage in the later lore about Satan's descent and imprisonment into the abyss cannot be underestimated. Cf. for example, Luke 18:10.

63. Ezek 28:1–8 seems to draw on a similar cluster of traditions about the antagonist's demotion when it unfolds its legend about the prince of Tyre:

"The word of the Lord came to me: Mortal, say to the prince of Tyre, Thus says the Lord God: Because your heart is proud and you have said, 'I am a god; I sit in the seat of the gods, in the heart of the seas,' yet you are but a mortal, and no god, though you compare your mind with the mind of a god. You are indeed wiser than Daniel; no secret is hidden from you; by your wisdom and your understanding you have amassed wealth for yourself, and have gathered gold and silver into your treasuries. By your great wisdom in trade you have increased your wealth, and your heart has become proud in your wealth. Therefore thus says the Lord God: Because you compare your mind with the mind of a god, therefore, I will bring strangers against you, the most terrible of the nations; they shall draw their swords against the beauty of your wisdom and defile your splendor. They shall thrust you down to the Pit, and you shall die a violent death in the heart of the seas" (NRSV).

64. Cf. *m. Yoma* 6:6: "He divided the thread of crimson wool and tied one half to the rock and the other half between its horns, and he pushed it from behind." Danby, *The Mishnah*, 170; also, *Barnabas* 7: "When this happens, the one who takes the goat leads it into the wilderness and removes the wool, and places it on a blackberry bush, whose buds we are accustomed to eat when we find it in the countryside." Ehrman, *The Apostolic Fathers*, 2.39.

65. Knibb, *The Ethiopic Book of Enoch*, 2.87–88.

66. The motif of throwing Asael onto jagged and sharp stones in *1 Enoch* 10 is also noteworthy in light of the tradition found in *Targum Pseudo-Jonathan*, telling how, during the ceremony of choosing the goats, their lots were thrown upon them. Thus, *Targum Pseudo-Jonathan* on Lev 16:8 reads: "And Aaron shall place equal lots on the two goats, one lot (marked) 'for the name of the Lord,' and the other (marked) 'for Azazel.' He shall shake them in the urn, take them out, and throw them on the goats." McNamara et al., *Targum Neofiti 1: Leviticus, Targum Pseudo-Jonathan; Leviticus,* 167.

67. Knibb, *The Ethiopic Book of Enoch*, 2.196.

68. Knibb, *The Ethiopic Book of Enoch*, 2.197.

69. It is possible that loosing of the band at the end of the ritual signified the forgiveness of the Israelite sins. Some studies point to the connection of the formulae of loosing with the theme of forgiveness. Cf. Hiers, "Binding and Loosing," 234.

70. Scholars have noted that the binding motif was very prominent in the tradition of the fall of the Watchers. R. Bauckham, *Jude, 2 Peter* (WBC, 50; Waco: Word Books, 1983) 53. On the binding motif, see also *1 Enoch* 13:1; 14:5; 18:16; 21:3–6; 54:3–5; 56:1–4; 88:1; *4Q203* 8:13; *Jub.* 5:6; 10:7–11; *2 Enoch* 7:2; *2 Baruch* 56:13; *Sib. Or.* 2.289; Origen, *Contra Celsum* 5:52.

71. *2 Enoch* 59:1–4 reads: "He who acts lawlessly with the soul of an animal acts lawlessly with his own soul. For a person brings one of the clean animals to make a sacrifice on account of sin, so that he may have healing for his soul. If he brings it to the sacrifice from clean animals and birds (and

cereals), then there is healing for that person, and he will heal his soul. Everything that has been given to you for food, bind by four legs, so as to perform the healing properly. And there is healing and he will heal his soul. And he who puts to death any kind of animal without bonds, puts his own soul to death and acts lawlessly with his own flesh." Andersen, "2 Enoch," 1.184.

72. Hiers, "Binding and Loosing," 235–239.

73. Cf. Tob 8:3: "The odor of the fish so repelled the demon that he fled to the remotest parts of Egypt. But Raphael followed him, and at once bound him there hand and foot" (NRSV).

74. The motif of the subterranean pit, as the place of punishment of the fallen angels, is often reiterated in the *Book of the Watchers*. *1 Enoch* 21:7–10 reads: "And from there I went to another place, more terrible than this, and I saw a terrible thing: (there was) a great fire there which burnt and blazed, and the place had a cleft (reaching) to the abyss, full of great pillars of fire which were made to fall; neither its extent nor its size could I see, nor could I see its source. Then I said: 'How terrible this place (is), and (how) painful to look at. Then Uriel, one of the holy angels who was with me, answered me. He answered me and said to me: 'Enoch, why do you have such fear and terror because of this terrible place, and before this pain ?' And he said to me: 'This place (is) the prison of the angels, and there they will be held forever.' " Knibb, *The Ethiopic Book of Enoch*, 2.108.

75. Knibb, *The Ethiopic Book of Enoch*, 2.89–90.

76. Hanson suggests that "[t]he Azazel episode involves an elaboration of the themes of punishment and restoration in the Shemihazah narrative through the application of motifs taken from the Yom Kippur ritual, especially as that ritual was interpreted in a tradition represented by the Pseudo-Jonathan Targum. As a result of various influences, primarily inner-Jewish in provenance, the simple ritual sending a scapegoat to the rugged, rocky hill of Azazel has become a description of the punishment of another divine figure." Hanson, "Rebellion in Heaven, Azazel, and Euhemeristic Heroes in *1 Enoch* 6–11," 225.

77. Hanson, "Rebellion in Heaven, Azazel, and Euhemeristic Heroes in *1 Enoch* 6–11," 224.

78. Hanson, "Rebellion in Heaven, Azazel, and Euhemeristic Heroes in *1 Enoch* 6–11," 224–225.

79. Knibb, *The Ethiopic Book of Enoch*, 2.198.

80. Knibb, *The Ethiopic Book of Enoch*, 2.138.

81. Vanderkam, *The Book of Jubilees*, 2.33.

82. "And Beliar shall be bounded by him. And he shall grant to his children the authority to trample on wicked spirits." H.C. Kee, "Testaments of the Twelve Patriarchs," *The Old Testament Pseudepigrapha* (2 vols.; ed. J. H. Charlesworth; New York: Doubleday, 1983–1985) 1.795.

83. Rev 20:1–3: "Then I saw an angel coming down from heaven, holding in his hand the key to the bottomless pit and a great chain. He seized the dragon, that ancient serpent, who is the Devil and Satan, and bound him for a thousand years, and threw him into the pit, and locked and sealed it over him, so that he would deceive the nations no more, until the thousand years were ended. After that he must be let out for a little while" (NRSV). Later Christian materials are also aware of such peculiar constellations. Thus, for example, the *Hypostasis of the Archons* (NHC, II, 95, 11–13) from Nag Hammadi library mentions that a fiery angel "bound Yaldabaoth and cast him down into Tartaros below the abyss." *Nag Nammadi Codex II, 2–7* (2 vols; ed. B. Layton; NHS, 20; Leiden: Brill, 1989) 1.255.

84. Richard Bauckham notes that ". . . the chains, to which Jude refers, are very prominent in the tradition of the fall of the Watchers. . . . The angels' imprisonment is only temporary, until the Day of Judgment when they will be transferred to the fire of Gehenna, but the chains are called 'eternal' . . . Jude's terminology seems here to depend on *1 Enoch* 10:5, where Asael is bound 'forever' . . ." R. Bauckham, *Jude, 2 Peter* (WBC, 50; Waco: Word Books, 1983) 53.

85. Bauckham notes that "Jude's reference is directly dependent on *1 Enoch* 6–19, which is the earliest extant account of the fall of the Watchers, and he shows himself closely familiar with those chapters. . . . Older exegetes understood Jude 6 to refer to the fall of Satan and his angels before the fall of Adam; but Jude's dependence on 1 Enoch is clear from the close parallels in this verse and also from the allusion in v. 7 to the fact that the angels' sin was sexual intercourse with mortal women." Bauckham, *Jude, 2 Peter*, 51–52.

86. The motif of chains is also found in Mark's accounts of Jesus' healing of the Gerasene demoniac (Mk 5:1–20). Concerning this motif, see A.T. Wright, "Evil Spirits in Second Temple Judaism: The Watcher Tradition as a Background to the Demonic Pericopes in the Gospels," *Henoch* 28 (2006) 141–159.

87. Bauckham suggests that "[t]he author of 2 Peter has followed Jude. He may not himself have known 1 Enoch and probably in any case could not expect his readers to be familiar with it . . . but he must have known the story of the fall of the Watchers, which was well known in contemporary Judaism, Hellenistic as well as Palestinian. In his rewriting of Jude 6 the specific verbal echoes of 1 Enoch have mostly been lost (a fact which is most easily explained if Jude is prior to 2 Peter), but this is probably accidental rather than a deliberate attempt to avoid echoes of 1 Enoch." Bauckham, *Jude, 2 Peter*, 248.

88. "For if God did not spare the angels when they sinned, but cast them into hell and committed them to chains of deepest darkness to be kept until the judgment" (NRSV).

89. Ryszard Rubinkiewicz has argued that ". . . the author of the *Apocalypse of Abraham* follows the tradition of *1 Enoch* 1–36. The chief of the fallen angels is Azazel, who rules the stars and most men. It is not difficult to find here the tradition of Genesis 6:1–4 developed according to the tradition of *1 Enoch*. Azazel is the head of the angels who plotted against the Lord and who impregnated the daughters of men. These angels are compared to the stars. Azazel revealed the secrets of heaven and is banished to the desert. Abraham, as Enoch, receives the power to drive away Satan. All these connections show that the author of the *Apocalypse of Abraham* drew upon the tradition of *1 Enoch*." Rubinkiewicz, "Apocalypse of Abraham," 1.685.

90. In this respect, Günter Stemberger notes that ". . . a more radical solution understands the Mishnaic descriptions as ideal forms of the cult, based exclusively on the biblical text and not at all reflecting the reality of the Second Temple period. . . ." Stemberger, "Yom Kippur in Mishnah Yoma," 121.

The Nourishment of Azazel

1. "For behold, the garment which in heaven was formerly yours has been set aside for him [Abraham]. . . ." Kulik, *Retroverting Slavonic Pseudepigrapha,* 20.

2. Kulik, *Retroverting Slavonic Pseudepigrapha,* 19.

3. *Apoc. Ab.* 9:7: "But for forty days abstain from every food which issues from fire, and from the drinking of wine, and from anointing [yourself] with oil." Kulik, *Retroverting Slavonic Pseudepigrapha,* 17.

4. D. Goodman, "Do Angels Eat?" *JJS* 37.2 (1986) 160–175 at 164.

5. Kulik, *Retroverting Slavonic Pseudepigrapha,* 20.

6. The concept of humans as the "food" of fire will appear again in *Apoc. Ab.* 31:2–3, this time coming from the lips, not of Azazel, but of God: "And I shall burn with fire those who mocked them ruling over them in this age and I shall commit those who have covered me with mockery to the reproach of the coming age. Since I have destined them to be food for the fire of hell, and ceaseless soaring in the air of the underground depths, the contents of a worm's belly." Kulik, *Retroverting Slavonic Pseudepigrapha*, 35.

7. *Apoc. Ab.* 23:7–8: "And behind the tree was standing, as it were, a serpent in form, but having hands and feet like a man, and wings on its shoulders: six on the right side and six on the left. And he was holding in his hands the grapes of the tree and feeding the two whom I saw entwined with each other." Kulik, *Retroverting Slavonic Pseudepigrapha*, 27.

8. See Goodman, "Do Angels Eat?"160–175; H.J. Hodges, *Food as Synecdoche in John's Gospel and Gnostic Texts* (Ph.D. diss.; University of Cal-

ifornia at Berkeley, 1995) 308–352; M. Leutzsch, "Essen Engel?: Über das Ernährungsverhalten himmlischer Wesen," in *Essen und Trinken in der Bibel: Ein literarisches Festmahl für Rainer Kessler zum 65. Geburtstag* (eds. M. Geiger et al.; Gütersloh: Gütersloher Verlagshaus, 2009) 254–268; E. Kobel, *Dining with John: Communal Meals and Identity Formation in the Fourth Gospel and Its Historical and Cultural Context* (BIS, 109; Leiden: Brill, 2011) 308–312.

9. Judg 13:15–16 reads: "Manoah said to the angel of the Lord, 'Allow us to detain you, and prepare a kid for you.' The angel of the Lord said to Manoah, 'If you detain me, I will not eat your food; but if you want to prepare a burnt offering, then offer it to the Lord' " (NRSV).

10. "And the Commander-in-chief said, 'Lord, all the heavenly spirits are incorporeal, and they neither eat nor drink.' " E.P. Sanders, "Testament of Abraham," *The Old Testament Pseudepigrapha* (2 vols.; ed. J. H. Charlesworth; New York: Doubleday, 1983–1985) 1.871–902 at 1.884.

11. Cf. Tob 12:19 "Although you were watching me, I really did not eat or drink anything—but what you saw was a vision" (NRSV).

12. See Philo, *De Abrahamo* 1:118 reads: "It is a marvel indeed that though they neither ate nor drank they gave the appearance of both eating and drinking." Colson and Whitaker, *Philo*, 6.61. For a similar tradition, see also *QG* 4:9.

13. See Josephus's *Ant.* 1:197 reads: "On their assenting, he ordered loaves of fine flour to be made forthwith and killed a calf and cooked it and brought it to them as they reclined under the oak; and they gave him to believe that they did eat." Thackeray and Markus, *Josephus*, 4.97.

14. Kobel, *Dining with John*, 309.

15. Cf. *Testament of Abraham* 6:4–5: "Sarah said, 'You must know, my lord, the three heavenly men who stayed as guests in our tent beside the oak of Mamre when you slaughtered the unblemished calf and set a table for them. After the meat had been eaten, the calf got up again and exultantly suckled its mother." Sanders, "Testament of Abraham," 1.885.

16. Cf. *Targ. Onq.* to Genesis 18:5–8; 19:1; *Targ. Neof.* to Genesis 18:8; *Targ. Ps.-J.* to Genesis 18:8. See also *Gen. Rab.* 48:14; *Lev. Rab.* 34:8; *b. Baba Metzia* 86b–87a.

17. Regarding this, see Hodges, *Food as Synecdoche in John's Gospel and Gnostic Texts*, 335–336, 339.

18. *2 Enoch* 56:2, the longer recension. Andersen, "2 Enoch," 1.182.

19. Andersen, "2 Enoch," 1.138.

20. Provenance of the oil/dew of resurrection in *2 Enoch* appears to be paradisal since it is portrayed with the same symbolism as oil coming from the Tree of Life. Thus, *2 Enoch* 8:3–4 reports that "the tree [of life] is indescribable for pleasantness and fine fragrance, and more beautiful than any (other) created thing that exists. And from every direction it has an

appearance which is gold-looking and crimson, and with the form of fire." Andersen, "2 Enoch," 1.114. Concerning the paradisal dew in *2 Enoch,* see A. Orlov, "Resurrection of Adam's Body: The Redeeming Role of Enoch-Metatron in 2 (Slavonic) Enoch," *The Theophaneia School: Jewish Roots of Eastern Christian Mysticism* (Scrinium, III; eds. B. Lourié and A. Orlov; St. Petersburg: Byzantinorossica, 2007) 385–389; Hodges, *Food as Synecdoche in John's Gospel and Gnostic Texts*, 336.

21. C. Burchard, "Joseph and Aseneth," *The Old Testament Pseudepigrapha* (2 vols.; ed. J. H. Charlesworth; New York: Doubleday, 1983–1985) 2.177–247 at 2.229. The parallelism between the dew and the manna is found also in *3 Bar.* 8:9–11 (Greek version): "And I said, 'Lord, what is this bird, and what is its name?' And the angel told me, 'His name is Phoenix.' 'And what does he eat?' And he told me, 'The manna of heaven and the dew of earth.'" H.E. Gaylord, "3 (Greek Apocalypse of) Baruch," *The Old Testament Pseudepigrapha* (2 vols.; ed. J.H. Charlesworth; New York: Doubleday, 1983–1985) 1.653–679 at 1.671. Cf. also *Zohar* II.62b: "The holy tree was arranged with twelve boundaries on four sides of the world, fortified by seventy branches, all corresponding to the pattern above. At that moment, holy dew trickled from the Concealed Ancient One, filling the head of the Short-Tempered One, the place called Heaven. Some of that dew of supernal holy light flowed and descended below, and as it descended, it dispersed into frozen flakes congealing below, as is written: fine as frost on the ground (Exodus 16:4). All those scions of faith went out and gathered and blessed the supernal Name over it. That manna emitted a fragrance like all the spices of the Garden of Eden, since it had flowed through there in descending. Once they placed it in front of them, they tasted whatever taste they desired and blessed the supernal King." Matt, *The Zohar: Pritzker Edition*, 4.338.

22. Ps 78:23–5: "Yet he commanded the skies above, and opened the doors of heaven; he rained down on them manna to eat, and gave them the grain of heaven. Mortals ate of the bread of angels; he sent them food in abundance" (NRSV).

23. Regarding the identification of Aseneth's honeycomb with manna, see V. Aptowitzer, "Asenath, the Wife of Joseph: A Haggadic Literary-Historical Survey," *HUCA* 1 (1924) 282–283; C. Burchard, *Untersuchungen zu Joseph und Aseneth: Überlieferung—Ortsbestimmung* (WUNT, 8; Tübingen: Mohr/Siebeck, 1965) 130; M. Philonenko, "Initiation et mystère dans Joseph et Aséneth," in *Initiation* (ed. C.J. Bleeker; SHR, 10; Leiden: Brill, 1965) 147–153 at 152–153; A. Lieber, "I Set a Table before You: The Jewish Eschatological Character of Aseneth's Conversion Meal," *JSP* 14 (2004) 63–77; R. Chesnutt, "Perceptions of Oil in Early Judaism and the Meal Formula in Joseph and Aseneth," *JSP* 14 (2005) 113–132 at 117–118; A.E. Portier-Young, "Sweet Mercy Metropolis: Interpreting Aseneth's Honeycomb," *JSP* 14 (2005)

133–157. With respect to the connection between the manna and the dew, see Portier-Young, "Sweet Mercy Metropolis," 142–143. Cf. also *Zohar* III.208a, in which the manna is identified both with the celestial dew and with the angelic food; it reads: "Similarly the manna which came down for the Israelites in the wilderness originated in the celestial dew from the most recondite spot, and at first its light would radiate to all worlds and the 'field of apples,' and the heavenly angels drew sustenance from it. . . ." Simon and Sperling, *The Zohar*, 5.311–312.

24. Thus, *Jos. Asen.*15:5–6 reads: "Behold, from today, you will be renewed and formed anew and made alive again, and you will eat blessed bread of life, and drink a blessed cup of immortality, and anoint yourself with blessed ointment of incorruptibility." Burchard, "Joseph and Aseneth," 2.226. Cf. also *Jos. Asen.* 8:5: "It is not fitting for a man who worships God, who will bless with his mouth the living God and eat blessed bread of life and drink a blessed cup of immortality and anoint himself with blessed ointment of incorruptibility. . . ." Burchard, "Joseph and Aseneth," 2.211–212.

25. Scholars have recognized the similarities in anointing between the two texts. Thus, Rivka Nir argues that "like Michael in *2 Enoch*, who took Enoch, undressed him of his earthly attire, anointed him with delightful oil, and clothed him in a vesture of glory (22.4–9), so the man of God took Aseneth and disrobed her of her earthly clothing and commanded her to don garments of glory and instructed her to anoint herself with the ointment of purity." R. Nir, *Joseph and Aseneth: A Christian Book* (HBM, 42; Sheffield: Phoenix Press, 2012) 134–135.

26. The motif of nourishment by means of the splendor of the divine form is in *11QPs*[a] XXII, line 4–5: "Generation after generation shall dwell in you, and generations of the devout (shall be) your splendour, those hungering for the day of your salvation and who rejoice in the abundance of your glory. . . . At your glorious breast they shall suckle . . ." García Martínez and E. Tigchelaar, *The Dead Sea Scrolls Study Edition*, 1177. Concerning this tradition, see C.C. Newman, *Paul's Glory-Christology: Tradition and Rhetoric* (NovTSup, 69; Leiden: Brill, 1992) 131.

27. Freedman and Simon, *Midrash Rabbah*, 6.844.

28. *Pesikta of Rav Kahana*, Piska 6.1. For a similar tradition see also *Pesikta Rabbati*, Piska 16.2.

29. Such inverse nourishing patterns are present, also, in the *Apocalypse of Abraham*, in which the first humans are fed by the grapes from the hands of Azazel.

30. Cf. also Gen 3:14: "The Lord God said to the serpent, "Because you have done this, cursed are you among all animals and among all wild creatures; upon your belly you shall go, and dust you shall eat all the days of your life" (NRSV).

31. Regarding the hunger motif in the *Primary Adam Books*, see G. Anderson, "The Penitence Narrative in the Life of Adam and Eve," *Literature on Adam and Eve. Collected Essays* (eds. G. Anderson, M. Stone, J. Tromp; SVTP, 15; Leiden: Brill, 2000) 6ff.

32. Concerning the food of angels, see: Ps 78:23–25: "Yet he commanded the skies above, and opened the doors of heaven; he rained down on them manna to eat, and gave them the grain of heaven. Mortals ate of the bread of angels; he sent them food in abundance" (NRSV). Wis 16:20 reads: "Instead of these things you gave your people food of angels, and without their toil you supplied them from heaven with bread ready to eat, providing every pleasure and suited to every taste" (NRSV).

33. *Primary Adam Books* 3:1 reads: "They arose and went about upon the earth, and they did not find food like the food by which they had been nourished in [the Garden]."Anderson and Stone, *A Synopsis of the Books of Adam and Eve*, 3E.

34. Anderson and Stone, *A Synopsis of the Books of Adam and Eve*, 5E.

35. Freedman and Simon, *Midrash Rabbah*, 3.542. Regarding rabbinic traditions of Moses' nourishment on the splendor of the *Shechinah*, see I. Chernus, *Mysticism in Rabbinic Judaism: Studies in the History of Midrash* (SJ, 11; Berlin: de Gruyter, 1982) 74–87. I am thankful to Prof. Moshe Idel for bringing my attention to Chernus's study.

36. The visionary nourishment on the Deity's fiery form is also reminiscent of the tradition found in *4 Ezra* 14:37–48, in which the scribe is offered a fiery drink from the arms of the Deity. Cf. B.M. Metzger, "The Fourth Book of Ezra," *The Old Testament Pseudepigrapha* (2 vols.; ed. J. H. Charlesworth; New York: Doubleday, 1983–1985) 1.554.

37. Freedman and Simon, *Midrash Rabbah*, 3.54–541. Cf. also *b. Ber.* 17a and *Pesikta Rabbati* 16.2.

38. "'. . . if thou goest into a city, thou must act according to its customs.' When Moses ascended on high, where there is no eating or drinking, he emulated the heavenly example." Freedman and Simon, *Midrash Rabbah*, 3.539.

39. Cf. *Gen. Rab.* 2:2: "R. Abbahu said: . . . 'The celestial beings [sc. the angels] and the terrestrial ones [sc. man] were created at the same time: yet the celestial beings are fed by the radiance of the *Shechinah*, whereas the terrestrial beings, if they do not toil, do not eat. Strange it is indeed!' "; also, *Exod. Rab.* 32:4: "The angels are sustained only by the splendour of the *Shechinah*, as it says, And Thou preservest them all, and the host of heaven worships Thee (Neh. 9, 6)." Freedman and Simon, *Midrash Rabbah*, 1.15.

40. Cf. *Zohar* II.63a: "Rabbi El'azar taught, 'From this manna the righteous are destined to eat in the world that is coming.' " Matt, *The Zohar: Pritzker Edition*, 4.342.

41. This idea of humankind's eschatological feeding is often juxtaposed, in the rabbinic materials, with imagery of Torah's study. Cf. *b. Babba Batra* 10a: "What is the meaning of the words, I shall be satisfied when I awake with thy likeness? R. Nahman b. Isaac said: This refers to the students of the Torah who banish sleep from their eyes in this world, and whom the Holy One, blessed be He, feasts with the resplendence of the Divine presence in the future world." Epstein, *The Babylonian Talmud. Babba Batra,* 10a. Also, *b. Sotah* 49a: "R. Judah, son of R. Hiyya said: Any disciple of the Sages who occupies himself with Torah in poverty will have his prayer heard; as it is stated: For the people shall dwell in Zion at Jerusalem; thou shalt weep no more; He will surely be gracious unto thee at the voice of thy cry; when He shall hear, He will answer thee, and it continues, And the Lord will give you bread in adversity and water in affliction. R. Abbahu said: They also satisfy him from the lustre of the *Shechinah*, as it is stated: Thine eyes shall see thy Teacher." Epstein, *The Babylonian Talmud. Sotah,* 49a.

42. Halperin, *Faces of the Chariot*, 111

43. Concerning the manna traditions, see: R. Meyer, "Manna," in *Theological Dictionary of the New Testament* (eds. G. Kittel and G. Friedrich; 10 vols.; Grand Rapids: Eerdmans, 1964–76) 4.462–66; P. Borgen, *Bread from Heaven: An Exegetical Study of the Concept of Manna in the Gospel of John and the Writings of Philo* (NovTSup, 10; Leiden: Brill, 1965); B. J. Malina, *The Palestinian Manna Tradition* (AGAJU, 7; Leiden: Brill, 1968); P. Maiberger, *Das Manna: Eine literarische, etymologische und naturkundliche Untersuchung* (2 vols; ÄAT, 6/1–2; Wiesbaden: Otto Harrassowitz, 1983); D. Merkur, *The Mystery of Manna: The Psychedelic Sacrament of the Bible* (Rochester: Park Street Press, 2000).

44. Cf. Goodman, "Do Angels Eat?" 161; Hodges, *Food as Synecdoche in John's Gospel and Gnostic Texts*, 308–309.

45. Pseudo-Philo, *Bibl. Ant.* 19:5 reads: "You know that you have eaten the bread of angels for forty years. And now behold I bless your tribes before my end comes. You know my toil that I have toiled for you from the time you went up from the land of Egypt." H. Jacobson, *A Commentary on Pseudo-Philo's Liber Antiquitatum Biblicarum, with Latin Text and English Translation* (2 vols.; AGAJU, 31; Leiden: Brill, 1996) 1.121.

46. Thus, *b. Yoma* 75b reads: "Our Rabbis taught: Man did eat the bread of the mighty, i.e., bread which ministering angels eat. This was the interpretation of R. Akiba." Epstein, *The Babylonian Talmud. Yoma*, 75b.

47. See Gen 3:6–7: "So when the woman saw that the tree was good for food, and that it was a delight to the eyes, and that the tree was to be desired to make one wise, she took of its fruit and ate; and she also gave some to her husband, who was with her, and he ate. Then the eyes of both were opened, and they knew that they were naked; and they sewed fig leaves together and made loincloths for themselves" (NRSV).

48. Lieber, "I Set a Table before You," 69–70.

49. R. Marcus, *Philo, Questions and Answers on Exodus* (Cambridge/London: Harvard University Press/Heinemann, 1949) 81–82.

50. Lieber, "I Set a Table before You," 70.

51. Lieber, "I Set a Table before You," 70.

52. For instance, Martha Himmelfarb observes that "the account in the *Apocalypse of Abraham* implicitly compares Abraham's ascent to Moses' experience at Sinai. Thus, for example, Abraham performs the sacrifice described in Genesis 15 at Mount Horeb (the name for Mount Sinai in some biblical sources) after forty days of fasting in the wilderness. The exegetical occasion for the association of Genesis 15 and Exodus 19–20 is the manifestation of the presence of God in smoke and fire in both passages." Himmelfarb, *Ascent to Heaven,* 62. Another scholar, Nancy Calvert, observes that "the similarity between Abraham's actions in chapter twelve and those of Moses are striking. He first travels to the mountain Horeb, known also in the Old Testament as Mt. Sinai, which is called 'God's mountain, glorious Horeb' in the Apocalypse of Abraham 12:3. Like Moses when he receives the law, Abraham spends forty days and nights on the mountain. Abraham is said neither to eat bread nor to drink water because his food 'was to see angel who was with me, and his discourse with me was my drink.' *Apoc. Ab.* 12:1–2. Philo reflects a Jewish tradition of Moses' time on the mount, saying that Moses neglected all meat and drink for forty days, because he had more excellent food than that in the contemplations with which he was inspired from heaven (*De Vita Mosis* II.69). Because Mt. Horeb and Mt. Sinai are names for the same mountain, Abraham receives his revelation from God in the same place that Moses received God's commandments. Finally, as the Lord 'was like a devouring fire on the top of the mountain' in the Exodus account, so the fire on top of Mt. Horeb burns the sacrifices over which Abraham and the angel ascend to heaven where God also appears as fire." Calvert, *Abraham Traditions in Middle Jewish Literature,* 274. Daniel Harlow also argues that "the patriarch's fasting 'for forty days and nights' marks one of several places in the apocalypse where the author models Abraham's experience on Moses's (Exod 34:28)." Harlow, "Idolatry and Alterity: Israel and the Nations in the Apocalypse of Abraham," 312. Cf. also Rubinkiewicz, *L'Apocalypse d'Abraham en vieux slave,* 58–60.

53. Kulik, *Retroverting Slavonic Pseudepigrapha*, 19.

54. Halperin, *Faces of the Chariot*, 111

55. Concerning this, see A. Orlov, " 'The Gods of My Father Terah': Abraham the Iconoclast and the Polemics with the Divine Body Traditions in the *Apocalypse of Abraham*," *JSP* 18.1 (2008) 33–53; idem, "Arboreal Metaphors and Polemics with the Divine Body Traditions in the *Apocalypse of Abraham*," *HTR* 102 (2009) 439–451.

56. Kulik, *Retroverting Slavonic Pseudepigrapha*, 13.

57. Cf. Ezek 1:27: "Upward from what appeared like the loins I saw something like gleaming amber, something that looked like fire enclosed all around; and downward from what looked like the loins I saw something that looked like fire, and there was a splendor all around" (NRSV); also, Ezek 8:2: "I looked, and there was a figure that looked like a human being; below what appeared to be its loins it was fire, and above the loins it was like the appearance of brightness, like gleaming amber" (NRSV). Cf. also Rev 1:15: ". . . his feet were like burnished bronze, refined as in a furnace, and his voice was like the sound of many waters" (NRSV).

58. *Apoc. Ab.* 15:14–17 reads: "And I said to him, 'Father Terah, do not bless your god Mar-Umath, do not praise him! Praise rather your god Bar-Eshath because, in his love for you he threw himself into the fire in order to cook your food.' And he said to me, 'And where is he now?' 'He has been reduced to ashes in the fury of the fire and become dust.' And he said, 'Great is the power of Bar-Eshath! I shall make another today, and tomorrow he will make my food!'" Kulik, *Retroverting Slavonic Pseudepigrapha*, 13.

59. "What are you doing, Abraham, on the holy heights, where no one eats or drinks, nor is there upon them food of men. But these will all be consumed by fire and they will burn you up. Leave the man who is with you and flee!" Kulik, *Retroverting Slavonic Pseudepigrapha*, 20.

60. Freedman and Simon, *Midrash Rabbah*, 4.261–262.

61. Freedman and Simon, *Midrash Rabbah*, 3.59. Cf. also *Exod. Rab.* 45:5: "R. Hoshayah Rabba said: Moses showed great respect in hiding his face, but Nadab and Abihu uncovered their heads and allowed their eyes to feed on the *Shechinah*, as it says, And upon the nobles of the children of Israel He laid not His hand; and they beheld God, and did eat and drink." Freedman and Simon, *Midrash Rabbah*, 3.523.

62. On rivers of fire, see Davila, *Hekhalot Literature in Translation*, 79. On rivers of fire see also *b. Hag.* 14a; *Exod. Rab.* 15:6; *Lam. Rab.* 3:8; *3 Enoch* 36:1–2; 40:1–4; *Zohar* I.201a; II.252b.

63. Cf. Davila, *Liturgical Works*, 139–140.

64. Schäfer et al., *Synopse*, 164.

65. M. Cohen, *The Shiᶜur Qomah: Texts and Recensions* (TSAJ, 9; Tübingen: Mohr/Siebeck, 1985)162–164.

66. James Davila notes that "in *Seder Rabba di-Bereshit* §182 . . . angels ascend a 'ladder of fire' to the heavenly throne room after returning from earth and bathing in rivers of fire to purify themselves." Davila, *Hekhalot Literature in Translation*, 101.

67. Orlov, *Dark Mirrors*, 18–19.

68. *Apoc. Ab.* 13:36: "And an impure bird flew down on the carcasses, and I drove it away. And the impure bird spoke to me and said, 'What are you doing, Abraham, on the holy heights, where no one eats or drinks, nor

is there upon them food of men. But these will all be consumed by fire and they will burn you up. Leave the man who is with you and flee! Since if you ascend to the height, they will destroy you.' " Kulik, *Retroverting Slavonic Pseudepigrapha,* 20. This passage is overlaid with an array of transformational concerns. It is clear that the demon does not want Abraham to undergo his further transition to the celestial state since it will lead to the antagonist's loss of celestial status—it is intriguing, also, that, right after Azazel's warning, we have a tradition of transference of the celestial garment of the fallen angel to the patriarch. As Dan Harlow rightly notes, "[C]learly Azazel recognizes an adversary in Abraham, whose going without food already makes him resemble the angels." Harlow, "Idolatry and Alterity: Israel and the Nations in the Apocalypse of Abraham," 314. David Halperin also notes, "[I]f Azazel can persuade Abraham not to make his ascent, he will perhaps be able to keep his own privileged status." Halperin, *Faces of the Chariot*, 111.

69. Cf. Chernus, *Mysticism in Rabbinic Judaism,* 74–75.

70. Kulik, *Retroverting Slavonic Pseudepigrapha*, 17.

71. *Jos. Asen.* 10:2: "[S]he ate no bread and drank no water," Burchard, "Joseph and Aseneth," 2.215; *Jos. Asen.*10:17: "And this way Aseneth did for seven days and she ate no bread and drank no water in those seven days of her humiliation." Burchard, "Joseph and Aseneth," 2.217. Cf. also *Jos. Asen.* 13:9; 18:3.

72. Scholars have noted that Aseneth's hospitality to the visiting angel is reminiscent of Abraham's hospitality in Genesis. As Andrea Lieber notes, "Aseneth offers to place a meal before the *anthropos*, in keeping with biblical traditions of hospitality associated with both Abraham in the Genesis narrative and Gideon in the book of Judges." Lieber, "I Set a Table before You," 68.

73. Kulik, *Retroverting Slavonic Pseudepigrapha*, 17; Rubinkiewicz, *L'Apocalypse d'Abraham en vieux slave,* 128; Philonenko-Sayar and Philonenko, *L'Apocalypse d'Abraham*, 58.

74. Kraemer, *When Aseneth Met Joseph*, 123. Cf. also E.M. Humphrey, *Joseph and Aseneth* (GAP, 8; Sheffield: Sheffield Academic Press, 2000) 69. The angel's reluctance to reveal his name to Aseneth might also indicate his role as the angel of the Tetragrammaton.

75. Concerning this motif, Anathea Portier-Young notes, "[O]bserving that its breath is also like the breath of the mouth of her visitor, she infers that the honeycomb has emanated from his mouth, having come into being by his speech (16.9). The angel confirms her suspicion, smiling at her understanding; she now demonstrates knowledge of heavenly mysteries (16.12)." Portier-Young, "Sweet Mercy Metropolis," 139.

76. Burchard, "Joseph and Aseneth," 2.228.

77. Burchard, "Joseph and Aseneth," 2.228.

78. Lieber, "I Set a Table before You," 68.

79. See, also, Matt 3:4: "And the tempter came and said to him, 'If you are the Son of God, command these stones to become loaves of bread.' But he answered, 'It is written, Man shall not live by bread alone, but by every word that proceeds from the mouth of God' " (NRSV).

80. Scholars have long noted a sharp opposition between the book of Deuteronomy and the Deuteronomic school, on the one hand, and early anthropomorphic developments, on the other. In fact, the Deuteronomic school is widely thought to have initiated the polemic against the anthropomorphic and corporeal conceptions of the Deity, which were subsequently adopted by the prophets Jeremiah and Deutero-Isaiah. Seeking to undermine ancient anthropomorphism, the book of Deuteronomy and the Deuteronomic school promulgated an anti-corporeal theology of the divine Name with its conception of the sanctuary or tabernacle as the exclusive dwelling abode of God's Name. Regarding these developments, see M. Weinfeld, *Deuteronomy and the Deuteronomic School* (Oxford: Clarendon Press, 1972) 191–201; T.N.D. Mettinger, *The Dethronement of Sabaoth. Studies in the Shem and Kabod Theologies* (ConBOT, 18; Lund: Wallin & Dalholm, 1982) 124.

81. M. Schneider, "Joseph and Aseneth and Early Jewish Mysticism," *Kabbalah* 3 (1998) 303–344 [Hebrew]; *idem*, *Scattered Traditions of Jewish Mysticism: Studies in Ancient Jewish Mysticism in Light of Traditions from the Apocrypha, the Pseudepigrapha, Hellenistic Literature, Christian and Islamic Sources* (SSLJM, 31; Los Angeles: Cherub Press, 2012) 11–79 [Hebrew]. Concerning Aseneth's conversion and the tradition of opening the statue's mouth with the divine Name, see also Philonenko, "Initiation et mystère dans Joseph et Aséneth," 147–153; C. Burchard, "The Present State of Research on Joseph and Aseneth," in *Religion, Literature, and Society in Ancient Israel, Formative Christianity and Judaism* (New Perspectives on Ancient Judaism, 2; eds. J. Neusner et al.; Lanham: University Press of America, 1987) 31–52; G. Bohak, "Asenath's Honeycomb and Onias' Temple: The Key to Joseph and Asenath," in *Proceedings of the Eleventh World Congress of Jewish Studies, Division A* (ed. D. Assaf; Jerusalem: Magness Press, 1994) 163–170; G.Y. Glazov, *The Bridling of the Tongue and the Opening of the Mouth in Biblical Prophecy* (JSOTSS, 311; Sheffield: Sheffield Academic Press, 2001) 379.

82. Regarding ancient rituals of the washing of the mouth and the opening of the mouth of cultic statues, see P.J. Boden, *The Mesopotamian Washing of the Mouth (Mīs Pî) Ritual* (Ph.D. diss. Johns Hopkins University, 1998); A. Berlejung, *Die Theologie der Bilder: Herstellung und Einweihung von Kultbildern in Mesopotamien und die alttestamentliche Bilderpolemik* (OBO, 162; Freiburg: Universitätsverlag, 1998); *Born in Heaven, Made on Earth: The Making of the Cult Image in the Ancient Near East* (ed. M.B. Dick; Winona Lake: Eisenbrauns, 1999); *The Induction of the Cult Image in Ancient Mesopotamia: The Mesopotamian Mīs Pî Ritual: Transliteration, Translation, and*

Commentary (eds. C. Walker and M.B. Dick; SAALT, 1; Helsinki: University of Helsinki, 2001); V.A. Hurowitz, "The Mesopotamian God Image, from Womb to Tomb," *JAOS* 123 (2003) 147–157; *Cult Image and Divine Representation in the Ancient Near East* (ed. N.H. Walls; ASOR, 10; Boston: American Schools of Oriental Research, 2005); V.A. Hurowitz, "What Goes In Is What Comes Out: Materials for Creating Cult Statues," in *Text, Artifact, and Image; Revealing Ancient Israelite Religion* (eds. G.M. Beckman and T.J. Lewis; BJS, 346; Providence, RI: Brown Judaic Studies, 2006) 3–23; G. K. Beale, *We Become What We Worship: A Biblical Theology of Idolatry* (Downers Grove, IL: Inter-Varsity Press, 2008); M. S. Smith, *God in Translation: Deities in Cross-Cultural Discourse in the Biblical World* (Grand Rapids: Eerdmans, 2010); M.J. Lundberg, "The Mis-Pi Rituals and Incantations and Jeremiah 10:1–16," in *Uprooting and Planting: Essays on Jeremiah for Leslie Allen* (ed. J. Goldingay; London: T&T Clark, 2007) 210–227.

83. M. Idel, "Hermeticism and Judaism," in *Hermeticism and the Renaissance: Intellectual History and the Occult in Early Modern Europe* (eds. I. Merkel and A. G. Debus; Washington, DC: Folger Library, 1988) 59–76; idem, *Golem: Jewish Magical and Mystical Traditions on the Artificial Anthropoid* (Albany: SUNY Press, 1990).

84. G. Scholem, "The Idea of the Golem," in *On the Kabbalah and Its Symbolism* (trans. R. Manheim, New York: Schocken, 1965) 159–165; E. L. Greenstein, "God's Golem: The Creation of the Human in Genesis 2," in *Creation in Jewish and Christian Tradition* (eds. H. Reventlow and Y. Hoffman; JSOTSS, 319; Sheffield: Sheffield Academic Press, 2002) 219–239. In later rabbinic testimonies, not only Golem, but also, some infamous biblical idols are brought to life through the placement of the divine Name in their mouths. One such story occurs in *Zohar* II.175a, in which the idol of King Nebuchadnezzar is vivified when a vessel of the Temple with the divine Name is put in its mouth: "King Nebuchadnezzar made an image of gold whose height was sixty cubits high and whose width was six cubits. Nebuchadnezzar said, 'The image that I saw had a head of gold and belly of silver. . . . I will make one all of gold, so that a lower coronet of gold will be upon its head.' It has been taught: On that day he gathered all peoples, nations, and tongues to worship that image, and he took one of the vessels of the Temple upon which was engraved the Holy Name and put it in the mouth of that image, and it began speaking grandly until Daniel came and approached the image, and said, 'I am the messenger of the supreme Lord. I decree upon you to leave here!' He invoked the Holy Name, and that vessel came out, and the image fell and broke. . . ." Matt, *The Zohar: Pritzker Edition*, 5.520; *Pirke de Rabbi Eliezer* 55 suggests that another infamous biblical idol—the Golden Calf—was created with the help of the divine Name; it reads: "They broke off their earrings which were in their own ears, and they gave (them) to Aaron, as it is

said, 'And all the people brake off the golden rings which were in their ears' (Ex. xxxii. 3). 'Which were in the ears of their wives' is not written here, but 'which were in their ears.' Aaron found among the earrings one plate of gold *upon which the Holy Name was written*, and engraved thereon was the figure of a calf, and that (plate) alone did he cast into the fiery furnace, as it is said, 'So they gave it me: and I cast it into the fire, and there came out this calf.' It is not written here, 'And I cast them in,' but 'And I cast it in the fire, and there came out this calf.' The calf came out lowing, and the Israelites saw it, and they went astray after it." Friedlander, *Pirke de Rabbi Eliezer*, 354–355. For in depth discussion of this tradition, see Scholem, *On the Kabbalah and Its Symbolism*, 182; Glazov, *The Bridling of the Tongue*, 382.

85. With respect to these traditions, see C. L. Beckerleg, *The "Image of God" in Eden* (Ph.D. diss.; Harvard University, 2009).

86. In both texts, the spiritual feeding has salvific and eschatological significance. It returns a human seer to the protological condition when the protoplast was fed by the splendor of the *Shechinah*. As Ira Chernus rightly noted, this tradition of the protoplast's spiritual nourishment appears to be reflected also in *3 Enoch*. Chernus, *Mysticism in Rabbinic Judaism*, 75–76. Thus, *3 Enoch* 5:3 tells that "the first man and his generation dwelt at the gate of the garden of Eden so that they might gaze at the bright image of the *Shechinah*." Alexander, "3 Enoch," 1.259. An early witness to such a tradition of the protoplast's feeding on the divine Glory might also be present in *2 Enoch*, in which the Deity orders the angel to open heavens so Adam will gain access to the vision of Glory.

87. Concerning these traditions, see Idel, *Golem*, 31, 91–92, 103, 139.

88. Cf. also 12:5: "My mouth is defiled from the sacrifices of the idols and from the tables of the gods of the Egyptians." Burchard, "Joseph and Aseneth," 2.221

89. *Jos. Asen.*10:12–13: "And Aseneth hurried and took all her gods that were in her chamber, the ones of gold and silver who were without number, and ground them to pieces/ and threw all the idols of the Egyptians through the window." Burchard, "Joseph and Aseneth," 2.218. Cf. also *Jos. Asen.* 13:11: "Behold now, all the gods whom I once used to worship in ignorance: I have now recognized that they were dumb and dead idols, and I have caused them to be trampled underfoot by men, and the thieves snatched those that were of silver and gold." Burchard, "Joseph and Aseneth," 2.223.

90. Ross Kraemer, for instance, observes: "Most obviously, the longer text contains two lengthy silent monologues (11.3–19) absent in the shorter version, whose motifs are also largely absent in the shorter text, including a great concern for the significance of the name of God. . . . The longer text thus displays considerably more interest in the name of God. . . . Interest in the divine name may point to the religious sensibilities of the redactors."

R. Kraemer, *When Aseneth Met Joseph: A Late Antique Tale of the Biblical Patriarch and His Egyptian Wife, Reconsidered* (New York: Oxford University Press, 1998) 54–56.

91. ". . . how shall I open my mouth to the Most High, and how name his terrible holy name." Burchard, "Joseph and Aseneth," 2.219.

92. Kraemer, *When Aseneth Met Joseph*, 121.

93. Kraemer, *When Aseneth Met Joseph*, 127.

94. Himmelfarb, *Ascent to Heaven*, 64; Rowland and Morray-Jones, *The Mystery of God*, 83.

95. See A. Orlov, *Heavenly Priesthood in the Apocalypse of Abraham* (Cambridge; Cambridge University Press, 2013) 53–58.

96. G. Scholem, *Major Trends in Jewish Mysticism* (New York: Schocken, 1954) 59–61; Dean-Otting, *Heavenly Journeys*, 252–253.

97. Kraemer, *When Aseneth Met Joseph*, 122.

98. "The angel refuses to tell her his name and so prevents her from singing hymns, presumably to him, and from glorifying him." Kraemer, *When Aseneth Met Joseph*, 127.

99. Kulik, *Retroverting Slavonic Pseudepigrapha*, 27.

100. The theme of physical and spiritual nourishment plays an important role in the extrabiblical elaborations of Abraham's story, in which he rejects the food of idols being then thrown into fire by Nimrod. In rabbinic literature his fiery ordeals are often tied to the Danielic tale about three Israelite youths, in which a motif of rejection of idolatrous food is juxtaposed, as in *Joseph and Aseneth*, with the alternative vision of the celestial being.

101. Although, here, Azazel, being in the form of the serpent, feeds Adam and Eve, according to some traditions, originally the protoplasts were responsible for nourishment of the serpent. Thus, for example, the Georgian version of the *Primary Adam Books* 16:2a reads: "Then the serpent came and the Devil told the serpent, 'I hear that you are wiser than all the animals and I have come to test your knowledge, for Adam gives food to all the animals, thus also to you.' " Anderson and Stone, *A Synopsis of the Books of Adam and Eve*, 49E. This motif points to the dynamics of exaltation and demotion that are dialectically manifest in an array of Jewish traditions of nourishment, in which the one who is fed and the one who is feeding are often situated in a hierarchical relationship. It is not coincidental that, both in *Apocalypse of Abraham* and *Joseph and Aseneth*, it is celestial beings (one who is demoted and the other in good standing) who are depicted as delivering nourishment to human beings. It depicts the creatures of the higher spiritual rank as ones who nourish the creatures of the lower realms. As Joel Hecker shows, in later Jewish mysticism, nourishment imagery is used as a metaphor signifying the flow of divine blessing from the upper worlds to the lower. See J. Hecker, *Mystical Bodies, Mystical Meals: Eating and Embodiment in Medieval Kabbalah*

(Raphael Patai Series in Jewish Folklore and Anthropology; Detroit: Wayne State University Press, 2005).

102. Daniel Harlow suggests that "the three of them appear in a *ménage à trois,* the man and woman entwined in an erotic embrace, the fallen angel in serpentine guise feeding them grapes." Harlow, "Idolatry and Alterity: Israel and the Nations in the Apocalypse of Abraham," 320.

103. See *Jos. Asen.* 8:5–6: ". . . It is not fitting for a man who worships God, who will bless with his mouth the living God and eat blessed bread of life and drink a blessed cup of immortality and anoint himself with blessed ointment of incorruptibility to kiss a strange woman who will bless with her mouth dead and dumb idols and eat from their table bread of strangulation and drink from their libation a cup of insidiousness and anoint herself with ointment of destruction." Burchard, "Joseph and Aseneth," 2.211–212. It is also intriguing that in *Joseph and Aseneth,* like in the *Apocalypse of Abraham,* the symbolism of angelic food is mirrored with the imagery of the food of corruption. Thus the formulae from Joseph's address to Aseneth in the beginning of the pseudepigraphon, which speaks of idolatrous food, are mirrored later in the text in description of angelic nourishment and anointing offered by the angel to the seer.

104. Burchard, "Joseph and Aseneth," 2.233.

105. Scholars have noted that in *Joseph and Aseneth* the spirit "is transferred through heavenly food and Joseph's kiss." V. Rabens, *The Holy Spirit And Ethics in Paul: Transformation and Empowering for Religious-Ethical Life* (2nd rev. ed.; WUNT, 2.283; Tübingen: Mohr/Siebeck, 2013) 11.

106. Burchard, "Joseph and Aseneth," 2.228.

107. Scholem, *On the Kabbalah and Its Symbolism,* 182.

108. *Pirke de Rabbi Eliezer* 55: "Rabbi Jehudah said: Sammael entered into it, and he was lowing to mislead Israel, as it is said, 'The ox knoweth his owner.'" Friedlander, *Pirke de Rabbi Eliezer,* 355.

109. "The serpent said, 'In what way or how can we expel him from the Garden?' Satan said to the serpent, 'Be you, in your form, a lyre for me and I will pronounce speech through your mouth, so that we may be able to help.' Then the two of them came to me and hung their feet around the wall of the Garden. When the angels ascended to the worship of the Lord, at that time Satan took on the form of an angel and began to praise God with angelic praises. I knelt down by the wall and attended to his praises. I looked and saw him in the likeness of an angel; when I looked again, I did not see him. Then he went and summoned the serpent and said to him, 'Arise, come to me so that I may enter into you and speak through your mouth as much as I will need to say.' At that time the serpent became a lyre for him, and he came again to the wall of the Garden. He cried out and said, 'Oh, woman, you who are blind in this Garden of delight, arise come to me and I will say

some words to you.'" Anderson and Stone, *A Synopsis of the Books of Adam and Eve*, 50E–52E. The tradition of Satan's metamorphosis into the living form of the serpent is also present in the Georgian version; it reads: "And the serpent told him, 'How can we have them excluded?' The devil replied and told the serpent, 'Be a sheath for me and I will speak to the woman through your mouth a word by which we will trick (them).' And the two of them came together and they allowed their heads to hang on the wall of the paradise at the time where the angels had ascended to bow down to God. Then the devil changed himself into the image of an angel; he praised the praises of the angels. And I was gazing in the direction of the enclosure to hear the praises. I stared and I saw him like an angel and at once he became invisible for he had gone forth to bring the serpent. And he told him, 'Arise and come and I will be with you and I will speak through your mouth that which it is proper for you to say.' He took on the form of the serpent (to go) close to the wall of paradise and the devil slipped inside the serpent and he allowed his head to hang on the wall of paradise. He cried out and said, 'Shame on you, woman, you who are in the paradise of Delight (and) who are blind! Come to me and I will tell you a certain secret word.'" Anderson and Stone, *A Synopsis of the Books of Adam and Eve*, 50E–52E.

110. Pseudepigraphical and rabbinic accounts depict this process of "possession" of a living form as Satan's "riding" of the serpent.

111. In this respect it is intriguing that in later Jewish mysticism the descent of Asael and Shemihazah from heaven is compared with the descent of the manna. The *Book of Zohar* III.208a reads: "The fact is, however, that after God cast Uzza and Azael down from their holy place, they went astray after the womenfolk and seduced the world also. It may seem strange that being angels they were able to abide upon the earth. The truth is, however, that when they were cast down the celestial light which used to sustain them left them and they were changed to another grade through the influence of the air of this world. Similarly the manna which came down for the Israelites in the wilderness originated in the celestial dew from the most recondite spot, and at first its light would radiate to all worlds and the 'field of apples,' and the heavenly angels drew sustenance from it, but when it approached the earth it became materialized through the influence of the air of this world and lost its brightness, becoming only like 'coriander seed.'" Simon and Sperling, *The Zohar*, 5.311–312.

The Messianic Scapegoat in the Apocalypse of Abraham

1. Kulik, *Retroverting Slavonic Pseudepigrapha*, 32–33.

2. Alexander Kulik conveys this consensus by affirming that "chapter 29, where a messianic (or anti-messianic) figure is introduced, is the most enigmatic in the entire writing." Kulik, *Retroverting Slavonic Pseudepigrapha*, 51.

3. See M.J. Lagrange, "Notes sur le messianisme au temps de Jesus," *RB* 14 (1905) 513; Box and Landsman, *The Apocalypse of Abraham*, 78; P. Riessler, *Altjüdisches Schrifttum außerhalb der Bibel* (Heidelberg: Kerle, 1927) 1267; Y. Kaufmann, "Abraham-Apokalypse," in: *Encyclopaedia Judaica. Das Judentum in Geschichte und Gegenwart* (eds. J. Klatzkin and I. Elbogen; 10 vols.; Berlin: Eschkol Publikations Gesellschaft, 1928–1934) 1.552–53; J. Licht, "Abraham, Apocalypse of," in: *Encyclopedia Judaica* (16 vols.; ed. C. Roth; Jerusalem: Keter, 1971) 2.127; R. Rubinkiewicz, "La vision de l'histoire dans l'Apocalypse d'Abraham," *ANRW* 2.19.1 (1979) 137–151 at 143–144; idem, *L'Apocalypse d'Abraham en vieux slave*, 66, 193; idem, "The Apocalypse of Abraham," 1.684; G.S. Oegema, *The Anointed and His People: Messianic Expectations from the Maccabees to Bar Kochba* (JSPSS, 27; Sheffield: Sheffield Academic Press, 1998) 214.

4. R.G. Hall, "The 'Christian Interpolation' in the *Apocalypse of Abraham*," *JBL* 107 (1988) 107–112; D. C. Harlow,"Anti-Christian Polemic in the Apocalypse of Abraham: Jesus as a Pseudo-Messiah in *Apoc. Ab.* 29.3–14," *JSP* 22.3 (2013) 167–183.

5. Harlow, "Idolatry and Alterity: Israel and the Nations in the *Apocalypse of Abraham*," 302–30.

6. Thus, for example, Rubinkiewicz observes that Azazel "who bows down and lowers his face, imitates Judas's gesture in the scene of Jesus' arrest (cf. Matt 26:47ff)." Rubinkiewicz, *L'Apocalypse d'Abraham en vieux slave*, 66. With respect to Judas as the scapegoat, see B. Dieckmann, *Judas als Sündenbock: Eine verhängnisvolle Geschichte von Angst und Vergeltung* (Munich: Kösel, 1991). Daniel Harlow argues that "the man in the vision bears an uncanny resemblance to Jesus of Nazareth. He does so in three respects: first, his being shamed and struck recall Jesus' passion, in particular his being flogged and humiliated by Roman soldiers and then being mocked at the foot of the cross; second, his being worshipped by the heathen and by some of Abraham's seed evokes veneration of Jesus by both Jews and non-Jews in the decades after his death; third, his being kissed by Azazel echoes not only Judas Iscariot's betrayal of Jesus with a kiss, known in all three of the Synoptic Gospels, but also the tradition known from the Gospels of Luke and John that Judas was possessed by Satan, who entered him and inspired him to hand Jesus over to the authorities." Harlow, "Anti-Christian Polemic in the Apocalypse of Abraham: Jesus as a Pseudo-Messiah in *Apoc. Ab.* 29.3–14," 175–176.

7. Some scholars also see in *Apoc. Ap.* 29 an allusion to the tradition of the Suffering Servant in the Book of Isaiah. Gillis Byrns Coleman notes

that the messianic figure's "sufferings . . . are reminiscent of Isaiah 53." G.B. Coleman, *The Phenomenon of Christian Interpolations into Jewish Apocalyptic Texts: A Bibliographical Survey and Methodological Analysis* (Ph.D. diss.; Vanderbilt University, 1976) 323. Coleman also adds that "it could perhaps be asked whether one would find anything specifically Christian here (any more than in Isaiah 53) if he were not looking for it." Coleman, *The Phenomenon of Christian Interpolations,* 323. It should be noted that some scholars have suggested that Deutero-Isaiah's tradition of the Suffering Servant was possibly influenced by the scapegoat imagery. See J.D. Watts, *Isaiah 34–66* (WBC, 25; Waco: Word Books, 1987) 231; J.N. Oswalt, *The Book of Isaiah. Chapters 40–66* (NICOT; Grand Rapids: Eerdmans, 1998) 377. For criticism of such parallels, see Stökl Ben Ezra, *The Impact of Yom Kippur on Early Christianity*, 117.

8. It is possible that the Yom Kippur settings are present in the New Testament materials, specifically in the story of Barabbas's release by Pilate, which appears in all four canonical gospels (Mark 15:6–15; Matthew 27:15–26; Luke 23:18–25; John 18:39–40). Yet, in these materials, Barabbas, not Jesus, assumes the functions of the scapegoat. Early Christian exegetes (cf. Origen, *Homily on Leviticus* 10:2:2) often emphasize this connection between Barabbas' episode and the Yom Kippur ritual of the two goats. Pseudo-Jerome's *Commentary on Mark* 15:11 also follows this line of interpretation: "The High Priests stirred up the crowds so they would ask for Barabbas, and so that they might crucify Jesus (cf. Mark 15:11). Here we have the two goats. One is termed ἀποπομαίος meaning 'the scapegoat.' He is set free with the sin of the people and sent into the desert of hell. The other goat is slain like a lamb for the sins of those who have been set free. The Lord's portion is always slaughtered. The portion of the devil, who is their master, is cast out, without restriction, into the infernal regions." M. Cahill, *The First Commentary on Mark. An Annotated Translation* (Oxford: Oxford University Press, 1998) 116. Regarding the scapegoat traditions in the canonical gospels, see A.H. Wratislaw, "The Scapegoat-Barabbas," *Expository Times* 3 (1891/92) 400–403; J.D. Crossan, *The Cross that Spoke: The Origins of the Passion Narrative* (San Francisco: Harper & Row, 1988) 114–159; Stökl Ben Ezra, *The Impact of Yom Kippur on Early Christianity*, 165–171; Maclean, "Barabbas, the Scapegoat Ritual, and the Development of the Passion Narrative," 309–334.

9. Crossan, *The Cross that Spoke,* 121.

10. Ehrman, *The Apostolic Fathers*, 2.37–41.

11. Stökl Ben Ezra, *The Impact of Yom Kippur on Early Christianity*, 154.

12. Stökl Ben Ezra, *The Impact of Yom Kippur on Early Christianity*, 152.

13. Concerning this motif, see J.C. Paget, *The Epistle of Barnabas* (WUNT, 2.64; Tübingen: Mohr/Siebeck, 1994) 138–140.

14. See Stökl Ben Ezra, *The Impact of Yom Kippur on Early Christianity*, 154.

15. *Iustini Martyris Dialogus Cum Tryphone* (ed. M. Marcovich; PTS, 47; Berlin/New York: De Gruyter, 1997) 137; *Justin Martyr: Dialogue avec Tryphon* (ed. and trans. P. Bobichon; Fribourg: Academic Press Fribourg, 2003) 284.

16. Falls, Halton, Slusser, *St. Justin Martyr, Dialogue with Trypho*, 62.

17. Stökl Ben Ezra, *The Impact of Yom Kippur on Early Christianity*, 156.

18. Crossan, *The Cross that Spoke*, 129.

19. Thus Daniel Stökl Ben Ezra observes that "this is shown, for example, by the reference to the death of the scapegoat, a fact Justin could not have learnt from the Bible or from Barnabas, but only from Jewish tradition." Stökl Ben Ezra, *The Impact of Yom Kippur on Early Christianity*, 156.

20. Stökl Ben Ezra, *The Impact of Yom Kippur on Early Christianity*, 156.

21. Cf. Isa 58:6 (LXX) ". . . λῦε πάντα σύνδεσμον ἀδικίας διάλυε στραγγαλιὰς βιαίων συναλλαγμάτων. . . ."

22. Another early influential Christian interpreter, Hippolytus of Rome, also shows his familiarity with the traditions that tie Jesus to the imagery of two goats of the Yom Kippur ceremony. Daniel Stökl Ben Ezra argues that the passage from Hippolytus of Rome's *Catenae on Proverbs* (Proverbs 30:31b (LXX)) that mentions "scarlet wool" "makes very plausible that it is a variety of the Yom Kippur typology known to *Barnabas*, Justin and Tertullian. . . ." Stökl Ben Ezra, *The Impact of Yom Kippur on Early Christianity*, 158. He, however, cautions that "the poetic form and the brevity of the fragment render an exact comparison difficult." Stökl Ben Ezra, *The Impact of Yom Kippur on Early Christianity*, 158.

23. Evans, *Tertullian. Adversus Marcionem*, 1.191. The nearly identical passage appears in *Against the Jews* 14:9, it reads: "In fact, thus also let me make an interpretation of the two goats that were offered at the fast. Do these not also show the two conditions of the Christ who is already come? They are indeed of the same age and appearance on account of the one and the same aspect of the Lord, because he will return in no other form, seeing that he has to be recognized by those from whom he has suffered injury. One of them, however, which was surrounded with scarlet, cursed and spat upon and perforated and punctured, was driven outside the city by the people to ruin, marked with obvious emblems of the suffering of Christ, who, having been surrounded with a scarlet garment, spat upon and knocked about with every physical violence, was crucified outside the city. The other, however, made an offering for offences, and given as food only to the priests of the temple, is marked with the proof of his second manifestation, because when all offences have been done away, the priests of the spiritual temple—that is, the church—were to enjoy as it were a feast of our Lord's grace, while the rest remain without a taste of salvation." Dunn, *Tertullian*, 103.

24. Crossan notes that "in the case of *Against Marcion* 3.7.7, however, we are not dealing with a third independent version of the two goats tradition

but rather with one which is dependent both on *Barnabas* 7 and on Justin, *Dialogue* 40." Crossan, *The Cross that Spoke*, 131.

25. Falls, Halton, Slusser, *St. Justin Martyr. Dialogue with Trypho*, 62.

26. "And in the same twelfth period of the close of my age I shall set up the man from your seed which you saw." Kilik, *Retroverting Slavonic Pseudepigrapha*, 32.

27. Kulik, *Retroverting Slavonic Pseudepigrapha*, 32.

28. Thus, for example, Marc Philonenko notes that the word "lot" (Slav. *частъ*) appears to be connected to the Hebrew גורל, a term attested to multiple times in the Qumran materials. Philonenko-Sayar and Philonenko, *L'Apocalypse d'Abraham. Introduction, texte slave, traduction et notes*, 33. Regarding the two lots, see also B. Philonenko-Sayar and M. Philonenko, *Die Apokalypse Abrahams* (JSHRZ, 5.5; Gütersloh: Mohn, 1982) 413–460 at 418; Rubinkiewicz, *L'Apocalypse d'Abraham en vieux slave*, 54.

29. For the biblical גורל terminology, see Lev 16:8–10.

30. See for example, *1QS* גורל בליעל (the lot of Belial); גורל קדושים (the lot of the holy ones); *1QM* גורל בני חושך (the lot of the sons of darkness); גורל חושך (the lot of darkness); *11Q13* גורל אנש[י] מל[כי] צדק (the men of the lot of Melchizedek).

31. Arie Rubinstein observes that "in the *Apocalypse of Abraham* . . . all nations, with the exception of the seed of Abraham, are the lot of Azazel, while the descendants of Abraham are the exclusive lot and heritage of God. So radical is this dualism in our Apocalypse that Abraham's descendants are shown to him spatially separated from Azazel and the nations which are with him." A. Rubinstein, "A Problematic Passage in the *Apocalypse of Abraham*," *JJS* 8 (1957) 45–50 at 47.

32. *Apoc. Ab.* 13:7: "And he said to him, 'Reproach is on you, Azazel! Since *Abraham's portion* (часть Аврамля) is in heaven, and *yours* is on earth. . . .'" Kulik, *Retroverting Slavonic Pseudepigrapha*, 20; Philonenko-Sayar and Philonenko, *L'Apocalypse d'Abraham*, 66.

33. Kulik, *Retroverting Slavonic Pseudepigrapha*, 32.

34. Cf. Stökl Ben Ezra, *The Impact of Yom Kippur on Early Christianity*, 31.

35. Danby, *The Mishnah*, 169.

36. Danby, *The Mishnah*, 170.

37. Ehrman, *The Apostolic Fathers*, 2.39.

38. Evans, *Tertullian. Adversus Marcionem*, 1.191.

39. Dunn, *Tertullian*, 103.

40. Crossan, *The Cross that Spoke*, 143.

41. Kulik, *Retroverting Slavonic Pseudepigrapha*, 20.

42. A. Orlov, *Dark Mirrors: Azazel and Satanael in Early Jewish Demonology* (Albany: SUNY Press, 2011) 44.

43. "и тече Азазилъ и поклонися и облобызавыи лице его и обратися и ста за нимъ." Philonenko-Sayar and Philonenko, *L'Apocalypse d'Abraham. Introduction, texte slave, traduction et notes*, 98–100.

44. Thus, the kiss of Azazel has often been considered by scholars (e.g. R. Hall, M. Philonenko) as an act of worship. Cf. Philonenko-Sayar and Philonenko, *Die Apocalypse Abrahams*, 450 n. xxix.

45. Thus, *m. Yoma* 4:1 reads: "He shook the casket and took up the two lots. On one was written 'For the Lord,' and on the other was written 'For Azazel.' " Danby, *The Mishnah*, 166.

46. Cf. Josephus, *Jewish War*, 5.235: "His head was covered by a tiara of fine linen, wreathed with blue, encircling which was another crown, of gold, whereon were embossed the sacred letters, to wit, four vowels." Thackeray and Markus, *Josephus*, 3.273.

47. Cf. *m. Yoma* 6:6: "What did he do? He divided the thread of crimson wool and tied one half to the rock and the other half between its horns, and he pushed it from behind; and it went rolling down, and before it had reached half the way down the hill it was broken in pieces. He returned and sat down beneath the last booth until nightfall. And from what time does it render his garments unclean? After he has gone outside the wall of Jerusalem. R. Simeon says: From the moment that he pushes it into the ravine." Danby, *The Mishnah*, 170. *m. Yoma* 6:8: "R. Ishmael says: Had they not another sign also?—a thread of crimson wool was tied to the door of the Sanctuary and when the he-goat reached the wilderness the thread turned white; for it is written, Though your sins be as scarlet they shall be as white as snow." Danby, *The Mishnah*, 170.

48. With respect to Azazel's mimesis of the divine *Kavod* in the *Apocalypse of Abraham,* see A. Orlov, " 'The Likeness of Heaven': *Kavod* of Azazel in the *Apocalypse of Abraham*," in *With Letters of Light: Studies in the Dead Sea Scrolls, Early Jewish Apocalypticism, Magic and Mysticism* (Ekstasis, 2; eds. D. Arbel and A. Orlov; Berlin; N.Y.: De Gruyter, 2010) 232–253.

49. Regarding erotic imagery in the *Apocalypse of Abraham,* see Harlow, "Idolatry and Alterity: Israel and the Nations in the *Apocalypse of Abraham*," 320; also, Orlov, " 'The Likeness of Heaven,' " 247.

50. Moreover, the theophanic dimension is even present in the earthly version of the revelation given to the high priest on Yom Kippur, in which he was given a disclosure of the intertwined pair of the Cherubim in the Holy of Holies. Thus, *b. Yoma* 54a reads: "R. Kattina said: Whenever Israel came up to the Festival, the curtain would be removed for them and the Cherubim were shown to them, whose bodies were intertwisted with one another, and they would be thus addressed: Look! You are beloved before God as the love between man and woman." Epstein, *The Babylonian Talmud. Yoma,* 54a. Cf. also *b. Yoma* 54b. Concerning this tradition, Rachel Elior observes

that while the early traditions about the cherubim, found "both in the Bible and elsewhere, imply varying degrees of proximity and contact—later tradition was more explicit, clearly indicating the identity of the cherubim as a mythical symbolization of reproduction and fertility, expressed in the form of intertwined male and female." R. Elior, *The Three Temples: On the Emergence of Jewish Mysticism* (Oxford: The Littman Library of Jewish Civilization, 2004) 67.

51. With respect to apocalyptic *imaginaires* of Yom Kippur, see Stökl Ben Ezra, *The Impact of Yom Kippur on Early Christianity*, 79–85.

52. *2 Enoch* 39:5: "But you, my children, see the right hand of one who helps you, a human being created identical to yourself, but I have seen the right hand of the Lord, helping me and filling heaven." Andersen, "2 Enoch," 1.162; M.I. Sokolov, "Материалы и заметки по старинной славянской литературе. Выпуск третий. VII. Славянская Книга Еноха Праведного. Тексты, латинский перевод и исследование. Посмертный труд автора приготовил к изданию М. Сперанский," *Чтения в Обществе Истории и Древностей Российских* 4 (1910) 1–167 at 38.

53. H. Jacobson, *The Exagoge of Ezekiel* (Cambridge: Cambridge University Press, 1983) 54.

54. Regarding this tradition, see R. Neis, "Embracing Icons: The Face of Jacob on the Throne of God," *Journal of Jewish Art & Visual Culture* 1 (2007) 36–54.

55. J.R. Davila, *Hekhalot Literature in Translation: Major Texts of Merkavah Mysticism* (SJJTP, 20; Leiden: Brill, 2013) 86; *Synopse zur Hekhalot-Literatur* (eds. P. Schäfer et al.; TSAJ, 2; Tübingen: Mohr/Siebeck, 1981) §163. See also *Hekhalot Rabbati* (*Synopse* §189): "Every single day, when the afternoon prayer arrives, the adorned King sits enthroned and exalts the living creatures. The word does not finish coming from His mouth before the holy living creatures go forth from under the throne of glory. From their mouth is fullness of chanting, with their wings is fullness of rejoicing, their hands make music, and their feet dance. They go around and surround their King; one from His right and one from His left, one from in front of Him and one from behind Him. They embrace and kiss Him and uncover their faces. They uncover and the King of glory covers His face, and the Aravot firmament is split like a siever before the King, before the adornment of the splendor of the attractiveness of the form of the loveliness of the compassion of the craving of the radiance of the light of the praise of the appearance of their faces, according to the word that is written, Holy, holy, holy (Isa 6:3)." Davila, *Hekhalot Literature in Translation*, 93–94.

56. It is noteworthy that the authors of the Slavonic apocalypse used erotic imagery in the depiction of another "theophany" of Azazel in chapter 23, in which he is depicted in conjugal union with Adam and Eve.

57. Concerning this tradition, see Orlov, "*Kavod* of Azazel," 245–252.

58. Moreover, Azazel's kiss might represent here, as in other portions of the book, an example of negative transformational mysticism, paralleling the eschatological reunification with God in the Holy of Holies.

59. Kulik, *Retroverting Slavonic Pseudepigrapha*, 32.

60. Rubinkiewicz observes that the phrase "with Azazel" can be interpreted in two ways: "In one, the phrase 'with Azazel' is construed with 'by the heathen' to mean that the heathen are being aided by Azazel in insulting, beating, and, presumably, also worshiping the man. In the other, 'with Azazel' is construed with the following participle to mean that both Azazel and the man are being worshiped." Rubinkiewicz and Lunt, "The Apocalypse of Abraham," 1.703.

61. Epstein, *The Babylonian Talmud. Yoma*, 66b.

62. *Hekhalot Rabbati* (*Synopse* §259).

63. Kissing the calves in the context of idolatrous practices is mentioned in the Book of Hosea 13:2: "Ephraim spake horror, and became guilty in Baal and now they sin more and more and have made them a molten image of their silver, even idols in their own intelligence, all of them the work of the craftsmen they say to them, Let the sacrificers of men kiss the calves."

64. *Apoc. Ab.* 29:6: "Azazel ran and worshiped, and having kissed his face he turned. . . ." Kulik, *Retroverting Slavonic Pseudepigrapha*, 32.

65. K. Jones, *Jewish Reactions to the Destruction of Jerusalem in A.D. 70: Apocalypses and Related Pseudepigrapha* (JSJSS, 151; Leiden: Brill, 2011) 265.

66. Cf. *Apoc. Ab.* 3:4; 3:8.

67. *Apoc. Ab.* 25:1: "I saw there the likeness of the idol of jealousy, as a likeness of a craftsman's [work] such as my father made, and its statue was of shining copper, and a man before it, and he was worshiping it. . . ." Kulik, *Retroverting Slavonic Pseudepigrapha*, 29.

68. R.G. Hall, *Revealed Histories. Techniques for Ancient Jewish and Christian Historiography* (JSPSS, 6; Sheffield: JSOT Press, 1991) 78.

69. Hall, "The 'Christian Interpolation' in the *Apocalypse of Abraham*," 108.

70. See Himmelfarb, *Ascent to Heaven in Jewish and Christian Apocalypses*, 62; N.L. Calvert, *Abraham Traditions in Middle Jewish Literature: Implications for the Interpretation of Galatians and Romans* (Ph.D. diss.; Sheffield University, 1993) 274.

71. Some midrashic materials try to connect the establishment of the Yom Kippur rites with the repentance of the Israelites after the idolatry of the Golden Calf. Later Jewish mysticism deepens this connection even further when it interprets the scapegoat ritual in light of the Golden Calf traditions. Thus some Jewish texts connect the Golden Calf episode with the beginning of the enigmatic practice of assigning a share to the Other Side in sacrificial

ritual. Isaiah Tishby, for instance, refers to the tradition found in the *Book of Zohar*, according to which "one of the consequences of Israel's sin with the Golden Calf was that 'the Other Side' was assigned a share in the sacrificial ritual." Tishby, *The Wisdom of the Zohar,* 891. The *Book of Zohar* II.242b tells that "from that day the only thing they could do was to give a portion of everything to 'the Other Side' through the mystery of the sacrifices, the libation, and the whole-offerings." Tishby, *The Wisdom of the Zohar*, 891. In the dualistic framework of the Zoharic tradition, the goat that is dispatched to Azazel comes to be understood as "the principal offering that is destined in its entirety for 'the Other Side.' " Tishby, *The Wisdom of the Zohar*, 821.

72. T. Prosic, "Kol Nidre: Speaking of the Unspoken (of)," *Bible and Critical Theory* 3.1 (2007) 1–14 at 8.

73. *Apoc. Ab.* 29:11–13: "And that you saw going out from the left side of the picture and those worshiping him, this means that many of the heathen will hope in him. And those of your seed you saw on the right side, some shaming and striking him, and some worshiping him, many of them will be misled on his account. And he will tempt those of your seed who have worshiped him." Kulik, *Retroverting Slavonic Pseudepigrapha*, 33.

74. Kulik, *Retroverting Slavonic Pseudepigrapha*, 51–52.

75. Kulik's strong belief in the messianic duo is also reflected in the title of the messianic section (*Apoc. Ab.* 29:4–13) of his English translation of the *Apocalypse of Abraham*, namely, "False and True Messiahs." Cf. Kulik, *Retroverting Slavonic Pseudepigrapha*, 32.

76. Kulik, *Retroverting Slavonic Pseudepigrapha*, 51.

77. Kulik, *Retroverting Slavonic Pseudepigrapha*, 51.

78. Concerning the concept of the two messiahs in Jewish lore, see C.C. Torrey, "The Messiah Son of Ephraim," *JBL* 66.3 (1947) 253–277; R.E. Brown, "The Messianism of Qumran," *CBQ* 19 (1957) 53–82; P.J. Kobelski, *Melchizedek and Melchireša*[c] (CBQMS, 10; Washington: Catholic Biblical Association of America, 1981) 70–71; J.J. Collins, *The Scepter and the Star: The Messiahs of the Dead Sea Scrolls and Other Ancient Literature* (N.Y.: Doubleday, 1995) 74–95; H. Lenowitz, *The Jewish Messiahs: From the Galilee to Crown Heights* (Oxford: Oxford University Press, 1998) 31ff.

79. Cf. *1QS* 9:9–11: "They should not depart from any counsel of the law in order to walk in complete stubbornness of their heart, but instead shall be ruled by the first directives which the men of the Community began to be taught until the prophet comes, and the Messiahs of Aaron and Israel." García Martínez and Tigchelaar, *The Dead Sea Scrolls Study Edition*, 91–93. *CD* 12:22–13:1: "And this is the rule of the assembly of the cam[ps]. Those who walk in them, in the time of wickedness until there arises the ‹messiah› of Aaron and Israel. . . ." García Martínez and Tigchelaar, *The Dead Sea Scrolls Study Edition*, 571. *CD* 14:19: ". . . [until there arises the messia]h of

Aaron and Israel. And their iniquity will be atoned [through meal and sin-offerings]. . . ." García Martínez and Tigchelaar, *The Dead Sea Scrolls Study Edition*, 575.*CD* 19:10: "These shall escape in the age of the visitation; but those that remain shall be delivered up to the sword when there comes the messiah of Aaron and Israel." García Martínez and Tigchelaar, *The Dead Sea Scrolls Study Edition*, 577. *CD* 20:1: ". . . until there arises the messiah out of Aaron and Israel. . . ." García Martínez and Tigchelaar, *The Dead Sea Scrolls Study Edition*, 579.

80. Scholars point out that this concept of the priestly and the princely Messiahs is present also in *Testament of Simeon* 7:2. Regarding this tradition, see J. Charlesworth, "From Jewish Messianology to Christian Christology," in *Judaisms and Their Messiahs at the Turn of the Christian Era* (eds. J. Neusner et al.; Cambridge: Cambridge University Press, 1987) 231.

81. There are several opinions about the provenance of this messianic figure. John Collins suggests that "while the origin of this figure (Messiah the son of Joseph) is obscure, he most probably reflects in some way the defeat and death of Bar Kokhba, whom Rabbi Akiba had hailed as messiah." Collins, *The Scepter and the Star*, 126. Yet Israel Yuval argues that the Messiah b. Joseph is best understood as a reflection of Jesus. I.J. Yuval, *Two Nations in Your Womb: Perceptions of Jews and Christians in Late Antiquity and the Middle Ages* (trans. B. Harshav and J. Chipman; Berkeley: University of California Press, 2006) 33–38.

82. Thus, for example, *b. Sukk.* 52a unveils the tradition of two messiahs: "Our Rabbis taught, The Holy One, blessed be He, will say to the Messiah, the son of David (May he reveal himself speedily in our days!), 'Ask of me anything, and I will give it to thee,' as it is said, I will tell of the decree etc. this day have I begotten thee, ask of me and I will give the nations for thy inheritance. But when he will see that the Messiah the son of Joseph is slain, he will say to Him, 'Lord of the Universe, I ask of Thee only the gift of life.' As to life, He would answer him, 'Your father David has already prophesied this concerning you,' as it is said, He asked life of thee, thou gavest it him, [even length of days for ever and ever]." Epstein, *The Babylonian Talmud. Sukkah*, 52a. Cf. also *b. Sukk.* 52b: "And the Lord showed me four craftsmen. Who are these 'four craftsmen'?—R. Hana b. Bizna citing R. Simeon Hasida replied: The Messiah the son of David, the Messiah the son of Joseph, Elijah and the Righteous Priest. R. Shesheth objected, If so, was it correct to write, These are the horns which scattered Judah, seeing that they came to turn [them] back?—The other answered him, Go to the end of the verse: These then are come to frighten them, to cast down the horns of the nations, which lifted up their horns against the Land of Judah, to scatter it etc. Why, said R. Shesheth to him, should I argue with Hana in Aggada?" Epstein, *The Babylonian Talmud. Sukkah*, 52b. Cf. also *Trg. to the Cant.* 4:5; 7:4.

83. The *Book of Zohar* I:25b, again, speaks of the same messianic pair; it reads: "According to another explanation, the words 'no shrub of the field was yet in the earth' refer to the first Messiah, and the words 'no herb of the field had yet sprung up' refer to the second Messiah. . . . This is also hinted at in the verse 'the scepter shall not depart from Judah nor the ruler's staff from between his feet,' 'the scepter' referring to the Messiah of the house of Judah, and 'the staff' to the Messiah of the house of Joseph." Sperling and Simon, *The Zohar*, 1.100–101. See also *b. San.* 98a and *Pesikta Rabbati* 36: "For seven years the Messiah, now referred to as Ephraim, will endure the suffering decreed for him even as God will endure the pain of Israel's banishment. At Israel's return from exile, God himself will go at the head of them. In the year in which the king Messiah will reveal himself. . . ." Braude, *Pesikta Rabbati*, 2.676.

84. In later Jewish messianic texts one can also find traces of a concept of another messianic dyad—the Jewish messiah and his opponent who will fight against him. Often these messianic opponents are associated with the Gentiles or their rulers. For example, in *Tg. Tos. Zech.* 12:10, one can find the following tradition: "I will place a spirit of true prophecy and prayerfulness upon the house of David and the inhabitants of Judah. Afterwards the Messiah of the lineage of Ephraim will emerge and fight a battle with Gog, but Gog will slay him in front of the gate of Jerusalem. Then they (i.e., Israel) will look to Me and seek from Me the reason why the nations have stabbed the Messiah of the lineage of Ephraim, and they will mourn him as a father and mother would mourn their only child, and they will grieve for him the way they would grieve for (the death of) a firstborn." J.C. Reeves, *Trajectories in Near Eastern Apocalyptic: A Postrabbinic Jewish Apocalypse Reader* (RBS, 45; Atlanta: SBL, 2005) 50. *Midrash Wa-Yosha*[c] attests to a similar tradition, in which the opponent of the Jewish messiah is a pagan king; it reads: "After that another king will arise, a wicked one and 'strong of face' and he will wage war with Israel for three months . . . He will come up to Jerusalem and kill the Messiah of the lineage of Joseph, as scripture attests: 'and they shall look to Me about the one whom they pierced, and they shall mourn for him like one who mourns an only child' (Zech. 12:10). After that the Messiah of the lineage of David will come, regarding which scripture affirms: 'and behold with the clouds of heaven one like a mortal man' (Dan 7:13), and it is written afterwards: 'he will have authority and royal dignity' (Dan 7:14). . . ." Reeves, *Trajectories in Near Eastern Apocalyptic*, 174.

85. Early development of a rudimentary concept of the false messiah who will serve as an eschatological opponent of the positive messianic figure is discernible in the Dead Sea Scrolls. In some Qumran materials (*11QMelch*, *4QAmram*, *4Q280*, etc.) various messianic characters, including Melchizedek, have their negative counterparts who bear conspicuous designations, such as

Melchireša[c], which come from deformation of the names of their messianic counterparts. In these materials, the messianic traditions are often overlaid with Yom Kippur imagery. Regarding these traditions, see Stökl Ben Ezra, *The Impact of Yom Kippur on Early Christianity*, 90–91.

86. Lenowitz, *The Jewish Messiahs: From the Galilee to Crown Heights*, 31.

87. Lenowitz, *The Jewish Messiahs: From the Galilee to Crown Heights*, 31.

88. As we have seen in these Christian traditions, Jesus is often portrayed as fulfilling the functions of both cultic animals: the scapegoat during his passion and the goat for YHWH after his resurrection or at the *parousia*.

89. "Then I shall sound the trumpet from the sky, and I shall send my chosen one, having in him one measure of all my power, and he will summon my people blamed among the heathen. . . ." Kulik, *Retroverting Slavonic Pseudepigrapha,* 34.

90. D. Matt, *The Zohar: Pritzker Edition* (12 vols.; Palo Alto, CA: Stanford University Press, 2003–) 2.170–173. See also *Zohar* I.190a: "This is the impure side, the Other Side, who stands perpetually before the blessed Holy One, bringing accusations of the sins of human beings, and who stands perpetually below, leading humans astray. . . . But the blessed Holy One feels compassion for Israel and has advised them how to save themselves from him. How? With a shofar on Rosh Hashanah, and on Yom Kippur with a goat, given to him so that he will disengage from them and occupy himself with that portion of his, as they have established." Matt, *The Zohar: Pritzker Edition*, 3.160–161; *Zohar* II.184b: "Come and see: The goat that Israel sends to the desert is in order to give a portion to that Other Side, with which to be occupied." Matt, *The Zohar: Pritzker Edition*, 6.37. *Pirke de Rabbi Eliezer* 46: "Sammael said before the Holy One, blessed be He: Sovereign of all the universe! Thou hast given me power over all the nations of the world, but over Israel Thou hast not given me power. He answered him, saying: Behold, thou hast power over them on the Day of Atonement if they have any sin, but if not, thou hast no power over them. Therefore they gave him a present on the Day of Atonement, in order that they should not bring their offering, as it is said, 'One lot for the Lord, and the other lot for Azazel.'" Friedlander, *Pirke de Rabbi Eliezer*, 363.

91. Tishby, *The Wisdom of the Zohar*, 892.

92. Tishby, *The Wisdom of the Zohar*, 892.

93. "ослаба от языкъ." Philonenko-Sayar and Philonenko, *L'Apocalypse d'Abraham*, 100.

94. Rubinkiewicz translates *oslaba* as "liberation, security, relaxation," tracing this term to Gk. *adeia, anesis.* Cf. Rubinkiewicz and Lunt, "The Apocalypse of Abraham," 1.703. Rubinstein also notes that *oslaba* is used

in the Slavonic Bible (for *anesis*) in Acts 24:23. A. Rubinstein, "Hebraisms in the Slavonic 'Apocalypse of Abraham,'" *JJS* 4 (1953) 108–115 at 113. *Oslaba* can also be translated as "loosing." In his messianic reinterpretation of the imagery of two sacrificial goats, Justin Martyr appears to be using similar terminology when he mentions the "loosing" the strangle of violent contracts: "[Y]ou shall recognize him whom you had subjected to shame, and who was a sacrificial offering for all sinners who are willing to repent and to comply with that fast which Isaiah prescribed when he said, *loosing the strangle of violent contracts*, (διασπῶντες στραγγαλιὰς βιαίων συναλλαγμάτων) and to observe likewise all the other precepts laid down by him (precepts which I have already mentioned and which all believers in Christ fulfill). You also know very well that the offering of the two goats, which had to take place during the fast, could not take place anywhere else except in Jerusalem." Marcovich, *Iustini Martyris Dialogus Cum Tryphone*, 137; Bobichon, *Justin Martyr: Dialogue avec Tryphon*, 284; Falls et al, *St. Justin Martyr. Dialogue with Trypho*, 62. Scholars have noticed that Justin Martyr seems to be reworking here the Septuagint version of Isa 58:6, a passage which speaks of loosing the bonds of injustice and the thongs of the yoke: "λῦε πάντα σύνδεσμον ἀδικίας διάλυε στραγγαλιὰς βιαίων συναλλαγμάτων." But Justin's quotation from the Septuagint has "διασπῶντες" instead of "διάλυε." With respect to the usage of this expression in Justin, see Skarsaune, *The Proof from Prophecy*, 55–56.

95. Reflecting on the misleading function of the false messiah in chapter 29, Alexander Kulik suggests that the Slavonic term *oslaba* might be connected with the notion of laxity in relation to the weakness in observance of the Torah, which the messianic man will bring to the Hebrews, misleading some of them. He points to some later rabbinic materials in which the false messiah brings neglect or laxity in upholding the Law. Kulik observes that "Greek counterparts of CS ослаба, ослабление, ослабѣние may also have negative connotations: 'willfulness'—Gk ἄνεσις or 'weakening,' 'laxity'—Gk. ἔκλυσις or παράλυσις (Mikl: 518; Srezn: 2.723–724; SRJa11-17: 13.1013). The last one might have rendered Heb. רפיון and relate to a pseudo-Messiah; cf. רפיון התורה 'laxity [= neglect] of the Law' (*Lam. Rab.* 1:4) or רפיון ידים מן התורה 'laxity of hands in upholding the Law' (*Midrash Tanhuma, Beshalah* 25)." Kulik, *Retroverting Slavonic Pseudepigrapha*, 51.

96. Rubinkiewicz thinks that the concept of liberation was present in the messianic traditions that constitute the conceptual basis of chapter 29. In his opinion the interpolator used an ancient text, a messianic apocryphal prophecy, which he inserted in the *Apocalypse of Abraham*, after adjusting it in line with Christian convictions. The original text presented the messianic figure as the liberator who would break the yoke of the heathen. Rubinkiewicz, *L'Apocalypse d'Abraham en vieux slave*, 66.

97. Robert Hall underlines this aspect arguing that "the man who is worshiped severs the unfaithful Jews from Abraham's seed and joins them to the Gentiles." Hall, "The 'Christian Interpolation' in the Apocalypse of Abraham," 108.

98. Lenowitz, *The Jewish Messiahs: From the Galilee to Crown Heights*, 31.

Adoil Outside the Cosmos: God Before and After Creation in the Enochic Tradition

1. The unique details of this cosmogonic account have been noted elsewhere. See A. Orlov, "Secrets of Creation in 2 (Slavonic) Enoch," in: A. Orlov, *From Apocalypticism to Merkabah Mysticism: Studies in the Slavonic Pseudepigrapha* (JSJSS, 114; Leiden: Brill, 2007) 175–195.

2. G. Scholem, *On the Mystical Shape of the Godhead: Basic Concepts in Kabbalah* (New York: Schocken, 1991) 98–101; M. Idel, *Ascensions on High in Jewish Mysticism: Pillars, Lines, Ladders* (Past Incorporated. CEU Studies in Humanities, 2; Budapest: Central European University Press, 2005) 75ff.

3. The longer recension, while preserving the general narrative structure of the shorter one, supplies some additional details. The longer recension of *2 Enoch* 25 reads: "And I commanded the lowest things: 'Let one of the invisible things descend visibly!' And Adoil descended, extremely large. And I looked at him, and, behold, in his belly he had a great light. And I said to him, 'Disintegrate yourself, Adoil, and let what is born from you become visible.' And he disintegrated himself, and there came out a very great light. And I was in the midst of the [great] light. And light out of light is carried thus. And the great age came out, and it revealed all the creation which I had thought up to create. And I saw how good it was. And I placed for myself a throne, and I sat down on it. And then to the light I spoke: 'You go up higher (than the throne), and be solidified [much higher than the throne], and become the foundation of the higher things.' And there is nothing higher than the light, except nothing itself. And again I bowed (?) myself and looked upward from my throne." Andersen, "2 Enoch," 1.144.

4. Andersen, "2 Enoch," 1.145.

5. Much scholarship has been devoted to clarifying the etymology of the enigmatic name of the great aeon. Many scholars consider the name to provide an important clue for understanding the origins of the text. Robert Henry Charles suggests that Adoil might be derived from the Hebrew יד אל, translated as the "hand of God." Charles, *APOT*, 2.445. Marc Philonenko supports this etymology, pointing to some Egyptian parallels in which "les premières créatures naissent du liquide séminal que le démiurge solitaire

avait fait jaillir au moyen de sa main." M. Philonenko, "La cosmogonie du 'livre des secrets d'Hénoch,'" in *Religions en Egypte hellénistique et romaine* (Paris: Presses Universitaires de France, 1969) 109–116 at 114. Léon Gry suggests that Adoil stems from אור אל, "the light of God." In his opinion, some letters in the Hebrew word אור, "light," were altered. *Resh* was read as *daleth*; *waw* was transposed. These alterations produced Adoil. See L. Gry, "Quelques noms d'anges ou d'êtres mystérieux en II Hénoch," *RB* 49 (1940) 201. André Vaillant suggests that the name might be derived from the Hebrew word עד with a suffix, "his eternity, his aeon." A. Vaillant, *Le Livre des secrets d'Hénoch: Texte slave et traduction française* (Textes publiés par l'Institut d'Études slaves, 4; Paris: L'Institut d'Études slaves, 1976) xi. Gershom Scholem criticizes this rendering, arguing that the Hebrew word עד cannot carry a pronominal suffix. G. Scholem, *Origins of the Kabbalah* (Princeton: Princeton University Press, 1987) 73. According to Scholem's own interpretation, Adoil derives from Sadoqil; see G. Scholem, "Die Lehre vom 'Gerechten' in der jüdischen Mystik," *ErJb* 27 (1958) 252. Józef Milik considers the name Adoil "a Greek and Semitic hybrid: Hades + El." Milik, *The Books of Enoch,* 113. Gilles Quispel derives it from *Adonai-el,* where the first element is the circumlocution for the Tetragrammaton. See Fossum, *The Name of God,* 288. I have previously proposed that the name Adoil might be connected with "El Gadol" (the Great God)—a designation for the primordial upper foundation in the creational narrative of the *Book of Zohar* (*Zohar* I.17b). In this respect it is intriguing that in *2 Enoch* Adoil is called "the large one" or "the great one." See A. Orlov, *The Enoch-Metatron Tradition* (TSAJ, 107; Tübingen: Mohr/Siebeck, 2005) 199.

6. Sokolov, "Материалы и заметки по старинной славянской литературе," 1.25.

7. Both recensions stress that Adoil's disintegration provides an important foundation on which the divine throne is established. The seat of the Deity thus serves, here, as the portentous locale from which God supervises the unfolding creation. The throne plays an important role in the process of creation, being depicted as the center of the created world.

8. His revelations, however, encompass not verbal but rather ontological disclosures, conveyed through the act of changing his nature. This mode of revelation is very important for our subsequent analysis of Enoch's role as the revealer and his "ontological" participation in the disclosure of the eschatological aeon.

9. "And Adoil descended, extremely large. And I looked at him, and, behold, in his belly he had a great light . . . there came out a very great light. And I was in the midst of the [great] light. And light out of light is carried thus." Andersen, "2 Enoch," 1.144.

10. Concerning the symmetry of *Urzeit* and *Endzeit* in the Jewish apocalyptic literature, see H. Gunkel, *Schöpfung und Chaos in Urzeit und*

Endzeit (Göttingen: Vandenhoeck und Ruprecht, 1895); D. Dimant, "Noah in Early Jewish Literature," in: *Biblical Figures Outside the Bible* (eds. M.E. Stone and T.A. Bergren; Harrisburg, PA: Trinity Press International, 1998) 123–150 at 135–136, 141; G.W.E. Nickelsburg, "Patriarchs Who Worry About Their Wives: A Haggadic Tendency in the Genesis Apocryphon," in: *Biblical Perspectives: Early Use and Interpretation of the Bible in Light of the Dead Sea Scrolls* (eds. M.E. Stone and E.G. Chazon; STDJ, 28. Leiden: Brill, 1998) 137–158 at 142–143; J.M. Scott, *On Earth as in Heaven: The Restoration of Sacred Time and Sacred Space in the Book of Jubilees* (JSJSS, 91; Leiden: Brill, 2005) 212–219.

11. Andersen, "2 Enoch," 1.145. The longer recension of *2 Enoch* 26:1–3 gives a similar portrayal: "And I called out a second time into the very lowest things, and I said, 'Let one of the invisible things come out visibly, solid.' And Arkhas came out, solid and heavy and very red. And I said, 'Open yourself up, Arkhas, and let what is born from you become visible!' And he disintegrated himself. There came out an age, dark, very large, carrying the creation of all lower things. And I saw how good it was. And I said to him, 'Come down low and become solid! And become the foundation of the lowest things!' And it came about. And he came down and became solid. And he became the foundation of the lowest things. And there is nothing lower than the darkness, except nothing itself." Andersen, "2 Enoch," 1.144.

12. See, for example, G.W. MacRae, "The Jewish Background of the Gnostic Sophia Myth," *NovT* 12 (1970) 86–101 at 90.

13. In his comments on the notion of the Heavenly Man in the hermetic tractate *Poimandres* and the gnostic *Apocryphon of John*, Roelef van den Broek notes that "both texts know the important notion of a heavenly Man—a notion that has to be explained through its Jewish background." Roelof van den Broek, "Gnosticism and Hermetism in Antiquity: Two Roads to Salvation," in *Gnosis and Hermeticism from Antiquity to Modern Times* (eds. R. van den Broek and W.J. Hanegraaf; Albany: SUNY Press, 1998) 1–20 at 15. Van den Broek traces the origins of this concept to Ezekiel 1:26, in which the prophet saw the Glory of God in the shape of a man. He then suggests that Ezekiel 1:26 "and a specific interpretation of the creation of man in Genesis eventually led to the myth of the heavenly Man." Van den Broek, "Gnosticism and Hermetism," 15.

14. *Poim*. 12: "Mind, the father of all, who is life and light, gave birth to a man like himself whom he loved as his own child. The man was most fair: he had the father's image; and god, who was really in love with his own form, bestowed on him all his craftworks." B.P. Copenhaver, *Hermetica. The Greek Corpus Hermeticum and the Latin Asclepius in a New English Translation, with Notes and Introduction* (Cambridge: Cambridge University Press, 1995) 3.

15. Regarding the Gnostic variants of this myth, see G. Quispel "Der Gnostische Anthropos und die jüdische Tradition," *ErJb* 22 (1953) 211–215;

I.S. Gilhus, *The Nature of the Archons: A Study in the Soteriology of a Gnostic Treatise from Nag Hammadi (CGII, 4)* (SOR, 12; Wiesbaden: Harrassowitz, 1985) 48ff.

16. *Poim.* 16: "Poimandres said: 'This is the mystery that has been kept hidden until this very day. When nature made love with the man, she bore a wonder most wondrous. In him he had the nature of the cosmic framework of the seven, who are made of fire and spirit, as I told you, and without delay nature at once gave birth to seven men, androgyne and exalted, whose natures were like these of the seven governors.'" Copenhaver, *Hermetica*, 4.

17. Jarl Fossum observes that "Adoil is thus the prime cosmogonic agent. Since he is the primordial *phos*, or—rather—the archetypal *phos*, which means 'man' as well as 'light.'" Fossum, *The Name of God*, 289–290.

18. With respect to the φως traditions, see G. Quispel, "Ezekiel 1:26 in Jewish Mysticism and Gnosis," *VC* 34 (1980) 1–13 at 6–7; Fossum, *The Name of* God, 280; idem, *The Image of the Invisible God: Essays on the Influence of Jewish Mysticism on Early Christology* (NTOA, 30; Fribourg: Universitätsverlag Freiburg Schweiz; Göttingen: Vanderhoeck & Ruprecht, 1995) 16–17; Copenhaver, *Hermetica*, 109.

19. "For this one, Adamas, is a light which radiated from the light; he is the eye of the light." *Gos. Egypt.* (NHC, IV, 61, 8–10). *Nag Hammadi Codices III, 2 and IV, 2: The Gospel of the Egyptians (The Holy Book of the Great Invisible Spirit)* (NHS, 4; eds. A. Böhlig and F. Wisse; Leiden: Brill, 1975) 93. Cf. also *On the Origin of the World* (NHC, II, 98, 23–31): "Now the eternal realm (aeon) of truth has no shadow outside it, *for the limitless light is everywhere within it.* But its exterior is shadow, which has been called by the name 'darkness.' From it, there appeared a force, presiding over the darkness. And the forces that came into being subsequent to them called the shadow 'the limitless chaos.'" *Nag Hammadi Codex II, 2–7* (2 vols., NHS, 21; ed. B. Layton; Leiden: Brill, 1989) 2.31.

20. *2 Enoch* 30:11–12: "And on the earth I assigned him to be a second angel, honored and great and glorious. And I assigned him to be a king, to reign on the earth, and to have my wisdom. And there was nothing comparable to him on earth, even among my creatures that exist." Andersen, "2 Enoch," 1.152.

21. Thus, for example, Jarl Fossum observes that in the Adoil account "the creation of the light has now become the result of its origination from angelic being, whose stomach issues the light." Fossum, *The Name of God*, 287.

22. *2 Enoch* 30:10 (longer recension). Andersen, "2 Enoch," 1.152.

23. *2 Enoch* 25:1 (longer recension). Andersen, "2 Enoch," 1.144.

24. Copenhaver, *Hermetica*, 3.

25. A similar list of components is found in the *Latin Life of Adam and Eve*, which offers a tradition of Adam's creation from the eight parts. Thus,

the Latin *Vita* 37 [55] reads: "It must be known that the body of Adam was formed of eight parts. The first part was of the dust of the earth, from which was made his flesh, and thereby he was sluggish. The next part was of the sea, from which was made his blood, and thereby he was aimless and fleeing. The third part was of the stones of the earth, from which his bones were made, and thereby he was hard and covetous. The fourth part was of the clouds, from which were made his thoughts, and thereby he was immoderate. The fifth part was of the wind, from which was made his breath, and thereby he was fickle. The sixth part was of the sun, from which were made his eyes, and thereby he was handsome and beautiful. The seventh part was of the light of the world, from which he was made pleasing, and thereby he had knowledge. The eighth part was of the Holy Spirit, from which was made his soul, and thereby are the bishops, priests, and all the saints and elect of God." Anderson and Stone, *A Synopsis of the Book of Adam and Eve,* 96E. Concerning the Adam Octipartite tradition attested in Latin, Old Irish, and Slavonic materials, see V. Jagić, "Slavische Beiträge zu den biblischen Apocryphen, I, Die altkirchenslavischen Texte des Adambuches," *Denkschriften der kaiserlichen Akademie der Wissenschaften. Philosophisch-historische Classe* 42 (1893) 44–47; M. Förster, "Adam's Erschaffung und Namengebung: Ein lateinisches Fragment des s.g. slawischen Henoch," *Archiv für Religionswissenschaft* 11 (1907–8) 477–529; *idem*, "Die mittelirische Version von Adams Erschaffung," *ZCP* 13 (1921) 47–48; M. McNamara, *The Apocrypha in the Irish Church* (Dublin: Dublin Institute for Advanced Studies, 1975) 21–23; C. Böttrich, *Adam als Mikrokosmos: eine Untersuchung zum slavischen Henochbuch* (JU, 59; Frankfurt am Main: Lang, 1995); G. Macaskill, *Revealed Wisdom and Inaugurated Eschatology in Ancient Judaism and Early Christianity* (JSJSS, 115; Leiden, Boston, 2007) 201.

26. The origin of this tradition of the seven elements of human nature can be traced to Plato's *Timaeus* 73B–76E. Regarding these conceptual developments, see R. van den Broek, "The Creation of Adam's Psychic Body in the *Apocryphon of John*," in his *Studies in Gnosticism and Alexandrian Christianity* (NHS, 39; Leiden: Brill, 1996) 67–85 at 75ff.

27. Although the lists of "properties" and "components" mentioned in *2 Enoch* 30 appear to have been heavily corrupted during the text's long transmission history, they are reminiscent of the lists of the planetary melothesia found in Ptolemy's *Tetrabiblos* 3:12, in which seven planets are put in correspondence with human "properties/faculties" (sight, touch, taste, smell, speech, thought, etc.) and with the "components" (bones, sinews, flesh, etc.) of the human body; it reads: "Saturn is lord of the right ear, the spleen, the bladder, the phlegm, and the bones; Jupiter is lord of touch, the lungs, arteries, and semen; Mars of the left ear, kidneys, veins, and genitals; the sun of the sight, the brain, heart, sinews, and all the right-hand parts; Venus of smell, the

liver, and the flesh; Mercury of speech and thought, the tongue, the bile, and the buttocks; the moon of taste and drinking, the stomach, belly, womb, and all the left-hand parts." F.E. Robbins, *Ptolemy, Tetrabiblos* (LCL; Cambridge: Harvard University Press/London: Heinemann, 1940) 319–320. Scholars note that although Ptolemy's compendium "is perhaps the best known of its kind, his list of correspondences between planets and faculties of the human body by no means goes back to Ptolemy's own invention. Such lists most probably stem from Hellenistic Egypt and can be traced back as far as the second century B.C.E." A. Toepel, "Planetary Demons in Early Jewish Literature," *JSP* 14 (2005) 231–238 at 235. Concerning the planetary melothesia, see also A. Bouché-Leclercq, *L'astrologie grecque* (Paris: Ernest Leroux, 1899) 319–325; W.H. Roscher, "Planeten," in: *Ausführliches Lexikon der griechischen und römischen Mythologie* (ed. W.H. Roscher; Leipzig: Teubner, 1902) 3.2535–2536; A. Touwaide, "Iatromathematik," in: *Der Neue Pauly. Enzyklopädie der Antike* (eds. H. Cancik and H. Schneider; Stuttgart: Metzler, 1998) 5.873; J. Reeves, "Reconsidering the Prophecy of Zardust," in: *A Multiform Heritage: Studies in Early Judaism and Christianity in Honor of Robert A. Kraft* (ed. B.G. Wright; SPHS, 24; Atlanta: Scholars, 1999) 167–182 at 177–182. The Jewish pseudepigraphical writings are also cognizant of the sevenfold system of human properties/faculties. Thus, *The Testament of Reuben* 2:3–8 provides a very similar cluster of traditions when it tells about seven spirits which were given to the protoplast at creation; it reads: "And seven other spirits are given to man at creation so that by them every human deed (is done). First is the spirit of life, with which man is created as a living being. The second is the spirit of seeing, with which comes desire. The third is the spirit of hearing, with which comes instruction. The fourth is the spirit of smell, with which is given taste for drawing air and breath. The fifth is the spirit of speech, with which comes knowledge. The sixth is the spirit of taste for consuming food and drink; by it comes strength, because in food is the substance of strength. The seventh is the spirit of procreation and intercourse, with which come sins through the fondness for pleasure." Kee, "Testaments of the Twelve Patriarchs," 1.782. For a discussion of these traditions, see Toepel, "Planetary Demons," 235ff.

28. Sokolov, "Материалы и заметки по старинной славянской литературе," 1.29–30.

29. Copenhaver, *Hermetica*, 4.

30. Regarding the Christian traditions of seven "first created" spirits, or the so-called *protoctists*, see B.G. Bucur, *Angelomorphic Pneumatology: Clement of Alexandria and Other Early Christian Witnesses* (SVC, 95; Leiden: Brill, 2009) 31–32; 38–39; 56–58; 69–70; 97–99; 135–138.

31. The tradition about the seven spirits or angels responsible for the origin of the humankind is also found in Irenaeus's account of Saturnilus's teaching. Cf. Irenaeus, *Haer.* I.24.1.

32. A.D. Nock and A.-J. Festugière, *Corpus Hermeticum* (4 vols.; Paris: Les Belles Lettres, 1954–60) 1.9.

33. Copenhaver, *Hermetica*, 2.

34. Andersen, "2 Enoch," 1.146.

35. Scholars have noted that "the easiest general clue to the identity of Archons lies in the sevenfold lists. These are given in the several versions of the document that have survived, in almost identical form—in the Berlin Codex version (BG 41, 16) and in the Codex II version from Nag Hammadi (C II 59, 26). In the BG version they are called 'the hebdomad of the week,' which seems to invite us to read them as the planetary powers of the successive days of the week." A.J. Welburn, "The Identity of the Archons in the 'Apocryphon Johannis,'" *VC* 32 (1978) 241–254 at 242.

36. *The Apocryphon of John. Synopsis of Nag Hammadi Codices II, 1; III, 1; and IV, 1 with BG 8502, 2* (NHMS, 33; eds. M. Waldstein and F. Wisse; Leiden: Brill, 1995) 71–73.

37. Waldstein and Wisse, *The Apocryphon of John. Synopsis of Nag Hammadi Codices II, 1; III, 1; and IV, 1 with BG 8502, 2*, 87–93. Cf. another version of this anthropogonic myth which is reflected in *On the Origin of the World* (NHC, II, 114, 29–115, 3) reads: "Since that day, the seven rulers have fashioned (*plassein*) man with his body resembling their body, but his likeness resembling the man that had appeared to them. His modeling (*plasma*) took place by parts, one at a time. And their leader fashioned the brain and the nervous system. Afterwards, he appeared as prior to him. He became a soul-endowed (*psykhikos*) man. And he was called Adam, that is, 'father,' according to the name of the one that existed before him." Layton, *Nag Hammadi Codex II, 2–7*, 2.65.

38. Layton, *Nag Hammadi Codex II, 2–7*, 2:37.

39. See Welburn, "The Identity of the Archons," 242. Cf. also Waldstein and Wisse, *The Apocryphon of John*, 88–111.

40. It should be noted that Van den Broek's chart of the correspondences between the Archons and the planets is based on Welburn's reconstruction. Welburn uses for his reconstruction the planetary lists found in *Pistis Sophia*, Origen, and other materials. See Welburn, "The Identity of the Archons," 244.

41. Van den Broek, "The Creation of Adam's Psychic Body," 76. It is noteworthy that the five elements mentioned here (bones, sinews, flesh, blood, and hair) are also mentioned in the two lists found in *2 Enoch* 30.

42. Andersen, "2 Enoch," 1.148–150. It should be noted that the tradition of the seven planetary spheres is also mentioned in *2 Enoch* 27:3, in which the Deity creates seven great circles: "And I made a foundation of light around the water. And I created seven great circles inside it, and I gave them an appearance of crystal, wet and dry, that is to say glass and ice. . . . And I appointed out to each one of them his route, to the seven stars, each one of

them in his own heaven, so that they might travel accordingly." Andersen, "2 Enoch,"1.146.

43. In this respect, Francis Andersen notes that the planetary "scheme could be no better than a garbled *Almagest* by some uninformed individual." Andersen, "2 Enoch," 1.149, footnote b.

44. Cf. *Contra Celsum* 6:22: "They associate the first with Kronos (Saturn), taking lead to refer to the slowness of the star; the second with Aphrodite (Venus), comparing her with the brightness and softness of tin; the third with Zeus (Jupiter), as the gate that has a bronze base and which is firm; the fourth with Hermes (Mercury), for both iron and Hermes, are reliable for all works and make money and are hard-working; the fifth with Ares (Mars), the gate which as a result of the mixture is uneven and varied in quality. . . ." H. Chadwick, *Origen: Contra Celsum* (Cambridge: Cambridge University Press, 1953) 334.

45. The planetary list found in *2 Enoch* appears to also deviate from the traditional list based on the ancient view of planets' distance from the earth—Saturn, Jupiter, Mars, Sun, Venus, Mercury, Moon. Cf. Chadwick, *Origen: Contra Celsum*, 335, footnote 2.

46. Van den Broek, "The Creation of Adam's Psychic Body," 70.

47. *Contra Celsum* 6:31: "And they say that the star Saturn is in sympathy with the lion-like Archon." Chadwick, *Origen: Contra Celsium*, 347. Regarding the identification between Kronos/Saturn and Ialdabaoth, see also W. Bousset, *Hauptprobleme der Gnosis* (FRLANT, 10; Göttingen: Vandenhoeck & Ruprecht, 1907) 351–355.

48. The shorter recension of *2 Enoch* 30:8 presents the tradition about Wisdom's creation of man in a very abbreviated form without any references to the pattern of seven; it reads: "When I had finished all this, I commanded my wisdom to create man." Andersen, "2 Enoch," 1.151.

49. It should be noted that, in Wis. 9:2 and Wis. 10:1–2, Wisdom is responsible for the formation, protection, deliverance, and strengthening of the protoplast: "[Who] by your wisdom have formed humankind," "Wisdom protected the first-formed father of the world, when he alone had been created; she delivered him from his transgression, and gave him strength to rule all things." Cf. also *2 Enoch* 30:12: "And I assigned him to be a king, to reign on the earth, and to have my wisdom." Andersen, "2 Enoch," 1.152.

50. In Prov 9:1, Wisdom is associated with the sevenfold cosmic structure: "Wisdom has built her house, she has hewn her seven pillars." Yet, in *2 Enoch* 30 and gnostic cosmogonies, this sevenfold pattern is applied to the creation of Adam's body. George MacRae suggests that "in the cosmogonic works it is conceivable that the seven Archons or planetary deities resulting from Sophia's fall are an application of the image in Prov 9:1, although the passage is certainly not the primary source of the idea of a sevenfold Demi-

urge." See his "The Jewish Background of the Gnostic Sophia Myth," *NovT* 12 (1970) 86–101 at 93.

51. See, for example, MacRae, "The Jewish Background of the Gnostic Sophia Myth," 90; D.J. Good, *Reconstructing the Tradition of Sophia in Gnostic Literature* (SBLMS, 32; Atlanta: Scholars, 1987) 69. Regarding the hypostatic Wisdom in early Enochic traditions, especially in chapter 42 of the *Book of the Similitudes,* see MacRae, "The Jewish Background of the Gnostic Sophia Myth," 91–92.

52. MacRae, "The Jewish Background of the Gnostic Sophia Myth," 90.

53. With respect to the imagery of Sophia in Gnostic materials, see G.C. Stead, "The Valentinian Myth of Sophia," *JTS* 20 (1969) 75–104; MacRae, "The Jewish Background of the Gnostic Sophia Myth," 86–101; U. Wilckens and G. Fohrer, "Sophia," in: *Theological Dictionary of the New Testament* (eds. G. Kittel and G. Friedrich; 10 vols.; Grand Rapids: Eerdmans, 1964–76) 7.465–526; E.M. Yamauchi, "The Descent of Ishtar, the Fall of Sophia, and the Jewish Roots of Gnosticism," *TB* 29 (1978) 143–175; K. Rudolph, "Sophia und Gnosis. Bemerkungen zum Problem 'Gnosis und Frühjudentum,'" in: K.-W. Tröger, *Altes Testament—Frühjudentum—Gnosis* (Berlin: Akademie, 1980) 220–237; J. Sieber, "The Barbelo Aeon as Sophia in Zostrianos and Related Tractates," in: *The Rediscovery of Gnosticism* (ed. B.L. Layton; Leiden: Brill, 1981) 2.788–795; J.E. Goehring, "A Classical Influence on the Gnostic Sophia Myth," *VC* 35 (1981) 16; Gilhus, *The Nature of the Archons*, 95–14; D.J. Good, "Sophia in Valentinianism," *The Second Century* 4 (1984) 193–201; *Images of the Feminine in Gnosticism* (ed. K. King; Harrisburg: Trinity Press International, 2000) 76–77; 96–112; 158–186; 211–227.

54. Concerning Sophia's connection with the origin of the seven rulers, see Good, *Reconstructing the Tradition*, 39ff.

55. Layton, *Nag Hammadi Codex II, 2-7*, 2:37.

56. "His thoughts became blind. And, having expelled his power—that is, the blasphemy he had spoken—he pursued it down to chaos and the abyss, his mother, at the instigation of Pistis Sophia (Faith Wisdom). And *she established each of his offspring in conformity with its power—after the pattern of the realms that are above*, for by starting from the invisible world the visible world was invented. As incorruptibility looked down into the region of the waters, her image appeared in the waters; and the authorities of the darkness became enamored of her." Layton, *Nag Hammadi Codex II, 2-7,* 1.235–237.

57. Cf. *2 Enoch* 48:1–5: ". . . the sun, so that he might travel along the seven celestial circles, which are appointed with 182 thrones so that he might descend to the shortest day, and once more 182 so that he might descend to the longest day. He also has two great thrones where he pauses when he turns around in this direction and in the other direction, higher than the

lunar thrones. From the month Tsivan, from the 17th day, he descends until the month Theved; and from the 17th day of Theved he ascends. And in this way the sun moves along all the celestial circles. When he comes close to the earth, then the earth is merry and makes its fruit grow. But when he goes away, then the earth laments, and the trees and all fruits have no productivity. All this is by measurement, and by the most precise measurement of the hours. He fixed it by measure, by *his own wisdom*, that is everything visible and invisible." Andersen, "2 Enoch," 1.174.

58. Regarding the Manichaean tradition about the eschatological dissolution of the world and the establishment of the new paradisal aeon outside of the world, see M. Heuser, "Manichaean Myth According to the Coptic Sources," in: M. Heuser and H.-J. Klimkeit, *Studies in Manichaean Literature and Art* (NHMS, 46; Leiden: Brill, 1998) 3–108 at 86. Cf. also *Keph.* 29: ". . . Yet, at the end, in the dissolution of the universe, this very counsel of life will gather itself in and sculpt its soul in the Last Statue. Its net is its Living Spirit, because with its Spirit it can hunt after the light and the life that is in all things; and build it upon its body." *The Kephalaia of the Teacher: The Edited Coptic Manichaean Texts in Translation with Commentary* (ed. I. Gardner; NHMS, 37; Leiden: Brill, 1995) 32.

59. Andersen, "2 Enoch," 1.191–193. The longer recension provides the following description that differs in several details from the account found in the shorter recension: "Listen my children! Before ever anything existed, and before ever any created thing was created, the Lord created the whole of his creation, visible and invisible. . . . And when the whole creation, visible and invisible, which the Lord has created, shall come to an end, then each person will go to the Lord's great judgment. And then all time will perish, and afterwards there will be neither years nor months nor days nor hours. They will be dissipated, and after that they will not be reckoned. But they will constitute a single age. And all the righteous, who escape from the Lord's great judgment, will be collected together into the great age. And the great age will come about for the righteous, and it will be eternal. And after that there will be among them neither weariness <nor sickness> nor affliction nor worry nor want nor debilitation nor night nor darkness. But they will have a great light, a great indestructible light, and paradise, great and incorruptible. For everything corruptible will pass away, and the incorruptible will come into being, and will be the shelter of the eternal residences." Andersen, "2 Enoch," 1.190–192.

60. According to the text, "all the righteous, who escape from the Lord's great judgment, will be collected together with [into] the great age."

61. The account describes the cataclysmic collapse of the spatial and temporal order that, according to the text, will lead to a situation when "all time will perish, and afterwards there will be neither years nor months

nor days nor hours. They will be dissipated, and after that they will not be reckoned. . . ."

62. Andersen, "2 Enoch," 1.194.

63. Andersen, "2 Enoch," 1.190.

64. For the influence of the Mesopotamian traditions on the Enochic materials, see H. Zimmern, "Urkönige und Uroffenbarung," in *Die Keilinschriften und das Alte Testament*, (2 vols.; ed. E. Schrader; Berlin: Reuther & Reichard, 1902–1903) 2.530–543; H. Ludin Jansen, *Die Henochgestalt: Eine vergleichende religionsgeschichtliche Untersuchung* (Oslo: Dybwad, 1939); P. Grelot, "La légende d'Hénoch dans les apocryphes et dans la Bible: Origine et signification," *RSR* 46 (1958) 5–26, 181–210; O. Neugebauer, "The 'Astronomical' Chapters of the Ethiopic Book of Enoch (72–82)," in: *The Book of Enoch, or I Enoch: A New English Edition with Commentary and Textual Notes* (eds. M. Black with J.C. VanderKam and O. Neugebauer; SVTP, 7; Leiden: Brill, 1985) 386–419 at 387; J. VanderKam, *Enoch and the Growth of an Apocalyptic Tradition* (CBQMS, 16; Washington: The Catholic Biblical Association of America, 1984); H. S. Kvanvig, *Roots of Apocalyptic: the Mesopotamian Background of the Enoch Figure and of the Son of Man* (WMANT, 61; Neukirchen-Vluyn: Neukirchener Verlag, 1988); Orlov, *The Enoch-Metatron Tradition*, 23–39.

65. For detailed analysis of the Mesopotamian sources about seven *apkallu*, see Kvanvig, *Roots of Apocalyptic: The Mesopotamian Background of the Enoch Figure and of the Son of Man*; A. Annus, "On the Origins of Watchers: A Comparative Study of the Antediluvian Wisdom in Mesopotamian and Jewish Traditions," *JSP* 19 (2010) 277–320.

66. See J.J. Finkelstein, "The Antediluvian Kings: A University of California Tablet," *JCS* 17 (1963) 50, n. 41; W.W. Hallo, "Antediluvian Cities," *JCS* 20 (1970) 62–63; T.C. Hartman, "Some Thoughts on the Sumerian King List and Genesis 5 and 11b," *JBL* 91 (1972) 25–32 at 28, n. 10; D.T. Bryan, "A Reevaluation of Gen 4 and 5 in Light of Recent Studies in Genealogical Fluidity," *ZAW* 99 (1987) 180–188.

67. Knibb, *The Ethiopic Book of Enoch*, 2.100.

68. With respect to this mediatorial office of the seventh antediluvian hero, see Orlov, *The Enoch-Metatron Tradition*, 59–70.

69. In his book about the symbolism of pillars in Jewish mysticism, Idel refers to a passage from the *Book of Bahir* that depicts the righteous person as the pillar reaching heaven: "There is a pillar from earth to heaven, and its name is *Tzaddiq*, according to the name of righteous men. And when there are righteous men in the world, then the pillar is strengthened, but if not—it becomes weak. And it supports the entire world, as it is written: 'the righteous are the foundation of the world.' But if it is weakened, it cannot support the world. This is the reason why even if there is only one righteous

[in the world], he maintains the world." *The Book of Bahir* (ed. D. Abrams; Los Angeles: The Cherub Press, 1994) 160–161. Idel points to an assumption about the dual status of the righteous, discernible in the passage from the *Book of Bahir*: there are righteous humans in the world, but there is also a cosmic righteous, and the former depend on the latter. Idel, *Ascensions on High in Jewish Mysticism*, 80. It is noteworthy that Idel traces the origins of this concept of the cosmic righteous to the conceptual developments found in the Slavonic Enoch wherein "the Great Aeon, which is identical to the foundation, passes for the righteous" (idem., 81). In light of this identification, Idel proposes that, in *2 Enoch*, the implicit connection might exist between the protological and eschatological foundations, the first represented by the primeval aeon Adoil and the second by the eschatological aeon, which is said to be the final place where all righteous of the world will be gathered.

70. It may be tempting to construe this rabbinic passage as a mere reference to the moral behavior that "sustains" the ethical order of the world. Idel, however, observes that the passage from the *Hagigah* has not only a moral but also a cosmological significance. He remarks that "the *Hagigah*, a short but highly influential passage, is a part of mythical cosmology rather than a mode of making sense of religious behavior. To be clear, the basic context of the discussion is cosmology, and its influence on the way in which the righteous should be understood is only an aside." Idel, *Ascensions on High*, 75.

71. One of the striking features found in the *Hagigah*'s account is a reference to the sevenfold nature of the world's foundation, a tradition also prominent in another passage from the *Zohar* that speaks of the seven pillars that sustain the creation. *Zohar* I.231a reads: "Rabbi Yose opened, saying, *On what were her pedestals sunk, or who laid her cornerstone?* (Job 38:6). This verse was spoken by the blessed Holy One, for when He created the world He created it solely upon pillars, the seven pillars of the world, as is written: *She has hewn her seven pillars* (Proverbs 9:1). Upon what those pillars stand is unknown, for that is a deep mystery, concealed of all concealed." Matt, *The Zohar: Pritzker Edition*, 3.396. It is intriguing that both *Hagigah*'s account and the *Zohar*, in their discussion of the foundation theme, mention a tradition about the seven pillars of Sophia from Prov 9:1, the tradition that might stand behind the motif of Sophia's creation of humanity from the seven elements.

72. *b. Hag.* 12b.

73. Thus, according to *Jub.* 4:23, thanks to Enoch, "the flood water did not come on any of the land of Eden because he was placed there as a sign and to testify against all people in order to tell all the deeds of history until the day of judgment." VanderKam, *The Book of Jubilees*, 2.28.

74. Idel, *Ascensions on High in Jewish Mysticism*, 85.

75. The term "world" in the angelic title appears to signify the entire creation. Peter Schäfer observes that in rabbinic literature the Prince of the

World is understood as an angel set over the whole creation. His duties include praying, together with the earth, for the coming of the Messiah, as well as praising God's creative work. P. Schäfer, *Rivalität zwischen Engeln und Menschen: Untersuchungen zur rabbinischen Engelvorstellung* (SJ, 8; Berlin: Walter de Gruyter, 1975) 55.

76. Regarding the role of Enoch as the Governor of the World in *2 Enoch*, see Orlov, *The Enoch-Metatron Tradition*, 159–161.

77. Cf. I.R. Tantlevskij, *Knigi Enoha* (Moscow/Jerusalem: Gesharim, 2000) 185.

78. Idel, *Ascensions on High in Jewish Mysticism*, 88.

79. One such description can be found in *Synopse* §12 (*3 Enoch* 9), which portrays the metamorphosis of Enoch's body into a gigantic corporeality, matching the world in length and breadth; it reads: "I was enlarged and increased in size till I matched the world in length and breath. He made to grow on me 72 wings, 36 on one side and 36 on the other, and each single wing covered the entire world." Alexander, "3 Enoch," 1.263.

80. It appears also that both Enoch and Adoil are envisioned in the text as the sacerdotal foundations. In our previous discussion about the primordial aeon Adoil, it was noted that he is identified with the upper sacred foundation that serves as the basis for the heavenly Temple, represented by the throne of God, which is depicted in the text as the center of the created order. It is intriguing that, similar to Adoil who serves as the upper foundation of the heavenly Temple, Enoch appears to be conceived as the sacerdotal foundation of the earthly Temple. In *2 Enoch*, immediately after Enoch's instructions to his sons before his second and final ascension to the highest heaven, the firstborn son of Enoch, Methuselah, and his brothers constructed an altar at Akhuzan, the exact location from which Enoch had been taken up. The place of the hero's departure, then, becomes the sacerdotal center of the earthly realm, where priestly initiations and expiatory sacrifices involving animal blood take place. It is no coincidence, therefore, that *2 Enoch* identifies the place Akhuzan as the center of the world. This arcane Slavonic word is traced by scholars to the Hebrew word אחזה, "special property of God," which, in Ezek 48:20–21, is applied to Jerusalem and the Temple. (Cf. Milik, *The Books of Enoch*, 114.) Here, similar to Adoil's protological role connected to the motif of the throne of the Deity, Enoch's eschatological role is tied to the idea of the earthly counterpart of the throne, the earthly Temple. The vertical axis of the throne and the Temple is thus explicitly reaffirmed in the text, as is the horizontal line connecting the protological and eschatological events. Later in the text, Akhuzan also receives the additional protological reaffirmation of being identified with the place of Adam's creation. Here, the protological and eschatological "pillars" are erected on the same place, and the starting point of creation becomes the place where eschatological consummation begins.

81. Andersen, "2 Enoch," 1.193. See also *2 Enoch* 66:7 (the longer recension): "How happy are the righteous who shall escape the Lord's great judgment; for they will be made to shine seven times brighter than the sun." Andersen, "2 Enoch," 1.194.

82. Enoch's metamorphosis before the Face is also repeated in *2 Enoch* 39.

83. Enoch's metamorphosis into a luminous celestial creature presupposes another eschatological trait mentioned in his descriptions of the final aeon of the righteous, namely, the state of incorruptibility. In *2 Enoch* 65:8–10, Enoch says that, at the end of times, all the righteous who will escape the Lord's great judgment will eventually attain the condition of incorruptibility since they "will be collected together into the great age . . . And they will have a great light, a great indestructible light, and paradise, great and incorruptible. For everything corruptible will pass away, and the incorruptible will come into being, and will be the shelter of the eternal residences." Andersen, "2 Enoch," 1.192. The longer recension's emphasis on the incorruptibility of the future condition of the righteous gathered in the final aeon seems, again, to recall the patriarch's newly acquired celestial state. One of the important features hinting at the patriarch's incorruptible nature is revealed during his brief visit to earth, when, after his luminous transformation God, sent him back to the lower realm to deliver final directions to his children. In *2 Enoch* 56, during Enoch's instructions, Methuselah asks his father for a blessing in order that he might prepare some food for him to eat. The translated hero, however, politely declines the offer to share earthly food lamenting that nothing earthly is agreeable with his current condition; it reads: "Listen, child! Since the time when the Lord anointed me with the ointment of his glory, food has not come into me, and earthly pleasure my soul does not remember; nor do I desire anything earthly." *2 Enoch* 56:2, the longer recension; Andersen, "2 Enoch," 1.182. In the shorter recension of *2 Enoch*, the patriarch's rejection of food is even more decisive; it reads: "Listen my child! Since the time when the Lord anointed me with ointment of my glory, it has been horrible for me, and food is not agreeable to me, and I have no desire for earthly food." Andersen, "2 Enoch," 1.183. In this passage, an important link is made between the changes in his nature during his luminous metamorphosis near the throne of Glory and his newly acquired condition of incorruptibility, which portends the future state of the righteous in the final aeon. Here, again, through his connection with the eschatological state of incorruptibility, Enoch appears to be fashioned as the first fruit of the future aeon of the righteous, or maybe even as one who is already joined to this final age. In this respect, it is notable that, in *2 Enoch* 55, Enoch tells his sons before his final departure that he shall go up to the highest heaven into his "eternal inheritance." Andersen, "2 Enoch," 1.182–183.

84. Regarding the Manichaean eschatological "Statue" made from the particles of light rescued by the elect, see G. Widengren, *Mani and Manichaeism* (New York: Holt, Rinehart and Winston, 1965) 68; M. Heuser, "Manichaean Myth According to the Coptic Sources," in: M. Heuser and H.-J. Klimkeit, *Studies in Manichaean Literature and Art* (NHMS, 46; Leiden: Brill, 1998) 3–108 at 86–87. Cf. also *Keph.* 54: "Then the summons and the obedience, the great counsel that came to the elements, which are set in conjunction. It mixed with them, it was established in silence. It bears up until the end time when it can arise and stand firm in the great fire. It will gather to it its own soul, and sculpt it in the Last Statue. You will also find it sweeps out and casts from it the pollution that is foreign to it. However, the life and the light that are in all things it gather in to it, and builds upon its body. Then when this Last Statue will be perfect in all its limbs, then it can become free and ascend from that great struggle through the Living Spirit its father, the one who comes and brings a limb. He brings it up from within this gathering, the melting down and destruction of all things." *Keph.* 75: "[T]he Last Statue will be sculpted from the remnant of all things." *Keph.* 81: "At the end also it can gather itself together and sculpt its own self in the Last Statue. And it separates light from darkness." *Keph.* 86: "Also another great and glorious work he will enact at the end is the Last Statue, which he will bring up to the aeons of light." Gardner, *The Kephalaia of the Teacher,* 58, 76, 83, and 89. Concerning the concept of the Last Statue as the corporeal gathering of the righteous souls, see, also, *Keph.* 149–150: "The fourth time when they weep is when the Statue will be taken up on the last day, and they will weep for the souls of the liars and blasphemers; for they may give . . . because their limbs have been severed . . . of the darkness. And also those souls, when the Statue will go up and they are left alone, they will weep in that will remain behind in affliction for ever. For they will be cut off and separated from the Last Statue. And it is a necessity to take these souls who are ready for loss as retribution for the deeds that they have done. They go in to this darkness and are bound with the darkness; just as they desired it and loved it, and placed their treasure with it. At that very moment, when the Last Statue rises up, they will weep. And they will scream out loud because they will be severed from the company of this great Statue. And they remain behind for ever. This great weeping is terrible, it occurs in front of the souls." Gardner, *The Kephalaia of the Teacher,* 157–158.

85. Cf. *Keph.* 71: "[F]rom when the First Man went down to the contest, till the time when the Statue comes in . . . this time . . . he appeared." *Keph.* 71: "[I]t is the time that occurred from the coming down of the First Man till the going up of the Last Statue." Gardner, *The Kephalaia of the Teacher,* 73.

86. Cf. *Keph.* 104: "The first death is from the time when the light fell to the darkness, and was mixed in with the rulers of darkness; until the

time when the light will become pure, and be separated from the darkness in that great fire. The reminder left behind there can build and add to the Last Statue." Gardner, *The Kephalaia of the Teacher,* 107–108.

87. In *2 Enoch* 33, the Lord tells the visionary that He himself is responsible for creating everything "from the highest foundation to the lowest, and to the end." Cf. *2 Enoch* 33:3 (the longer recension). Andersen, "2 Enoch," 1.156. The shorter recension also stresses the totality of the creative work of the Deity; it reads: "I have contrived it all—I created from the lowest foundation and up to the highest and out to the end." Andersen, "2 Enoch," 1.157. *2 Enoch's* emphasis on the Deity's role as the Creator shows a significant parallel to the Jewish mystical imagery, in which God is sometimes referred as *Yoser Bereshit*, "the Creator."

88. Cf. Orlov, *The Enoch-Metatron Tradition*, 191.

89. The access of the seventh antediluvian hero to the cosmological secrets is already manifested in the Enmeduranki tradition, in which Enmeduranki receives the secret of heaven and the underworld. Later rabbinic materials also emphasize the expertise of Enoch-Metatron in the secrets of creation. Regarding these developments, see Orlov, *The Enoch-Metatron Tradition*, 31–34.

90. N. Deutsch, *Guardians of the Gate: Angelic Vice Regency in Late Antiquity* (Brill's Series in Jewish Studies, 22; Leiden: Brill, 1999) 44–45. See also Bousset, *Hauptprobleme der Gnosis*, 200; Fossum, *The Name of God*, 310ff.

91. Freedman and Simon, *Midrash Rabbah*, 1.36.

92. Fossum, *The Name of God*, 310.

93. Fossum, *The Name of God*, 301.

94. *2 Enoch* 40:2 (the shorter recension): "I have fully counted the stars, a great multitude innumerable." Andersen, "2 Enoch," 1.165. In Psalm 147:4, God counts the number of all the stars. See, also, Ezekiel the Tragedian, *Exagoge* 79–80: "A multitude of stars fell before my knees and I counted them all." Jacobson, *The Exagoge of Ezekiel*, 55.

95. Deutsch, *Guardians of the Gate,* 99. With respect to the eschatological pillar of the souls in the Manichaean and Zoharic traditions, see Idel, *Ascensions on High in Jewish Mysticism*, 101–133.

96. *b. Avodah Zarah* 3b depicts Metatron as a teacher of the souls of those who died in their childhood; it reads: "What then does God do in the fourth quarter?—He sits and instructs the school children, as it is said, Whom shall one teach knowledge, and whom shall one make to understand the message? Them that are weaned from the milk. Who instructed them theretofore?—If you like, you may say Metatron, or it may be said that God did this as well as other things. And what does He do by night?—If you like you may say, the kind of thing He does by day; or it may be said that He rides a light cherub, and floats in eighteen thousand worlds; for it is said,

The chariots of God are myriads, even thousands shinan." See Epstein, *The Babylonian Talmud. Avodah Zarah,* 3b.

97. *Synopse* §75 (*3 Enoch* 48C:12) attests to a similar tradition; it reads: "Metatron sits for three hours every day in the heaven above, and assembles all the souls of the dead that have died in their mother's wombs, and of the babes that have died at their mothers' breasts, and of the schoolchildren beneath the throne of glory, and sits them down around him in classes, in companies, and in groups, and teaches them Torah, and wisdom, and haggadah, and tradition, and he completes for them their study of the scroll of the Law, as it is written, 'To whom shall one teach knowledge, whom shall one instruct in the tradition? Them that are weaned from the milk, them that are taken from the breasts.'" Alexander, "3 Enoch," 1.313; Schäfer, Schlüter, von Mutius, *Synopse zur Hekhalot-Literatur*, 36–37. A similar tradition is also found in the *Alphabet of R. Akiba*. See S. A. Wertheimer, *Batei Midrashot* (2 vols.; Jerusalem: Mossad Harav Kook, 1950–53) 2.333–477.

98. Metatron's role as the leader of the souls might also be reflected in an obscure passage from *Zohar* II.161b, in which one can find a description of the mysterious angelic "officer" put in charge of the souls; it reads: "And even today, all inhabitants of the world, before they come to this world, all stand in their images as they exist in this world, in a single treasure-house, where all souls of the world are clothed in their images. As they are about to descend to this world, the blessed Holy One calls upon one official whom He has appointed over all souls destined to descend to this world, and says to him, 'Go, bring Me the spirit of so-and-so.' At that moment the soul comes, clothed in the image of this world, and the official presents her before the Holy King. The blessed Holy One speaks to her and adjures her that when she descends to this world she will engage in Torah in order to know Him and to know the mystery of faith." Matt, *The Zohar: Pritzker Edition*, 5.431. Here, similar to the Metatron passages found in *b. Avod. Zar.* and *Sefer Hekhalot*, one sees, again, the motif of the importance of the study of the Torah that coincides with the tradition about the angelic captain of the souls. The description found in the *Zohar* also refers to the imagery of the storehouse of the souls, which in its turn brings to memory the motifs found in the Slavonic apocalypse, with its imagery of the protological and eschatological reservoirs, in the form of the womb of the primordial aeon Adoil and the final aeon during which all the righteous souls will be gathered.

99. It is possible that, like the Manichaean traditions, Metatron is also understood as the "Last Statue" or the corporeal collection of all righteous souls. Cf. *Keph.* 165: "Again, when the sun sinks from the universe and sets, and all people go in to their hiding places and houses and conceal themselves; this also pertains to the mystery of the end, as it presages the consummation of the universe. For, when all the light will be purified and redeemed in the

universe at the last, the collector of all things, the Last Statue, will gather in and sculpt itself. It is the last hour of the day, the time when the Last Statue will go up to the aeon of light." Gardner, *The Kephalaia of the Teacher,* 174.

100. It is intriguing that *Numbers Rabbah* 12:12 depicts Metatron as being in charge of the souls of the righteous whom he offers as the atonement for the sins of Israel; it reads: "R. Simeon expounded: When the Holy One, blessed be He, told Israel to set up the Tabernacle He intimated to the ministering angels that they also should make a Tabernacle, and when the one below was erected the other was erected on high. The latter was the tabernacle of the youth whose name was Metatron, and therein he offers up the souls of the righteous to atone for Israel in the days of their exile." Freedman and Simon, *Midrash Rabbah,* 5.482–483.

The Veneration Motif in the Temptation Narrative of the Gospel of Matthew: Lessons from the Enochic Tradition

1. Scholars believe that the stories of Jesus' temptation by Satan found in the Gospel of Matthew and the Gospel of Luke originated from Q. See T.J. Donaldson, *Jesus on the Mountain: A Study in Matthean Theology* (JSNTSS, 8; Sheffield: JSOT Press, 1985) 242–243; W.D. Davies and D.C. Allison, Jr., *The Gospel According to Saint Matthew* (3 vols; Edinburgh: T & T Clark, 1988) 1.351; C.M. Tuckett, "The Temptation Narrative in Q," in: *The Four Gospels. Festschrift Frans Neirynck* (eds. F. van Segbroeck et al.; 3 vols.; BETL, 100; Leuven: Peeters, 1992) 1.479–507. Both Matthew and Luke are also informed by the temptation narrative found in the Gospel of Mark. The fact that Matthew and Luke both start with the temptation in the wilderness might suggest that both of them were influenced by Mark's account. Cf. N.H. Taylor, "The Temptation of Jesus on the Mountain: A Palestinian Christian Polemic against Agrippa I," *JSNT* 83 (2001) 27–49 at 33. The Gospel of Matthew then follows this first temptation with the second one in the Temple, and the third on the mountain. In contrast to the Gospel of Matthew, the Gospel of Luke, places as second a temptation from a high place, then concludes with the temptation in the Temple. Matthew and Luke thus exhibit some differences in the order of the temptations. The majority of scholars think that the Gospel of Matthew attests the original order of the temptation narrative, while the Gospel of Luke represents the inversion of this original order. Cf., for example, J. Dupont, *Les tentations de Jésus au desert* (StudNeot, 4; Bruges: Desclée de Brouwer, 1968) 290; J. A. Fitzmyer, *The Gospel According to Luke* (2 vols; AB, 28; Garden City, 1981, 1985) 1.507–508; Donaldson, *Jesus on the Mountain: A Study in Matthean Theology,* 88; Davies and Allison, *The Gospel According to Saint Matthew,* 1.364.

2. This intense presence of apocalyptic motifs in the temptation narrative reflects the general tendency of the gospel. Some scholars have argued that in the Gospel of Matthew, "the apocalyptic perspective holds a much more prominent place than in any of the other Gospels." D. Hagner, "Apocalyptic Motifs in the Gospel of Matthew: Continuity and Discontinuity," *HBT* 7 (1985) 53–82 at 53.

3. Luke, like Mark, states that Satan's temptation of Jesus in the wilderness lasted a forty-day period. In contrast, Matthew's account seems to emphasize the length of Jesus' fast by claiming that he *fasted* forty days and forty nights. Davies and Allison note that "in Matthew all temptation appears to come only after the fast; in Luke Jesus is tempted during the forty day period. Matthew's version, in which the forty days go with the fasting, is closer to Exod 32:28," Davies and Allison, *The Gospel According to Saint Matthew*, 1.359.

4. Luigi Schiavo suggests that the expression that opens the account of the temptation of Jesus in Q—"ἤγετο ἐν τῷ πνεύματι" ("he was led/taken up by the spirit")—"characterizes the narrative as a transcendental experience of religious ecstasy. The verb, which always appears in the passive, indicates an action that comes from outside. The expression at Q 4.1, ἤγετο ἐν τῷ πνεύματι, albeit with literary variations, occurs in various texts of the New Testament and intertestamental literature (*1 Enoch* 71.1, 5; *Ascension of Isaiah* 6.9; Rev 1.10; 4.2; 17.3; 21.10; Mt. 4.1; Lk 4:1; Ezek 3.14), always in relation to accounts of visions." L. Schiavo, "The Temptation of Jesus: The Eschatological Battle and the New Ethic of the First Followers of Jesus in Q," *JSNT* 25 (2002) 141–164 at 144–145.

5. "Moses entered the cloud, and went up on the mountain. Moses was on the mountain for forty days and forty nights" (NRSV).

6. "He got up, and ate and drank; then he went in the strength of that food forty days and forty nights to Horeb the mount of God" (NRSV).

7. For the discussion of the forty-day motif, see S.R. Garrett, *The Temptations of Jesus in Mark's Gospel* (Grand Rapids: Eerdmans, 1998) 57; B. Gerhardsson, *The Testing of God's Son* (ConBNT, 2.1; Lund: Gleerup, 1966) 41–43; H.A. Kelly, "The Devil in the Desert," *CBQ* 26 (1964) 190–220 at 196.

8. Regarding Satan and Satan's traditions, see: G. Anderson, "The Exaltation of Adam and the Fall of Satan," in: *Literature on Adam and Eve. Collected Essays* (eds. G. Anderson et al.; SVTP, 15; Brill: Leiden, 2000) 83–110; C. Breytenbach and P.L. Day, "Satan," in: *Dictionary of Deities and Demons in the Bible* (eds. K. van der Toorn et al.; Leiden: Brill, 1995) 726–732; J. Dan, "Samael and the Problem of Jewish Gnosticism," in: *Perspectives on Jewish Thought and Mysticism* (eds. A.L. Ivry, E.R. Wolfson and A. Arkush; Amsterdam: Harwood Academic Publishers, 1998) 257–276; P.L. Day, *An Adversary in Heaven: Satan in the Hebrew Bible* (HSM, 43; Atlanta: Scholars, 1988); N. Forsyth, *The Old Enemy: Satan and the Combat Myth* (Princeton: Princeton

University Press, 1987); H.E. Gaylord, "How Satanael Lost His '-el,'" *JJS* 33 (1982) 303–309; V.P. Hamilton, "Satan," in: *Anchor Bible Dictionary* (6 vols.; ed. D.N. Freedman; New York: Doubleday, 1992) 5.985–998; H.A. Kelly, *Towards the Death of Satan: The Growth and Decline of Christian Demonology* (London: Chapman, 1968); idem, *Satan: A Biography* (Cambridge: Cambridge University Press, 2006); R.S. Kluger, *Satan in the Old Testament* (SJT, 7; Evanston: Northwestern University Press, 1967); A. Lods, "Les origines de la figure de satan, ses fonctions à la cour céleste," in: *Mélanges syriens offerts à Monsieur René Dussaud* (2 vols.; eds. J.-A. Blanchet et al.; Paris: P. Geuthner, 1939) 2.649–660; E.H. Pagels, "The Social History of Satan, the 'Intimate Enemy': A Preliminary Sketch," *HTR* 84:2 (1991) 105–128; idem, "The Social History of Satan, 2: Satan in the New Testament Gospels," *JAAR* 62:1 (1994) 17–58; idem, *The Origin of Satan* (New York: Vintage Books, 1996); idem, "The Social History of Satan, 3: John of Patmos and Ignatius of Antioch: Contrasting Visions of 'God's People,'" *HTR* 99 (2006) 487–505; C.A. Patrides, "The Salvation of Satan," *JHI* 28 (1967) 467–478; J.B. Russell, *Satan: The Early Christian Tradition* (Ithaca: Cornell University Press, 1981); M. Schneider, "The Myth of the Satan in the *Book of Bahir*," *Kabbalah* 20 (2009) 287–343 [Hebrew]; R. Stichel, "Die Verführung der Stammeltern durch Satanael nach der Kurzfassung der slavischen Baruch-Apocalypse," in: *Kulturelle Traditionen in Bulgarien* (eds. R. Lauer and P. Schreiner; AAWG, 177; Göttingen: Vandenhoeck & Ruprecht, 1989) 116–128; M.E. Stone, *Adam's Contract with Satan. The Legend of the Cheirograph of Adam* (Bloomington: Indiana University Press, 2002); idem, "'Be You a Lyre for Me': Identity or Manipulation in Eden," *The Exegetical Encounter between Jews and Christians in Late Antiquity* (eds. E. Grypeou and H. Spurling; JCPS, 18; Leiden: Brill, 2009) 87–99.

9. See, for example, Davies and Allison, *The Gospel According to Saint Matthew*, 1.364; D. Sim, *Apocalyptic Eschatology in the Gospel of Matthew* (Cambridge: Cambridge University Press, 1996).

10. A. Orlov, "Satan and the Visionary: Apocalyptic Roles of the Adversary in the Temptation Narrative of the Gospel of Matthew," in Orlov, *Dark Mirrors*, 107–112.

11. Some early Christian interpreters saw the temptation of Jesus as the reversal of Adam's sins. Cf., for example, Justin, *Dial.* 103; Irenaeus, *Adv. Haer.* 5.21.2. On this see D.C. Allison, Jr., "Behind the Temptations of Jesus: Q 4:1–13 and Mark 1:12–13," in: *Authenticating the Activities of Jesus* (eds. B.D. Chilton and C. Evans; NTTS, 28/2; Leiden: Brill, 2002) 196.

12. W.A. Schultze, "Der Heilige und die wilden Tiere. Zur Exegese von Mc. 1. 13b," *ZNW* 46 (1955) 280–83; A. Feuillet, "L'épisode de la tentation d'après l'Evangile selon saint Marc (I,12–13)," *EB* 19 (1960) 49–73; J. Jeremias, "Adam," *TDNT*, 1.141–143; *idem*, "Nachwort zum Artikel von H.-G. Leder," *ZNW* 54 (1963) 278–279; A. Vargas-Machuca, "La tentación de Jesús

según Mc. 1,12–13¿Hecho real o relato de tipo haggádico?" *EE* 48 (1973) 163–190; P. Pokorný, "The Temptation Stories and Their Intention," *NTS* 20 (1973–74) 115–27; J. Gnilka, *Das Evangelium nach Markus* (2 vols; EKKNT, 2.1–2; Zürich: Benziger; Neukirchen-Vluyn: Neukirchener Verlag, 1978–79) 1.58; R.A. Guelich, *Mark 1–8:26* (WBC, 34A; Dallas: Word, 1989) 38–39; R. Bauckham, "Jesus and the Wild Animals (Mark 1:13): A Christological Image for an Ecological Age," in *Jesus of Nazareth: Lord and Christ: Essays on the Historical Jesus and New Testament Christology* (eds. J.B. Green and M. Turner; Grand Rapids: Eerdmans, 1994) 3–21; J. Gibson, *Temptations of Jesus in Early Christianity* (JSNTSS, 112; Sheffield: Sheffield Academic Press, 1995) 65–66; Allison, "Behind the Temptations of Jesus: Q 4:1–13 and Mark 1:12–13," 196–199.

13. J. Jeremias, *New Testament Theology* (New York: Scribner, 1971) 69. The theme of alienation between humanity and animals looms large in the *Book of Jubilees*. It receives further development in the *Primary Adam Books*, in which Eve and Seth encounter a hostile beast.

14. Jeremias, *New Testament Theology*, 69–70.

15. Jeremias, *New Testament Theology*, 70.

16. Bauckham, "Jesus and the Wild Animals (Mark 1:13): A Christological Image for an Ecological Age," 6.

17. In this respect, Allison and Davies remark that "in Mk 1.12–13 Jesus is probably the last Adam (cf. Rom 5.12–21; 1 Cor 15.42–50; Justin, *Dial.* 103; *Gospel of Philip* 71.16–21; Irenaeus. *Adv. haer.* 5.21.2). He, like the first Adam, is tempted by Satan. But unlike his anti-type, he does not succumb, and the result is the recovery of paradise (cf. *Testament of Levi* 18.10): the wild beasts are tamed and once again a man dwells with angels and is served by them." Davies and Allison, *The Gospel According to Saint Matthew*, 1.356.

18. Allison, "Behind the Temptations of Jesus: Q 4:1–13 and Mark 1:12–13," 198.

19. Allison, "Behind the Temptations of Jesus: Q 4:1–13 and Mark 1:12–13," 196.

20. Allison, "Behind the Temptations of Jesus: Q 4:1–13 and Mark 1:12–13," 199.

21. The suggestion that the veneration motif found in the temptation story might be connected to the theme of worship of Jesus in Matthew is hinted by the usage of the verb προσκυνέω. Larry Hurtado suggests that the "pattern of preference for προσκυνέω, with its strong associations with cultic worship, suggests that Matthew has chosen to make these scenes all function as foreshadowings of the exalted reverence of Jesus familiar to his Christian readers in their collective worship. . . . The net effect of Matthew's numerous omissions and insertions of προσκυνέω in cases where Jesus is the recipient of homage is a consistent pattern. It is not simply a matter of preference

of one somewhat synonymous word for others. Matthew reserves the word προσκυνέω for the reverence of Jesus given by disciples and those who are presented as sincerely intending to give him homage. As Günther Bornkamm, Gerhard Barth, and Heinz Joachim Held concluded from their analysis of scenes where Jesus is the recipient of the gesture in Matthew, προσκυνέω is used 'only in the sense of genuine worship of Jesus.'" L. Hurtado, *How On Earth Did Jesus Become A God?: Historical Questions About Earliest Devotion to Jesus* (Grand Rapids: Eerdmans, 2005) 143.

22. Hurtado, in his analysis of usage of the verb προσκυνέω in the New Testament, which both Matthew and Luke use in their temptation narratives (Matt 4:9; Luke 4:7), suggests that "the term προσκυνέω is a recurrent feature of Matthew's narrative vocabulary, with thirteen occurrences, a frequency exceeded only by the twenty-four uses in Revelation among the New Testament writings." Hurtado, *How On Earth Did Jesus Become a God?: Historical Questions About Earliest Devotion to Jesus,* 142–143. In the Gospels προσκυνέω "appears twice in Mark, three times in Luke (in two passages), eight times in John (in three passages), and thirteen times in Matthew (in nine distinguishable passages)." Hurtado, *How On Earth Did Jesus Become a God?: Historical Questions About Earliest Devotion to Jesus,* 142.

23. Cf. Matt 2:2: "ἤλθομεν προσκυνῆσαι αὐτῷ"; Matt 2:8 "ὅπως κἀγὼ ἐλθὼν προσκυνήσω αὐτῷ." With respect to these formulae, scholars note that in some LXX passages "ἔρχομαι followed by προσκυνέω denotes a cultic action." Davies and Allison, *The Gospel According to Saint Matthew,* 1.236. Similarly, in the temptation narrative, προσκυνέω is also placed in the cultic context. Cf., for example, Matt 4:10: "Κύριον τὸν θεόν σου προσκυνήσεις καὶ αὐτῷ μόνῳ λατρεύσεις."

24. Cf. Matt 2:11: "και πεσόντες προσεκύνησαν αὐτῳ"; Matt 4:9: "πεσὼν προσκυνήσῃς μοι." Scholars note that similar terminological constellations occur also in Ps 72. 11; Dan 3.5–7; Josephus, *Ant.* 7.95; 9.11; Acts 10.25; 1 Cor 14.25; Rev 4.10; 7.11; 22.8. Concerning this, see Davies and Allison, *The Gospel According to Saint Matthew,* 1.248.

25. D.C. Allison, "The Magi's Angel (Matt. 2:2, 9–10)," in: D.C. Allison, Jr., *Studies in Matthew: Interpretation Past and Present* (Grand Rapids: Baker Academic, 2005) 17–41. Cf. also D.C. Allison, Jr., "What Was the Star That Guided the Magi?" *BR* 9 (1993) 24; Bucur, *Angelomorphic Pneumatology: Clement of Alexandria and Other Early Christian Witnesses*, 93.

26. Cf. Gen 2:8: "And the Lord God planted a garden in Eden, in the east; and there he put the man whom he had formed" (NRSV).

27. With respect to the cultic functions of frankincense and myrrh, as ingredients in incense, Dale Allison notes that "frankincense was an odoriferous gum resin from various trees and bushes which had a cultic usage in the ancient world. According to Exod 30:34–8, it was a prescribed ingredient of

sacred incense. According to Lev 24.7, it was to be offered with the bread of the Presence. According to Lev 2.1–2, 14–6; 6.14–8, it was added to cereal offerings. . . . Myrrh was a fragrant gum resin from trees . . . a component of holy anointing oil, and an ingredient in incense." D.C. Allison, Jr., *Matthew: A Shorter Commentary* (London and New York: T & T Clark, 2004) 27. The magi's gifts also include gold, a material that is mentioned in the description of Eden in Gen 2:11. In relation to this, Gordon Wenham observes that "if Eden is seen as a super sanctuary, this reference to gold can hardly be accidental for the most sacred items of tabernacle furniture were made of or covered with 'pure gold.'" Wenham, "Sanctuary Symbolism in the Garden of Eden Story," 22. With respect to the connections between gold of Eden and the materials used for decoration of the tabernacle and priestly vestments in the Book of Exodus, see also D. Chilton, *Paradise Restored: A Biblical Theology of Dominion* (Ft. Worth: Dominion Press, 1985).

28. Jacques van Ruiten argues that, in *Jubilees*, "the Garden of Eden is seen as a Temple, or, more precisely as a part of the Temple: the room which is in the rear of the Temple, where the ark of the covenant of the Lord is placed, and which is often called 'Holy of Holies.'" Such an understanding of Eden as the temple presupposes the protoplast's role as a sacerdotal servant. In relation to this, van Ruiten suggests that, according to the author of *Jubilees*, Adam is acting as a prototypical priest as he burns incense at the gate of the Garden of Eden. Van Ruiten puts this description in parallel with a tradition found in Exodus, which tells that the incense was burned in front of the Holy of Holies. Van Ruiten, "Visions of the Temple in the Book of Jubilees," 215–228; idem, "Eden and the Temple: The Rewriting of Genesis 2:4–3:24 in the Book of Jubilees," 76.

29. *Jub.* 3:27 reads: "On that day, as he was leaving the Garden of Eden, he burned incense as a pleasing fragrance—frankincense, galbanum, stacte, and aromatic spices—in the early morning when the sun rose at the time when he covered his shame." VanderKam, *The Book of Jubilees*, 2.20. Regarding the Edenic incense, see also *1 Enoch* 29–32: "And there I saw . . . vessels of the fragrance of incense and myrrh. . . ." Knibb, *The Ethiopic Book of Enoch*, 2.117–123; Sirach 24:15: ". . . like cassia and camel's thorn I gave forth perfume, and like choice myrrh I spread my fragrance, like galbanum, onycha, and stacte, and like the odor of incense in the tent." (NRSV); Armenian *LAE* 29:3 reads: "Adam replied and said to the angels, 'I beseech you, let (me) be a little, so that I may take sweet incenses with me from the Garden, so that when I go out of here, I may offer sweet incenses to God, and offerings, so that, perhaps, God will hearken to us.'" Anderson and Stone, *A Synopsis of the Books of Adam and Eve*, 72E.

30. Previous studies have identified the connection between the magi story and the birth of a priestly child (Noah, Melchizedek, Moses) in some

Jewish accounts. In the gifts that the magi brought to the child, these studies see the sacerdotal items. Thus, for example, Crispin Fletcher-Louis observes that, "[I]t is noteworthy that at the birth of Jesus, of course, there is signaled the child's priestly identity in the gift of gold, frankincense and myrrh (cf. Exod 30:23; 28:5, 6, 8 etc.) from the magi (Matt 2:11)." C. Fletcher-Louis, *All the Glory of Adam. Liturgical Anthropology in the Dead Sea Scrolls* (STDJ, 42; Leiden: Brill, 2002) 53.

31. Concerning this tradition, Allison and Davies note that "of the many legends that later came to surround the magi and their gifts, one of the most pleasing is found in the so-called *Cave of Treasures* (6th cent. AD). Adam, we are told, had many treasures in paradise, and when he was expelled therefrom he took what he could with him—gold, frankincense, and myrrh. Upon his death, Adam's sons hid their father's treasures in a cave, where they lay undisturbed until the magi, on their way to Bethlehem, entered the cave to get gifts for the Son of God. In this legend, Matthew's story has become the vehicle for a very Pauline idea, namely, that Jesus is the second Adam." Davies and Allison, *The Gospel According to Saint Matthew* 1.251.

32. Cf. Matt 2:8: "Πορευθέντες ἐξετάσατε ἀκριβῶς περὶ τοῦ παιδίου: ἐπὰν δὲ εὕρητε ἀπαγγείλατέ μοι, ὅπως κἀγὼ ἐλθὼν προσκυνήσω αὐτῷ."

33. Matt 17:6: "καὶ ἀκούσαντες οἱ μαθηταὶ ἔπεσαν ἐπὶ πρόσωπον αὐτῶν καὶ ἐφοβήθησαν σφόδρα."

34. The motif of the disciples' veneration is reminiscent of the one performed by the magi. Thus, Allison and Davies note that "the magi do not simply bend their knees (cf. 17.14; 18.29). They fall down on their faces. This is noteworthy because there was a tendency in Judaism to think prostration proper only in the worship of God (cf. Philo, *Leg. Gai.* 116; *Decal.* 64; Mt 4.9–10; Acts 10.25–6; Rev 19.10; 22.8–9)." Davies and Allison, *The Gospel According to Saint Matthew,* 1.248. Robert Gundry notes that "they (the magi) knelt down before him with heads to the ground." R.H. Gundry, *Matthew: A Commentary on His Handbook for a Mixed Church under Persecution* (Grand Rapids: Eerdmans, 1994) 31.

35. Another unique Matthean occurrence of this motif is found in Matt 18:26, in which one can find a familiar constellation of "πεσὼν" and "προσεκύνει." Gundry observes that, besides the magi story, "Matthew inserts the same combination of falling down and worshiping in 4:9 and uses it in unique material at 18:26." He further notes that, "[I]n particular, πεσόντες sharpens Matthew's point, for in 4:9 falling down will accompany worship in the alternatives of worshiping God and worshiping Satan, and without parallel it describes the response of the disciples who witnessed the transfiguration (17:6)." 31–32. Gundry, *Matthew: A Commentary on His Handbook for a Mixed Church under Persecution*, 31–32.

36. The general scholarly consensus holds that the apocalypse was composed before the destruction of the Second Temple in 70 CE. In his first systematic exploration of the text published in 1896, R. H. Charles used references to the Temple practices found in the Slavonic apocalypse as main proofs for his hypothesis of the early date of the apocalypse which he placed in the first century CE before the destruction of the Second Temple. Charles and scholars after him noted that the text gives no indication that the catastrophe of the destruction of the Temple had already occurred at the time of the book's composition. Critical readers of the pseudepigraphon would have some difficulties finding any explicit expression of feelings of sadness or mourning about the loss of the sanctuary. Affirmations of the value of animal sacrifice and Enoch's halakhic instructions found in *2 Enoch* 59 also appear to be fashioned not in the "preservationist," mishnaic-like mode but rather as if they reflected sacrificial practices that still existed when the author was writing his book. There is also an intensive and consistent effort on the part of the author to legitimize the central place of worship, which through the reference to the place Akhuzan—a cryptic name for the temple mountain in Jerusalem—is explicitly connected in *2 Enoch* with the Jerusalem Temple. Further, the Slavonic apocalypse also contains a direct command to visit the Temple three times a day, advice that would be difficult to fulfill if the sanctuary had already been destroyed. On the date of *2 Enoch* see R.H. Charles and W. R. Morfill, *The Book of the Secrets of Enoch* (Oxford: Clarendon Press, 1896) xxvi; R.H. Charles and N. Forbes, "The Book of the Secrets of Enoch," *The Apocrypha and Pseudepigrapha of the Old Testament* (2 vols.; ed. R.H. Charles; Oxford: Clarendon Press, 1913) 2. 429; Milik, *The Books of Enoch*, 114; C. Böttrich, *Das slavische Henochbuch* (JSHRZ, 5; Gütersloh: Gütersloher Verlaghaus, 1995) 813; Orlov, *The Enoch-Metatron Tradition*, 323–328; idem, "The Sacerdotal Traditions of 2 Enoch and the Date of the Text," in: *New Perspectives on 2 Enoch: No Longer Slavonic Only* (eds. A. Orlov, G. Boccaccini, J. Zurawski; Studia Judaeoslavica, 4; Leiden: Brill, 2012) 103–116.

37. Andersen, "2 Enoch," 1.138. The tradition of the angelic veneration of Enoch is attested to in both recensions of *2 Enoch*. Cf. *2 Enoch* 22:6–7 in Ms. J (longer recension): "And the Lord said to his servants, sounding them out, 'Let Enoch join in and stand in front of my face forever!' And the Lord's glorious ones did obeisance and said, 'Let Enoch yield in accordance with your word, O Lord !' " Andersen, "2 Enoch," 1.138. *2 Enoch* 22:6–7 in Ms. A (shorter recension): "The Lord said, 'Let Enoch come up and stand in front of my face forever!' And the glorious ones did obeisance and said, 'Let him come up!' " Andersen, "2 Enoch," 1.139.

38. Latin *LAE* 13:2: "When God blew into you the breath of life and your countenance and likeness were made in the image of God, Michael led

you and made you worship in the sight of God." Armenian *LAE* 13:2: "When God breathed his spirit into you, you received the likeness of his image. Thereupon, Michael came and made you bow down before God." Anderson and Stone, *A Synopsis of the Books of Adam and Eve,* 16E.

39. Latin *LAE* 13:2–14:1: "The Lord God then said: 'Behold, Adam, I have made you in our image and likeness.' Having gone forth Michael called all the angels saying: 'Worship the image of the Lord God, just as the Lord God has commanded.'" Armenian *LAE* 13:2–14:1: "God said to Michael, 'Behold I have made Adam in the likeness of my image.' Then Michael summoned all the angels, and God said to them, 'Come, bow down to god whom I made.'" Anderson and Stone, *A Synopsis of the Books of Adam and Eve*, 16E.

40. Latin *LAE* 14:2–15:1: "Michael himself worshipped first then he called me and said: 'Worship the image of God Jehovah.' I answered: 'I do not have it within me to worship Adam.' When Michael compelled me to worship, I said to him: 'Why do you compel me? I will not worship him who is lower and later than me. I am prior to that creature. Before he was made, I had already been made. He ought to worship me.' Hearing this, other angels who were under me were unwilling to worship him." Armenian *LAE* 14:2–15:1: "Michael bowed first He called me and said. 'You too, bow down to Adam.' I said, Go away, Michael! I shall not bow [down] to him who is posterior to me, for I am former. Why is it proper [for me] to bow down to him? The other angels, too, who were with me, heard this, and my words seemed pleasing to them and they did not prostrate themselves to you, Adam." Anderson and Stone, *A Synopsis of the Books of Adam and Eve*, 16E–17E.

41. W.R. Morfill and R.H. Charles, *The Book of the Secrets of Enoch* (Oxford: Oxford University Press, 1896) 28.

42. M.E. Stone, "The Fall of Satan and Adam's Penance: Three Notes on the *Books of Adam and Eve,*" *Literature on Adam and Eve. Collected Essays* (eds. G. Anderson, M. Stone, J. Tromp; SVTP, 15; Brill: Leiden, 2000) 47.

43. The tradition of the angelic veneration of humanity was forgotten in later Enochic lore. Often these later developments help us to clarify the obscure details of the early tradition by providing additional insight into the distorted mosaic of their patterns. *3 Enoch* is also cognizant of the tradition of the angelic veneration portraying the celestial citizens bowing down, as in the Slavonic apocalypse, before the translated seventh antediluvian hero. *Sefer Hekhalot* 4:1–10 depicts Rabbi Ishmael questioning his celestial guide Metatron about his name "Youth": "R. Ishmael said: I said to Metatron: '. . . you are greater than all the princes, more exalted than all the angels, more beloved than all the ministers . . . why, then, do they call you "Youth" in the heavenly heights?' He answered: 'Because I am Enoch, the son of Jared . . . the Holy One, blessed be he, appointed me in the height as a prince and a ruler among the ministering angels. Then three of the ministering angels, Uzzah, Azzah, and Azael, came and laid charges against

me in the heavenly height. They said before the Holy One, blessed be He, "Lord of the Universe, did not the primeval ones give you good advice when they said, Do not create man!" . . . And once they all arose and went to meet me and prostrated themselves before me, saying Happy are you, and happy your parents, because your Creator has favored you. Because I am young in their company and mere youth among them in days and months and years—therefore they call me 'Youth.'" Alexander, "3 Enoch," 1.258–259. Commenting on this passage, Gary Anderson suggests that if "we remove those layers of the tradition that are clearly secondary . . . we are left with a story that is almost identical to the analog we have traced in the Adam and Eve literature and II Enoch." G. Anderson, "The Exaltation of Adam and the Fall of Satan," *Literature on Adam and Eve. Collected Essays* (eds. G. Anderson, M. Stone, J. Tromp; SVTP, 15; Brill: Leiden, 2000) 107. Anderson further notes that the acclamation of Enoch as "Youth," in *Sefer Hekhalot*, is intriguing because the reason *3 Enoch* supplies for this title is deceptively simple and straightforward: "Because I am young in their company and a mere youth among them in days and months and years—therefore they call me 'Youth.'" Anderson proposes that the title might point to its Adamic provenance since the explanation for the epithet "youth" recalls the reason for the angelic refusal to worship Adam in the *Vita* on the basis of his inferiority to them by way of his age. Anderson, "The Exaltation of Adam and the Fall of Satan," 108.

44. Stone, "The Fall of Satan and Adam's Penance," 48.

45. In this respect, it should be noted that scholars have demonstrated that *2 Enoch* has more parallels with the Gospel of Matthew than with any other book in the New Testament. Regarding this, see C. Böttrich, *Weltweisheit, Menschheitsethik, Urkult: Studien zum slavischen Henochbuch* (WUNT, 2/50; Tübingen: Mohr/Siebeck, 1992) 219–221.

46. Allison and Davies discuss the visionary mold of these traditions of transportation, noting that "Whether we are to think of a visionary experience (so Theodore of Mopsuestia in PG 66.721a and other Antiochene theologians) or of a miraculous teleportation (cf. Acts 8.39–40; *2 Bar.* 6.3; *Apoc. Zeph.* frag, in Clement of Alexandria, *Strom.* 5.11.77; *L. Proph. Hab.* 4–7; and the Catholic stories of bilocating saints, such as those about St. Martin de Porres) is unclear (cf. 2 Cor 12.2!), although 4.8 ('and he showed him all the kingdoms of the world') may argue for the former possibility." Davies and Allison, *The Gospel According to Saint Matthew*, 1.364.

47. Concerning the transportation of Jesus in the temptation narrative, see also Schiavo, "The Temptation of Jesus: The Eschatological Battle and the New Ethic of the First Followers of Jesus in Q," 147–148.

48. With respect to this, Schiavo notes that "on his journey, Jesus is also accompanied, but this time by the Devil, a fallen angel, whose function is to lead him and show him his dominion and power on earth." Schiavo, "The

Temptation of Jesus: The Eschatological Battle and the New Ethic of the First Followers of Jesus in Q," 147.

49. "Then Moses went up from the plains of Moab to Mount Nebo, to the top of Pisgah, which is opposite Jericho, and the Lord showed him the whole land: Gilead as far as Dan, all Naphtali, the land of Ephraim and Manasseh, all the land of Judah as far as the Western Sea, the Negeb, and the Plain—that is, the valley of Jericho, the city of palm trees—as far as Zoar. The Lord said to him, 'This is the land of which I swore to Abraham, to Isaac, and to Jacob, saying, 'I will give it to your descendants'; I have let you see it with your eyes, but you shall not cross over there' " (NRSV).

50. J. Dupont, "L'arrière-fond biblique du récit des tentations de Jésus," *NTS* 3 (1957) 287–304 at 297.

51. Thus, for example, Allison and Davies observe that "the three temptations exhibit a spatial progression, from a low place to a high place. The first takes place in the desert, the second on a pinnacle in the temple, the third on a mountain from which all the kingdoms of the world can be seen. This progression corresponds to the dramatic tension which comes to a climax with the third temptation." Davies and Allison, *The Gospel According to Saint Matthew*, 1.352

52. Schiavo argues that "there is no doubt that the account of the temptation can be read in the wider context of the heavenly journey. With regard to the way the experience is prepared and the nature of the experience, it appears truly to be a journey, even if its content is quite different." Schiavo "The Temptation of Jesus: The Eschatological Battle and the New Ethic of the First Followers of Jesus in Q," 147.

53. *1 Enoch* 25:3 reads: "And he answered me, saying: 'This high mountain which you saw, whose summit is like the throne of the Lord, is the throne where the Holy and Great One, the Lord of Glory, the Eternal King, will sit when he comes down to visit the earth for good.' " Knibb, *The Ethiopic Book of Enoch*, 2.113.

54. *Exagoge* 67–90 reads: "Moses: I had a vision of a great throne on the top of Mount Sinai and it reached till the folds of heaven. A noble man was sitting on it, with a crown and a large scepter in his left hand. He beckoned to me with his right hand, so I approached and stood before the throne. He gave me the scepter and instructed me to sit on the great throne. Then he gave me a royal crown and got up from the throne. I beheld the whole earth all around and saw beneath the earth and above the heavens. A multitude of stars fell before my knees and I counted them all. They paraded past me like a battalion of men. Then I awoke from my sleep in fear." Jacobson, *The Exagoge of Ezekiel,* 54–55.

55. Thus, for example, in *3 Enoch* 45:1–4 one can find the following tradition about the *Pargod*: "R. Ishmael said: Metatron said to me: Come and I will show you the curtain of the Omnipresent One which is spread before

the Holy One, blessed be he, and on which are printed all the generations of the world and their deeds, whether done or to be done, till the last generation. . . . the kings of Judah and their generations, their deeds and their acts; the kings of Israel and their generations, their deeds and their acts; the kings of the gentiles and their generations, their deeds and their acts. . . ." Alexander, "3 Enoch," 1.295–298.

56. Regarding this, see also Orlov, *Heavenly Priesthood in the Apocalypse of Abraham*, 159–178.

57. Thus, for example, Schiavo notes that "in the *Apocalypse of Abraham* . . . Abraham is led in the body by an angel to the throne of God. . . . From there, Abraham sees heaven with the throne of God, before his descent to the earth and the history of the world until the judgment. The similarity between this text and Q 4.1–13 is striking: Jesus, like Abraham, is transported bodily, on a journey to the sky. From up there, he contemplates the temple and the earth (earthly kingdoms)." Schiavo, "The Temptation of Jesus: The Eschatological Battle and the New Ethic of the First Followers of Jesus in Q," 147–148.

58. Thus, for example, according to *4Q180* 1.1–3, "all ages" are engraved on the heavenly tablets; it reads: "Interpretation concerning the ages which God has made: An age to conclude [all that there is] and all that will be. Before creating them he determined [their] operations [according to the precise sequence of the ages,] one age after another age. And this is engraved on the [heavenly] tablets [for the sons of men,] [for] /[a]ll/ the ages of their dominion." García-Martínez and Tigchelaar, *The Dead Sea Scrolls Study Edition*, 1.371. Furthermore, according to *1 Enoch* 81:1–2, by looking at the heavenly tablets, the seventh antediluvian hero was able to learn about every human action: "And he said to me: 'O Enoch, look at the book of the tablets of heaven, and read what is written upon them, and learn *every individual act.*' And I looked at everything in the tablets of heaven, and I read everything which was written, and I noted everything." Knibb, *The Ethiopic Book of Enoch*, 2.186.

59. On this tradition see Orlov, *The Enoch-Metatron Tradition*, 165–176.

60. Cf. *b. Hag.* 15a: "It is taught as a tradition that on high there is no sitting and no emulation, and no back, and no weariness." Epstein, *The Babylonian Talmud. Hagiga*, 15a; *Merkavah Rabbah* (*Synopse* §672): "He said: the sages taught: above there is no standing, and no sitting, no jealousy and no rivalry, and no duplicity and no affliction." Schäfer et al., *Synopse zur Hekhalot-Literatur*, 246.

61. Hugo Odeberg may be the first scholar to have discovered the characteristics of the Prince of the Presence in the longer recension of *2 Enoch*. He demonstrated, in his synopsis of the parallel passages from *2* and *3 Enoch*, that the phrase "stand before my face forever," found in the Slavonic apocalypse does not serve there merely as a typical Hebraism "to be in the presence," but

establishes the angelic status of Enoch as Metatron, the Prince of the Presence. Odeberg, *3 Enoch*, 1.55. Charles Gieschen's research also reinforces this position; Gieschen argues that Enoch's "standing" in front of the face of the Lord forever conclusively indicates the status of a principal angel. He further observes that "those who stand immediately before the throne are usually the principal angels, i.e., the Angels of the Presence." C.A. Gieschen, *Angelomorphic Christology: Antecedents and Early Evidence* (AGAJU, 42; Leiden: Brill, 1998) 158, n. 17.

62. Matt 4:5: "καὶ ἔστησεν αὐτὸν ἐπὶ τὸ πτερύγιον τοῦ ἱεροῦ." Luke 4:9: "καὶ ἔστησεν ἐπὶ τὸ πτερύγιον τοῦ ἱεροῦ."

63. Concerning the Mosaic typology in the Gospel of Matthew, see D.C. Allison, Jr., *The New Moses: A Matthean Typology* (Minneapolis: Fortress, 1994).

64. Jacobson, *The Exagoge of Ezekiel*, 54.

65. Georgian *LAE* 13:2: "And Michael came; he presented you. . . ." Anderson and Stone, *A Synopsis of the Books of Adam and Eve*, 16E.

66. Georgian *LAE* 13:2: ". . . and made you bow down before God." Anderson and Stone, *A Synopsis of the Books of Adam and Eve*, 16E.

67. Georgian *LAE* 14:1–2: "Then Michael came; he summoned all the troops of angels and told them, 'Bow down before the likeness and the image of the divinity.' And then, when Michael summoned them and all had bowed down to you, he summoned me also." Anderson and Stone, *A Synopsis of the Books of Adam and Eve*, 16E.

68. Matt 4:5: "Then the devil took him to the holy city and placed him on the pinnacle of the temple . . ." (NRSV).

69. Matt 4:6a: ". . . saying to him, 'If you are the Son of God, throw yourself down . . .' " (NRSV).

70. Matt 4:6b: ". . . for it is written, 'He will command his angels concerning you,' and 'On their hands they will bear you up, so that you will not dash your foot against a stone' " (NRSV).

71. Thus the deification of Adam is especially evident in the Armenian *LAE* 14:1: "Then Michael summoned all the angels, and God said to them, 'Come, bow down to god whom I made.' " Anderson and Stone, *A Synopsis of the Books of Adam and Eve*, 16E. *2 Enoch* also emphasizes the supraangelic status of its hero when it tells him that he is above the angels by being placed closer to the Deity than Gabriel and, by revelation, closer to the mysteries of creation that God never revealed to the angels.

72. Jarl Fossum's research demonstrates that the motif of the God's opposition to the veneration of Adam by the angels appears in several forms in the rabbinic literature. Fossum differentiates three major forms of this tradition: "(1) The angels mistake Adam for God and want to exclaim 'Holy' before him, whereupon God lets sleep fall upon Adam so it becomes clear that the latter is human; (2) all creatures mistake Adam for their creator and wish

to bow before him, but Adam teaches them to render all honor to God as their true creator; (3) the angels mistake Adam for God and wish to exclaim 'Holy' before him, whereupon God reduces Adam's size." J. Fossum, "The Adorable Adam of the Mystics and the Rebuttals of the Rabbis," in: *Geschichte-Tradition-Reflexion. Festschrift für Martin Hengel zum 70. Geburtstag* (3 vols; eds. H. Cancik, H. Lichtenberger, and P. Schäfer; Tübingen: Mohr/Siebeck, 1996) 1.529–539. An important similarity can be detected between these Adamic traditions and the Metatron accounts. In *b. Hag.* 15a, for instance, God punished Metatron with sixty fiery lashes. Alan Segal observes that "just as Metatron needed correction for the false impression he gave Aher, so Adam needs correction for the false impression given the angels." A. Segal, *Two Powers in Heaven: Early Rabbinic Reports about Christianity and Gnosticism* (SJLA, 25; Leiden: Brill, 1977) 112. Indeed, in the Adamic "two powers" accounts, the protoplast is disciplined in various ways, including the reduction of his stature. Thus from *Gen. R.* 8:10 one can learn that when God created man in his own image "the ministering angels mistook him [for a divine being] and wished to exclaim 'Holy' before Him. . . . What did the Holy One, blessed be He, do? He caused sleep to fall upon him, and so all knew that he was [only a mortal] man." Freedman and Simon, *Midrash Rabbah*, 1.61. In the *Alphabet of Rabbi Akiba* the angels' erroneous behavior is explained through reference to Adam's gigantic body; it reads: "This teaches that initially Adam was created from the earth to the firmament. When the ministering angels saw him, they were shocked and excited by him. At that time they all stood before the Holy One, blessed be He, and said to Him; 'Master of the Universe! There are two powers in the world, one in heaven and one on earth.' What did the Holy One, blessed be He, do then? He placed His hand on him, and decreased him, setting him at one thousand cubits." M. Idel, "Enoch is Metatron," *Imm* 24/25 (1990) 220–240 at 226. For the Hebrew text, see Wertheimer, *Batei Midrashot*, 2.333–477. *Pesikta de Rab Kahana* 1:1 reflects the same tradition: "Said R. Aibu, 'At that moment the first man's stature was cut down and diminished to one hundred cubits.'" *Pesiqta de Rab Kahana* (tr. J. Neusner; 2 vols.; Atlanta; Scholars, 1987) 1.1.

73. Regarding Enoch-Metatron's title יהוה הקטן, see Orlov, *The Enoch-Metatron Tradition*, 136–143.

Primordial Lights: The Logos and Adoil in the Johannine Prologue and 2 Enoch

1. C. Rowland, "John 1.51, Jewish Apocalyptic and Targumic Tradition," *NTS* 30 (1984) 498–507 at 500.

2. Andersen, "2 Enoch," 1.142–144.

3. Andersen, "2 Enoch," 1.143–145.

4. Concerning the etymology of the name Adoil, see A. Orlov, "Secrets of Creation in 2 (Slavonic) Enoch," in: idem, *From Apocalypticism to Merkabah Mysticism: Studies in the Slavonic Pseudepigrapha* (JSJSS, 114; Leiden: Brill, 2007) 191–194.

5. Alan Segal, among others, regarding the demiurgic role of Adoil, notes that "some relationship between God's principal angel and His agent at creation may be possible in traditions about the angel Adoil." Segal, *Two Powers in Heaven,* 189. April DeConick also sees Adoil as a demiurgic agent. She notes that "the creative activity of the heavenly Man is highlighted in another Jewish Alexandrian source, the story of Adoil found in *2 Enoch*." A. DeConick, *Recovering the Original Gospel of Thomas: A History of the Gospel and Its Growth* (London: T&T Clark, 2005) 201.

6. Some scholars have difficulties seeing these demiurgic qualities of Adoil. Masanobu Endo argues that, although Adoil is personified and functions as one who obeys the command of God, he is not an agent, but rather, he is an object which is transformed and created. Endo notes that "both Adoil and Arkhas are personified and function as those who obey the command of God; however they are not described as the agents, but rather as the objects which are transformed and created." M. Endo, *Creation and Christology: A Study on the Johannine Prologue in the Light of Early Jewish Creation Accounts* (WUNT, 2.149; Tübingen: Mohr/Siebeck, 2002) 21.

7. Emphasis mine.

8. Charles, *APOT*, 2.445.

9. Fossum, *The Name of God,* 288.

10. See *Sifre to Deuteronomy. Pisqa* 338. *Sifre to Deuteronomy. An Analytical Translation* (tr. J. Neusner; BJS, 101; 2 vols., Atlanta: Scholars, 1987) 2.392. Cf. also *3 Enoch* 48D (*Synopse* §§77–80).

11. Some additional details about the nature and qualities of Adoil are also found in chapter 65 of *2 Enoch,* in which the beginning of creation is invoked again in the context of the mysteries of the last days. Scholars have noted that the protological account in *2 Enoch* 25, dealing with the establishment of the created order, appears to correspond with the order of eschatological events in chapter 65, in which, during his short visit to earth, Enoch conveys to his children some eschatological secrets. The patriarch reveals that in the eschatological time all the righteous of the world will be incorporated into a luminous entity: the aeon of the righteous. The description of this final aeon bears some striking similarities to the primordial aeon Adoil depicted in chapter 25. The last aeon in many ways restores and mirrors the first aeon and the depiction of the last aeon provides additional hints at the qualities and nature of Adoil. The patriarch begins his retelling with the familiar theme of the primeval aeon already mentioned in chapter 25. These protological events

are then set in parallel with the cluster of eschatological events that, according to the authors of the apocalypse, will reintegrate the remnant of the creation into a single aeonic entity which will collect all the righteous of the world. It appears that the righteous, here, as in later Jewish mysticism, are understood as gatherers of the divine light dispersed during the disintegration of Adoil who will collect the primordial light into a new eschatological vessel. The final consummation of the chosen creation into a single aeon mirrors the initial protological disintegration of Adoil that once gave birth to the multiplicity of created forms. This eschatological depiction, which reflects the protological realities, again demonstrates Adoil's preexistence. The portrayal of the final aeon underlines its atemporal nature when it says "then the time periods will perish, and there will be neither years nor months nor days, and hours will no longer be counted." Andersen, "2 Enoch," 1.191–193. The final aeon also reaffirms the anthropomorphic qualities of Adoil since it will be eschatologically reassembled from the remnant of humankind.

12. ". . . the light had not yet opened up."

13. Endo rightly observes that "darkness is pre-existent at the beginning of creation, and it is the foundation of the lowest things." Endo, *Creation and Christology,* 22.

14. Andersen, "2 Enoch," 1.145. The longer recension of *2 Enoch* 26:1–3 offers a similar depiction: "And I called out a second time into the very lowest things, and I said, 'Let one of the invisible things come out visibly, solid.' And Arkhas came out, solid and heavy and very red. And I said, 'Open yourself up, Arkhas, and let what is born from you become visible!' And he disintegrated himself. There came out an age, dark, very large, carrying the creation of all lower things. And I saw how good it was. And I said to him, 'Come down low and become solid! And become the foundation of the lowest things!' And it came about. And he came down and became solid. And he became the foundation of the lowest things. And there is nothing lower than the darkness, except nothing itself." Andersen, "2 Enoch," 1.144.

15. *2 Enoch* 33:4 (longer recension) reads: "And there is no adviser and no successor to my creation. I am self-eternal and not made by hands. My thought is without change. My wisdom is my adviser and my deed is my word." Andersen, "2 Enoch," 1.156.

16. Endo, *Creation and Christology*, 22.

17. The shorter recension of *2 Enoch* 30:8 reads: "When I had finished all this, I commanded (повелѣх) my wisdom to create man." Andersen, "2 Enoch," 1.151. The longer recension of *2 Enoch* 30:8 reads: "And on the sixth day I commanded (повелѣх) my wisdom to create man out of the seven components." Andersen, "2 Enoch," 1.150.

18. For example, Charles Kingsley Barrett suggests that "Col 1:15–20 shows as clearly as does John 1:1–18 the use of language drawn from Jewish

speculations about Wisdom." C.K. Barrett, *The Gospel According to St. John* (2nd ed.; London: SPCK, 1978) 154.

19. Martin Hengel notes that in Wis 9:1 "the creative word of God and the personified Sophia appear in a *parallelismus membrorum*: 'O God of my fathers, Lord of mercy who hast made all things by thy word and by thy wisdom hast formed man.' Word and wisdom of God are here nearly identified." M. Hengel, "The Prologue of the Gospel of John as the Gateway to Christological Truth," in *The Gospel of John and Christian Theology* (eds. R. Bauckham and C. Mosser; Grand Rapids: Eerdmans, 2008) 265–294 at 274.

20. "And there is no adviser and no successor to my creation . . . My wisdom is my adviser and my deed is my word." Andersen, "2 Enoch," 1.156.

21. Cf. *2 Enoch* 24: "Before anything existed at all, from the very beginning (испръва)." Andersen, "2 Enoch," 1.142.

22. R. Brown, "The Prologue of the Gospel of John," *RevExp* 62 (1965) 429–439 at 430–431.

23. F.F. Bruce, *The Gospel of John: Introduction, Exposition and Notes* (Grand Rapids: Eerdmans, 1994) 32.

24. R. Brown, *The Gospel According to John I-XII*, (AB, 29; Garden City, N.Y.: Doubleday, 1966) 26.

25. Bruce notes that "our Evangelist has no mere literary personification in mind. The personal status which he ascribes to the Word is a matter of real existence; the relation which the Word bears to God is a personal relation: 'the Word was with God.'" Bruce, *The Gospel of John: Introduction, Exposition, and Notes*, 30.

26. Brown, "The Prologue of the Gospel of John," 431.

27. Brown, *The Gospel According to John I-XII*, 4.

28. *2 Enoch* 24 (the shorter recension): "[N]ot even to my angels have I explained my secrets, nor related to them their composition, nor my endless and inconceivable creation which I conceived, as I am making them known to you today." Andersen, "2 Enoch," 1.143.

29. John 1:10: "He was in the world, and the world came into being through him; yet the world did not know him" (NRSV).

30. Concerning the Prologue's "mystery" language, Paul Lamarche highlights its soteriological dimension. He suggests that "if we compare John with the Pauline corpus we find that the Logos corresponds exactly to the mystery which, for Paul, is embodied in the divine person of Christ. And it is probably no accident that in one passage in Paul the words 'logos' and 'mystery' are found side by side; it is not Paul's mission, 'which was given to me for you [the Colossians], to make the word of God (*ton logon tou theou*) fully known, the mystery (*to mystērion*) hidden for ages and generations but now made manifest' (Col. 1:25f.). No doubt the Pauline Logos and Johannine are not identical; nevertheless the link established by Paul between the Word of

God and mystery can pave the way for a more profound understanding of the Word as mystery—inner word, hidden mystery, plan of God." P. Lamarche, "The Prologue of John," in: *The Interpretation of John* (2nd ed.; ed. J. Ashton; Edinburgh: T&T Clark, 1997) 47–66 at 53.

31. Peder Borgen notes that "John 1:1–8 seems to draw on learned Jewish exegesis, wherein Logos, דבר and light, אור are connected on the basis of Gen. 1:3." P. Borgen, "Logos Was the True Light: Contributions to the Interpretation of the Prologue of John," *NovT* 14 (1972) 115–130 at 192.

32. N.R. Petersen, *The Gospel of John and Sociology of Light: Language and Characterization in the Fourth Gospel* (Valley Forge: Trinity Press International, 1993) 72.

33. R. Bultmann, *The Gospel of John. A Commentary* (Philadelphia: Westminster, 1971) 32.

34. Barrett notes that the choice of the term *logos* points both to the demiurgic and revelatory roles, the functions already associated with this terminology in the Septuagint. He notes that *logos* "is a very frequent word in the Greek Old Testament; here special attention may be drawn to two groups of passages. In the former the word is creative . . . in the latter, the word of the Lord is the prophet's message, that is, the means by which God communicates his purpose to his people . . . Both creation and revelation are in mind in the Johannine Prologue, and the rest of the gospel encourages us to suppose that the influence of the Old Testament may be found here." Barrett, *The Gospel According to St. John*, 153.

35. Brown, *The Gospel According to John I-XII*, 25.

36. J. Ashton, *Studying John: Approaches to the Fourth Gospel* (Oxford: Clarendon, 1994) 20–21.

37. Brown, *The Gospel According to John I-XII*, 6. He further notes that "with the appearance of 'came into being' (ἐγένετο) in verse 3 we are in the sphere of creation. All that is created is intimately related to the Word, for it was created not only through him, but also in him. We find the same idea in the hymn of Col 1. 16: 'For in him were all things created . . . all things were created by him and in him.' The same unity that exists between the Word and his creation will be applied in John 15:5 to Jesus and the Christian: 'Apart from me you can do nothing.'" Brown, *The Gospel According to John I-XII*, 25.

38. Andersen, "2 Enoch," 1.144–145, emphasis mine.

39. This tradition that can be further illuminated by Col 1:15–16: "He is the image of the invisible God, the firstborn of all creation; for in him all things in heaven and on earth were created, things visible and invisible, whether thrones or dominions or rulers or powers—all things have been created through him and for him" (NRSV).

40. Cf. Phil 2:5–8: "Let the same mind be in you that was in Christ Jesus, who, though he was in the form of God, did not regard equality with

God as something to be exploited, but emptied himself, taking the form of a slave, being born in human likeness. And being found in human form, he humbled himself and became obedient to the point of death—even death on a cross" (NRSV).

41. DeConick, *Recovering the Original Gospel of Thomas,* 201. See, also, A. DeConick, *Seek to See Him: Ascent and Vision Mysticism in the Gospel of Thomas* (SVC, 33; Leiden: Brill, 1996) 66–67.

42. Cf. *Keph.* 165: "Again, when the sun sinks from the universe and sets, and all people go in to their hiding places and houses and conceal themselves; this also pertains to the mystery of the end, as it presages the consummation of the universe. For, when all the light will be purified and redeemed in the universe at the last, the collector of all things, the Last Statue, will gather in and sculpt itself. It is the last hour of the day, the time when the Last Statue will go up to the aeon of light." Gardner, *The Kephalaia of the Teacher,* 174. Cf. also *Keph.* 104: "The first death is from the time when the light fell to the darkness, and was mixed in with the rulers of darkness; until the time when the light will become pure, and be separated from the darkness in that great fire. The reminder left behind there can build and add to the Last Statue." Gardner, *The Kephalaia of the Teacher,* 107–108. Regarding the Manichaean eschatological "Statue" made from the particles of light rescued by the elect, see Widengren, *Mani and Manichaeism*, 68; Heuser, "Manichaean Myth According to the Coptic Sources," 86–87.

43. Cf. *Conf.* 41: ". . . you who have enrolled yourself as children of one and the same Father, who is not mortal but immortal—God's Man (ἄνθρωπον Θεοῦ), who being the Word (λόγος) of the Eternal. . . ." Colson and Whitaker, *Philo,* 4.32–33; *Conf.* 146: "And many names are his, for he is called, 'the Beginning,' and the Name of God, and His Word (λόγος), and the Man after His image." Colson and Whitaker, *Philo*, 4.88–91.

44. T. Tobin, "The Prologue of John and Hellenistic Jewish Speculation," *CBQ* 52 (1990) 252–69 at 267. Alan Segal also notes that "Philo identifies the heavenly man with the Logos, which is identified with God's archangel and principal helper in creation." Segal, *Two Powers in Heaven*, 189.

45. Tobin, "The Prologue of John and Hellenistic Jewish Speculation," 267.

46. Tobin, "The Prologue of John and Hellenistic Jewish Speculation," 267.

47. John Painter notes that "in John the darkness and the light are antithetical. Each excludes the other." J. Painter, "Rereading Genesis in the Prologue of John?" in: *Neotestamentica et Philonica. Studies in Honor of Peder Borgen* (eds. D.E. Aune, T. Seland, J.H. Ulrichsen; Leiden: Brill 2003) 182. With respect to the motif of primordial light and darkness in the Johannine Prologue, see also P. Borgen, *Philo, John and Paul: New Perspectives on Judaism and Early Christianity* (BJS, 131; Atlanta: Scholars, 1987) 89–92.

48. Tobin, "The Prologue of John and Hellenistic Jewish Speculation," 254.

49. Andersen, "2 Enoch," 1.191–193.

50. J. Ashton, "The Transformation of Wisdom," in: J. Ashton, *Studying John: Approaches to the Fourth Gospel* (Oxford: Clarendon, 1994) 7.

51. N.F. Denzey, "Genesis Traditions in Conflict? The Use of Some Exegetical Traditions in the Trimorphic Protennoia and the Johannine Prologue," *VC* 55 (2001) 20–44 at 28.

52. The tension between aural and anthropomorphic manifestations of the Deity can be traced to the Hebrew Bible, in which the anthropomorphic imagery of the Priestly tradition was contested by the aural paradigm of the divine Name promulgated by the Deuteronomic school. Concerning the tensions between the paradigms of the divine Name and the divine Form in biblical materials, see Weinfeld, *Deuteronomy and the Deuteronomic School*, 191–201; Mettinger, *The Dethronement of Sabaoth. Studies in the Shem and Kabod Theologies*, 124.

Conclusion

1. P. Schäfer, *The Origins of Jewish Mysticism* (Tübingen: Mohr/Siebeck, 2009) 5.

2. Schäfer, *The Origins of Jewish Mysticism*, 11–14. Cf. also Himmelfarb, *Ascent to Heaven*, 106–114; Halperin, *The Faces of the Chariot*, 359–363; P. Schäfer, "The Aim and Purpose of Early Jewish Mysticism. Gershom Scholem Reconsidered," in P. Schäfer, *Hekhalot-Studien* (TSAJ, 19; Tübingen: Mohr/Siebeck, 1988) 277–295; idem, *The Hidden and Manifest God: Some Major Themes in Early Jewish Mysticism* (Albany: SUNY Press, 1992) 150–155; M.D. Swartz, *Scholastic Magic: Ritual and Revelation in Early Jewish Mysticism* (Princeton: Princeton University Press, 1996) 29; 153–157; 170–172; 210–212.

3. Scholem argued that "subterranean but effective, and occasionally still traceable, connections exist between these later mystics and the groups which produced a large proportion of the pseudepigrapha and apocalypses of the first century before and after Christ." Scholem, *Major Trends*, 42.

4. Scholem, *Major Trends*, 67.

5. Regarding the various streams of the Metatron tradition, Scholem argued that "one aspect identifies Metatron with Jahoel or Michael and knows nothing of his transfiguration from a human being into an angel. The talmudic passages concerned with Metatron are of this type. The other aspect identifies Metatron with the figure of Enoch as he is depicted in apocalyptic literature. . . . When the Book of Hekhaloth, or 3 Enoch, was composed, the two aspects had already become intertwined." G. Scholem, *Jewish Gnosticism,*

Merkabah Mysticism, and Talmudic Tradition (New York: The Jewish Theological Seminary, 1965) 51

6. E. Wolfson, *Luminal Darkness: Imaginal Gleanings from Zoharic Literature* (Oxford: Oneworld, 2007) 1. Wolfson further notes that like the kabbalists of the Castilian circle, the author of the *Zohar* understands a demonic realm, called by him *Sitra Ahra*, the 'Other Side,' as structurally mirroring the divine realm: both realms are constituted by ten powers. Wolfson, *Luminal Darkness*, 2.

7. Tishby, *The Wisdom of the Zohar*, 450. Eitan Fishbane notes that the "prominent dimension of zoharic mythology is the perennial cosmic struggle between good and evil, metaphysical forces that are rooted in particular components of the tenfold divine structure. The divine self, like the world of human experience, is depicted as dominated by a tense polarity between the Right Side (Hesed—Love/Compassion) and the Left Side (Gevurah/Din—Severity/Judgment). . . ." E.P. Fishbane, "The Zohar: Masterpiece of Jewish Mysticism," in *Jewish Mysticism and Kabbalah: New Insights and Scholarship* (ed. F.E. Greenspahn; New York and London: New York University Press, 2011) 49–67 at 54.

8. Joseph Dan traces the conceptual crystallization of the demonic counterpart of the sefirotic system to a representative of the Castilian school by arguing that "the first kabbalistic dualistic system was presented in a brief treatise written by Rabbi Isaac ben Jacob ha-Cohen, entitled Treatise on the Emanations on the Left. This treatise, written in Castile about 1265, describes a parallel system of seven divine evil powers, the first of which is called Samael and the seventh, feminine one is called Lilith. While both of these figures have a long history in Jewish writings before Rabbi Isaac, it seems that he was the first to bring them together and present them as a divine couple, parallel to God and the *Shekhinah*, who rule over a diverse structure of evil demons, who struggle for dominion in the universe against the powers of goodness, the emanations on the right." J. Dan, *Kabbalah: A Very Short Introduction* (Oxford: Oxford University Press, 2006) 50.

9. Tishby, *The Wisdom of the Zohar*, 451.

10. ". . . the demonic realm, which vis-à-vis the divine is considered to be the left. . . ." Wolfson, *Luminal Darkness*, 2. Wolfson notes that "already in the *Sefer ha-Bahir*, the first literary source based on a theosophic doctrine of emanations to emerge in medieval Europe, Satan is identified as one of the divine 'attributes,' the 'left hand' 'whose name is evil' and 'who is set on the north side of God.'" Wolfson, *Luminal Darkness*, 31. Wolfson adds that "in the kabbalistic circles of Castile, however, the demonic is presented not simply as one of the powers of God, but rather as a realm fully complementing that of the divine." Wolfson, *Luminal Darkness*, 31

11. Cf. *Apoc. Ab.* 22:1–2; 29:11.

12. Tishby, *The Wisdom of the Zohar*, 451.

13. Cf. *Apoc. Ab.* 23:4–11; *Zohar* I.152b–153a. Concerning this imagery, see Orlov, "'The Likeness of Heaven': *Kavod* of Azazel in the Apocalypse of Abraham," 232–253.

14. Reflecting on the antagonism of the divine and demonic in later Jewish mysticism, Joseph Dan notes that "the formulation of the powers of evil as an independent enemy of the divine, and the description of human life as being conducted in a dualistic universe in which evil and good are in constant struggle, is the contribution of the kabbalah to Jewish worldview." Dan, *Kabbalah,* 50.

15. Wolson notes that "the author of the Zohar, like his Castilian predecessors, was concerned with the problem of the origin of evil and the etiological relation of the divine to the demonic." He further notes that "the dualistic posture in this circle is not of an ontological or metaphysical sort. That is, the kabbalistic conception . . . explicitly states that the one God makes both good and evil, light and dark, the good and evil impulses of the human individual. Against this conceptual background we must understand these kabbalists' concern with the question of the genesis of the demonic left side. The underlying assumption here is that even the demonic derives from a stage in the emanative process. The demonic is thus depicted as an extension of a divine attribute, usually identified as judgment, rather than as an autonomous power." Wolfson, *Luminal Darkness*, 3 and 31–32.

16. In relation to this concept, Elliot Wolfson notes that, "according to these kabbalists, the 'emanations of the left' have their origin in and are sustained by the left side of the divine realm itself. That is to say, therefore, that the demonic has a root within the divine. This gnostic theme is developed repeatedly in the Zohar; indeed, it forms one of the essentially characteristic doctrines of the work." Wolfson, *Luminal Darkness*, 2.

17. Fishbane, "The Zohar: Masterpiece of Jewish Mysticism," 54.

18. Tishby, *The Wisdom of the Zohar*, 452.

19. See, for example, *Zohar* I.52a.

20. Tishby, *The Wisdom of the Zohar*, 452. Tishby demonstrates that in the *Zohar* "an account of the victory of 'the Other Side,' described as the entrance of the monster into the sea of the *Shekhinah* and into the rivers that flow from it." Tishby, *The Wisdom of the Zohar*, 452.

21. Whitney, *Two Strange Beasts*, 117.

22. Regarding this development, see I. Jacobs, *The Midrashic Process: Tradition and Interpretation in Rabbinic Judaism* (Cambridge: Cambridge University Press, 1995) 158; M.A. Fishbane, *The Exegetical Imagination: On Jewish Thought and Theology* (Cambridge, Mass.: Harvard University Press, 1998) 41–55; idem, *Biblical Myth and Rabbinic Mythmaking* (Oxford: Oxford University Press, 2003) 273–285; A. Orlov, "What is Below?: Mysteries of

Leviathan in Jewish Pseudepigrapha and Mishnah Hagigah 2:1," in *Hekhalot Literature in Context: From Byzantium to Babylonia* (eds. R. Boustan et al.; Tübingen: Mohr/Siebeck, 2013) 313–322.

23. Tishby, *The Wisdom of the Zohar*, 452.

24. Tishby, *The Wisdom of the Zohar*, 453.

25. Tishby notes that in later Jewish mysticism "several commandments are explained as being bribes offered to *sitra ahra*, including, for example, the goat that is dispatched to Azazel, the heifer that has its neck broken, the washing of the hands after meals, and the animal hair on the phylacteries." Tishby, *The Wisdom of the Zohar*, 453.

26. Tishby, *The Wisdom of the Zohar*, 453. Wolfson notes that "in the Zohar, the *mitswot* have one of two purposes: either to strengthen and sustain the realm of holiness by maintaining the flow of divine light from the uppermost grades to the lowest, or to neutralize the forces of evil so they do not interfere with the unity of the holy realm. Sacrifices in particular, according to the *Zohar*, are an instance where we quite literally 'give the devil his due.' That is, a portion of every sacrifice is set aside for *Sitra Ahra*, the one exception being the *olah*, the burnt offering, which according to Scripture is burnt entirely for God." Wolfson, *Luminal Darkness*, 37.

27. Tishby, *The Wisdom of the Zohar*, 453. Tishby explores the connection between the weakening of the sacerdotal presence and the power of the Other Side in the Zoharic tradition which believed that "when the tabernacle was erected the *Shekhinah* became very powerful, and the strength of 'the Other Side' diminished, and were it not for Israel's subsequent iniquities 'the Other Side' would not have been able to exercise any further authority. But once they had returned to their evil ways 'the Other Side' recovered, 'and from that day the only thing they could do was to give portion of everything to 'the Other Side' through the mystery of the sacrifices, the libations, and the whole-offerings.' With the cessation of sacrifices at the destruction of the Temple, 'the Other Side' has to be appeased and kept at bay through correct devotion during the statutory evening prayer, uttered at night-time when the husks rule the world." Tishby, *The Wisdom of the Zohar*, 454.

28. Tishby, *The Wisdom of the Zohar*, 452.

29. ". . . in the language of the Zohar, Satan would have been removed from the sanctuary (*Shekhinah*) and the side of holiness would have ascended upwards." Wolfson, *Luminal Darkness*, 38.

30. Tishby, *The Wisdom of the Zohar*, 452.

31. Schäfer, *The Origins of Jewish Mysticism*, 11.

32. J.L. Hagen, "No Longer 'Slavonic' Only: 2 Enoch Attested in Coptic from Nubia," in *New Perspectives on 2 Enoch: No Longer Slavonic Only* (eds. A. Orlov, G. Boccaccini, J. Zurawski; SJS, 4; Leiden: Brill, 2012) 7–34.

33. Cf. Charles and Morfill, *The Book of the Secrets of Enoch*, xvii.

34. Thus, Wolfson observes that "Egypt, according to the symbolic map of the *Zohar*, represents the demonic left side." Wolfson, *Luminal Darkness*, 3.

35. Concerning these traditions, see Wolfson, *Luminal Darkness*, 4–5.

36. *Zohar* I.83a. D. Matt, *The Zohar: The Book of Enlightenment* (Classics of Western Spirituality; New York: Paulist Press, 1983) 63.

Bibliography

I. Texts and Translations

Abdullaeva, Firiuza. *Персидская Кораническая экзегетика: Тексты, переводы, комментарии*. С.-Петербург: Петербургское Востоковедение, 2000.

Abrams, Daniel. *The Book of Bahir*. Los Angeles: The Cherub Press, 1994.

Albeck, Chanoch. *Midrash Bereshit Rabbati*. Jerusalem: Mekitse Nirdamim, 1940.

Alexander, Philip. "3 (Hebrew Apocalypse of) Enoch." In *The Old Testament Pseudepigrapha*. Edited by J.H. Charlesworth, 1.223–315. 2 vols. New York: Doubleday, 1983–1985.

Allison, Dale. *Matthew: A Shorter Commentary*. London and New York: T&T Clark, 2004.

Andersen, Francis. "2 (Slavonic Apocalypse of) Enoch." In *The Old Testament Pseudepigrapha*. Edited by J.H. Charlesworth, 1.91–221. 2 vols. New York: Doubleday, 1983–1985.

Anderson, Gary and Stone, Michael. *A Synopsis of the Books of Adam and Eve. Second Revised Edition*. EJL 17. Atlanta: Scholars, 1999.

Aune, David. *Revelation 17–22*. WBC 52C. Nashville, TN: T. Nelson, 1998.

Barrett, Charles. *The Gospel According to St. John*. London: SPCK, 1978.

Bauckham, Richard. *Jude, 2 Peter*. WBC 50. Waco, TX: Word Books, 1983.

Black, Matthew. *The Book of Enoch or 1 Enoch*. SVTP 7. Leiden: Brill, 1985.

Bobichon, Philippe. *Justin Martyr: Dialogue avec Tryphon*. Fribourg: Academic Press Fribourg, 2003.

Böhlig, Alexander et al. *Nag Hammadi Codices III, 2 and IV, 2: The Gospel of the Egyptians (The Holy Book of the Great Invisible Spirit)*. NHS 4. Leiden: Brill, 1975.

Böttrich, Christfried. *Das slavische Henochbuch*. JSHRZ 5. Gütersloh: Gütersloher Verlaghaus, 1995.

Box, George Herbert and Landsman, Joseph. *The Apocalypse of Abraham. Edited, with a Translation from the Slavonic Text and Notes*. TED 1.10. London, New York: The Macmillan Company, 1918.

Braude, William. *Pesikta Rabbati*. 2 vols. YJS 18. New Haven, CT: Yale University Press, 1968.

Brown, Raymond. *The Gospel According to John I-XII*. AB 29. Garden City, NY: Doubleday, 1966.

Bruce, Frederick. *The Gospel of John: Introduction, Exposition and Notes*. Grand Rapids, MI: Eerdmans, 1994.

Bultmann, Rudolph. *The Gospel of John. A Commentary*. Philadelphia: Westminster, 1971.

Burchard, Christoph. "Joseph and Aseneth." In *The Old Testament Pseudepigrapha*. Edited by J. H. Charlesworth, 2.177–247. 2 vols. New York: Doubleday, 1983–1985.

Cahill, Michael. *The First Commentary on Mark. An Annotated Translation*. Oxford: Oxford University Press, 1998.

Cassuto, Umberto. *A Commentary on the Book of Genesis*. Jerusalem: Magnes, 1989.

Chadwick, Henry. *Origen: Contra Celsum*. Cambridge: Cambridge University Press, 1953.

Charles, Robert Henry. *The Book of Enoch*. Oxford: Clarendon Press, 1893.

———. *The Apocrypha and Pseudepigrapha of the Old Testament*. 2 vols. Oxford: Clarendon Press, 1913.

Charles, Robert Henry and Morfill, William Richard. *The Book of the Secrets of Enoch*. Oxford: Clarendon Press, 1896.

Charlesworth, James. "Prayer of Manasseh." In *The Old Testament Pseudepigrapha*. Edited by J.H. Charlesworth, 2.625–37. 2 vols. New York: Doubleday, 1983–1985.

Cohen, Martin. *The Shiᶜur Qomah: Texts and Recensions*. TSAJ 9. Tübingen: Mohr/Siebeck, 1985.

Colson, Francis Henry and Whitaker, George Herbert. *Philo*. 10 vols. LCL. Cambridge, Massachusetts: Harvard University Press, 1929–1964.

Copenhaver, Brian. *Hermetica. The Greek Corpus Hermeticum and the Latin Asclepius in a New English Translation, with Notes and Introduction*. Cambridge: Cambridge University Press, 1995.

Danby, Herbert. *The Mishnah*. Oxford: Oxford University Press, 1992.

Davies, William and Allison, Dale. *The Gospel According to Saint Matthew*. 3 vols. Edinburgh: T & T Clark, 1988.

Davila, James. *Hekhalot Literature in Translation: Major Texts of Merkavah Mysticism*. SJJTP 20. Leiden: Brill, 2013.

Dunn, Geoffrey. *Tertullian*. London: Routledge, 2004.

Ehrman, Bart. *The Apostolic Fathers*. LCL. 2 vols. Cambridge, Massachusetts: Harvard University Press, 2003.

Epstein, Isidore. *The Babylonian Talmud.* London: Soncino, 1935–1952.

Evans, Ernest. *Tertullian. Adversus Marcionem.* 2 vols. Oxford, Clarendon Press, 1972.

Fitzmyer, Joseph. *The Gospel According to Luke.* 2 vols. AB 28, 28A. Garden City, NY: Doubleday, 1981.

Freedman, Harry and Simon, Maurice. *Midrash Rabbah.* 10 vols. London: Soncino, 1961.

Friedlander, Gerald. *Pirke de Rabbi Eliezer.* 2nd ed. New York: Hermon Press, 1965.

García Martínez, Florentino and Tigchelaar, Eibert. *The Dead Sea Scrolls Study Edition.* 2 vols. Leiden: Brill, 1997.

Gardner, Iain. *The Kephalaia of the Teacher: The Edited Coptic Manichaean Texts in Translation with Commentary.* NHMS 37. Leiden: Brill, 1995.

Gaylord, Harry. "3 (Greek Apocalypse of) Baruch." In *The Old Testament Pseudepigrapha.* Edited by J.H. Charlesworth, 1.653–79. 2 vols. New York: Doubleday, 1983–1985.

Gnilka, Joachim. *Das Evangelium nach Markus.* 2 vols. EKKNT 2.1–2. Zürich: Benziger; Neukirchen-Vluyn: Neukirchener Verlag, 1978–79.

Guggenheimer, Heinrich. *The Jerusalem Talmud. Tractates Pesahim and Yoma. Edition, Translation and Commentary.* SJ 74. Berlin: De Gruyter, 2013.

Gundry, Robert. *Matthew: A Commentary on His Handbook for a Mixed Church under Persecution.* Grand Rapids, MI: Eerdmans, 1994.

Hanhart, Robert. *Sacharja.* BKAT 14/7. Neukirchen-Vluyn: Neukirchener Verlag, 1990.

Isaac, Ephraim. "1 (Ethiopic Apocalypse of) Enoch." In *The Old Testament Pseudepigrapha.* Edited by J.H. Charlesworth, 1.5–89. 2 vols. New York: Doubleday, 1983–1985.

Jacobson, Howard. *The Exagoge of Ezekiel.* Cambridge: Cambridge University Press, 1983.

———. *A Commentary on Pseudo-Philo's Liber Antiquitatum Biblicarum, with Latin Text and English Translation.* 2 vols. AGAJU 31. Leiden: Brill, 1996.

Jagić, Vatroslav. "Slavische Beiträge zu den biblischen Apocryphen, I, Die altkirchenslavischen Texte des Adambuches." *Denkschriften der kaiserlichen Akademie der Wissenschaften. Philosophisch-historische Classe* 42 (1893): 44–47.

Jellinek, Adolph. *Beth ha-Midrash.* 6 vols. Jerusalem: Wahrmann, 1967.

Kee, Howard. "Testaments of the Twelve Patriarchs." In *The Old Testament Pseudepigrapha.* Edited by J.H. Charlesworth, 1.775–828. 2 vols. New York: Doubleday, 1983–1985.

Knibb, Michael. *The Ethiopic Book of Enoch: A New Edition in the Light of the Aramaic Dead Sea Fragments.* 2 vols. Oxford: Clarendon Press, 1978.

Kulik, Alexander. *Retroverting Slavonic Pseudepigrapha: Toward the Original of the Apocalypse of Abraham*. TCS 3. Atlanta: Scholars, 2004.

Lauterbach, Jacob. *Mekhilta de-Rabbi Ishmael: A Critical Edition on the Basis of the Manuscripts and Early Editions with an English Translation, Introduction and Notes*. 2 vols. Philadelphia: The Jewish Publication Society, 2004.

Layton, Bentley. *Nag Hammadi Codex II, 2–7*. 2 vols. NHS 20. Leiden: Brill, 1989.

Maher, Michael. *Targum Pseudo-Jonathan: Genesis*. ArBib 1B. Collegeville, MN: Liturgical Press, 1992.

Marcovich, Miroslav. *Iustini Martyris Dialogus Cum Tryphone*. PTS 47. Berlin/New York: De Gruyter, 1997.

Marcus, Ralph. *Philo. Questions and Answers on Genesis*. LCL. Cambridge/London: Harvard University Press/Heinemann, 1949.

———. *Philo, Questions and Answers on Exodus*. LCL. Cambridge/London: Harvard University Press/Heinemann, 1949.

Matt, Daniel. *The Zohar: The Book of Enlightenment*. Classics of Western Spirituality. New York: Paulist Press, 1983.

———. *The Zohar: Pritzker Edition*. 12 vols. Palo Alto, CA: Stanford University Press, 2003.

McCrindle, John. *The Christian Topography of Cosmas, an Egyptian Monk. Translated from the Greek, and Edited with Notes and Introduction*. Cambridge: Cambridge University Press, 2010.

McNamara, Martin. *Targum Neofiti 1: Genesis*. ArBib 1A. Collegeville, MN: Liturgical Press, 1992.

McNamara, Martin et al. *Targum Neofiti 1, Leviticus; Targum Pseudo-Jonathan, Leviticus*. ArBib 3. Collegeville, MN: Liturgical Press, 1994.

Metzger, Bruce. "The Fourth Book of Ezra." In *The Old Testament Pseudepigrapha*. Edited by J. H. Charlesworth, 1.517–559. 2 vols. New York: Doubleday, 1983–85.

Milgrom, Jacob. *Leviticus 1–16: A New Translation with Introduction and Commentary*. AB 3. New York: Doubleday, 1991.

Milik, Józef Tadeusz. *The Books of Enoch: Aramaic Fragments of Qumrân Cave 4*. Oxford: Clarendon Press, 1976.

Neusner, Jacob. *Sifre to Deuteronomy. An Analytical Translation*. BJS 101. 2 vols. Atlanta: Scholars, 1987.

———. *Pesiqta de Rab Kahana*. 2 vols. Atlanta: Scholars, 1987.

Nickelsburg, George. *1 Enoch 1: A Commentary on the Book of 1 Enoch: Chapters 1–36; 81–108*. Hermeneia. Minneapolis: Fortress, 2001.

Nickelsburg, George and VanderKam, James. *1 Enoch 2: A Commentary on the Book of 1 Enoch: Chapters 37–82*. Hermeneia, Minneapolis: Fortress, 2012.

Nock, Arthur and Festugière, André-Jean. *Corpus Hermeticum*. 4 vols. Paris: Les Belles Lettres, 1954–60.

Odeberg, Hugo. *3 Enoch or the Hebrew Book of Enoch*. New York: KTAV, 1973.

Olson, Daniel. *Enoch. A New Translation: The Ethiopic Book of Enoch, or 1 Enoch*. North Richland Hills, TX: Bibal Press, 2004.

Oswalt, John. *The Book of Isaiah. Chapters 40–66*. NICOT. Grand Rapids, MI: Eerdmans, 1998.

Paget, James. *The Epistle of Barnabas*. WUNT 2.64. Tübingen: Mohr/Siebeck, 1994.

Philonenko-Sayar, Belkis and Philonenko, Marc. *L'Apocalypse d'Abraham. Introduction, texte slave, traduction et notes*. Semitica 31. Paris: Librairie Adrien-Maisonneuve, 1981.

———. *Die Apokalypse Abrahams*. JSHRZ 5.5. Gütersloh: Mohn, 1982.

———. "Apocalypse d'Abraham." In *La Bible. Écrits intertestamentaires*. Edited by A. Dupont-Sommer et al., 1691–1730. Paris: La Bibliothèque de la Pléiade, 1987.

Robbins, Frank. *Ptolemy, Tetrabiblos*. LCL. Cambridge: Harvard University Press/London: Heinemann, 1940.

Rubinkiewicz, Ryszard. *L'Apocalypse d'Abraham en vieux slave. Introduction, texte critique, traduction et commentaire*. ŹM 129. Lublin: Towarzystwo Naukowe Katolickiego Uniwersytetu Lubelskiego, 1987.

Rubinkiewicz, Ryszard and Lunt, Horace. "Apocalypse of Abraham." In *The Old Testament Pseudepigrapha*. Edited by J. H. Charlesworth, 1.681–705. 2 vols. New York: Doubleday, 1983–1985.

Sanders, E. P. "Testament of Abraham." In *The Old Testament Pseudepigrapha*. Edited by J. H. Charlesworth, 1.871–902. 2 vols. New York: Doubleday, 1983–1985.

Schäfer, Peter, Schlüter, Margaret and von Mutius, Hans George. *Synopse zur Hekhalot-Literatur*. TSAJ 2. Tübingen: Mohr/Siebeck, 1981.

Shutt, Robert. "Letter of Aristeas." In *The Old Testament Pseudepigrapha*. Edited by J.H. Charlesworth, 2.7–34. 2 vols. New York: Doubleday, 1983–1985.

Slusser, Michael. *St. Justin Martyr. Dialogue with Trypho*. Washington, DC; Catholic University of America Press, 2003.

Sokolov, Matvej Ivanovich. "Материалы и заметки по старинной славянской литературе. Выпуск третий. VII. Славянская Книга Еноха Праведного. Тексты, латинский перевод и исследование. Посмертный труд автора приготовил к изданию М. Сперанский." *Чтения в Обществе Истории и Древностей Российских* 4 (1910): 1–167.

Sperling, Harry and Simon, Maurice. *The Zohar*. 5 vols. London and New York: Soncino, 1933.

Thackeray, Henry St. J., and Markus, Ralph. *Josephus*. 10 vols. LCL. Cambridge: Harvard University Press, 1926–65.
Tiller, Patrick. *A Commentary on the Animal Apocalypse of 1 Enoch*. EJL 4. Atlanta: Scholars, 1993.
Uhlig, Siegbert. *Das äthiopische Henochbuch*. JSHRZ 5.6. Gütersloh: Gütersloher Verlaghaus Mohn, 1984.
Vaillant, André. *Le Livre des secrets d'Hénoch: Texte slave et traduction française*. Textes publiés par l'Institut d'Études slaves 4. Paris: L'Institut d'Études slaves, 1976.
VanderKam, James. *The Book of Jubilees*. 2 vols. CSCO 510–11. Scriptores Aethiopici 87–88. Leuven: Peeters, 1989.
Waldstein, Michael and Wisse, Frederik. *The Apocryphon of John. Synopsis of Nag Hammadi Codices II, 1; III, 1; and IV, 1 with BG 8502, 2*. NHMS 33. Leiden: Brill, 1995.
Walton, John. *Genesis*. NIVAC. Grand Rapids, MI: Zondervan, 2001.
Watts, John. *Isaiah 34–66*. WBC 25. Waco, TX: Word Books, 1987.
Wertheimer, Solomon. *Batei Midrashot*. 2 vols. Jerusalem: Mosad Harav Kook, 1950–53. [Hebrew]

II. Secondary Literature

Adelman, Rachel. *The Return of the Repressed: Pirqe De-Rabbi Eliezer and the Pseudepigrapha*. JSJSS 140. Leiden: Brill, 2009.
Alexander, Philip. *The Mystical Texts: Songs of the Sabbath Sacrifice and Related Manuscripts*. LSTS 61. London: T&T Clark, 2005.
Allison, Dale. *The New Moses: A Matthean Typology*. Minneapolis: Fortress Press, 1993.
———. "What Was the Star That Guided the Magi?" *BR* 9 (1993): 20–24.
———. "Behind the Temptations of Jesus: Q 4:1–13 and Mark 1:12–13." In *Authenticating the Activities of Jesus*. Edited by B.D. Chilton and C. Evans, 195–213. NTTS 28/2. Leiden: Brill, 2002.
———. "The Magi's Angel (Matt. 2:2, 9–10)." In *Studies in Matthew: Interpretation Past and Present*. Edited by D.C. Allison, 17–41. Grand Rapids, MI: Baker Academic, 2005.
Anderson, Gary. "The Penitence Narrative in the Life of Adam and Eve." In *Literature on Adam and Eve. Collected Essays*. Edited by G. Anderson, M.E. Stone, and J. Tromp, 3–42. SVTP 15. Leiden: Brill, 2000.
———. "The Exaltation of Adam and the Fall of Satan." In *Literature on Adam and Eve. Collected Essays*. Edited by G. Anderson, M.E. Stone, and J. Tromp, 83–110. SVTP 15. Brill: Leiden, 2000.
Angel, Joseph. *Otherworldly and Eschatological Priesthood in the Dead Sea Scrolls*. STDJ 86. Leiden: Brill, 2010.

Annus, Amar. "On the Origins of Watchers: A Comparative Study of the Antediluvian Wisdom in Mesopotamian and Jewish Traditions." *JSP* 19 (2010): 277–320.

Aptowitzer, Victor. "Asenath, the Wife of Joseph: A Haggadic Literary-Historical Survey." *HUCA* 1 (1924): 282–83.

———. "The Celestial Temple as Viewed in the Aggadah." In *Binah: Studies in Jewish Thought*. Edited by J. Dan, 1–29. New York: Praeger, 1989.

Arbel, Daphna. *Beholders of Divine Secrets: Mysticism and Myth in the Hekhalot and Merkavah Literature*. Albany, NY: SUNY Press, 2003.

Ashton, John. *Studying John: Approaches to the Fourth Gospel*. Oxford: Clarendon, 1994.

Balentine, Samuel. *The Torah's Vision of Worship*. Minneapolis: Fortress Press, 1999.

Bamberger, Bernard. *Fallen Angels: Soldiers of Satan's Realm*. Philadelphia: Jewish Publication Society, 1952.

Barker, Margaret. *The Gate of Heaven: The History and Symbolism of the Temple in Jerusalem*. London: SPCK, 1991.

———. *Creation: A Biblical Vision for the Environment*. London: T&T Clark, 2010.

Barton, George. "The Origin of the Names of Angels and Demons in the Extra-Canonical Apocalyptic Literature to 100 A.D." *JBL* 31 (1912): 156–167.

Bauckham, Richard. "Jesus and the Wild Animals (Mark 1:13): A Christological Image for an Ecological Age." In *Jesus of Nazareth: Lord and Christ: Essays on the Historical Jesus and New Testament Christology*. Edited by J.B. Green and M. Turner, 3–21. Grand Rapids, MI: Eerdmans, 1994.

Beale, Gregory. *The Temple and the Church's Mission*. NSBT 17. Downers Grove, IL: Intervarsity Press, 2004.

———. *We Become What We Worship: A Biblical Theology of Idolatry*. Downers Grove, IL: Inter-Varsity Press, 2008.

Beckerleg, Catherine Leigh. *The "Image of God" in Eden*. Ph.D. diss. Harvard University, 2009.

Begg, Christopher. "Rereading of the 'Animal Rite' of Genesis 15 in Early Jewish Narratives." *CBQ* 50 (1988): 36–46.

Ben-Dov, Jonathan. "Exegetical Notes on Cosmology in the Parables of Enoch." In *Enoch and the Messiah Son of Man: Revisiting the Book of Parables*. Edited by G. Boccaccini, 143–150. Grand Rapids, MI: Eerdmans, 2007.

Berlejung, Angelika. *Die Theologie der Bilder: Herstellung und Einweihung von Kultbildern in Mesopotamien und die alttestamentliche Bilderpolemik*. OBO 162. Freiburg: Universitätsverlag, 1998.

Bhayro, Siam. *The Shemihazah and Asael Narrative of 1 Enoch 6–11: Introduction, Text, Translation and Commentary with Reference to Ancient Near Eastern and Biblical Antecedents*. AOAT 322. Münster: Ugarit-Verlag, 2005.

———. "Noah's Library: Sources for 1 Enoch 6:11." *JSP* 15 (2006): 163–177.

Bietenhard, Hans. *Die himmlische Welt im Urchristentum und Spätjudentum*. WUNT 2. Tübingen: Mohr/Siebeck, 1951.

Blair, Judit. *De-Demonising the Old Testament: An Investigation of Azazel, Lilith, Deber, Qeteb and Reshef in the Hebrew Bible*. FAT 2.37. Tübingen: Mohr/Siebeck, 2009.

Bloch-Smith, Elizabeth. " 'Who is the King of Glory?' Solomon's Temple and Its Symbolism." In *Scripture and Other Artifacts. Essays on the Bible and Archeology in Honor of Philip J. King*. Edited by M. Coogan et al., 19–31. Louisville, KY: Westminster, 1994.

Blocher, Henri. "Zacharie 3. Josué et le Grand Jour des Expiations." *ETR* 54 (1979): 264–270.

Boccaccini, Gabriele. *Middle Judaism. Jewish Thought, 300 B.C.E. to 200 C.E.* Minneapolis: Fortress, 1991.

———. *Roots of Rabbinic Judaism*. Grand Rapids, MI: Eerdmans, 2002.

Boden, Peggy Jean. *The Mesopotamian Washing of the Mouth (Mīs Pî) Ritual*. Ph.D. diss. Johns Hopkins University, 1998.

Bohak, Gideon. "Asenath's Honeycomb and Onias' Temple: The Key to Joseph and Asenath." In *Proceedings of the Eleventh World Congress of Jewish Studies, Division A*. Edited by D. Assaf, 163–70. Jerusalem: Magness Press, 1994.

———. *Joseph and Aseneth and the Jewish Temple in Heliopolis*. Atlanta: Scholars, 1996.

Borgen, Peder. *Bread from Heaven: An Exegetical Study of the Concept of Manna in the Gospel of John and the Writings of Philo*. NovTSup 10. Leiden: Brill, 1965.

———. "Logos Was the True Light: Contributions to the Interpretation of the Prologue of John." *NovT* 14 (1972): 115–130.

———. *Philo, John and Paul: New Perspectives on Judaism and Early Christianity*. BJS 131. Atlanta: Scholars, 1987.

Böttrich, Christfried. *Weltweisheit, Menschheitsethik, Urkult: Studien zum slavischen Henochbuch*. WUNT 2/50. Tübingen: Mohr/Siebeck, 1992.

———. *Adam als Mikrokosmos: eine Untersuchung zum slavischen Henochbuch*. JU 59. Frankfurt am Main: Lang, 1995.

Bouché-Leclercq, Auguste. *L'astrologie grecque*. Paris: Ernest Leroux, 1899.

Bousset, Wilhelm. *Hauptprobleme der Gnosis*. FRLANT 10. Göttingen: Vandenhoeck & Ruprecht, 1907.

Breytenbach, Cilliers and Peggy L. Day. "Satan." In *Dictionary of Deities and Demons in the Bible*. Edited by K. van der Toorn, B. Becking and P.W. van der Horst, 726–732. Leiden: Brill, 1995.

Brown, Raymond. "The Messianism of Qumran." *CBQ* 19 (1957): 53–82.

———. "The Prologue of the Gospel of John." *RevExp* 62 (1965): 429–439.

Bryan, David. "A Reevaluation of Gen 4 and 5 in Light of Recent Studies in Genealogical Fluidity." *ZAW* 99 (1987): 180–188.

Buber, Martin. *Die Schrift und ihre Verdeutschung*. Berlin: Schocken, 1936.

Bucur, Bogdan. *Angelomorphic Pneumatology: Clement of Alexandria and Other Early Christian Witnesses*. SVC 95. Leiden: Brill, 2009.

Burchard, Christoph. *Untersuchungen zu Joseph und Aseneth: Überlieferung—Ortsbestimmung*. WUNT 8. Tübingen: Mohr/Siebeck, 1965.

———. "The Present State of Research on Joseph and Aseneth." In *Religion, Literature, and Society in Ancient Israel, Formative Christianity and Judaism*. Edited by J. Neusner, 31–52. New Perspectives on Ancient Judaism 2. Lanham: University Press of America, 1987.

Burrows, Eric. "Some Cosmological Patterns in Babylonian Religion." In *The Labyrinth. Further Studies in the Relation between Myth and Ritual in the Ancient World*. Edited by S. H. Hooke, 45–70. London: SPCK; New York: Macmillan, 1935.

Calvert, Nancy Lynn. *Abraham Traditions in Middle Jewish Literature: Implications for the Interpretation of Galatians and Romans*. Ph.D. diss. University of Sheffield, 1993.

Caquot, André. "גער." In *Theological Dictionary of the Old Testament*. Edited by G.J. Botterweck and H. Ringgren. 3.49–53. Grand Rapids, MI.: Eerdmans, 1979.

Carmichael, Calum. "The Origin of the Scapegoat Ritual." *VT* 50 (2000): 167–82.

Charlesworth, James. "From Jewish Messianology to Christian Christology." In *Judaisms and Their Messiahs at the Turn of the Christian Era*. Edited by J. Neusner et al., 225–264. Cambridge: Cambridge University Press, 1987.

Chernus, Ira. *Mysticism in Rabbinic Judaism: Studies in the History of Midrash*. SJ 11. Berlin: de Gruyter, 1982.

Chesnutt, Randal. "Perceptions of Oil in Early Judaism and the Meal Formula in Joseph and Aseneth." *JSP* 14 (2005): 113–132.

Chilton, David. *Paradise Restored: A Biblical Theology of Dominion*. Ft. Worth: Dominion Press, 1985.

Coleman, Gillis. *The Phenomenon of Christian Interpolations into Jewish Apocalyptic Texts: A Bibliographical Survey and Methodological Analysis*. Ph.D. diss. Vanderbilt University, 1976.

Collins, John. "Methodological Issues in the Study of 1 Enoch." *SBLSP* 13.1 (1978): 315–322.

———. "A Throne in the Heavens: Apotheosis in Pre-Christian Judaism." In *Death, Ecstasy, and Other Worldly Journeys*. Edited by J.J. Collins and M. Fishbane, 43–57. Albany, NY: SUNY Press, 1995.

———. *The Scepter and the Star: The Messiahs of the Dead Sea Scrolls and Other Ancient Literature*. ABRL 10. New York: Doubleday, 1995.

Crone, Patricia. “The Book of the Watchers in the Qur’an.” In *Exchange and Transmission across Cultural Boundaries: Philosophy, Mysticism and Science in the Mediterranean World.* Edited by H. Ben-Shammai, S. Shaked, and S. Stroumsa, 16–51. Jerusalem: The Israel Academy of Sciences and Humanities, 2013.

Crossan, John Dominic. *The Cross that Spoke: The Origins of the Passion Narrative.* San Francisco: Harper & Row, 1988.

Dan, Joseph. “Samael, Lilith, and the Concept of Evil in Early Kabbalah.” *AJSR* 5 (1980): 17–40.

———. “Samael and the Problem of Jewish Gnosticism.” In *Perspectives on Jewish Thought and Mysticism.* Edited by A. Altmann, A.L. Ivry and E.R. Wolfson, 257–276. Amsterdam: Harwood Academic Publishers, 1998.

———. *Kabbalah: A Very Short Introduction.* Oxford: Oxford University Press, 2006.

Davila, James. “The Hodayot Hymnist and the Four Who Entered Paradise.” *RevQ* 17/65–68 (1996): 457–478.

Day, Peggy. *An Adversary in Heaven: Satan in the Hebrew Bible.* HSM 43. Atlanta: Scholars, 1988.

DeConick, April. *Seek to See Him: Ascent and Vision Mysticism in the Gospel of Thomas.* SVC 33. Leiden: Brill, 1996.

———. *Recovering the Original Gospel of Thomas: A History of the Gospel and Its Growth.* London: T&T Clark, 2005.

Denzey, Nicola Frances. “Genesis Traditions in Conflict? The Use of Some Exegetical Traditions in the Trimorphic Protennoia and the Johannine Prologue.” *VC* 55 (2001): 20–44.

De Roo, Jacqueline. “Was the Goat for Azazel Destined for the Wrath of God?” *Bib* 81 (2000): 233–241.

Deutsch, Nathaniel. *Guardians of the Gate: Angelic Vice Regency in Late Antiquity.* Brill’s Series in Jewish Studies 22. Leiden: Brill, 1999.

Dick, Michael. *Born in Heaven, Made on Earth: The Making of the Cult Image in the Ancient Near East.* Winona Lake: Eisenbrauns, 1999.

Dick, Michael and Walker, Christopher. *The Induction of the Cult Image in Ancient Mesopotamia: The Mesopotamian Mīs Pî Ritual: Transliteration, Translation, and Commentary.* SAALT 1. Helsinki: University of Helsinki, 2001.

Dieckmann, Bernhard. *Judas als Sündenbock: Eine verhängnisvolle Geschichte von Angst und Vergeltung.* Munich: Kösel, 1991.

Dimant, Devorah. *The Fallen Angels in the Dead Sea Scrolls and the Related Apocrypha and Pseudepigrapha.* Ph.D. diss. Hebrew University of Jerusalem, 1974. [Hebrew]

———. “1 Enoch 6–11: A Methodological Perspective.” *SBLSP* 17 (1978): 323–339.

———. "Noah in Early Jewish Literature." In *Biblical Figures Outside the Bible*. Edited by M.E. Stone and T.A. Bergren, 123–50. Harrisburg: Trinity Press International, 1998.

———. "1 Enoch 6–11: A Fragment of a Parabiblical Work." *JJS* 53 (2002): 223–237.

Donaldson, Terence. *Jesus on the Mountain: A Study in Matthean Theology*. JSNTSS 8. Sheffield: JSOT, 1985.

Dorman, Anke. " 'Commit Injustice and Shed Innocent Blood.' Motives behind the Institution of the Day of Atonement in the Book of Jubilees." In *The Day of Atonement: Its Interpretation in Early Jewish and Christian Traditions*. Edited by T. Hieke and T. Nicklas, 47–61. TBN 15. Leiden: Brill, 2012.

Douglas, Mary. *Purity and Danger: An Analysis of Concepts of Pollution and Taboo*. London: Praeger, 1969.

Drawnel, Henryk. "The Punishment of Asael (1 En 10:4–8) and Mesopotamian Anti-Witchcraft Literature." *RevQ* 25 (2012): 369–394.

Dupont, Jacques. "L'arrière-fond biblique du récit des tentations de Jésus." *NTS* 3 (1957): 287–304.

———. *Les tentations de Jésus au desert*. StudNeot 4. Bruges: Desclée de Brouwer, 1968.

Ego, Beate. *"Im Himmel wie auf Erden."* WUNT 2.34. Tübingen: Mohr/Siebeck, 1989.

Elior, Rachel. "From Earthly Temple to Heavenly Shrines: Prayer and Sacred Song in the Hekhalot Literature and Its Relation to Temple Traditions." *JSQ* 4 (1997): 217–267.

———. *The Three Temples: On the Emergence of Jewish Mysticism*. Oxford: The Littman Library of Jewish Civilization, 2004.

Emerton, John. "Binding and Loosing—Forgiving and Retaining," *JTS* 13 (1962): 325–331.

Endo, Masanobu. *Creation and Christology: A Study on the Johannine Prologue in the Light of Early Jewish Creation Accounts*. WUNT 2.149. Tübingen: Mohr/Siebeck, 2002.

Fahd, Toufy. "Anges, démons et djinns en Islam." In: *Génies, anges et démons*. 153–214. SO 8. Paris: Seuil, 1971.

Fallon, Francis. *The Enthronement of Sabaoth: Jewish Elements in Gnostic Creation Myths*. NHS 10. Leiden: Brill, 1978.

Fauth, Wolfgang. "Auf den Spuren des biblischen Azazel (Lev 16): Einige Residuen der Gestalt oder des Namens in jüdisch-aramäischen, griechischen, koptischen, äthiopischen, syrischen und mandäischen Texten." *ZAW* 110 (1998): 514–534.

Feinberg, Charles Lee. "The Scapegoat of Leviticus Sixteen." *BSac* 115 (1958): 320–331.

Feuillet, André. "Le récit lucanien de la tentation (Lc 4, 1–13)." *Bib* 40 (1959): 613–631.

———. "L'épisode de la tentation d'après l'Evangile selon saint Marc (I, 12–13)." *EstBib* 19 (1960): 49–73.

Finkelstein, Jacob. "The Antediluvian Kings: A University of California Tablet." *JCS* 17 (1963): 39–51.

Finlan, Stephen. *Problems with Atonement: The Origins of, and Controversy About, the Atonement Doctrine*. Collegeville, MN: Liturgical Press, 2005.

Fishbane, Eitan. "The Zohar: Masterpiece of Jewish Mysticism." In *Jewish Mysticism and Kabbalah: New Insights and Scholarship*. Edited by F.E. Greenspahn, 49–67. New York and London: New York University Press, 2011.

Fishbane, Michael. *Text and Texture*. New York: Schocken, 1979.

———. *The Exegetical Imagination: On Jewish Thought and Theology*. Cambridge, MA.: Harvard University Press, 1998.

———. *Biblical Myth and Rabbinic Mythmaking*. Oxford: Oxford University Press, 2003.

Fletcher-Louis, Crispin. "The Revelation of the Sacral Son of Man: The Genre, History of Religions Context and the Meaning of the Transfiguration." In *Auferstehung—Resurrection*. Edited by F. Avemarie and H. Lichtenberger, 247–298. Tübingen: Mohr/Siebeck, 2001.

———. *All the Glory of Adam: Liturgical Anthropology in the Dead Sea Scrolls*. STDJ 42. Leiden: Brill, 2002.

———. "The Aqedah and the Book of the Watchers (*1 Enoch* 1–36)." In *Studies in Jewish Prayer*. Edited by R. Hayward and B. Embry, 1–33. JSSSS 17. Oxford: Oxford University Press, 2005.

Förster, Max. "Adam's Erschaffung und Namengebung: Ein lateinisches Fragment des s.g. slawischen Henoch." *Archiv für Religionswissenschaft* 11 (1907–8): 477–529.

———. "Die mittelirische Version von Adams Erschaffung." *ZCP* 13 (1921): 47–48.

Forsyth, Neil. *The Old Enemy: Satan and the Combat Myth*. Princeton: Princeton University Press, 1987.

Fossum, Jarl. *The Name of God and the Angel of the Lord: Samaritan and Jewish Mediation Concepts and the Origin of Gnosticism*. WUNT 36. Tübingen: Mohr/Siebeck, 1985.

———. *The Image of the Invisible God: Essays on the Influence of Jewish Mysticism on Early Christology*. NTOA 30. Fribourg: Universitätsverlag Freiburg Schweiz; Göttingen: Vanderhoeck & Ruprecht, 1995.

———. "The Adorable Adam of the Mystics and the Rebuttals of the Rabbis." In *Geschichte-Tradition-Reflexion. Festschrift für Martin Hengel zum*

70. Geburtstag. Edited by H. Cancik, H. Lichtenberger and P. Schäfer, 1.529–539. 3 vols. Tübingen: Mohr/Siebeck, 1996.

Freedman, David Noel. "Temple Without Hands." In *Temples and High Places in Biblical Times: Proceedings of the Colloquium in Honor of the Centennial of Hebrew Union College-Jewish Institute of Religion, Jersualem, 14–16 March 1977*. Edited by A. Biran, 21–30. Jerusalem: Hebrew Union College-Jewish Institute of Religion, 1981.

García Martínez, Florentino. *Qumran and Apocalyptic*. STDJ 9. Leiden: Brill, 1992.

———. "Man and Woman: Halakhah Based upon Eden in the Dead Sea Scrolls." In *Paradise Interpreted: Representations of Biblical Paradise in Judaism and Christianity*. Edited by G. Luttikhuizen, 95–115. TBN 2. Leiden: Brill, 1999.

Garrett, Susan. *The Temptations of Jesus in Mark's Gospel*. Grand Rapids, MI: Eerdmans, 1998.

Gaylord, Harry. "How Satanael Lost His '-el.'" *JJS* 33 (1982): 303–309.

Geiger, Abraham. "Einige Worte über das Buch Henoch." *JZWL* 3 (1864–65): 196–204.

Gerhardsson, Birger. *The Testing of God's Son: Matt. 4:1–11 & Par, An Analysis of An Early Christian Midrash*. ConBNT 2.1. Lund: Gleerup, 1966.

Gibson, Jeffrey. *Temptations of Jesus in Early Christianity*. JSNTSS 112. Sheffield: Sheffield Academic Press, 1995.

Gieschen, Charles. *Angelomorphic Christology: Antecedents and Early Evidence*. AGAJU 42. Leiden: Brill, 1998.

Gilhus, Ingvild. *The Nature of the Archons: A Study in the Soteriology of a Gnostic Treatise from Nag Hammadi (CGII, 4)*. SOR 12. Wiesbaden: Harrassowitz, 1985.

Ginzberg, Louis. *Legends of the Jews*. 7 vols. Baltimore: John Hopkins University Press, 1998.

Glazov, Gregory. *The Bridling of the Tongue and the Opening of the Mouth in Biblical Prophecy*. JSOTSS 311. Sheffield: Sheffield Academic Press, 2001.

Goehring, James. "A Classical Influence on the Gnostic Sophia Myth." *VC* 35 (1981): 16–23.

Good, Deirdre. "Sophia in Valentinianism." *The Second Century* 4 (1984): 193–201.

———. *Reconstructing the Tradition of Sophia in Gnostic Literature*. SBLMS 32. Atlanta: Scholars, 1987.

Goodman, David. "Do Angels Eat?" *JJS* 37 (1986): 160–175.

Görg, Manfred. "Beobachtungen zum sogenannten Azazel-Ritus." *BN* 33 (1986): 10–16.

Grabbe, Lester. "The Scapegoat Tradition: A Study in Early Jewish Interpretation." *JSJ* 18 (1987): 165–179.

Grelot, Pierre. "La légende d'Hénoch dans les apocryphes et dans la Bible: Origine et signification." *RSR* 46 (1958): 5–26, 181–210.

Greenstein, Edward. "God's Golem: The Creation of the Human in Genesis 2." In *Creation in Jewish and Christian Tradition*. Edited by H. Reventlow and Y. Hoffman, 219–239. JSOTSS 319. Sheffield: Sheffield Academic Press, 2002.

Gruenwald, Ithamar. *Apocalyptic and Merkavah Mysticism*. AGAJU 14. Leiden: Brill, 1980.

Gry, Léon. "Quelques noms d'anges ou d'êtres mysterieux en II Hénoch." *RB* 49 (1940): 195–203.

Guelich, Robert. *Mark 1–8:26*. WBC 34A. Dallas: Word, 1989.

Gunkel, Hermann. *Schöpfung und Chaos in Urzeit und Endzeit*. Göttingen: Vandenhoeck und Ruprecht, 1895.

Hagen, Joost. "No Longer 'Slavonic' Only: *2 Enoch* Attested in Coptic from Nubia." In *New Perspectives on 2 Enoch: No Longer Slavonic Only*. Edited by A. Orlov, G. Boccaccini, J. Zurawski, 7–34. SJS 4. Leiden: Brill, 2012.

Hagner, Donald. "Apocalyptic Motifs in the Gospel of Matthew: Continuity and Discontinuity." *HBT* 7 (1985): 53–82.

Hall, Robert. "The 'Christian Interpolation' in the *Apocalypse of Abraham*." *JBL* 107 (1988): 107–112.

———. *Revealed Histories. Techniques for Ancient Jewish and Christian Historiography*. JSPSS 6. Sheffield: JSOT Press, 1991.

Hallo, William. "Antediluvian Cities." *JCS* 20 (1970): 57–67.

Halperin, David. *The Merkabah in Rabbinic Literature*. New Haven, American Oriental Society, 1980.

———. "Heavenly Ascension in Ancient Judaism: The Nature of the Experience." *SBLSP* 26 (1987): 218–231.

———. *The Faces of the Chariot: Early Jewish Responses to Ezekiel's Vision*. TSAJ 16. Tübingen: Mohr/Siebeck, 1988.

Hamerton-Kelly, Robert. "The Temple and the Origins of Jewish Apocalyptic." *VT* 20 (1970): 1–15.

Hamilton, Victor. "Satan." In *Anchor Bible Dictionary*. Edited by D.N. Freedman, 5.985–998. 6 vols. New York: Doubleday, 1992.

Hanson, Paul. "Rebellion in Heaven, Azazel, and Euhemeristic Heroes in *1 Enoch* 6–11." *JBL* 96 (1977): 195–233.

Harlow, Daniel. "Idolatry and Alterity: Israel and the Nations in the *Apocalypse of Abraham*." In *The "Other" in Second Temple Judaism. Essays in Honor of John J. Collins*. Edited by D.C. Harlow, M. Goff, K.M. Hogan and J.S. Kaminsky, 302–330. Grand Rapids, MI: Eerdmans, 2011.

———. "Anti-Christian Polemic in the Apocalypse of Abraham: Jesus as a Pseudo-Messiah in *Apoc. Ab.* 29.3–14." *JSP* 22.3 (2013): 167–183.

Hartman, Thomas. "Some Thoughts on the Sumerian King List and Genesis 5 and 11b." *JBL* 91 (1972): 25–32

Hayward, Robert. *The Jewish Temple: A Non-Biblical Sourcebook.* London: Routledge, 1996.

Hecker, Joel. *Mystical Bodies, Mystical Meals: Eating and Embodiment in Medieval Kabbalah.* Raphael Patai Series in Jewish Folklore and Anthropology. Detroit: Wayne State University Press, 2005.

Heller, Bernard. "La chute des anges: Shemhazai, Ouzza et Azaël." *REJ* 60 (1910): 202–212.

Helm, Robert. "Azazel in Early Jewish Literature." *AUSS* 32 (1994): 217–226.

Hengel, Martin. "The Prologue of the Gospel of John as the Gateway to Christological Truth." In *The Gospel of John and Christian Theology.* Edited by R. Bauckham and C. Mosser, 265–294. Grand Rapids, MI: Eerdmans, 2008.

Heuser, Manfred. "Manichaean Myth According to the Coptic Sources." In *Studies in Manichaean Literature and Art.* Edited by M. Heuser and H. Klimkeit, 3–108. NHMS 46. Leiden: Brill, 1998.

Hiers, Richard. "'Binding and Loosing': The Matthean Authorizations." *JBL* 104 (1985): 233–250.

Himmelfarb, Martha. "From Prophecy to Apocalypse: The Book of the Watchers and Tours of Heaven." In *Jewish Spirituality: From the Bible Through the Middle Ages.* Edited by A. Green, 145–165. New York: Crossroad, 1986.

———. "Apocalyptic Ascent and the Heavenly Temple." *SBLSP* 26 (1987): 210–217.

———. *Ascent to Heaven in Jewish and Christian Apocalypses.* New York/Oxford: Oxford University Press, 1993.

———. "The Practice of Ascent in the Ancient Mediterranean World." In *Death, Ecstasy, and Other Worldly Journeys.* Edited by J.J. Collins and M. Fishbane, 123–137. Albany, NY: SUNY Press, 1995.

Hodges, Horace. *Food as Synecdoche in John's Gospel and Gnostic Texts.* Ph.D. diss. University of California at Berkeley, 1995.

Hofius, Otfried. *Der Vorhang vor dem Thron Gottes.* WUNT 14. Tübingen: Mohr/Siebeck, 1972.

Humphrey, Edith McEwan. *Joseph and Aseneth.* GAP 8. Sheffield: Sheffield Academic Press, 2000.

Hurowitz, Victor. "Inside Solomon's Temple." *BR* 10.2 (1994): 24–36.

———. "The Mesopotamian God Image, from Womb to Tomb," *JAOS* 123 (2003): 147–157.

———. "What Goes In Is What Comes Out: Materials for Creating Cult Statues." In *Text, Artifact, and Image; Revealing Ancient Israelite Religion.*

Edited by G.M. Beckman and T.J. Lewis, 3–23. BJS 346. Providence, RI: Brown Judaic Studies, 2006.

Hurtado, Larry. *How On Earth Did Jesus Become A God?: Historical Questions About Earliest Devotion To Jesus.* Grand Rapids, MI: Eerdmans, 2005.

Idel, Moshe. "The Evil Thought of the Deity." *Tarbiz* 49 (1980): 356–364. [Hebrew]

———. "The Origin of Alchemy According to Zosimos and a Hebrew Parallel." *REJ* 145 (1986): 117–124.

———. "Hermeticism and Judaism." In *Hermeticism and the Renaissance: Intellectual History and the Occult in Early Modern Europe.* Edited by I. Merkel and A.G. Debus, 59–76. Washington, D.C.: Folger Shakespeare Library, 1988.

———. "Enoch is Metatron." *Imm* 24/25 (1990): 220–240.

———. *Golem: Jewish Magical and Mystical Traditions on the Artificial Anthropoid.* Albany, NY: SUNY Press, 1990.

———. *Ascensions on High in Jewish Mysticism: Pillars, Lines, Ladders.* Past Incorporated. CEU Studies in Humanities 2. Budapest: Central European University Press, 2005.

Jacobs, Irving. *The Midrashic Process: Tradition and Interpretation in Rabbinic Judaism.* Cambridge: Cambridge University Press, 1995.

Janowski, Bernd. *Sühne als Heilsgeschehen: Studien zur Sühnetheologie der Priesterschrift und zur Wurzel KPR im Alten Orient und im Alten Testament.* WMANT 55. Neukirchen-Vluyn: Neukirchener Verlag, 1982.

———. "Azazel." In *Dictionary of Deities and Demons in the Bible.* Edited by K. van der Toorn, B. Becking and P.W. van der Horst, 240–248. Leiden: Brill, 1995.

———. "Die heilige Wohnung des Höchsten. Kosmologische Implikationen der Jerusalemer Tempeltheologie." In *Gottesstadt und Gottesgarten. Zu Geschichte und Theologie des Jerusalemer Tempels.* Edited by O. Keel and E. Zenger, 24–68. QD 191. Freiburg: Herder, 2002.

———. "Der Tempel als Kosmos-Zur kosmologischen Bedeutung des Tempels in der Umwelt Israels." In *Egypt—Temple of the Whole World-Ägypten-Tempel der Gesamten Welt. Studies in Honour of Jan Assmann.* Edited by S. Meyer, 163–186. SHR 97. Leiden: Brill, 2003.

Jeremias, Joachim. "Nachwort zum Artikel von H.-G. Leder." *ZNW* 54 (1963): 278–279.

———. "Adam." In *Theological Dictionary of the New Testament.* Edited by G. Kittel and G. Friedrich, 1.141–143. 10 vols. Grand Rapids, MI: Eerdmans, 1964–1976.

———. *New Testament Theology.* New York: Scribner, 1971.

Jones, Kenneth. *Jewish Reactions to the Destruction of Jerusalem in A.D. 70: Apocalypses and Related Pseudepigrapha.* JSJSS 151. Leiden: Brill, 2011.

Jung, Leo. *Fallen Angels in Jewish, Christian, and Mohammedan Literature*. Philadelphia: Dropsie College for Hebrew and Cognate Learning, 1926.

Jürgens, Benedikt. *Heiligkeit und Versöhnung: Levitikus 16 in seinem literarischen Kontext*. New York: Herder, 2001.

Kaplan, Chaim. "The Hidden Name." *JSOR* 13 (1929): 181–184.

Kaufmann, Yeḥezkel. "Abraham-Apokalypse." In *Encyclopaedia Judaica. Das Judentum in Geschichte und Gegenwart*. Edited by J. Klatzkin and I. Elbogen, 1.552–553. 10 vols. Berlin: Eschkol Publikations Gesellschaft. 1928–1934.

Kearney, Peter. "Creation and Liturgy: The P Redaction of Ex 25–40." *ZAW* 89.3 (1977): 375–378.

Kelly, Henry Ansgar. "The Devil in the Desert." *CBQ* 26 (1964): 190–220.

———. *Towards the Death of Satan: The Growth and Decline of Christian Demonology*. London: Chapman, 1968.

———. *Satan: A Biography*. Cambridge: Cambridge University Press, 2006.

King, Karen. *Images of the Feminine in Gnosticism*. Harrisburg: Trinity Press International, 2000.

Kluger, Rivkah. *Satan in the Old Testament*. SJT 7. Evanston: Northwestern University Press, 1967.

Kobel, Esther. *Dining with John: Communal Meals and Identity Formation in the Fourth Gospel and Its Historical and Cultural Context*. BIS 109. Leiden: Brill, 2011.

Kobelski, Paul. *Melchizedek and Melchirešaᶜ*. CBQMS 10. Washington: Catholic Biblical Association of America, 1981.

Koester, Craig. *The Dwelling of God: The Tabernacle in the Old Testament, Intertestamental Jewish Literature and the New Testament*. CBQMS 22. Washington: Catholic Biblical Association of America, 1989.

Kraemer, Ross. *When Aseneth Met Joseph: A Late Antique Tale of the Biblical Patriarch and His Egyptian Wife, Reconsidered*. New York: Oxford University Press, 1998.

Kulik, Alexander. "К датировке 'Откровения Авраама.'" In *In Memoriam of Ja. S. Lur'e*. Edited by N.M. Botvinnik and Je.I. Vaneeva, 189–195. St. Petersburg: Fenix, 1997.

———. *Apocalypse of Abraham: Towards the Lost Original*. Ph.D. diss. Hebrew University of Jerusalem, 2000.

———. "'The Mysteries of Behemoth and Leviathan' and the Celestial Bestiary of 3 Baruch." *Le Muséon* 122 (2009): 291–329.

Kümmel, Hans. "Ersatzkönig und Sündenbock." *ZAW* 80 (1986): 289–318.

Kvanvig, Helge. *Roots of Apocalyptic: The Mesopotamian Background of the Enoch Figure and of the Son of Man*. WMANT 61. Neukirchen-Vluyn: Neukirchener Verlag, 1988.

Lagrange, Marie-Joseph. "Notes sur le messianisme au temps de Jesus." *RB* 14 (1905): 481–514.

Lamarche, Paul. "The Prologue of John." In *The Interpretation of John*. Edited by J. Ashton, 47–66. Edinburgh: T&T Clark, 1997.

Lambert, Wilfred. "Enmeduranki and Related Matters." *JCS* 21 (1967): 126–138.

Lenowitz, Harris. *The Jewish Messiahs: From the Galilee to Crown Heights*. Oxford: Oxford University Press, 1998.

Leutzsch, Martin. "Essen Engel?: Über das Ernährungsverhalten himmlischer Wesen." In *Essen und Trinken in der Bibel: Ein literarisches Festmahl für Rainer Kessler zum 65. Geburtstag*. Edited by M. Geiger et al., 254–268. Gütersloh: Gütersloher Verlagshaus, 2009.

Levenson, Jon. "The Temple and the World." *JR* 64 (1984): 275–298.

———. *Sinai and Zion*. San Francisco: Harper & Row, 1985.

———. "The Jerusalem Temple in Devotional and Visionary Experience." In *Jewish Spirituality: From the Bible Through the Middle Ages*. Edited by A. Green, 32–59. New York: Crossroad, 1986.

———. *Creation and the Persistence of Evil: The Jewish Drama of Divine Omnipotence*. San Francisco: Harper & Row, 1988.

Levy, Ralph. *The Symbolism of the Azazel Goat*. Bethesda: International Scholars Publication, 1998.

Licht, Jacob. "Abraham, Apocalypse of." In *Encyclopedia Judaica*. Edited by C. Roth, 2.127. 16 vols. Jerusalem: Keter, 1971.

Lieber, Andrea. "I Set a Table before You: The Jewish Eschatological Character of Aseneth's Conversion Meal." *JSP* 14 (2004): 63–77.

Liebes, Yehuda. *Studies in the Zohar*. Albany, NY: SUNY Press, 1993.

Littmann, Enno. "Harut und Marut." In *Festschrift Friedrich Carl Andreas*. 70–87. Leipzig: Harrassowitz, 1916.

Lods, Adolphe. "Les origines de la figure de satan, ses fonctions à la cour céleste." In *Mélanges syriens offerts à Monsieur René Dussaud*. Edited by J.-A. Blanchet, F. Cumont and G. Contenau, 2.649–660. 2 vols. Paris: P. Geuthner, 1939.

Loretz, Oswald. *Leberschau, Sündenbock, Asasel in Ugarit und Israel: Leberschau und Jahwestatue in Psalm 27, Leberschau in Psalm 74*. UBL 3. Altenberge: CIS-Verlag, 1985.

Lourié, Basil. "Propitiatorium in the Apocalypse of Abraham." In *The Old Testament Apocrypha in the Slavonic Tradition: Continuity and Diversity*. Edited by L. DiTommaso and C. Böttrich, 267–277. TSAJ 140. Tübingen: Mohr/Siebeck, 2011.

Ludin Jansen, Herman. *Die Henochgestalt: Eine vergleichende religionsgeschichtliche Untersuchung*. Oslo: Dybwad, 1939.

Lundberg, Marilyn. "The Mis-Pi Rituals and Incantations and Jeremiah 10:1–16." In *Uprooting and Planting: Essays on Jeremiah for Leslie Allen*. Edited by J. Goldingay, 210–227. London: T&T Clark, 2007.

Macaskill, Grant. *Revealed Wisdom and Inaugurated Eschatology in Ancient Judaism and Early Christianity*. JSJSS 115. Leiden: Brill, 2007.

Maclean, Jennifer. "Barabbas, the Scapegoat Ritual, and the Development of the Passion Narrative." *HTR* 100 (2007): 309–334.

MacRae, George. *Some Elements of Jewish Apocalyptic and Mystical Tradition and Their Relation to Gnostic Literature*. 2 vols. Ph.D. diss. University of Cambridge, 1966.

Maiberger, Paul. *Das Manna: Eine literarische, etymologische und naturkundliche Untersuchung*. 2 vols. ÄAT 6. Wiesbaden: Otto Harrassowitz, 1983.

Malina, Bruce. *The Palestinian Manna Tradition*. AGAJU 7. Leiden: Brill, 1968.

McDonough, Sean. *YHWH at Patmos: Rev. 1:4 in Its Hellenistic and Early Jewish Setting*. WUNT 2.107. Tübingen: Mohr/Siebeck, 1999.

McNamara, Martin. *The Apocrypha in the Irish Church*. Dublin: Dublin Institute for Advanced Studies, 1975.

McNicol, Allan. "The Heavenly Sanctuary in Judaism: A Model for Tracing the Origin of the Apocalypse." *JRS* 13 (1987): 66–94.

Menasce, Jean de. "Une légende indo-iranienne dans l'angélologie judéomusulmane: à propos de Hârût et Mârût." *EA* 1 (1947): 10–18.

Merkur, Daniel. *The Mystery of Manna: The Psychedelic Sacrament of the Bible*. Rochester: Park Street Press, 2000.

Mettinger, Tryggve. *The Dethronement of Sabaoth. Studies in the Shem and Kabod Theologies*. ConBOT 18. Lund: Wallin & Dalholm, 1982.

Metzger, Martin. "Keruben und Palmetten als Dekoration im Jerusalemer Heiligtum und Jahwe, 'der Nahrung gibt allem Fleisch.'" In *Zion-Ort der Begegnung. FS L. Klein*. Edited by F. Hahn et al., 503–529. BBB 90. Bodenheim: Athenäum Hain Hanstein, 1993.

Meyer, Rudolf. "Manna." In *Theological Dictionary of the New Testament*. Edited by G. Kittel and G. Friedrich, 4.462–466. 10 vols. Grand Rapids, MI: Eerdmans, 1964–1976.

Meyers, Carol. "Sea, Molten." In *Anchor Bible Dictionary*. Edited by D.N. Freedman, 5.1061–1062. 6 vols. New York: Doubleday, 1992.

Milgrom, Jacob. *Studies in Cultic Theology and Terminology*. SJLA 36. Leiden: Brill, 1983.

Molenberg, Corrie. "A Study of the Roles of Shemihaza and Asael in 1 Enoch 6–11." *JSJ* 35 (1984): 136–146.

Morland, Kjell. *The Rhetoric of Curse in Galatians: Paul Confronts Another Gospel*. Atlanta: Scholars, 1995.

Morray-Jones, Christopher. "Transformational Mysticism in the Apocalyptic-Merkabah Tradition." *JJS* 43 (1992): 1–31.

———. *A Transparent Illusion: The Dangerous Vision of Water in Hekhalot Mysticism: A Source-critical and Tradition-historical Inquiry.* JSJSS 59. Leiden: Brill, 2002.

Neis, Rachel. "Embracing Icons: The Face of Jacob on the Throne of God." *Journal of Jewish Art & Visual Culture* 1 (2007): 36–54.

Neugebauer, Otto. "The 'Astronomical' Chapters of the Ethiopic Book of Enoch (72–82)." In *The Book of Enoch, or I Enoch: A New English Edition with Commentary and Textual Notes.* Edited by M. Black with J.C. VanderKam and O. Neugebauer, 386–419. SVTP 7. Leiden: Brill, 1985.

Newman, Carey. *Paul's Glory-Christology: Tradition and Rhetoric.* NovTSup 69. Leiden: Brill, 1992.

Newsom, Carol. "The Development of *1 Enoch* 6–19: Cosmology and Judgment." *CBQ* 42 (1980): 310–329.

———. " 'He Has Established for Himself Priests': Human and Angelic Priesthood in the Qumran Sabbath Shirot." In *Archaeology and History in the Dead Sea Scrolls: The New York University Conference in Memory of Yigael Yadin.* Edited by L.H. Schiffman, 101–120. JSPSS 8. Sheffield: JSOT Press, 1990.

Nickelsburg, George. "Apocalyptic and Myth in 1 Enoch 6–11." *JBL* 96 (1977): 383–405.

———. "The Apocalyptic Construction of Reality in 1 Enoch." In *Mysteries and Revelations: Apocalyptic Studies since the Uppsala Colloquium.* Edited by J.J. Collins, 51–64. JSPSS 9. Sheffield: JSOT Press, 1991.

———. "Patriarchs Who Worry About Their Wives: A Haggadic Tendency in the Genesis Apocryphon." In *Pseudepigraphic Perspectives: The Apocrypha and the Pseudepigrapha in Light of the Dead Sea Scrolls.* Edited by E. Chazon and M. E. Stone, 137–158. STDJ 31. Leiden: Brill, 1999.

Nir, Rivka. *Joseph and Aseneth: A Christian Book.* HBM 42. Sheffield: Phoenix Press, 2012.

Noort, Ed. "Gan-Eden in the Context of the Mythology of the Hebrew Bible." In *Paradise Interpreted: Representations of Biblical Paradise in Judaism and Christianity.* Edited by G. Luttikhuizen, 21–36. TBN 2. Leiden: Brill, 1999.

Oegema, Gerbern. *The Anointed and His People: Messianic Expectations from the Maccabees to Bar Kochba.* JSPSS 27. Sheffield: Sheffield Academic Press, 1998.

Olson, Daniel. "1 Enoch." In *Eerdmans Commentary on the Bible*. Edited by J.D.G. Dunn and J.W. Rogerson, 904–941. Grand Rapids, MI: Eerdmans, 2003.

Orlov, Andrei. "Celestial Choir-Master: The Liturgical Role of Enoch-Metatron in *2 Enoch* and the Merkabah Tradition." *JSP* 14 (2004): 3–24.

———. *The Enoch-Metatron Tradition*. TSAJ 107. Tübingen: Mohr/Siebeck, 2005.

———. "Secrets of Creation in 2 (Slavonic) Enoch." In *From Apocalypticism to Merkabah Mysticism: Studies in the Slavonic Pseudepigrapha*. Edited by A. Orlov, 175–195. JSJSS 114. Leiden: Brill, 2007.

———. "Resurrection of Adam's Body: The Redeeming Role of Enoch-Metatron in 2 (Slavonic) Enoch." In *The Theophaneia School: Jewish Roots of Eastern Christian Mysticism*. Edited by B. Lourié and A. Orlov, 385–389. Scrinium 3. St. Petersburg: Byzantinorossica, 2007.

———. " 'The Gods of My Father Terah': Abraham the Iconoclast and the Polemics with the Divine Body Traditions in the *Apocalypse of Abraham*." *JSP* 18.1 (2008): 33–53.

———. "Eschatological Yom Kippur in the *Apocalypse of Abraham*. Part I. The Scapegoat Ritual." In *Symbola Caelestis. Le symbolisme liturgique et paraliturgique dans le monde chrétien*. Edited by A. Orlov and B. Lourié, 79–111. Scrinium 5. Piscataway: Gorgias Press, 2009.

———. "Arboreal Metaphors and Polemics with the Divine Body Traditions in the *Apocalypse of Abraham*." *HTR* 102 (2009): 439–451.

———. " 'The Likeness of Heaven': *Kavod* of Azazel in the Apocalypse of Abraham." In *With Letters of Light: Studies in the Dead Sea Scrolls, Early Jewish Apocalypticism, Magic and Mysticism*. Edited by D. Arbel and A. Orlov, 232–253. Ekstasis 2. Berlin: De Gruyter, 2010.

———. *Dark Mirrors: Azazel and Satanael in Early Jewish Demonology*. Albany, NY: SUNY Press, 2011.

———. "Satan and the Visionary: Apocalyptic Roles of the Adversary in the Temptation Narrative of the Gospel of Matthew." In *Dark Mirrors: Azazel and Satanael in Early Jewish Demonology*. Edited by A. Orlov, 107–112. Albany, NY: SUNY Press, 2011.

———. "The Sacerdotal Traditions of *2 Enoch* and the Date of the Text." In *New Perspectives on 2 Enoch: No Longer Slavonic Only*. Edited by A. Orlov, G. Boccaccini, J. Zurawski, 103–116. SJS 4. Leiden: Brill, 2012.

———. *Heavenly Priesthood in the Apocalypse of Abraham*. Cambridge; Cambridge University Press, 2013.

———. "What is Below?: Mysteries of Leviathan in the Early Jewish Accounts and Mishnah Hagigah 2:1." In *Hekhalot Literature in Context: From*

Byzantium to Babylonia. Edited by R. Boustan et al., 313–322. Tübingen: Mohr/Siebeck, 2013.

Pagels, Elaine. "The Social History of Satan, the 'Intimate Enemy': A Preliminary Sketch." *HTR* 84 (1991): 105–128.

———. "The Social History of Satan, 2: Satan in the New Testament Gospels." *JAAR* 62 (1994): 17–58.

———. *The Origin of Satan*. New York: Vintage Books, 1996.

———. "The Social History of Satan, 3: John of Patmos and Ignatius of Antioch: Contrasting Visions of 'God's People.'" *HTR* 99 (2006): 487–505.

Painter, John. "Rereading Genesis in the Prologue of John?" In *Neotestamentica et Philonica. Studies in Honor of Peder Borgen*. Edited by D.E. Aune, T. Seland, J.H. Ulrichsen, 179–201. Leiden: Brill, 2003.

Parry, Donald. "Garden of Eden: Prototype Sanctuary." In *Temples of the Ancient World: Ritual and Symbolism*. Edited by D.W. Parry, 126–151. Provo: Deseret, 1994.

Patai, Raphael. *Man and Temple in Ancient Jewish Myth and Ritual*. New York: KTAV, 1967.

Patrides, Constantinos. "The Salvation of Satan." *JHI* 28 (1967): 467–478.

Petersen, Norman. *The Gospel of John and Sociology of Light: Language and Characterization in the Fourth Gospel*. Valley Forge: Trinity Press International, 1993.

Philonenko, Marc. "Initiation et mystère dans Joseph et Aséneth." In *Initiation*. Edited by C.J. Bleeker, 147–153. SHR 10. Leiden: Brill, 1965.

———. "La cosmogonie du 'livre des secrets d'Hénoch.'" In *Religions en Egypte hellénistique et romaine*, 109–116. Paris: Presses Universitaires de France, 1969.

Pokorný, Petr. "The Temptation Stories and Their Intention." *NTS* 20 (1973–1974): 115–127.

Portier-Young, Anathea. "Sweet Mercy Metropolis: Interpreting Aseneth's Honeycomb." *JSP* 14 (2005): 133–157.

Prosic, Tamara. "Kol Nidre: Speaking of the Unspoken (of)," *Bible and Critical Theory* 3.1 (2007): 1–14.

Quispel, Gilles. "Der gnostische Anthropos und die jüdische Tradition." *ErJb* 22 (1953): 195–234.

———. "Ezekiel 1:26 in Jewish Mysticism and Gnosis." *VC* 34 (1980): 1–13.

Rabens, Volker. *The Holy Spirit and Ethics in Paul: Transformation and Empowering for Religious-Ethical Life*. 2nd rev. ed. WUNT 2.283. Tübingen: Mohr/Siebeck, 2013.

Reed, Annette Yoshiko. *Fallen Angels and the History of Judaism and Christianity: The Reception of Enochic Literature*. Cambridge: Cambridge University Press, 2005.

Reeves, John. *Jewish Lore in Manichaean Cosmogony: Studies in the Book of Giants Traditions.* Cincinnati: Hebrew Union College Press, 1992.

———. "Reconsidering the Prophecy of Zardust." In *A Multiform Heritage: Studies in Early Judaism and Christianity in Honor of Robert A. Kraft.* Edited by B.G. Wright, 167–182. SPHS 24. Atlanta: Scholars, 1999.

———. *Trajectories in Near Eastern Apocalyptic: A Postrabbinic Jewish Apocalypse Reader.* RBS 45. Atlanta: SBL, 2005.

Richard, Marcel. "Les fragments du commentaire de S. Hippolyte sur les Proverbes de Solomon." *Le Muséon* 79 (1966): 65–94.

Riessler, Paul. *Altjüdisches Schrifttum außerhalb der Bibel.* Heidelberg: Kerle, 1927.

Roscher, Wilhelm. "Planeten." In *Ausführliches Lexikon der griechischen und römischen Mythologie.* Edited by W.H. Roscher, 3.2535–2536. Leipzig: Teubner, 1902.

Rowland, Christopher. "The Visions of God in Apocalyptic Literature." *JSJ* 10 (1979): 137–154.

———. "John 1.51, Jewish Apocalyptic and Targumic Tradition." *NTS* 30 (1984): 498–507.

Rowland, Christopher and Morray-Jones, Christopher. *The Mystery of God: Early Jewish Mysticism and the New Testament.* CRINT 12. Leiden: Brill, 2009.

Rubinkiewicz, Ryszard. "La vision de l'histoire dans l'Apocalypse d'Abraham." *ANRW* 2.19.1 (1979): 137–151.

Rubinstein, Arie. "Hebraisms in the Slavonic 'Apocalypse of Abraham.'" *JJS* 4 (1953): 108–115.

———. "A Problematic Passage in the Apocalypse of Abraham." *JJS* 8 (1957): 45–50.

Rudman, Dominic. "A Note on the Azazel-goat Ritual." *ZAW* 116 (2004): 396–401.

Rudolph, Kurt. "Sophia und Gnosis. Bemerkungen zum Problem 'Gnosis und Frühjudentum.'" In *Altes Testament-Frühjudentum-Gnosis.* Edited by K.-W. Tröger, 220–237. Berlin: Akademie, 1980.

Russell, Jeffrey. *Satan: The Early Christian Tradition.* Ithaca: Cornell University Press, 1981.

Schäfer, Peter. *Rivalität zwischen Engeln und Menschen: Untersuchungen zur rabbinischen Engelvorstellung.* SJ 8. Berlin: Walter de Gruyter, 1975.

———. "Tempel und Schöpfung. Zur Interpretation einiger Heiligtumstraditionen in der rabbinischen Literatur." In *Studien zur Geschichte und Theologie des rabbinischen Judentums.* Edited by P. Schäfer, 122–133. AGAJU 15. Leiden: Brill, 1978.

———. "The Aim and Purpose of Early Jewish Mysticism. Gershom Scholem Reconsidered." In *Hekhalot-Studien*. Edited by P. Schäfer, 277–295. TSAJ 19. Tübingen: Mohr/Siebeck, 1988.

———. *The Hidden and Manifest God: Some Major Themes in Early Jewish Mysticism*. Albany, NY: SUNY Press, 1992.

———. *The Origins of Jewish Mysticism*. Tübingen: Mohr/Siebeck, 2009.

Schiavo, Luigi. "The Temptation of Jesus: The Eschatological Battle and the New Ethic of the First Followers of Jesus in Q." *JSNT* 25 (2002): 141–164.

Schneider, Michael. "Joseph and Aseneth and Early Jewish Mysticism." *Kabbalah* 3 (1998): 303–344. [Hebrew]

———. "The Myth of the Satan in the *Book of Bahir*." *Kabbalah* 20 (2009): 287–343. [Hebrew]

———. *Scattered Traditions of Jewish Mysticism: Studies in Ancient Jewish Mysticism in Light of Traditions from the Apocrypha, the Pseudepigrapha, Hellenistic Literature, Christian and Islamic Sources*. SSLJM 31. Los Angeles: Cherub Press, 2012. [Hebrew]

Scholem, Gershom. "The Kabbalah of of R. Jacob and R. Isaac, the Sons of R. Jacob ha-Kohen." *Madda^cei ha-Yahadut* 2 (1927): 165–293. [Hebrew]

———. *Major Trends in Jewish Mysticism*. New York: Schocken, 1954.

———. "Die Lehre vom 'Gerechten' in der jüdischen Mystik." *ErJb* 27 (1958): 237–297.

———. "The Idea of the Golem." In *On the Kabbalah and Its Symbolism*. Translated by R. Manheim, 159–165. New York: Schocken, 1965.

———. *Jewish Gnosticism, Merkabah Mysticism, and Talmudic Tradition*. New York: The Jewish Theological Seminary, 1965.

———. *Origins of the Kabbalah*. Princeton: Princeton University Press, 1987.

———. *On the Mystical Shape of the Godhead: Basic Concepts in Kabbalah*. New York: Schocken, 1991.

Schroer, Silvia. *In Israel gab es Bilder. Nachrichten von darstellender Kunst im Alten Testament*. OBO 74. Freiburg: Universitätsverlag; Gottingen: Vandenhoeck & Ruprecht, 1987.

Schultze, Wilhelm. "Der Heilige und die wilden Tiere. Zur Exegese von Mc. 1. 13b." *ZNW* 46 (1955): 280–283.

Schwartz, Daniel. "Two Pauline Allusions to the Redemptive Mechanism of the Crucifixion." *JBL* 102 (1983): 259–283.

Scott, James. *On Earth as in Heaven: The Restoration of Sacred Time and Sacred Space in the Book of Jubilees*. JSJSS 91. Leiden: Brill, 2005.

Scullion, James. *A Traditio-historical Study of the Day of Atonement*. Ph.D. diss. Catholic University of America, 1990.

Segal, Alan. *Two Powers in Heaven: Early Rabbinic Reports about Christianity and Gnosticism*. SJLA 25. Leiden: Brill, 1977.

———. "Heavenly Ascent in Hellenistic Judaism, Early Christianity, and Their Environment." *ANRW* 2.23.2 (1980): 1333–1394.

Shaked, Shaul. *Dualism in Transformation: Varieties of Religion in Sasanian Iran.* London: School of Oriental and African Studies, 1994.

Shea, William. "Azazel in the Pseudepigrapha." *JATS* 13 (2002): 1–9.

Sieber, John. "The Barbelo Aeon as Sophia in Zostrianos and Related Tractates." In *The Rediscovery of Gnosticism.* Edited by B.L. Layton, 2.788–795. 2 vols. Leiden: Brill, 1981.

Sim, David. *Apocalyptic Eschatology in the Gospel of Matthew.* Cambridge: Cambridge University Press, 1996.

Skarsaune, Oskar. *The Proof from Prophecy: A Study in Justin Martyr's Proof-Text Tradition: Text-Type, Provenance, Theological Profile.* NovTSup 56. Leiden: Brill, 1987.

Smith, Mark. "Biblical and Canaanite Notes to the Songs of the Sabbath Sacrifice from Qumran." *RevQ* 12 (1987): 585–588.

———. *God in Translation: Deities in Cross-Cultural Discourse in the Biblical World.* Grand Rapids, MI: Eerdmans, 2010.

Sokoloff, Michael. "Notes on the Aramaic Fragments of Enoch from Qumran Cave 4." *Maarav* 1 (1978–1979): 197–224.

Stadelmann, Luis. *The Hebrew Conception of the World. A Philological and Literary Study.* Rome: Biblical Institute, 1970.

Stager, Lawrence. "Jerusalem and the Garden of Eden." In *Frank Moore Cross Festschrift.* Edited by B.A. Levine et al., 183–194. Eretz Israel 26. Jerusalem: Israel Exploration Society, 1999.

———. "Jerusalem as Eden." *BAR* 26 (2000): 36–47.

Stead, Christopher. "The Valentinian Myth of Sophia." *JTS* 20 (1969): 75–104.

Stemberger, Günter. "Yom Kippur in Mishnah Yoma." In *The Day of Atonement: Its Interpretation in Early Jewish and Christian Traditions.* Edited by T. Hieke and T. Nicklas, 121–138. TBN 15. Leiden: Brill, 2012.

Stichel, Rainer. "Die Verführung der Stammeltern durch Satanael nach der Kurzfassung der slavischen Baruch-Apocalypse." In *Kulturelle Traditionen in Bulgarien.* Edited by R. Lauer and P. Schreiner, 116–128. AAWG 177. Göttingen: Vandenhoeck & Ruprecht, 1989.

Stökl Ben Ezra, Daniel. "Yom Kippur in the Apocalyptic Imaginaire and the Roots of Jesus' High Priesthood." In *Transformations of the Inner Self in Ancient Religions.* Edited by J. Assmann and G. Stroumsa, 349–366. SHR 83. Leiden: Brill, 1999.

———. "The Biblical Yom Kippur, the Jewish Fast of the Day of Atonement and the Church Fathers." *SP* 34 (2002): 493–502.

———. *The Impact of Yom Kippur on Early Christianity: The Day of Atonement from Second Temple Judaism to the Fifth Century.* WUNT 163. Tübingen: Mohr/Siebeck, 2003.

———. "Fasting with Jews, Thinking with Scapegoats: Some Remarks on Yom Kippur in Early Judaism and Christianity, in Particular 4Q541, Barnabas 7, Matthew 27 and Acts 27." In *The Day of Atonement. Its Interpretations in Early Jewish and Christian Traditions*. Edited by T. Hieke and T. Nicklas, 165–188. TBN 18. Leiden: Brill, 2011.

Stone, Michael. "Apocalyptic Literature." In *Jewish Writings of the Second Temple Period: Apocrypha, Pseudepigrapha, Qumran Sectarian Writings, Philo, Josephus*. Edited by M.E. Stone, 383–441. CRINT 2.2. Assen: Van Gorcum, 1984.

———. "The Fall of Satan and Adam's Penance: Three Notes on the Books of Adam and Eve." In *Literature on Adam and Eve. Collected Essays*. Edited by G. Anderson, M. Stone and J. Tromp, 43–56. SVTP 15. Brill: Leiden, 2000.

———. *Adam's Contract with Satan. The Legend of the Cheirograph of Adam*. Bloomington: Indiana University Press, 2002.

———. " 'Be You a Lyre for Me': Identity or Manipulation in Eden." In *The Exegetical Encounter between Jews and Christians in Late Antiquity*. Edited by E. Grypeou and H. Spurling, 87–99. JCPS 18. Leiden: Brill, 2009.

Strange, John. "The Idea of Afterlife in Ancient Israel: Some Remarks on the Iconography in Solomon's Temple." *PEQ* 117 (1985): 35–40.

Strobel, August. "Das jerusalemische Sündenbock-Ritual. Topographische und landeskundliche Überlegungen zur Überlieferungsgeschichte von Lev. 16, 10.21f." *ZDPV* 103 (1987): 141–68.

Swartz, Michael. *Scholastic Magic: Ritual and Revelation in Early Jewish Mysticism*. Princeton: Princeton University Press, 1996.

Tantlevskij, Igor. *Knigi Enoha*. Moscow/Jerusalem: Gesharim, 2000. [Russian]

Tawil, Hayim. "Azazel the Prince of the Steppe: A Comparative Study." *ZAW* 92 (1980): 43–59.

Taylor, Nicholas. "The Temptation of Jesus on the Mountain: A Palestinian Christian Polemic against Agrippa I." *JSNT* 83 (2001): 27–49.

Tigchelaar, Eibert. *Prophets of Old and the Day of the End: Zechariah, the Book of Watchers and Apocalyptic*. OS 35. Leiden: Brill, 1996.

Tishby, Isaiah. *The Doctrine of Evil and the "Kelippah" in Lurianic Kabbalism*. Jerusalem: Magnes, 1984. [Hebrew]

———. *The Wisdom of the Zohar: An Anthology of Texts*. 3 vols. London: The Littman Library of Jewish Civilization, 1989.

Tobin, Thomas. "The Prologue of John and Hellenistic Jewish Speculation." *CBQ* 52 (1990): 252–269.

Toepel, Alexander. "Planetary Demons in Early Jewish Literature." *JSP* 14 (2005): 231–238.

Torrey, Charles. "The Messiah Son of Ephraim." *JBL* 66.3 (1947): 253–277.

Touwaide, Alain. "Iatromathematik." In *Der Neue Pauly. Enzyklopädie der Antike*. Edited by H. Cancik and H. Schneider, 5.873. Stuttgart: Metzler, 1998.

Tuckett, Christopher. "The Temptation Narrative in Q." In *The Four Gospels. Festschrift Frans Neirynck*. Edited by F. van Segbroeck, C.M. Tuckett, G. Van Belle, and J. Verheyden, 1.479–507. 3 vols. BETL 100. Leuven: Peeters, 1992.

Vajda, Georges. "Harut wa-Marut." In *Encyclopaedia of Islam*. Edited by B. Lewis et al., 3.236b–237. Leiden: Brill, 1971.

Van den Broek, Roelof. "Gnosticism and Hermetism in Antiquity: Two Roads to Salvation." In *Gnosis and Hermeticism from Antiquity to Modern Times*. Edited by R. van den Broek and W.J. Hanegraaf, 1–20. Albany, NY: SUNY Press, 1998.

———. "The Creation of Adam's Psychic Body in the *Apocryphon of John*." In *Studies in Gnosticism and Alexandrian Christianity*. Edited by R. van den Broek, 67–85. NHS 39. Leiden: Brill, 1996.

VanderKam, James. *Enoch and the Growth of an Apocalyptic Tradition*. CBQMS 16. Washington, D.C.: The Catholic Biblical Association of America, 1984.

Van Ruiten, Jacques. "Eden and the Temple: The Rewriting of Genesis 2:4–3:24 in the Book of Jubilees." In *Paradise Interpreted: Representations of Biblical Paradise in Judaism and Christianity*. Edited by G.P. Luttikhuizen, 63–94. TBN 2. Leiden: Brill, 1999.

———. "Visions of the Temple in the Book of Jubilees." In *Gemeinde ohne Tempel/Community without Temple: Zur Substituierung und Transformation des Jerusalemer Tempels und seines Kults im Alten Testament, antiken Judentum und frühen Christentum*. Edited by B. Ego et al., 215–228. WUNT 118. Tübingen: Mohr/Siebeck, 1999.

Van Seters, John. "Solomon's Temple: Fact and Ideology in Biblical and Near Eastern Historiography." *CBQ* 59 (1997): 45–57.

Vargas-Machuca, Antonio. "La tentación de Jesús según Mc. 1,12–13¿Hecho real o relato de tipo haggádico?" *EE* 48 (1973): 163–190.

Walls, Neal. *Cult Image and Divine Representation in the Ancient Near East*. ASOR 10. Boston: American Schools of Oriental Research, 2005.

Weinfeld, Moshe. *Deuteronomy and the Deuteronomic School*. Oxford: Clarendon Press, 1972.

———. "Sabbath, Temple and the Enthronement of the Lord—The Problem of the Sitz im Leben of Genesis 1:1–2:3." In *Mélanges bibliques et orientaux en l'honneur de M. Henri Cazelles*. Edited by A. Caquot and M. Delcor, 501–512. Kevelaer: Butzon & Bercker, 1981.

———. "Social and Cultic Institutions in the Priestly Source against Their ANE Background." In *Proceedings of the Eighth World Congress of Jewish Studies*, 95–129. Jerusalem: Magnes Press, 1983.

Weippert, Helga. "Die Kesselwagen Salomos." *ZDPV* 108 (1992): 8–41.

Welburn, Andrew. "The Identity of the Archons in the 'Apocryphon Johannis.'" *VC* 32 (1978): 241–254.

Wenham, Gordon. "Sanctuary Symbolism in the Garden of Eden Story." In *Proceedings of the Ninth World Congress of Jewish Studies, Division A: The Period of the Bible*, 19–25. Jerusalem: World Union of Jewish Studies, 1986.

Whitney, William K. Jr. *Two Strange Beasts: Leviathan and Behemoth in Second Temple and Early Rabbinic Judaism.* HSM 63. Winona Lake, IN.: Eisenbrauns, 2006.

Widengren, Geo. *Mani and Manichaeism.* New York: Holt, Rinehart and Winston, 1965.

Wilckens, Ulrich and Fohrer, Georg. "Sophia." In *Theological Dictionary of the New Testament.* Edited by G. Kittel and G. Friedrich, 7.465–526. 10 vols. Grand Rapids, MI: Eerdmans, 1964–1976.

Wise, Michael. "4QFlorilegium and the Temple of Adam." *RevQ* 15/57–58 (1991): 103–132.

Wolfson, Elliot. "Left Contained in the Right: A Study in Zoharic Hermeneutics."*AJSR* 11 (1986): 27–52.

———. "Light through Darkness: The Ideal of Human Perfection in the Zohar." *HTR* 81 (1988): 73–95.

———. *Luminal Darkness: Imaginal Gleanings from Zoharic Literature.* Oxford: Oneworld, 2007.

Wratislaw, Albert. "The Scapegoat-Barabbas." *ET* 3 (1891/92): 400–403.

Wright, Archie. *The Origin of the Evil Spirits: The Reception of Genesis 6.1–4 in Early Jewish Literature.* WUNT 2.198. Tübingen: Mohr/ Siebeck, 2005.

———. "Evil Spirits in Second Temple Judaism: The Watcher Tradition as a Background to the Demonic Pericopes in the Gospels." *Henoch* 28 (2006): 141–159.

Wright, David. *The Disposal of Impurity: Elimination Rites in the Bible and in Hittite and Mesopotamian Literature.* SBLDS 101. Atlanta: Scholars, 1987.

Yamauchi, Edwin. "The Descent of Ishtar, the Fall of Sophia, and the Jewish Roots of Gnosticism." *TB* 29 (1978): 143–175.

Yuval, Israel. *Two Nations in Your Womb: Perceptions of Jews and Christians in Late Antiquity and the Middle Ages.* Translated by B. Harshav and J. Chipman. Berkeley: University of California Press, 2006.

Zatelli, Ida. "The Origin of the Biblical Scapegoat Ritual: The Evidence of Two Eblaite Texts." *VT* 48 (1998): 254–263.

Zimmern, Heinrich. "Urkönige und Uroffenbarung." In *Die Keilinschriften und das Alte Testament.* Edited by E. Schrader, 2.530–543. 2 vols. Berlin: Reuther & Reichard, 1902–1903.

Zwickel, Wolfgang. *Der salomonische Tempel.* KAW 83. Mainz: Von Zabern, 1999.

Index